10453439

ACCA

TAXATION (TX – UK)

FA 2017

STUDY TEXT

BPP Learning Media is an **ACCA Approved Content Provider**. This means we work closely with ACCA to ensure this Study Text contains the information y~~ou need to pass~~ your exam.

In this Study Text, which has been reviewed by the **ACCA examining t~~eam~~**

D1439380

- **Highlight** the **most important elements** in the syllabus and the **key skills** you nee~~d~~
- **Signpost** how each chapter links to the syllabus and the study guide
- **Provide** lots of **exam focus points** demonstrating what is expected of you in the exam
- **Emphasise key points** in regular **fast forward summaries**
- **Test your knowledge** in quick quizzes
- **Examine your understanding** in our **practice question bank**
- **Reference** all the important topics in our **full index**

BPP's **Practice & Revision Kit** also supports the Taxation (TX – UK) syllabus.

FOR EXAMS IN JUNE 2018, SEPTEMBER 2018, DECEMBER 2018 AND MARCH 2019

BPP
LEARNING MEDIA

First edition 2007
Eleventh edition October 2017

ISBN 9781 5097 1532 9
(Previous 9781 5097 0787 4)
eISBN 9781 5097 1534 3

British Library Cataloguing-in-Publication Data
A catalogue record for this book is available from the
British Library

Published by

BPP Learning Media Ltd
BPP House, Aldine Place
142–144 Uxbridge Road
London W12 8AA

www.bpp.com/learningmedia

Printed in the United Kingdom

Your learning materials, published by BPP Learning
Media Ltd, are printed on paper obtained from traceable
sustainable sources.

We are grateful to the Association of Chartered Certified
Accountants for permission to reproduce past examination
questions. The suggested solutions in the practice answer bank
have been prepared by BPP Learning Media Ltd, unless otherwise
stated.

Contents

Helping you to pass

As an ACCA **Approved Content Provider**, BPP Learning Media gives you the **opportunity** to use study materials reviewed by the ACCA examining team. By incorporating the examining team's comments and suggestions regarding the depth and breadth of syllabus coverage, the BPP Learning Media Study Text provides excellent, **ACCA-approved** support for your studies.

The PER alert!

Before you can qualify as an ACCA member, you not only have to pass all your exams but also fulfil a three year **practical experience requirement** (PER). To help you to recognise areas of the syllabus that you might be able to apply in the workplace to achieve different performance objectives, we have introduced the '**PER alert**' feature. You will find this feature throughout the Study Text to remind you that what you are **learning to pass** your ACCA exams is **equally useful to the fulfilment of the PER requirement**.

Your achievement of the PER should be recorded in your online *My Experience* record.

Tackling studying

Studying can be a daunting prospect, particularly when you have lots of other commitments. The **different features** of the Study Text, the **purposes** of which are explained fully on the **Chapter features** page, will help you whilst studying and improve your chances of **exam success**.

Developing exam awareness

Our Texts are completely **focused** on helping you pass your exam.

Our advice on **Studying Taxation (TX – UK)** outlines the **content** of the paper and the **necessary skills** you are expected to be able to demonstrate.

Exam focus points are included within the chapters to highlight when and how specific topics were examined, or how they might be examined in the future.

Exam references are provided to the September 2016 and December 2016 full exams. Subsequently, only a selection of constructed response questions (CRQ) were released by ACCA. Exam references post December 2016 do not represent a full exam. The references should be taken as a guide. BPP Learning Media and ACCA do not advocate question spotting.

Testing what you can do

Testing yourself helps you develop the skills you need to pass the exam and also confirms that you can recall what you have learnt.

We include **Questions** – lots of them – both within chapters and in the **Practice Question Bank**, as well as **Quick Quizzes** at the end of each chapter to test your knowledge of the chapter content.

Chapter features

Each chapter contains a number of helpful features to guide you through each topic.

Topic list

Topic list	Syllabus reference

Tells you what you will be studying in this chapter and the relevant section numbers, together with ACCA syllabus references.

Introduction

Puts the chapter content in the context of the syllabus as a whole.

Study Guide

Links the chapter content with ACCA guidance.

Exam Guide

Highlights how examinable the chapter content is likely to be and the ways in which it could be examined.

FAST FORWARD »

Summarises the content of main chapter headings, allowing you to preview and review each section easily.

Examples

Demonstrate how to apply key knowledge and techniques.

Key terms

Definitions of important concepts that can often earn you easy marks in exams.

Exam focus points

Tell you when and how specific topics were examined, or how they may be examined in the future.

Formula to learn

Formulae that are not given in the exam but which have to be learnt.

PER alert

Gives you a useful indication of syllabus areas that closely relate to performance objectives in your Practical Experience Requirement (PER).

Question

Gives you essential practice of techniques covered in the chapter.

Chapter Roundup

A full list of the Fast Forwards included in the chapter, providing an easy source of review.

Quick Quiz

A quick test of your knowledge of the main topics in the chapter.

Practice Question Bank

Found at the back of the Study Text with more comprehensive chapter questions. Cross referenced for easy navigation.

Studying Taxation (TX – UK)

Note on exam name (F6 UK)

This text is valid for exams from June 2018 to March 2019. From the September 2018 session, a new naming convention is being introduced for all of the exams in the ACCA Qualification, so from that session, the name of the exam will be Taxation (TX – UK). June 2018 is the first session of a new exam year for tax, and the exam name continues to be F6 Taxation (UK). Since this name change takes place during the validity of this text, both the old and new names have been used.

As the name suggests, this paper examines the **basic principles of taxation**. This is a very important area for certified accountants as many areas of practice involve a consideration of taxation issues. It also provides a **foundation for Advanced Taxation (ATX – UK)** which will be chosen by those who work in a tax environment.

Members of the Taxation (TX – UK) examining team have written **several technical articles** including two on Inheritance Tax, two on chargeable gains, one on groups, two on VAT, one on benefits, one on motor cars, one on adjustment of profit and one on Finance Act 2017. All these articles are available on the ACCA website. Make sure you read them to gain further insight into what the Taxation (TX – UK) examining team is looking for.

1 What Taxation (TX – UK) is about

You are introduced to the rationale behind – and the functions of – **the tax system**. The syllabus then considers the **separate taxes** that an accountant would need to have a detailed knowledge of, such as **income tax from self-employment**, **employment and investments**, the **corporation tax** liability of individual companies and groups of companies, the **national insurance contribution** liabilities of both employed and self employed persons, the **value added tax** liability of businesses, the **chargeable gains** arising on disposals of investments by both individuals and companies, and the **inheritance tax** liabilities arising on chargeable lifetime transfers and on death.

You will be expected to have a **detailed knowledge** of these taxes, but **no previous knowledge is assumed**. You should **study the basics** carefully and **learn the pro forma computations**. It then becomes straightforward to complete these by slotting in figures from your detailed workings.

As well as being able to calculate tax liabilities, you may be required to **explain the basis of the calculations**, **apply tax planning techniques** for individuals and companies and **identify the compliance issues** for each major tax through a variety of business and personal scenarios and situations.

2 What skills are required?

- Be able to **integrate** knowledge and understanding from across the syllabus to enable you to complete detailed computations of tax liabilities.
- Be able to **explain** the underlying principles of taxation by providing a simple summary of the rules and how they apply to the particular situation.
- Be able to **apply** tax planning techniques by identifying available options and testing them to see which has the greater effect on tax liabilities.

3 How to improve your chances of passing

- There is no choice in this paper, all questions have to be answered. You must therefore study the **entire syllabus**, there are no short-cuts.
- The first section of the paper consists of 15 **objective test questions**, worth two marks each. These will inevitably cover a **wide range of the syllabus**.

- The second section of the paper consists of three scenarios each being tested with 5 **objective test questions,** worth two marks each. You must make sure you **understand the scenario** before attempting the related questions.

- Practising longer questions set in the third section of the paper under **timed conditions** is essential. BPP's **Practice & Revision Kit** contains 10 mark and 15 mark questions on all areas of the syllabus.

- **Answer all parts** of the question. Even if you cannot do all of the calculation elements, you will still be able to gain marks in the discussion parts.

- **Answer selectively** – the examining team will expect you to consider carefully what is relevant and significant enough to include in your answer. Don't include unnecessary information.

- Keep an eye out for **articles** as the **examining team** will use **Student Accountant** to communicate with students.

The exam

Computer-based exams

ACCA have commenced the launch of computer-based exams (CBEs) for this paper. They have been piloting CBEs in limited markets since September 2016 with the aim of rolling out into all markets internationally over a five-year period. Paper-based examinations will be run in parallel while the CBEs are phased in. BPP materials have been designed to support you, whichever exam option you choose.

Exam duration

The syllabus is assessed in both computer-based (CBE) and paper-based (PBE) exam formats. PBE exams are 3 hours 15 minutes in duration to reflect the manual effort required to write up your solutions. CBE exams are 3 hours and 20 minutes in duration to reflect the 10 extra marks for seeded questions included in CBE exams.

At each sitting, there is only one version of the PBE; however, as of March 2017, CBE questions will be extracted from a bank of questions, meaning for CBEs you may not necessarily be sitting the same exam as your neighbour. To ensure that the exams remain fair and equivalent, ACCA have included 10 additional marks of seeded questions. You will not be able to determine which question is the seeded content and all questions are quality assured and set to the same standard as the rest of the exam. Having seeded content feeds into the rigorous processes that ACCA have been working on with worldwide experts to ensure all students can be confident that the new CBEs will be fair and equivalent for all.

For more information on these changes and when they will be implemented, please visit the ACCA website: www.accaglobal.com/uk/en/student/exam-support-resources/fundamentals-exams-study-resources/f1/technical-articles/201617-changes.html

Format of the exam

The exam format is the same irrespective of the mode of delivery and will comprise three exam sections:

Section	Style of question type	Description	Proportion of exam, %
A	Objective test (OT)	15 questions × 2 marks	30
B	Objective test (OT) case	3 questions × 10 marks Each question will contain 5 subparts each worth 2 marks	30
C	Constructed Response (Long questions)	1 question × 10 marks 2 questions × 15 marks	40
Total			100

Section A and B questions will be selected from the entire syllabus. The paper version of these objective test questions contains multiple choice only and the computer-based versions will contain a variety. The responses to each question or subpart in the case of OT cases are marked automatically as either correct or incorrect by computer.

The 10 mark Section C questions can come from any part of the syllabus. The 15 mark Section C questions will mainly focus on the following syllabus areas but a minority of marks can be drawn from any other area of the syllabus:

- Income tax (syllabus area B)
- Corporation tax (syllabus area E)

The responses to these questions are human marked.

Syllabus and Study Guide

The complete Taxation (TX – UK) syllabus and study guide can be found by visiting the exam resource finder on the ACCA website: www.accaglobal.com/uk/en/student/exam-support-resources.html

UK tax system

Introduction to the UK tax system

1

Topic list	Syllabus reference
1 The overall function and purpose of taxation in a modern economy	A1(a)
2 Different types of taxes	A1(b), (c)
3 Principal sources of revenue law and practice	A2(a)–(c), (e), (f)
4 Tax avoidance and tax evasion	A2(d), (g)

Introduction

We start our study of tax with an introduction to the UK tax system.

First, we consider briefly the purpose of raising taxes, focussing on economic, social and environmental factors. We next consider the specific UK taxes, both revenue and capital, and also direct and indirect.

We see how the collection of tax is administered in the UK, and where the UK tax system interacts with overseas tax jurisdictions.

Finally, we highlight the difference between tax avoidance and tax evasion and explain the need for a professional and ethical approach in dealing with tax. In particular, we look at the situation where a client has failed to disclose information to the tax authorities.

When you have finished this chapter you should be able to discuss the broad features of the tax system. In the following chapters we will consider specific UK taxes, starting with income tax.

Study guide

		Intellectual level
A1	**The overall function and purpose of taxation in a modern economy**	
(a)	Describe the purpose (economic, social etc) of taxation in a modern economy.	1
(b)	Explain the difference between direct and indirect taxation.	2
(c)	Identify the different types of capital and revenue tax.	1
A2	**Principal sources of revenue law and practice**	
(a)	Describe the overall structure of the UK tax system.	1
(b)	State the different sources of revenue law.	1
(c)	Describe the organisation of HM Revenue & Customs (HMRC) and its terms of reference.	1
(d)	Explain the difference between tax avoidance and tax evasion, and the purposes of the General Anti-Abuse Rule (GAAR).	1
(e)	Appreciate the interaction of the UK tax system with that of other tax jurisdictions.	2
(f)	Appreciate the need for double taxation agreements.	2
(g)	Explain the need for an ethical and professional approach.	2

Exam guide

You may be asked a question on a specific topic from this part of the syllabus in either Section A or Section B. An example would be to identify sources of revenue law. You are unlikely to be asked a whole Section C question on this part of the syllabus. You may, however, be asked to comment on one aspect, such as the difference between tax avoidance and tax evasion or how to act if a client has failed to disclose information to the tax authorities, as part of a question.

1 The overall function and purpose of taxation in a modern economy

FAST FORWARD

Economic, social and environmental factors may affect the government's tax policies.

1.1 Economic factors

In terms of economic analysis, government **taxation represents a withdrawal from the UK economy** while its expenditure acts as an injection into it. So the government's net position in terms of taxation and expenditure, together with its public sector borrowing policies, has an effect on the level of economic activity within the UK.

The government favours longer-term planning, and regularly sets out proposed plans for expenditure. These show the proportion of the economy's overall resources which will be allocated by the government and how much will be left for the private sector.

This can have an effect on demand for particular types of goods, eg health and education on the one hand, which are predominately the result of public spending, and consumer goods on the other, which results from private spending. Changing demand levels will have an impact on employment levels within the different sectors, as well as on the profitability of different private sector suppliers.

Within that overall proportion left in the private sector, **the government uses tax policies to encourage and discourage certain types of activity**.

It **encourages**:

(a) **Saving** on the part of the individual, by offering tax incentives such as tax-free individual savings accounts (ISAs) and tax relief on pension contributions

(b) **Donations to charities** through the Gift Aid scheme

(c) **Entrepreneurs** who build their own business, through reliefs from capital gains tax

(d) **Investment in plant and machinery** through capital allowances

(e) **Marriage and civil partnerships** through the transferable personal allowance (marriage allowance). Civil partners are members of a same sex couple which has registered as a civil partnership under the Civil Partnerships Act 2004. Same sex couples can also marry in England, Wales and Scotland (but not Northern Ireland).

It **discourages**:

(a) **Smoking** and **alcoholic drinks**, through the duties placed on each type of product
(b) **Motoring**, through fuel duties

Governments can and do argue that these latter taxes and duties to some extent mirror the extra costs to the country as a whole of such behaviours, such as the cost of coping with smoking related illnesses. However, the government needs to raise money for spending in areas where there are no consumers on whom the necessary taxes can be levied, such as defence, law and order, overseas aid and the cost of running the government and Parliament.

1.2 Social factors

Social justice lies at the heart of politics, since what some think of as just is regarded by others as completely unjust. Attitudes to the redistribution of wealth are a clear example.

In a free market some individuals generate greater amounts of income and capital than others and once wealth has been acquired, it tends to grow through the reinvestment of investment income received. This can lead to the rich getting richer and the poor poorer, with economic power becoming concentrated in relatively few hands.

Some electors make the value judgement that these trends should be countered by **taxation policies which redistribute income and wealth** away from the rich towards the poor. This is one of the key arguments in favour of some sort of capital gains tax and inheritance tax, taxes which, relative to the revenue raised, cost a great deal to collect.

Different taxes have different social effects:

(a) **Direct taxes** based on income and profits (income tax), gains (capital gains tax) or wealth (inheritance tax) **tax only those who have these resources**.

(b) **Indirect taxes** paid by the consumer (value added tax – VAT) **discourage spending** and encourage saving. Lower or nil rates of tax can be levied on essentials, such as food.

(c) **Progressive taxes** such as income tax, where the proportion of the income or gains paid over in tax increases as income/gains rise, **target those who can afford to pay**. Personal allowances and the rates of taxation can be adjusted so as to ensure that those on very low incomes pay little or no tax.

(d) Taxes on capital or wealth ensure that people cannot avoid taxation by having an income of zero and just living off the sale of capital assets.

Almost everyone would argue that taxation should be **equitable** or 'fair', but there are many different views as to what is equitable.

An **efficient tax** is one where the costs of collection are low relative to the tax paid over to the government. The government publishes figures for the administrative costs incurred by government departments in

operating the taxation systems, but there are also compliance costs to be taken into account. Compliance costs are those incurred by the taxpayer, whether they be the individual preparing tax returns under the self assessment system or the employer operating the Pay As You Earn (PAYE) system to collect income tax or the business collecting VAT. Some of the more equitable taxes may be less efficient to collect.

1.3 Environmental factors

The taxation system accommodates environmental concerns to a certain extent, especially concerns about renewable and non-renewable sources of energy and global warming.

Examples of tax changes which have been introduced for environmental reasons are:

(a) The **climate change levy**, raised on businesses in proportion to their consumption of energy. Its claimed purpose is to encourage reduced consumption.

(b) The **landfill tax** levied on the operators of landfill sites on each tonne of rubbish/waste processed at the site. Its claimed purpose is to encourage recycling by taxing waste which has to be stored.

(c) The changes to rules on the **lease or purchase of cars**, and taxation of **cars and private fuel provided for employees** to be dependent on carbon dioxide (CO_2) emissions. Its claimed purpose is to encourage the manufacture and purchase of low CO_2 emission cars to reduce emissions into the atmosphere caused by driving.

Only the last of these will be directly felt by individuals, even if the other taxes are passed on by being factored into a business's overheads.

2 Different types of taxes

FAST FORWARD ▶▶ Central government raises revenue through a wide range of taxes. Tax law is made by statute.

2.1 Taxes in the UK

Central government raises revenue through a wide range of taxes on income and capital which may be direct or indirect. The primary source of tax law is statute.

The main taxes, their incidence and their sources, are set out in the table below.

Tax	Suffered by	Source
Income tax	Individuals Partnerships	Capital Allowances Act 2001 (CAA 2001); Income Tax (Earnings and Pensions) Act 2003 (ITEPA 2003); Income Tax (Trading and Other Income) Act 2005 (ITTOIA 2005); Income Tax Act 2007 (ITA 2007)
Corporation tax	Companies	CAA 2001 as above, Corporation Tax Act 2009 (CTA 2009), Corporation Tax Act 2010 (CTA 2010)
Capital gains tax	Individuals Partnerships Companies (which pay tax on capital gains in the form of corporation tax)	Taxation of Chargeable Gains Act 1992 (TCGA 1992)
Inheritance tax	Individuals Trustees	Inheritance Tax Act 1984 (IHTA 1984)
Value added tax	**Businesses**, both incorporated and unincorporated	Value Added Tax Act 1994 (VATA 1994)

You will also meet National Insurance. **National insurance is payable by employers, employees and the self employed.**

Further details of all these taxes are found later in this Study Text.

The **other taxes** referred to in the previous section, such as landfill tax, are **not examinable** in Taxation (TX – UK). In addition, **devolved taxes** for Scotland, Wales and Northern Ireland are **not examinable** in Taxation (TX – UK).

Finance Acts are passed each year, incorporating proposals set out in the **Budget**. They make changes which apply mainly to the tax year ahead. **This Study Text includes the provisions of the Finance Act 2017.** This is the **Finance Act examinable** in the sessions in **June 2018, September 2018, December 2018 and March 2019**. If there are **any further Finance Acts 2017**, such Acts are **not examinable** in these sessions.

2.2 Revenue and capital taxes

Revenue taxes are those charged on income. In this Study Text we cover:

- **Income tax**
- **Corporation tax** (on income profits)
- **National insurance**

Capital taxes are those charged on capital gains or on wealth. In this Study Text we cover:

- **Capital gains tax**
- **Corporation tax** (on capital gains)
- **Inheritance tax**

2.3 Direct and indirect taxes   9/16

Direct taxes are those charged on **income, gains and wealth**. **Income tax, national insurance, corporation tax**, **capital gains tax** and **inheritance tax** are **direct taxes**. Direct taxes are collected directly from the taxpayer.

Indirect taxes are those **paid by the consumer to the supplier** who then passes the tax to the government. **Value added tax** is an indirect tax.

3 Principal sources of revenue law and practice

Tax is administered by Her Majesty's Revenue & Customs (HMRC).

3.1 The overall structure of the UK tax system

3.1.1 Her Majesty's Treasury

Her Majesty's Treasury formally imposes and collects taxation. The management of the Treasury is the responsibility of the Chancellor of the Exchequer.

3.1.2 Her Majesty's Revenue & Customs (HMRC)

The administrative function for the collection of tax is undertaken by HMRC.

The HMRC staff are referred to in the tax legislation as **'Officers of Revenue and Customs'**. They are responsible for supervising the self-assessment system and raising queries about tax liabilities.

3.1.3 Crown Prosecution Service (CPS)

The **Crown Prosecution Service (CPS)** provides legal advice and institutes and conducts criminal prosecutions in England and Wales where there has been an investigation by HMRC.

3.1.4 Tax Tribunal

Tax appeals are heard by the **Tax Tribunal** which is made up of **two tiers**:

(a)   **First Tier Tribunal**
(b)   **Upper Tribunal**

The **First Tier Tribunal deals with most cases** other than complex cases. The **Upper Tribunal deals with complex cases** which either involve an important issue of tax law or a large financial sum. The Upper Tribunal **also hears appeals** against decisions of the First Tier Tribunal. We look at the appeals system in more detail later in this Study Text.

3.2 Different sources of revenue law   12/16

FAST FORWARD

> The sources of revenue law are Acts of Parliament, Statutory Instruments and case law.

As stated above, taxes are imposed by statute. This comprises not only **Acts of Parliament** but also regulations laid down by **Statutory Instruments**. Statute is interpreted and amplified by **case law**.

HMRC also issue:

- **Statements of practice**, setting out how they intend to apply the law

- **Extra-statutory concessions**, setting out circumstances in which they will not apply the strict letter of the law where it would be unfair

- A wide range of **explanatory leaflets**

- **Revenue and Customs Brief** – this gives HMRC's view on specific points

- The **Internal Guidance**, a series of manuals used by HMRC staff

- **Agent Update**, for tax practitioners

Although the HMRC publications do not generally have the force of law, some of the VAT notices do where power has been delegated under regulations. This applies, for example, to certain administrative aspects of the cash accounting scheme.

3.3 The interaction of the UK tax system with that of other tax jurisdictions

3.3.1 The European Union (EU)

FAST FORWARD

> UK membership of the European Union (EU) has a significant effect on UK taxes, in particular VAT. This will continue until the UK leaves the EU.

Membership of the European Union (EU) has a significant effect on UK taxes although there is no general requirement imposed on the EU member states to move to a common system of taxation nor to harmonise their individual tax systems. The states may, however, agree jointly to enact specific laws, known as 'Directives', which provide for a common code of taxation within particular areas of their taxation systems.

The most important example to date is **Value Added Tax (VAT)**, where the UK is obliged to pass its laws in conformity with the rules laid down in the European legislation. The VAT Directives still allow for a certain amount of flexibility between member states, eg in setting rates of taxation. There are only limited examples of Directives in the area of Direct Taxes, generally concerned with cross-border dividend and interest payments and corporate reorganisations.

However, under the EU treaties, member states are also obliged to permit freedom of movement of workers, freedom of movement of capital and freedom to establish business operations within the EU. These treaty provisions have '**direct effect**', ie a taxpayer is entitled to claim that a UK tax provision is ineffective because it **breaches one or more of the freedoms** guaranteed under European Law.

The European Court of Justice has repeatedly held that taxation provisions which discriminate against non-residents (ie treat a non-resident less favourably than a resident in a similar situation) are contrary to European Law, unless there is a very strong public interest justification.

There are provisions regarding the **exchange of information** between European Union Revenue authorities.

The long term implications of the **process which has started for the UK to leave the EU** are not fully known. However, until the UK has gone through this process, **EU rules will continue to apply to the UK**.

3.3.2 Other countries

In general, the rules of tax jurisdictions of other countries do not have a direct interaction with UK tax. However, the UK has entered into **double tax agreement** with various countries, as discussed below.

3.4 Double taxation agreements

Double taxation agreements are designed to protect against the risk of double taxation where the same income or gains are taxable in two countries.

Double Taxation agreements between two countries are primarily designed to protect against the risk of double taxation where the same income or gains are taxable in two countries.

For example, an individual may have a **source of income which is taxed in the country in which the income arose** but **is also taxed in the individual's country of residence**. The agreement could provide that the **income is only to be taxed in one country** or that **credit is to be given for tax arising in one country against the tax charge in the other country**.

Double taxation agreements may also include **non-discrimination provisions** which prevent a foreign national from being treated more harshly than a national of a country.

Double taxation agreements also usually include rules for the **exchange of information** between the different Revenue authorities.

4 Tax avoidance and tax evasion

One of the competencies you require to fulfil Performance Objective 17 Tax planning and advice of the PER is to advise clients responsibly about the differences between tax planning, tax avoidance and tax evasion. You can apply the knowledge you obtain from this section of the Study Text to help to demonstrate this competence.

Tax avoidance is the legal minimisation of tax liabilities; tax evasion is illegal.

4.1 Tax evasion

Tax evasion consists of seeking to pay too little tax by deliberately misleading HMRC by either:

(a) **Suppressing information to which they are entitled** (eg failing to notify HMRC that you are liable to tax, understating income or gains or omitting to disclose a relevant fact; for example, that business expenditure had a dual motive), or

(b)   **Providing them with deliberately false information** (eg deducting expenses which have not been incurred or claiming capital allowances on plant that has not been purchased).

Tax evasion is illegal. Minor cases of tax evasion have generally been settled out of court on the payment of penalties. However, there is now a **statutory offence of evading income tax**, which enables such matters as deliberate failure to operate PAYE to be dealt with in magistrates' courts.

Serious cases of tax evasion, particularly those involving fraud, will continue to be the subject of **criminal prosecutions** which may lead to **fines and/or imprisonment on conviction**.

4.2 Tax avoidance

Tax avoidance is more difficult to define.

In a very broad sense, it could include **any legal method of reducing your tax burden**, eg taking advantage of tax shelter opportunities explicitly offered by tax legislation such as ISAs. However, the term is more commonly used in a more narrow sense, to denote complex arrangements designed to produce unintended tax advantages for the taxpayer.

The effectiveness of tax avoidance schemes has often been examined in the courts. Traditionally the tax rules were applied to the legal form of transactions, although this principle was qualified in later cases. It was held that the courts could disregard transactions which were preordained and solely designed to avoid tax.

Traditionally, the response of HMRC has been to seek to mend the **loopholes** in the law as they come to their attention. In general, there is a presumption that the effect of such changes should not be backdated.

There are **disclosure obligations** on promoters of certain tax **avoidance schemes**, and on taxpayers, to provide details to HMRC of any such schemes used by the taxpayer. This enables HMRC to introduce anti avoidance measures at the earliest opportunity.

4.3 The distinction between avoidance and evasion

The **distinction between tax evasion and tax avoidance should generally be clear cut**, since tax avoidance is an entirely legal activity and does not entail misleading HMRC. However, some tax avoidance arrangements may be subject to the General Anti-Abuse Rule (GAAR) discussed below.

Care should also be taken in giving advice in some circumstances. For example, a taxpayer who does not return income or gains because they wrongly believe that they have successfully avoided having to pay tax on them may, as a result, be accused of tax evasion.

4.4 General Anti-Abuse Rule (GAAR)

FAST FORWARD

There is a General Anti-Abuse Rule (GAAR) which enables HMRC to counteract tax advantages arising from abusive tax arrangements.

Tax avoidance is usually targeted with legislation which applies in specific circumstances. **The GAAR provides additional means for HMRC to 'counteract' tax advantages arising from abusive 'tax arrangements'**, ie arrangements that involve obtaining a **tax advantage** as (one of) their main purpose(s).

Arrangements are **abusive** if they **cannot be regarded as a reasonable course of action**, for example, where they **lead to unintended results involving one or more contrived or abnormal steps and exploit any shortcomings in the tax provisions**.

Examples of abusive arrangements include those that result in:

- Significantly less income, profits or gains;
- Significantly greater deductions or losses, or
- A claim for the repayment or crediting of tax that has not been, and is unlikely to be, paid.

A 'tax advantage' includes:

- Relief or increased relief from tax
- Repayment or increased repayment of tax
- Avoidance or reduction of a charge to tax
- Avoidance of a possible assessment to tax
- Deferral of a payment of tax or advancement of a repayment of tax
- Avoidance of an obligation to deduct or account for tax

HMRC may counteract tax advantages arising by, for example, increasing the taxpayer's tax liability. HMRC must follow certain procedural requirements and, if it makes any adjustments, these must be on a 'just and reasonable' basis.

4.5 The need for an ethical and professional approach

FAST FORWARD

If a client makes a material error or omission in a tax return, or fails to file a tax return, and does not correct the error, omission or failure when advised, the accountant should cease to act for the client, inform HMRC of this cessation and make a money laundering report.

Under self assessment, all taxpayers (whether individuals or companies) are responsible for disclosing their taxable income and gains and the deductions and reliefs they are claiming against them.

Many taxpayers arrange for their accountants to prepare and submit their tax returns. **The taxpayer is still the person responsible for submitting the return and for paying whatever tax becomes due**; the accountant is only acting as the taxpayer's agent.

The practising accountant often acts for taxpayers in their dealings with HMRC and situations can arise where the accountant has concerns as to whether the taxpayer is being honest in providing information to the accountant for onward transmission.

How the accountant deals with such situations is a matter of **professional judgement**, but in deciding what to do, the accountant will be expected to uphold the standards of the Association of Chartered Certified Accountants. The accountant must act **honestly** and **objectively**, with **due care and diligence**, and showing the highest standards of **integrity**.

If an accountant learns of a material error or omission in a client's tax return or of a **failure to file a required tax return**, the accountant has a responsibility to **advise the client of the error, omission or failure** and **recommend that disclosure be made to HMRC**.

If the client, after having had a reasonable time to reflect, does not correct the error, omission or failure or authorise the accountant to do so on the client's behalf, the accountant should **inform the client in writing that it is not possible for the accountant to act for that client.**

The accountant should also **notify HMRC that the accountant no longer acts for the client but should not provide details of the reason for ceasing to act.**

An accountant whose client refuses to make disclosure to HMRC, after having had notice of the error, omission or failure and a reasonable time to reflect, **must also report the client's refusal and the facts surrounding it to the Money Laundering Reporting Officer within the accountancy firm or to the appropriate authority (National Crime Agency) if the accountant is a sole practitioner.**

Accountants who suspect or are aware of tax evasion activities by a client may themselves commit an offence if they do not report their suspicions. The accountant must not disclose to the client, or any one else, that such a report has been made if the accountant knows or suspects that to do so would be likely to prejudice any investigation which might be conducted following the report as this might constitute the criminal offence of 'tipping-off'.

Exam focus point

You may be asked to explain how you, as a trainee Chartered Certified Accountant, should deal with a situation where a client is evading tax, for example by not disclosing income or gains to HMRC.

Chapter Roundup

- Economic, social and environmental factors may affect the government's tax policies.

- Central government raises revenue through a wide range of taxes. Tax law is made by statute.

- Tax is administered by HM Revenue & Customs (HMRC).

- The sources of revenue law are Acts of Parliament, Statutory Instruments and case law.

- UK membership of the European Union (EU) has a significant effect on UK taxes, in particular value added tax (VAT). This will continue until the UK leaves the EU.

- Double taxation agreements are designed to protect against the risk of double taxation where the same income or gains are taxable in two countries.

- Tax avoidance is the legal minimisation of tax liabilities; tax evasion is illegal.

- There is a General Anti-Abuse Rule (GAAR) which enables HMRC to counteract tax advantages arising from abusive tax arrangements.

- If a client makes a material error or omission in a tax return, or fails to file a tax return, and does not correct the error, omission or failure when advised, the accountant should cease to act for the client, inform HMRC of this cessation and make a money laundering report.

Quick Quiz

1   What is the difference between a direct and an indirect tax?

2   What is an Extra Statutory Concession?

3   How might a double taxation agreement benefit a UK taxpayer who has income arising in a country which has such an agreement with the UK?

4   Tax avoidance is legal. True/False?

5   When may HMRC use the General Anti-Abuse Rule (GAAR)?

Answers to Quick Quiz

1   A direct tax is one charged on income or gains; an indirect tax is paid by a consumer to the supplier, who then passes it to HMRC.

2   An Extra Statutory Concession is a relaxation by HMRC of the strict rules where their imposition would be unfair.

3   The agreement could provide that the income is only to be taxed in one country or that credit is to be given for tax arising in one country against the tax charge in the other country.

4   True. Tax avoidance is legal; tax evasion is illegal.

5   The GAAR may be used by HMRC where a taxpayer has used abusive tax arrangements to obtain a tax advantage.

Now try the question below from the Practice Question Bank

Number	Type	Marks	Time
Q1	Section A	2	4 mins
Q2	Section A	2	4 mins
Q3	Section A	2	4 mins

Income tax and national insurance contributions

Computing taxable income and the income tax liability

2

Topic list	Syllabus reference
1 Scope of income tax	B1(a)
2 Computing taxable income	B5(a)
3 Types of income	B4(g), B5(a)
4 Tax exempt income	B4(h), B7(c)
5 Qualifying interest	B5(e)
6 Personal allowance	B5(b)
7 Computing income tax liability and income tax payable	B4(g), B5(d)
8 Accrued income scheme	B4(i)
9 Gift aid	B5(f)
10 Child benefit income tax charge	B5(g), B7(c)
11 Transferable personal allowance	B5(c), B7(c)
12 Married couples and couples in a civil partnership	B5(h), B7(b),(c)

Introduction

In the previous chapter we considered the UK tax system generally. Now we look at income tax, which is the tax applied on the income individuals make from their jobs, their businesses and their savings and investments. We consider the scope of income tax and see how to collect together all of an individual's income in a personal tax computation, and we also see which income can be excluded as being exempt from tax.

Next, we look at the circumstances in which interest paid can be deducted in the income tax computation.

Each individual is entitled to a personal allowance and only if that is exceeded will any tax be due. We then learn how to work out the income tax liability on taxable income and how much tax remains to be paid in cash.

We consider how the accrued income scheme applies to interest on UK Government securities (gilts). We see how donations to charity under the gift aid scheme can save tax. We also look at the income tax charge in relation to child benefit. We then consider the relief given by the transferable amount of the personal allowance between spouses/civil partners. Finally we consider how married couples or civil partners are subject to income tax and how they can minimise their tax liabilities.

In the next chapter we look at employment income.

Study guide

		Intellectual level
B1	**The scope of income tax**	
(a)	Explain how the residence of an individual is determined.	1
B4	**Property and investment income**	
(g)	Compute the tax payable on savings and dividends income.	2
(h)	Recognise the treatment of individual savings accounts (ISAs) and other tax exempt investments.	1
(i)	Understand how the accrued income scheme applies to UK Government securities (gilts).	1
B5	**The comprehensive computation of taxable income and income tax liability**	
(a)	Prepare a basic income tax computation involving different types of income.	2
(b)	Calculate the amount of personal allowance available.	2
(c)	Understand the impact of the transferable amount of personal allowance for spouses and civil partners.	2
(d)	Compute the amount of income tax payable.	2
(e)	Explain the treatment of interest paid for a qualifying purpose.	2
(f)	Understand the treatment of gift aid donations and charitable giving.	1
(g)	Explain and compute the child benefit tax charge.	1
(h)	Understand the treatment of property owned jointly by a married couple, or by a couple in a civil partnership.	1
B7	**The use of exemptions and reliefs in deferring and minimising income tax liabilities**	
(b)	Understand how a married couple or a couple in a civil partnership can minimise their tax liabilities.	2
(c)	Basic income tax planning.	2

Exam guide

Section A questions on the topics in this chapter may include identification of different types of income or calculation of the personal allowance. They could also include a simple computation of income tax liability on one type of income, or a computation of the child benefit income tax charge. Section B questions on the topics in this chapter could focus on tax implications of various types of income and the treatment of married couples/civil partners.

It is likely that you will have to prepare a full computation of income tax liability (and possibly income tax payable) in a Section C question, in a 15 mark question or a 10 mark question. You should familiarise yourself with the layout of the computation, and the three types of income: non-savings, savings and dividends. It is then a simple matter of slotting the final figures into the computation from supporting workings for the different types of income.

Gift aid donations could feature in a question in any section. You will come across the technique of increasing the basic rate and higher rate limits again when you deal with pensions later in this Study Text.

Throughout this chapter, you should be aware of basic income tax planning such as investing in sources of exempt income. We will also deal with some tax planning for spouses/civil partners in Section 12.

1 Scope of income tax

1.1 Residence   9/16, 12/16

1.1.1 Statutory residence test

FAST FORWARD

> An individual will automatically be non-UK resident if they meet any of the automatic overseas tests. An individual, who does not meet any of the automatic overseas tests, will automatically be UK resident if they meet any of the automatic UK tests. An individual who has not met any of the automatic overseas tests nor any of the automatic UK tests will be UK resident if they meet the sufficient ties test.

A taxpayer's **residence** has important consequences in establishing the **tax treatment of their UK and overseas income and capital gains. Statute sets out tests to determine whether or not an individual is UK resident in a tax year.**

The **operation of the tests** can be summarised as follows.

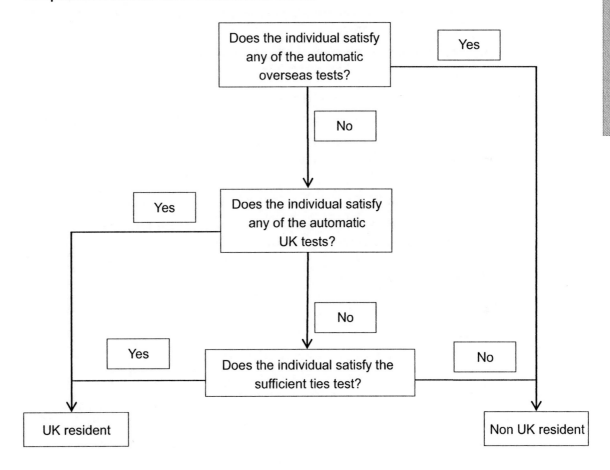

1.1.2 Automatic overseas tests

The automatic overseas tests must be considered first.

The **automatic overseas tests** treat an individual as **not resident in the UK in a tax year** if that individual:

(a)   **Spends less than 16 days in the UK in that tax year** and **was resident in the UK for one or more of the three previous tax years** (typically someone who is leaving the UK); or

(b)   **Spends less than 46 days in the UK in that tax year** and **was not resident in the UK for any of the previous three tax years** (typically someone who is arriving in the UK); or

(c)   **Works full-time overseas throughout that tax year** and **does not spend more than 90 days in the UK during that tax year.**

1.1.3 Automatic UK tests

If **none of the automatic overseas tests are met**, then the **automatic UK tests are considered.**

The **automatic UK tests treat an individual as UK resident in a tax year** if that individual:

(a) **Spends 183 days or more in the UK** during that tax year; or

(b) Has a **home in the UK** and **no home overseas**; or

(c) **Works full-time in the UK** during that tax year.

1.1.4 Sufficient UK ties tests

If the **individual meets none of the automatic overseas tests and none of the automatic UK tests,** the **'sufficient ties' test** must be considered.

The **sufficient ties test** compares the **number of days spent in the UK** and the **number of connection factors or 'ties' to the UK.**

An **individual who was not UK resident in any of the previous three tax years** (typically someone who is arriving in the UK) must determine whether any of the following ties apply:

(a) **UK resident close family** eg spouse/civil partner, child under the age of 18, but not including parents or grandparents

(b) **Available UK accommodation in which the individual spends at least one night during the tax year**

(c) **Substantive UK work** (employment or self-employment)

(d) **More than 90 days spent in the UK in either or both of the previous two tax years**

An **individual who was UK resident in any of the previous three tax years** (typically someone who is leaving the UK) must also determine whether any of the ties in (a) to (d) above apply plus whether an additional tie applies:

(e) **Present in the UK at midnight for the same or more days** in that tax year than in any other country

The following table shows **how an individual's UK residence status is found** by comparing **the number of days in the UK** during a tax year and the **number of UK ties:**

Days in UK	Previously resident	Not previously resident
Less than 16	Automatically not UK resident	Automatically not UK resident
Between 16 and 45	Resident if 4 UK ties (or more)	Automatically not UK resident
Between 46 and 90	Resident if 3 UK ties (or more)	Resident if 4 UK ties
Between 91 and 120	Resident if 2 UK ties (or more)	Resident if 3 UK ties (or more)
Between 121 and 182	Resident if 1 UK tie (or more)	Resident if 2 UK ties (or more)
183 or more	Automatically UK resident	Automatically UK resident

Exam focus point

> This table will be given in the Tax Rates and Allowances section of the examination paper.

1.1.5 Days spent in UK

Generally, **if a taxpayer is present in the UK at the end of a day (ie midnight)**, that **day counts as a day spent by the taxpayer in the UK.**

Exam focus point

> The detailed rules in the statutory residence test are quite complex (and have been simplified here), especially those in regard to work and having a home in the UK or overseas. **These more complex aspects are not examinable in Taxation (TX – UK).**

1.1.6 Examples

(a) James spent 40 days in the UK during the tax year 2017/18. He had not previously been resident in the UK. James did not work during 2017/18.

James is arriving in the UK. He satisfies one of the automatic overseas tests since he spent less than 46 days in the UK in 2017/18 and was not resident in the UK for any of the previous three tax years. James is therefore not UK resident for the tax year 2017/18.

(b) Caroline had not previously been resident in the UK before she arrived on 6 April 2017. She spent 60 days in the UK during the tax year 2017/18. She did not work during 2017/18. Her only home during 2017/18 is in the UK.

Caroline is arriving in the UK. She does not satisfy any of the automatic overseas tests since she spends 46 days or more in the UK and does not work overseas. She satisfies one of the automatic UK tests since her only home is in the UK. Caroline is therefore UK resident for the tax year 2017/18.

(c) Miranda had always been resident in the UK before the tax year 2017/18 and has previously spent more than 90 days in the UK in every tax year. Miranda does not work during 2017/18. Miranda is married to Walter who is UK resident in 2017/18. They own a house in the UK which is available to them for the whole of 2017/18. On 6 April 2017, Miranda bought an overseas apartment where she spent 285 days during 2017/18. The remaining 80 days were spent in her UK house.

Miranda is leaving the UK. She does not satisfy any of the automatic overseas tests since she spends 16 days or more in the UK and does not work overseas. She does not satisfy any of the automatic UK tests since she spends less than 183 days in the UK, has an overseas home and does not work in the UK. The 'sufficient ties' test is therefore relevant. Miranda has three UK ties:

(i) Close family resident in the UK (spouse);

(ii) Available accommodation in the UK in which she spends at least one night in the tax year; and

(iii) More than 90 days spent in the UK in both of the previous two tax years.

Miranda spends between 46 and 90 days in the UK in 2017/18, and was previously resident. These three ties are therefore sufficient to make her UK resident in 2017/18.

(d) Norman has not been resident in, or visited, the UK in any tax year before 2017/18. On 6 April 2017, he bought a house in the UK and spent 160 days in the UK during the tax year 2017/18. Norman also has an overseas house in which he spent the remainder of the tax year 2017/18. Norman did not work in 2017/18 and his close family members are not UK resident in 2017/18.

Norman is arriving in the UK. He does not satisfy any of the automatic overseas tests since he spends 46 days or more in the UK and does not work overseas. He does not satisfy any of the automatic UK tests as he spent less than 183 days in the UK, has an overseas home and does not work in the UK. The 'sufficient ties' test is therefore relevant. Norman spends between 121 and 182 days in the UK during 2017/18, and has not previously been resident and so he would need two UK ties to be UK resident for that tax year. Since Norman has only one tie with the UK in 2017/18 (available accommodation), he is not UK resident for the tax year 2017/18.

1.2 Tax consequences of residence

An individual who is UK resident is taxed on worldwide income.

Generally, a **UK resident is liable to UK income tax on their UK and overseas income** whereas a **non-UK resident is liable to UK income tax only on income arising in the UK**. We deal with the capital gains tax consequences later in this Study Text.

Exam focus point

> The taxation of the overseas income of a UK resident and the taxation of non-UK residents is **outside the scope** of the Taxation (TX – UK) syllabus.

In a personal income tax computation, we bring together, for each tax year, income from all sources, splitting the sources into non-savings, savings and dividend income.

An individual's income from all sources is brought together (aggregated) in a personal tax computation for each tax year.

Key terms

> The **tax year**, or **fiscal year**, or **year of assessment** runs from 6 April to 5 April. For example, the tax year 2017/18 runs from 6 April 2017 to 5 April 2018.

In the computation, three columns are needed to distinguish between non-savings income, savings income and dividend income. Here is an example. All items are explained later in this Study Text.

RICHARD: INCOME TAX COMPUTATION 2017/18

	Non-savings income £	Savings income £	Dividend income £	Total £
Income from employment	50,150			
Building society interest		1,400		
Dividends			6,000	
Total income	50,150	1,400	6,000	
Less qualifying interest paid	(2,000)			
Net income	48,150	1,400	6,000	55,550
Less personal allowance	(11,500)			
Taxable income	36,650	1,400	6,000	44,050

	£
Income tax	
Non savings income	
£33,500 × 20%	6,700
£3,150 (36,650 – 33,500) × 40%	1,260
Savings income	
£500 × 0%	0
£900 (1,400 – 500) × 40%	360
Dividend income	
£5,000 × 0%	0
£1,000 (6,000 – 5,000) × 32.5%	325
Tax liability	8,645
Less tax suffered	
PAYE tax on salary (say)	(8,050)
Tax payable	595

Key terms

> **Total income** is all income subject to income tax. Each of the amounts which make up total income is called a component. **Net income** is total income after qualifying interest and trade losses. **Taxable income** is net income less the personal allowance.

Income tax is charged on **taxable income**. Non-savings income is dealt with first, then savings income and then dividend income. We look at how to compute the income tax liability later in this chapter.

2.1 The complete proforma for computing taxable income

Here is a complete proforma computation of taxable income. It is probably too much for you to absorb at this stage, but refer back to it as you come to the chapters dealing with the types of income shown. You will also see how trading losses fit into the proforma later in this Study Text.

	Non-savings income £	Savings income £	Dividend income £	Total £
Trading income	X			
Employment income	X			
Pension income	X			
Property business income	X			
Bank/building society interest		X		
Other interest (eg gilt interest)		X		
Dividends	—	—	X	
Total income	X	X	X	
Less qualifying interest paid	(X)	(X)	(X)	
Net income	X	X	X	X
Less personal allowance	(X)	(X)	(X)	
Taxable income	X	X	X	X

3 Types of income

 FAST FORWARD

Income must be classified according to the nature of the income as different computational rules apply to different types of income.

 One of the competencies you require to fulfil Performance Objective 15 Tax computations and assessments of the PER is to extract and analyse data from financial records and filing information relevant to the preparation of tax computations and related supporting documents. You can apply the knowledge you obtain from this section of the Study Text to help to demonstrate this competence.

3.1 Classification of income

All income received must be **classified** according to the nature of the income. This is because different computational rules apply to different types of income. Income can then be further classified as non-savings, savings or dividend income. The main types of income are:

- **Income from employment (employment income, non-savings income)**
- **Pension income (non-savings income)**
- **Profits of trades, professions and vocations (trading income, non-savings income)**
- **Income from property letting (property business income, non-savings income)**
- **Interest income (savings income)**
- **Dividends (dividend income)**

3.2 Non-savings income

The rules for computing **employment income**, **trading income** and **property business income** will be covered in later chapters. These types of income are **non-savings income**. **Pension income** is also non-savings income.

3.3 Savings income

Savings income is interest. Interest is paid on bank and building society accounts, most National Savings & Investments (NS&I) products, on government securities (gilts) such as treasury stock, and on company loan stock.

 BPP LEARNING MEDIA

Part B Income tax and national insurance contributions | **2: Computing taxable income and the income tax liability** 23

3.4 Dividend income

Dividend income consists of **dividends** received as a result of ownership of shares. Dividends are paid without deduction of tax (paid gross).

4 Tax exempt income

FAST FORWARD

Income from certain investments, such as those held in individual savings accounts (ISAs), is exempt from income tax.

4.1 Types of tax exempt investments

One of the competencies you require to fulfil Performance Objective 17 Tax planning and advice of the PER is to mitigate and/or defer tax liabilities through the use of standard reliefs, exemptions and incentives. You can apply the knowledge you obtain from this section of the Study Text to help to demonstrate this competence.

Income from certain investments is exempt from income tax. They are therefore useful for tax planning to minimise tax from investments.

4.2 Individual savings accounts (ISAs)   12/16

Key term

ISAs are tax efficient savings accounts. There are two types of ISA.

- Cash ISA (which only has a cash component)
- Stocks and shares ISA (which primarily has a stocks and shares component, although cash may be held in a stocks and shares ISA if the provider allows this)

The annual subscription limit **for ISAs is £20,000 per tax year (2017/18)**. This can be invested in cash, stocks and shares, or any combination of the two. An individual can **withdraw money from a flexible cash ISA** and **replace it in the same tax year without the replaced cash counting towards the ISA subscription limit.**

Dividend income and interest received from ISAs is exempt from income tax, whether it is paid out to the investor or retained and reinvested within the ISA. Similarly, **capital gains made within a ISA are exempt from capital gains tax.** The introduction of the savings income nil rate band and the dividend nil rate band (see later in this chapter) means that ISAs are not as advantageous as they were previously. However, **additional rate taxpayers and individuals who have already used their savings income nil band will still benefit from using a cash ISA. The main benefit of using a stocks and shares ISA is the capital gains tax exemption** where an individual already uses the annual exempt amount (see later in this Study Text).

24   **2: Computing taxable income and the income tax liability** | Part B Income tax and national insurance contributions

BPP LEARNING MEDIA

4.3 Savings certificates

Savings certificates are issued by National Savings and Investments (NS&I). They may be fixed rate certificates or index linked and are for fixed terms of between two and five years. On maturity the profit is tax exempt. This profit is often called interest.

4.4 Premium bonds

Prizes received from premium bonds are exempt from tax.

4.5 Child benefit

Child benefit is a benefit paid to people responsible for caring for at least one child. It is usually paid to the mother of the child.

Child benefit is usually exempt from income tax. However, an **income tax charge** applies if a taxpayer receives child benefit (or their partner receives child benefit) and has **adjusted net income over £50,000 in a tax year**. This charge is covered later in this chapter.

5 Qualifying interest   6/17

FAST FORWARD

Qualifying interest is given tax relief by being deducted from total income to compute net income.

An individual who pays interest on a loan in a tax year is entitled to relief in that tax year if the loan is for one of the following purposes:

(a) **Loan to buy plant or machinery for partnership use.** Interest is allowed for three years from the end of the tax year in which the loan was taken out. If the plant or machinery is used partly for private use, the allowable interest is apportioned.

(b) **Loan to buy plant or machinery for employment use.** Interest is allowed for three years from the end of the tax year in which the loan was taken out. If the plant or machinery is used partly for private use, the allowable interest is apportioned.

(c) **Loan to buy interest in employee-controlled company.** The company must be an unquoted trading company resident in the UK with at least 50% of the voting shares held by employees.

(d) **Loan to invest in a partnership.** The investment may be a share in the partnership or a contribution to the partnership of capital or a loan to the partnership. The individual must be a partner (other than a limited partner) and relief ceases when they cease to be a partner.

(e) **Loan to invest in a co-operative.** The investment may be shares or a loan. The individual must spend the greater part of their time working for the co-operative.

Tax relief is given by deducting the interest from total income to calculate net income for the tax year in which the interest is paid. For Taxation (TX – UK) purposes it is deducted from **non-savings income first, then from savings income and lastly from dividend income**.

Exam focus point

There are some situations where this order of set off will not be the most beneficial but such a scenario **will not be examined** in Taxation (TX – UK).

Question

In 2017/18, Frederick has trading income of £45,000, savings income of £4,320 and dividend income of £6,000. Frederick pays interest of £1,370 in 2017/18 on a loan to invest in a partnership. What is Frederick's net income for 2017/18?

Answer

	Non-savings income £	Savings income £	Dividend income £	Total £
Total income	45,000	4,320	6,000	55,320
Less qualifying interest paid	(1,370)			
Net income	43,630	4,320	6,000	53,950

6 Personal allowance (PA)   6/17

FAST FORWARD

All individuals are entitled to a personal allowance (PA). It is deducted from net income, first against non savings income, then against savings income and lastly against dividend income. The PA is reduced by £1 for every £2 that adjusted net income exceeds £100,000 and can be reduced to nil.

Once income from all sources has been aggregated and any qualifying interest deducted, the remainder is the taxpayer's net income. An allowance, the **personal allowance**, is **deducted from net income**. Like qualifying interest, for Taxation (TX – UK) purposes it reduces **non-savings income first, then savings income and lastly dividend income**.

Exam focus point

There are some situations where this order of set off will not be the most beneficial but such a scenario **will not be examined** in Taxation (TX – UK).

All individuals (including children) **are entitled to a PA of £11,500.**

However, if the **individual's adjusted net income exceeds £100,000**, the **PA is reduced by £1 for each £2 by which adjusted net income exceeds £100,000 until the PA is nil (which is when adjusted net income is £123,000 or more).**

Key term

Adjusted net income is net income less the gross amounts of personal pension contributions and gift aid donations.

Exam focus point

The examining team have stated that if adjusted net income clearly exceeds £123,000, there is no need to perform the calculations to restrict the personal allowance. A simple statement that no personal allowance is available because adjusted net income exceeds £123,000 is sufficient.

We will look at personal pension contributions and gift aid donations later in this Study Text and revisit this topic again then. At the moment, we will look at the situation where net income and adjusted net income are the same amounts.

Question   Personal allowance

In 2017/18, Clare receives employment income of £95,000, bank interest of £8,000 and dividends of £7,500. Calculate Clare's taxable income for 2017/18.

	Non-savings income £	Savings income £	Dividend income £	Total £
Employment income	95,000			
Bank interest		8,000		
Dividends			7,500	
Net income (N)	95,000	8,000	7,500	110,500
Less PA (W)	(6,250)			
Taxable income	88,750	8,000	7,500	104,250

Working	£
Net income	110,500
Less income limit	(100,000)
Excess	10,500
PA	11,500
Less half excess £10,500 × ½	(5,250)
	6,250

Note. Where there is no qualifying interest, so that total income is the same as net income, it is acceptable just to state the net income at this stage of the computation.

7 Computing income tax liability and income tax payable

FAST FORWARD

To work out the income tax liability on the taxable income, first compute the tax on non-savings income, then on savings income and, finally, on dividend income. Tax reducers reduce tax on income at a set rate of relief. To work out tax payable, deduct tax paid under Pay As You Earn (PAYE). If tax deducted under PAYE exceeds the tax liability, the excess will be repayable.

PER alert

One of the competencies you require to fulfil Performance Objective 15 Tax computations and assessments of the PER is to prepare or contribute to the computation or assessment of tax computations for individuals. You can apply the knowledge you obtain from this section of the Study Text to help to demonstrate this competence.

Key terms

The **income tax liability** is the amount of tax charged on the individual's taxable income. **Income tax payable** is the balance of the income tax liability still to be settled in cash.

7.1 Introduction

Income tax payable is computed on an individual's taxable income using the proforma in shown earlier in this chapter. The tax rates are applied to taxable income first to non-savings income, then to savings income and finally to dividend income. We will start by looking at taxpayers who only have non-savings income, then to taxpayers who have both non-savings and savings income and, finally, to taxpayers who have non-savings income, savings income, and dividend income.

7.2 Computations with non-savings income only

Taxpayers with non-savings income only may pay income tax at basic rate, higher rate and additional rate.

7.2.1 Basic rate on non-savings income

The **basic rate of tax** on non-savings income is **20%** for 2017/18. The **basic rate limit** for 2017/18 is £33,500.

7.2.2 Higher rate on non-savings income

The **higher rate of tax** on non-savings income is **40%** for 2017/18. The **higher rate limit** for 2017/18 is £150,000.

Question	Basic rate and higher rate on non-savings income

In 2017/18 Jem has trading income of £43,000 and property business income of £8,500. Calculate Jem's tax liability for 2017/18.

Answer

	Non-savings income £
Trading income	43,000
Property business income	8,500
Net income	51,500
Less PA	(11,500)
Taxable income	40,000

Income tax

	£
Non-savings income	
£33,500 × 20%	6,700
£6,500 (40,000 – 33,500) × 40%	2,600
Tax liability	9,300

7.2.3 Additional rate on non-savings income

The **additional rate of tax** on non-savings income is **45%** for 2017/18. **This rate applies to non-savings income in excess of the higher rate limit which is £150,000 in 2017/18.**

Question	All rates of tax on non-savings income

In 2017/18 Milo has employment income of £145,000 and property business income of £10,800. Calculate Milo's tax liability for 2017/18.

	Non-savings income £
Employment income	145,000
Property business income	10,800
Net income/taxable income (no PA available as net income exceeds £123,000)	155,800

Income tax

	£
Non-savings income	
£33,500 × 20%	6,700
£116,500 (150,000 – 33,500) × 40%	46,600
£5,800 (155,800 – 150,000) × 45%	2,610
Tax liability	55,910

7.3 Computations with non-savings income and savings income only

7.3.1 Savings income starting rate

There is a **tax rate of 0% for savings income up to £5,000 (the savings income starting rate limit)**. This rate is called the **savings income starting rate. The savings income starting rate only applies where the savings income falls wholly or partly below the starting rate limit.**

Remember that income tax is charged first on non-savings income. So, in most cases, an individual's non-savings income will exceed the savings income starting rate limit and the savings income starting rate will not be available on savings income.

7.3.2 Savings income basic, higher and additional rates

The **basic rate of tax** for savings income is **20%** for 2017/18. The **higher rate of tax** for savings income is **40%** for 2017/18. The **additional rate of tax** for savings income is **45%** for 2017/18.

7.3.3 Savings income nil rate band

There is a **tax rate of 0%** for **savings income** within the **savings income nil rate band.** The savings income nil rate band for 2017/18 is **£1,000** if the individual is a **basic rate taxpayer** and **£500** if the individual is a **higher rate taxpayer.** There is **no savings income nil rate band** for **additional rate taxpayers.**

The **savings income nil rate band** counts towards the **basic rate limit of £33,500.**

Exam focus point

> The detailed rules for establishing whether an individual is a higher rate or additional rate taxpayer for the purpose of computing the availability of the savings income nil rate band are quite complicated and are **not examinable** in Taxation (TX – UK). Therefore, in any question involving the savings income nil rate band, it will be quite clear which tax rate is applicable.

 Question   Savings income starting rate and savings income nil rate band

In 2017/18 Alicia has trading income of £14,100 and bank interest of £8,000. Calculate Alicia's tax liability for 2017/18.

Answer

	Non-savings income £	Savings income £	Total £
Trading income	14,100		
Bank interest		8,000	
Net income	14,100	8,000	22,100
Less PA	(11,500)		
Taxable income	2,600	8,000	10,600

Income tax

	£
Non-savings income	
£2,600 × 20%	520
Savings income	
£2,400 (5,000 – 2,600) × 0% (savings starting rate)	0
£1,000 × 0% (savings income nil rate band)	0
£4,600 (8,000 – 2,400 – 1,000) × 20%	920
Tax liability	1,440

Question — Savings nil rate, basic rate and higher rate with savings income

In 2017/18 Joe has employment income of £41,800 and bank interest of £5,200. Calculate Joe's tax liability for 2017/18.

Answer

	Non-savings income £	Savings income £	Total £
Employment income	41,800		
Bank interest		5,200	
Net income	41,800	5,200	47,000
Less PA	(11,500)		
Taxable income	30,300	5,200	35,500

Income tax

	£
Non-savings income	
£30,300 × 20%	6,060
Savings income	
£500 × 0% (savings income nil rate band – higher rate taxpayer)	0
£2,700 (33,500 – 30,300 – 500) × 20%	540
£2,000 (5,200 – 500 – 2,700) × 40%	800
Tax liability	7,400

Question — All rates of tax with savings income

In 2017/18 Maddie has trading income of £146,800 and building society interest of £6,700. Calculate Maddie's tax liability for 2017/18.

	Non-savings income £	Savings income £	Total £
Trading income	146,800		
Building society interest		6,700	
Net income/taxable income (no PA available)	146,800	6,700	153,500

Maddie is not entitled to the PA as her net income exceeds £123,000.

Income tax

	£
Non-savings income	
£33,500 × 20%	6,700
£113,300 (146,800 – 33,500) × 40%	45,320
Savings income	
£3,200 (150,000 – 146,800) × 40%	1,280
£3,500 (6,700 – 3,200) × 45%	1,575
Tax liability	54,875

No savings income nil rate band is available because Maddie is an additional rate taxpayer.

7.4 Computations with non-savings, savings and dividend income 12/16

7.4.1 Dividend income basic, higher and additional rates

The **basic rate of tax** for dividend income is **7.5%** for 2017/18. The **higher rate of tax** for dividend income is **32.5%** for 2017/18. The **additional rate of tax** for dividend income is **38.1%** for 2017/18.

7.4.2 Dividend nil rate band

There is a **tax rate of 0%** for **dividend income** within the **dividend nil rate band.** The dividend nil rate band is **£5,000** for **all taxpayers**.

The **dividend nil rate band** counts towards the **basic rate limit of £33,500 and the higher rate limit of £150,000.**

Question   Dividend nil rate, basic rate and higher rate with dividend income

In 2017/18 Margery has employment income of £55,450, building society interest of £1,600 and dividends of £15,000. Calculate Margery's tax liability for 2017/18.

Answer

	Non-savings income £	Savings income £	Dividend income £	Total £
Employment income	55,450			
BSI		1,600		
Dividends			15,000	
Net income	55,450	1,600	15,000	72,050
Less PA	(11,500)			
Taxable income	43,950	1,600	15,000	60,550

Income tax

	£
Non-savings income	
£33,500 × 20%	6,700
£10,450 (43,950 – 33,500) × 40%	4,180
Savings income	
£500 × 0% (savings income nil rate band – higher rate taxpayer)	0
£1,100 (1,600 – 500) × 40%	440
Dividend income	
£5,000 × 0% (dividend nil rate band)	0
£10,000 (15,000 – 5,000) × 32.5%	3,250
Tax liability	14,570

Question		All rates of tax with dividend income

In 2017/18 Julian has employment income of £148,000, bank interest of £6,250 and dividends of £20,000. Calculate Julian's tax liability for 2017/18.

Answer	

	Non-savings income £	Savings income £	Dividend income £	Total £
Employment income	148,000			
Bank interest		6,250		
Dividends			20,000	
Net income/taxable income (no PA available)	148,000	6,250	20,000	174,250

Julian is not entitled to the PA as his net income exceeds £123,000.

Income tax

	£
Non-savings income	
£33,500 × 20%	6,700
£114,500 (148,000 – 33,500) × 40%	45,800
Savings income	
£2,000 (150,000 – 148,000) × 40%	800
£4,250 (6,250 – 2,000) × 45%	1,912
Dividend income	
£5,000 × 0%	0
£15,000 (20,000 – 5,000) × 38.1%	5,715
Tax liability	60,927

No savings income nil rate band is available because Julian is an additional rate taxpayer.

7.4.3 Tax reducers

Tax reducers do not affect income; they reduce tax on income. The relevant tax reducers for Taxation (TX – UK) are:

- **Transferable PA** (marriage allowance). This is dealt with later in this chapter.
- **Property business financial costs**. This is dealt with later in this Study Text.

Tax reducers are deducted in computing an individual's income tax liability. The tax liability can only be reduced to zero; a tax reducer cannot create a repayment.

7.5 Steps in computing the income tax liability and income tax payable

We now summarise the **steps required to compute the income tax liability.**

Step 1   **The first step in preparing a personal tax computation is to set up three columns.**
One column for non-savings income, one for savings income and one for dividend income. Add up income from different sources. The sum of these is known as 'total income'. Deduct qualifying interest and trade losses to compute 'net income'. Deduct the PA to compute 'taxable income'.

Step 2   **Deal with non-savings income first**
Any non-savings income up to the basic rate limit of £33,500 is taxed at 20%. Non-savings income between the basic rate limit and the higher rate limit of £150,000 is taxed at 40%. The maximum non-savings income to which the higher rate applies is therefore £(150,000 – 33,500) = £116,500. Any further non-savings income is taxed at 45%.

Step 3   **Now deal with savings income**
Savings income below the savings income starting rate limit of £5,000 is taxed at the savings income starting rate of 0%. Then tax savings income covered by the savings income nil rate band (for basic rate and higher rate taxpayers) at 0%. Any remaining savings income up to the basic rate limit of £33,500 is taxed at 20%. Savings income between the basic rate limit and the higher rate limit of £150,000 is taxed at 40%. Any further savings income is taxed at 45%.

Step 4   **Lastly, tax dividend income**
The first £5,000 is within the dividend nil rate band and is taxed at 0%. Other dividend income below the basic rate limit of £33,500 is taxed at 7.5%. Dividend income between the basic rate limit and the higher rate limit of £150,000 is taxed at 32.5%. Any further dividend income is taxed at 38.1%.

Step 5   **Add the amounts of tax together.**

Step 6   Once tax has been computed, **deduct any available tax reducers** (eg transferable PA, property business finance costs – see later in this Study Text).

Step 7   Calculate the amount of any **child benefit income tax charge** and **pension annual allowance charge** (see later in this Study Text) add to the tax remaining after step 6. The resulting figure is the **income tax liability**.

The following **additional step** is needed to compute income tax payable when the income tax liability has been calculated.

Step 8   **Deduct tax paid under PAYE.**

Question	Calculation of income tax payable

In 2017/18, Michael has employment income of £58,300 (PAYE deducted £6,100), bank interest of £4,250 and dividends of £7,500. He pays qualifying interest of £3,000. How much income tax is payable by Michael in 2017/18?

	Non-savings income £	Savings income £	Dividend income £	Total £
Employment income	58,300			
Bank interest		4,250		
Dividends			7,500	
Total income	58,300	4,250	7,500	
Less qualifying interest paid	(3,000)			
Net income	55,300	4,250	7,500	67,050
Less personal allowance	(11,500)			
Taxable income	43,800	4,250	7,500	55,550

Income tax	£
Non-savings income	
£33,500 × 20%	6,700
£10,300 (43,800 – 33,500) × 40%	4,120
Savings income	
£500 × 0% (savings income nil rate band – higher rate taxpayer)	0
£3,750 (4,250 – 500) × 40%	1,500
Dividend income	
£5,000 × 0%	0
£2,500 (7,500 – 2,500) × 32.5%	812
Tax liability	13,132
Less PAYE	(6,100)
Tax payable	7,032

7.6 Calculating additional tax due 6/17

FAST FORWARD Calculating additional tax due, for example when a new source of income is acquired, can often be done by working at the margin.

Often a taxpayer is interested in looking at the after tax return from a particular investment or transaction. In each of the following examples we will **calculate the additional tax due as a result of acquiring a new source of income.** This is sometimes called 'working at the margin' as it relates to the marginal rate of tax which is the rate that the taxpayer has to pay on each additional pound of income received. Note how it is **not necessary here to use the full income tax proforma and therefore is a useful way of saving time in the exam.**

7.7 Examples: Additional tax due

(a) Kate has employment income each tax year of £70,000. Her grandfather dies leaving her a number of houses which are rented out to tenants. She has property business income of £25,000 during 2017/18. Kate's employment income uses up her PA of £11,500 and the basic rate band of £33,500 (total £45,000) so the additional tax due as a result of receiving the property business income can be calculated simply as £25,000 × 40% = £10,000.

(b) Kate has employment income each tax year of £44,000. Her grandfather dies leaving her a number of houses which are rented out to tenants. She has property business income of £25,000 during 2017/18.

The additional tax due as a result of receiving the property business income can be calculated as follows:

Amount remaining below basic rate limit:
£33,500 – (£44,000 – £11,500) = £1,000

	£
£1,000 @ 20%	200
£24,000 (25,000 – 1,000) @ 40%	9,600
Additional tax due	9,800

(c)   Kate has employment income each tax year of £99,000. Her grandfather dies leaving her a number of houses which are rented out to tenants. She has property business income of £25,000 during 2017/18. Income tax on property business income is all at the higher rate. In addition, Kate will no longer be entitled to the PA since her net income is £(99,000 + 25,000) = £124,000.

The additional tax due is therefore calculated as follows:

	£
Higher rate tax on property business income £25,000 @ 40%	10,000
Tax on income previously covered by PA £11,500 @ 40%	4,600
Additional tax due	14,600

(d)   Kate has employment income each tax year of £175,000. She has property business income of £25,000 during 2017/18. Kate's employment income uses up the basic rate band of £33,500 and the higher rate band of £116,500 (total £150,000) so the property business income will be taxed at the additional rate. Kate's existing income is of such a level that she is not entitled to the PA, even before the property business income is received, and so there is no further impact on additional tax due. The additional tax due as a result of receiving the property business income therefore can be calculated simply as £25,000 × 45% = £11,250.

8 Accrued income scheme

The accrued income scheme ensures that a taxpayer who sells a gilt is taxed on any interest income included in the proceeds. Similarly, relief is given to the purchaser of the gilt for the interest included in the price paid.

8.1 Introduction

If the **owner of UK Government securities (known as gilt-edged securities or 'gilts')** sells them before a particular date, **that individual will not be entitled to the next interest payment**. The new owner will receive it. However, **the sale proceeds received by the seller includes interest accrued to the date of sale**. Since gilts are exempt from capital gains tax (see later in this Study Text), this would be a way of avoiding tax on this interest without the special rules of the accrued income scheme described in this section.

However, if securities are sold on or after a particular date, they are sold **excluding interest** and the **original owner is entitled to the whole of the next interest payment and will be taxed on it under the usual income tax rules**. However, **the sale proceeds will exclude interest accruing after the date of sale so that this accrued interest effectively goes to the purchaser**. Again, the usual tax rules do not reflect the actual receipt of interest and so the accrued income scheme applies to reflect the situation.

The **accrued income scheme only applies** where the seller **holds securities with a nominal value exceeding £5,000** during the tax year in which the interest period ends.

8.2 How the accrued income scheme works

Under the **accrued income scheme**, where **gilts are transferred at a price which includes interest, the accrued interest reflected in the value of gilts is taxed as savings income on the seller.** This is because the seller is treated as entitled to the proportion of interest which has accrued since the last interest payment. The buyer is entitled to relief against the interest they receive equal to the amount taxable on the seller.

Conversely, **where the transfer is excluding interest, the seller will receive the whole of the next interest payment. They will be entitled to relief for the amount of interest assessed on the purchaser. The purchaser is treated as entitled to the proportion of the interest accrued between the sale and the next payment date and it is taxed as savings income.**

Exam focus point

> The accrued income scheme also applies to securities other than gilts, such as corporate bonds. However, in Taxation (TX – UK), **any question on the accrued income scheme will be confined to gilts.**

Question
Accrued income scheme

Owen owned £10,000 (nominal value) 5% UK Government Loan Stock. Interest was payable on 30 June and 31 December each year. Owen sold the loan stock to Yvonne on 30 November 2017 for sale proceeds of £11,208 including accrued interest of £208 for the period between 1 July 2017 and 30 November 2017 (£10,000 × 5% × 5/12). What are the amounts taxable on Owen and Yvonne as savings income in respect of the loan stock for 2017/18?

Answer

Owen

	£
Interest received 30.6.17	
£10,000 × 5% × 6/12	250
Accrued interest deemed received 31.12.17	
£10,000 × 5% × 5/12	208
Total taxable as savings income	458

Yvonne

	£
Interest received 31.12.17	
£10,000 × 5% × 6/12	250
Less relief for accrued interest (amount taxable on Owen)	
£10,000 × 5% × 5/12	(208)
Total taxable as savings income (ie 1 month of interest £10,000 × 5% × 1/12)	42

Exam focus point

> The accrued income scheme rules may seem complicated but remember that the aim is to tax each taxpayer on the interest which relates to their period of ownership, regardless of whether it was actually received by the buyer or the seller.

9 Gift aid

 FAST FORWARD

> Increase the basic rate limit and the higher rate limit by the gross amount of any gift aid payment to give tax relief at the higher and additional rates.

9.1 Gift aid donations

Key term

> One-off and regular charitable gifts of money qualify for tax relief under the **gift aid scheme** provided the donor gives the charity a gift aid declaration.

Gift aid declarations can be made in writing, electronically through the internet or orally over the phone. A declaration can cover a one-off gift or any number of gifts made after a specified date (which may be in the past).

The gift must not be repayable and must not confer any more than a minimal benefit on the donor.

9.2 Tax relief for gift aid donations

A gift aid donation is treated as though it is paid net of basic rate tax (20%). This gives basic rate tax relief when the payment is made. For example, if the taxpayer wants the charity to receive a donation of £1,000, they would only need to make a payment to the charity of £800. The charity reclaims the 20% tax relief that the taxpayer has received, resulting in a gross gift of £1,000.

Additional tax relief for higher rate and additional rate taxpayers is given in the personal tax computation by increasing the donor's basic rate limit and higher rate limit by the gross amount of the gift. To arrive at the gross amount of the gift you must multiply the amount paid by 100/80. In the above example, the gross amount would be the amount paid of £800 × 100/80 = £1,000. The effect of increasing the basic rate limit is to increase the amount on which basic rate tax is payable. This is sometimes called 'extending the basic rate band'.

The effect of increasing the higher rate limit is simply to preserve the amount of taxable income on which higher rate tax is payable.

No additional relief is due for basic rate taxpayers. Increasing the basic rate limit is irrelevant as taxable income is below this limit.

Question   Gift aid with higher rate relief

In 2017/18, James has employment income of £69,135. This is his only income for the tax year. In September 2017 he paid £8,000 (net) under the gift aid scheme. Compute James' income tax liability for 2017/18.

Answer

		Non-savings income
		£
Employment income/Net income		69,135
Less PA		(11,500)
Taxable income		57,635

Income tax	£	£
Basic rate	43,500 (W) × 20%	8,700
Higher rate	14,135 × 40%	5,654
	57,635	14,354

Working: Basic rate limit £33,500 + (£8,000 × 100/80) = £43,500

In 2017/18, Matt has trading income of £182,000. This is his only income for the tax year. In January 2018, he made a gift aid donation of £12,000 (net). Compute Matt's income tax liability for 2017/18.

Answer

		Non-savings income £
Taxable income (no PA as income over £123,000)		182,000

Income tax	£	£
Basic rate	48,500 (W1) × 20%	9,700
Higher rate	116,500 (W2) × 40%	46,600
Additional rate	17,000 × 45%	7,650
	182,000	63,950

Workings

1   Basic rate limit £33,500 + (£12,000 × 100/80) = £48,500

2   Higher rate limit £150,000 + (£12,000 × 100/80) = £165,000. The higher rate band is therefore £(165,000 − 48,500) = £116,500 ie the same as usual £(150,000 − 33,500).

9.3 Adjusted net income

Key term

> **Adjusted net income** is net income less the gross amounts of personal pension contributions and gift aid donations.

The restrictions on the PA are calculated in relation to adjusted net income.

Question   **Adjusted net income**

Margaretta earns a salary of £112,000 in 2017/18. In January 2018, she made a gift aid donation of £5,000. Compute Margaretta's income tax liability for 2017/18.

Answer

		Non-savings income £
Employment income/Net income		112,000
Less PA (W1)		(8,625)
Taxable income		103,375

Income tax	£	£
Basic rate (W2)	39,750 × 20%	7,950
Higher rate	63,625 × 40%	25,450
	103,375	33,400

Workings

1 PA

	£
Net income	112,000
Less: gift aid donation £5,000 × 100/80	(6,250)
Adjusted net income	105,750
Less income limit	(100,000)
Excess	5,750
PA	11,500
Less half excess £5,750 × ½	(2,875)
	8,625

2 Basic rate limit

£33,500 + (£5,000 × 100/80)   **£39,750**

Where an individual has an adjusted net income between £100,000 and £123,000, the effective rate of tax on the income between these two amounts will usually be 60%. This is calculated as 40% (the higher rate on income) plus 40% of half (ie 20%) of the excess adjusted net income over £100,000 used to restrict the PA. The individual should consider **making personal pension contributions and/or gift aid donations to reduce adjusted net income to below £100,000.**

10 Child benefit income tax charge

FAST FORWARD

There is an income tax charge to recover child benefit if the recipient or their partner has adjusted net income over £50,000 in a tax year.

An **income tax charge** applies if a taxpayer receives child benefit (or their partner receives child benefit) and the taxpayer has **adjusted net income over £50,000 in a tax year. Adjusted net income is defined in the same way as for the restriction of the PA** described earlier in this chapter. The effect of the charge is to recover child benefit from taxpayers who have higher incomes.

A 'partner' is a **spouse,** a **civil partner,** or an **unmarried partner** where the couple are **living together as though they were married or were civil partners.**

If the taxpayer has **adjusted net income over £60,000,** the charge is equal to the **full amount of child benefit received.**

If the taxpayer has **adjusted net income between £50,000 and £60,000,** the charge is **1% of the child benefit amount for each £100 of adjusted net income in excess of £50,000. The calculation,** at all stages, **is rounded down to the nearest whole number.**

Exam focus point

This information will be given in the Tax Rates and Allowances in the examination paper.

If **both partners have adjusted net income in excess of £50,000,** the **partner with the higher adjusted net income** is liable for the charge.

The child benefit income tax charge is collected through the self-assessment system (dealt with later in this Study Text). This includes the need for **taxpayers to submit tax returns,** which can be time consuming and costly. To avoid this, **taxpayers can opt not to receive child benefit at all** so that the income tax charge does not apply.

Samantha is divorced and has two children aged ten and six. She has net income of £56,000 in 2017/18. Samantha made personal pension contributions of £4,500 (gross) during 2017/18. She receives child benefit of £1,788 in 2017/18. Calculate Samantha's child benefit income tax charge for 2017/18.

Answer

	£
Net income	56,000
Less personal pension contributions (gross)	(4,500)
Adjusted net income	51,500
Less threshold	(50,000)
Excess	1,500
÷ £100	15
Child benefit income tax charge: 1% × £1,788 × 15	268

Tutorial note

If Samantha had made an extra gross personal pension contribution of £1,500 during 2017/18, her adjusted net income would not have exceeded £50,000 and she would not have been subject to the child benefit income tax charge.

11 Transferable personal allowance

 FAST FORWARD

An individual is permitted to transfer £1,150 of their PA to their spouse/civil partner, in certain circumstances, giving a tax reducer of £230.

11.1 Transferable personal allowance

An individual can elect to transfer £1,150 of their PA to their spouse/civil partner if certain conditions are met. This is sometimes known as the marriage allowance.

Exam focus point

The transferable amount of PA will be given to you in the Tax Rates and Allowances in the examination paper.

11.2 Conditions

Neither the spouse/civil partner making the transfer nor the spouse/civil partner receiving the transfer can be a higher rate or additional rate taxpayer.

11.3 Method of giving relief

The spouse/civil partner receiving the transfer does not have an increased PA. **Instead, they are entitled to a tax reducer of £1,150 × 20% = £230. The tax reducer reduces the individual's tax liability.** If the individual has a tax liability of less than £230, the tax reducer reduces the tax liability to nil.

Alec and Bertha are a married couple. In the tax year 2017/18, Alec has net income of £10,000 and Bertha has net income of £25,500. All their income is non-savings income. Alec has made an election to transfer part of his PA to Bertha. Show Alec and Bertha's taxable income for 2017/18 and compute Bertha's income tax liability.

Answer

Alec

	Non-savings income
	£
Net income	10,000
Less PA £(11,500 – 1,150)	(10,350)
Taxable income	0

Bertha

	Non-savings income
	£
Net income	25,500
Less PA	(11,500)
Taxable income	14,000

Income tax	
£14,000 × 20%	2,800
Less marriage allowance tax reducer £1,150 × 20%	(230)
Income tax liability	2,570

11.4 Election

The election for transfer of the PA is made to HMRC online by the spouse/civil partner making the transfer.

For the tax year 2017/18, if the election is made before 6 April 2018 it will have effect for 2017/18 and subsequent tax years unless it is cancelled by the transferor spouse/civil partner or circumstances change (eg divorce or a tax reduction is not actually obtained). If the election for the tax year 2017/18 is made on or after 6 April 2018 it must be made within four years of the end of the tax year (ie by 5 April 2022) and will only apply for the tax year 2017/18.

The couple, as a whole, will save tax through the election if the net income of the transferor is below £11,500.

12 Married couples and couples in a civil partnership

Spouses and civil partners are separate taxpayers but should ensure that each spouse/civil partner uses their savings income nil rate band and dividend nil rate band. Income on property held jointly by married couples and civil partners is treated as if it were shared equally unless they make a joint declaration of the actual shares of ownership.

⚠ **PER alert**

One of the competencies you require to fulfil Performance Objective 17 Tax planning and advice of the PER is to review the situation of an individual or entity advising on any potential tax risks and/or additional tax minimisation measures. You can apply the knowledge you obtain from this section of the Study Text to help to demonstrate this competence.

12.1 Spouses and civil partners

Spouses and civil partners are taxed as two separate people. Each spouse/civil partner is entitled to a personal allowance depending on their income. Spouses and civil partners should ensure, where possible, that **each spouse/civil partner uses their savings income nil rate band and dividend nil rate band**.

12.2 Example: Income tax planning for spouses/civil partners (1)

Liam and Joe are a married couple. In 2017/18, Liam has trading profits of £180,000 and receives building society interest of £300 and Joe has a salary of £88,000 and receives dividends of £11,000. Since Liam is an additional rate taxpayer, he is not entitled to the savings income nil rate band but he has not utilised his dividend nil rate band. Joe has not utilised his savings income nil rate band of £500 (higher rate taxpayer) and has exceeded his dividend nil rate band of £5,000. Liam should therefore transfer his building society funds to Joe thus saving income tax of £300 × 45% = £135. Joe should transfer shares producing £5,000 of dividends to Liam thus saving income tax of £5,000 × 32.5% = £1,625.

12.3 Joint property

When spouses/civil partners jointly own income-generating property, it is assumed that they are entitled to equal shares of the income.

If the spouses/civil partners are not entitled to equal shares in the income-generating property, they may make a joint declaration to HMRC, specifying the proportion to which each is entitled. These proportions are used to tax each of them separately, in respect of income arising on or after the date of the declaration.

12.4 Example: Income tax planning for spouses/civil partners (2)

Brian is a higher rate taxpayer who owns a rental property producing £27,000 of property income on which he pays tax at 40%, giving him a tax liability of £10,800. His spouse, Mary, has no income. If Brian transfers only 5% of the asset to Mary, they will be treated as jointly owning the property and will each be taxed on 50% of the income. Brian's tax liability will be reduced to £5,400.

Mary's liability is then calculated as follows:

	£
Net income	13,500
Less PA	(11,500)
Taxable income	2,000
Tax on £2,000 × 20%	400

This gives an overall tax saving of £(5,400 – 400) = £5,000. This could alternatively be calculated as £11,500 × 40% = £4,600 plus £2,000 × 20% = £400 giving the total saving of £5,000.

Chapter Roundup

- An individual will automatically be non-UK resident if they meet any of the automatic overseas tests. An individual, who does not meet any of the automatic overseas tests, will automatically be UK resident if they meet any of the automatic UK tests. An individual who has not met any of the automatic overseas tests nor any of the automatic UK tests will be UK resident if they meet the sufficient ties test.

- An individual who is UK resident is taxed on worldwide income.

- In a personal income tax computation, we bring together, for each tax year, income from all sources, splitting the sources into non-savings, savings and dividend income.

- Income must be classified according to the nature of the income as different computational rules apply to different types of income.

- Income from certain investments, such as those held in Individual Savings Accounts (ISAs), is exempt from income tax.

- Qualifying interest is given tax relief by being deducted from total income to compute net income.

- All individuals are entitled to a personal allowance (PA). It is deducted from net income, first against non savings income, then against savings income and lastly against dividend income. The PA is reduced by £1 for every £2 that adjusted net income exceeds £100,000 and can be reduced to nil.

- To work out the income tax liability on the taxable income, first compute the tax on non-savings income, then on savings income and, finally, on dividend income. Tax reducers reduce tax on income at a set rate of relief. To work out tax payable, deduct tax paid under Pay As You Earn (PAYE). If tax deducted under PAYE exceeds the tax liability, the excess will be repayable.

- Calculating additional tax due, for example when a new source of income is acquired, can often be done by working at the margin.

- The accrued income scheme ensures that a taxpayer who sells a gilt is taxed on any interest income included in the proceeds. Similarly, relief is given to the purchaser of the gilt for the interest included in the price paid.

- Increase the basic rate limit and the higher rate limit by the gross amount of any gift aid payment to give tax relief at the higher and additional rates.

- There is an income tax charge to recover child benefit if the recipient or their partner has adjusted net income over £50,000 in a tax year.

- An individual is permitted to transfer £1,150 of their PA to their spouse/civil partner, in certain circumstances, giving a tax reducer of £230.

- Spouses and civil partners are separate taxpayers but should ensure that each spouse/civil partner uses their savings income nil rate band and dividend nil rate band. Income on property held jointly by married couples and civil partners is treated as if it were shared equally unless they make a joint declaration of the actual shares of ownership.

Quick Quiz

1   If an individual meets none of the automatic overseas tests and none of the automatic UK tests of residence in a tax year, what determines whether the individual is resident in the UK?

2   What are the tax advantages of holding investments in an individual savings account (ISA)?

3   Income tax on non-savings income is charged at _ % below the basic rate limit, at _% between the basic rate limit and the higher rate limit, and at _% above the higher rate limit. Fill in the blanks.

4   How is dividend income taxed?

5   Ingrid owned £30,000 (nominal value) 4% UK Government Loan Stock. Interest was payable on 31 March and 30 September each year. Ingrid sold the loan stock on 31 July 2017 including interest. What is the amount of savings income taxable on Ingrid in respect of the loan stock for 2017/18?

6   If Dennis has taxable income of £34,200 and makes gift aid payments of £400, on how much of his income will he pay higher rate tax?

7   Mike and Matt are a married couple. Mike owns 25% of an investment property and Matt owns 75%. How will the income be taxed?

Answers to Quick Quiz

1   The number of ties the individual has to the UK and the number of days spent in the UK that year. Whether the individual is leaving the UK or arriving in the UK also determines how many ties are to be satisfied for UK residence.

2   Dividend income and interest received from ISAs are exempt from income tax. Capital gains made within an ISA are exempt from capital gains tax.

3   Income tax on non-savings income is charged at **20%** below the basic rate limit, at **40%** between the basic rate limit and the higher rate limit, and at **45%** above the higher rate limit.

4   Dividend income within the dividend nil rate band is taxed at 0%. Any remaining dividend income below the basic rate limit is taxed at 7.5%, at 32.5% between the basic rate limit and the higher rate limit, and at 38.1% above the higher rate limit.

5   Accrued interest to date of sale £30,000 × 4% × 4/12 (1 April to 31 July) = £400. This is an application of the accrued income scheme.

6   The basic rate limit is increased by £400 × 100/80 = £500 to £34,000. Dennis will be liable to higher rate tax on £34,200 − £34,000 = £200.

7   Mike and Matt will each be taxed on 50% of the income from the investment property unless they make a joint declaration to specify the actual proportions in which case Mike will be taxed on 25% of the income and Matt on 75%.

Now try the questions below from the Practice Question Bank

Number	Type	Marks	Time
Q4	Section A	2	4 mins
Q5	Section A	2	4 mins
Q6	Section A	2	4 mins
Q7	Section A	2	4 mins
Q8	Section A	2	4 mins
Q9	Section C	10	18 mins
Q10	Section C	15	27 mins
Q11	Section C	15	27 mins

Employment income

Topic list	Syllabus reference
1 Employment and self employment	B2(a)
2 Basis of assessment for employment income	B2(b), B2(c)
3 Allowable deductions	B2(c), B2(d)
4 Statutory approved mileage allowances	B2(c), B2(e)
5 Charitable donations under the payroll deduction scheme	B5(f)

Introduction

In the previous chapters we saw how to construct the income tax computation. Now we start to look in greater detail at the different types of income that people may receive so that the income can be slotted into the computation.

Many people earn money by working. We look at the important distinction between employment and self employment, so that we can consider the way in which people are taxed on the wages or salaries from their jobs.

Sometimes employees may incur expenses when carrying out their jobs. We look at the rules determining when these can be deducted from employment income for tax purposes. We also look at the rules covering mileage payments made by employers to employees who use their own cars for business journeys. Finally, employees can make tax efficient contributions to charity under the payroll giving scheme.

In the next chapter we look at how benefits received as a result of employment are taxed and at how tax is deducted from employment income under the Pay As You Earn (PAYE) system.

Study guide

		Intellectual level
B2	**Income from employment**	
(a)	Recognise the factors that determine whether an engagement is treated as employment or self-employment.	2
(b)	Recognise the basis of assessment for employment income.	2
(c)	Recognise the income assessable.	2
(d)	Recognise the allowable deductions, including travelling expenses.	2
(e)	Discuss the use of the statutory approved mileage allowances.	2
B5	**The comprehensive computation of taxable income and income tax liability**	
(f)	Understand the treatment of charitable giving.	1

Exam guide

You are very likely to be asked a question concerning at least one aspect of employment taxation in your exam. This could range from identifying the date on which earnings are received in Section A or Section B to a discussion of the distinction between employment and self employment in Section C, either as part of a 15 mark question or a 10 mark question.

1 Employment and self employment

FAST FORWARD

Employment involves a contract of service whereas self employment involves a contract for services. The distinction between employment and self employment is decided by looking at all the facts of the engagement.

1.1 Employment income

Employment income includes income arising from an employment under a **contract of service**.

Some people, however, set themselves up in business and carry out work for customers under a **contract for services**.

Before we can calculate employment income, we must be sure that the individual is employed rather than self employed. This can only be decided by looking at all the facts of the engagement.

1.2 Employment and self employment

Exam focus point

Many of the tax rules have come about as a result of legal cases. In the exam you are not required to know the relevant cases. However, we have included the case names in the Study Text for your information.

It can be difficult to distinguish between employment (receipts taxable as earnings) and self employment (profits taxable as trading income). Employment involves a contract of service, whereas self employment involves a contract for services. Taxpayers tend to prefer self employment, because the rules on deductions for expenses are more generous.

Factors which may be of importance include:

- The degree of control exercised over the person doing the work (a high level of control indicates employment)

- Whether the worker must accept further work (if yes, indicates employment)

- Whether the person who has offered work must provide further work (if yes, indicates employment)

- Whether the worker provides their own equipment (if yes, indicates self-employment)

- Whether the worker is entitled to employment benefits such as sick pay, holiday pay and pension facilities (entitlement indicates employment)

- Whether the worker hires their own helpers (if yes, indicates self-employment)

- What degree of financial risk the worker takes (if high risk, indicates self-employment)

- What degree of responsibility for investment and management the worker has (if most of responsibility is the worker's, indicates self-employment)

- Whether the worker can profit from sound management (if can do so, indicates self-employment)

- Whether the worker can work when they choose (if can do so, indicates self-employment)

- Whether the worker works for a number of different people or organisations (working for just one person or organisation indicates employment)

- The wording used in any agreement between the worker and the person for whom they perform work (but not conclusive about the actual legal relationship between them)

Relevant cases include:

(a) *Edwards v Clinch 1981*

A civil engineer acted occasionally as an inspector on temporary unplanned appointments.

Held: There was no ongoing office which could be vacated by one person and held by another so the fees received were from self employment not employment.

(b) *Hall v Lorimer 1994*

A vision mixer was engaged under a series of short-term contracts.

Held: The vision mixer was self employed, not because of any one detail of the case but because the overall picture was one of self-employment.

(c) *Carmichael and Anor v National Power plc 1999*

Individuals engaged as visitor guides on a casual 'as required' basis were not employees. An exchange of correspondence between the company and the individuals was not a contract of employment as there was no provision as to the frequency of work and there was flexibility to accept work or turn it down as it arose. Sickness, holiday and pension arrangements did not apply and neither did grievance and disciplinary procedures.

A worker's status also affects national insurance contributions (NIC). The self employed generally pay less than employees. NICs are covered later in this Study Text.

2 Basis of assessment for employment income

General earnings are taxed in the year of receipt. Money earnings are generally received on the earlier of the time payment is made and the time entitlement to payment arises.

2.1 Outline of the charge

Employment income includes income arising from an employment under a contract of service and the income of office holders, such as directors. The term 'employee' is used in this Study Text to mean anyone who receives employment income (ie both employees and directors).

General earnings are an employee's earnings (see key term below) plus the 'cash equivalent' of any taxable non-monetary benefits.

Key term

> **'Earnings'** means any salary, wage or fee, any gratuity or other profit or incidental benefit obtained by the employee if it is money or money's worth (something of direct monetary value or convertible into direct monetary value) or anything else which constitutes a reward of the employment.

Taxable earnings from an employment in a tax year are the general earnings received in that tax year.

2.2 When are earnings received?   9/16, 6/17

2.2.1 General earnings consisting of money

General earnings consisting of money are treated as received at the earlier of:

- **The time when payment is made**
- **The time when a person becomes entitled to payment of the earnings**

If the employee is a **director** of a company, earnings from the company are received on the **earliest** of:

- The earlier of the two alternatives given in the general rule (above)
- The time when the amount is **credited in the company's accounting records**
- **The end of the company's period of account** (if the amount was determined by then)
- The **time the amount is determined** (if after the end of the company's period of account)

Question   Receipt of money earnings

Josephine and Vincent are employed by D plc. Josephine is a director of D plc. Vincent is not a director of D plc. D plc makes up its accounts to 31 March each year.

Bonuses were awarded by D plc as follows:

Josephine: £5,000. This amount was determined by the directors on 28 February 2018 and credited to Josephine's director's account on 10 March 2018, subject to a condition that she was could not draw down the bonus until 15 April 2018, on which date she became entitled to payment of the bonus. Josephine was actually paid the bonus on 28 April 2018.

Vincent: £3,000. Vincent became entitled to be paid this bonus on 31 March 2017, but agreed that payment should be delayed due to D plc's cash flow problems. He was actually paid the bonus on 30 April 2017.

Explain when each of the bonuses is received for the purposes of employment income and so determine the tax year in which it will be taxed.

Josephine

Josephine is a director and so her bonus is received for the purposes of employment income on the earliest of:

Time payment made:	28 April 2018
Time of entitlement:	15 April 2018
Credited in records	10 March 2018
End of period of account	31 March 2018 (amount determined before end of period)

The earliest of these dates is 10 March 2018 and so this is the date of receipt of the bonus. The tax year in which the bonus is taxed is therefore 2017/18.

Vincent

Vincent is not a director so his bonus is received for the purposes of employment income on the earlier of:

Time payment made:	30 April 2017
Time of entitlement:	31 March 2017

The earlier of these dates is 31 March 2017 and so this is the date of receipt of the bonus. The tax year in which the bonus is taxed is therefore 2016/17.

2.2.2 General earnings consisting taxable benefits

Taxable benefits (see next chapter) are generally treated as received when they are provided to the employee.

2.2.3 Pension income

The receipts basis does not apply to pension income. Pension income is taxed on the amount accruing in the tax year, whether or not it has actually been received in that year.

2.3 Net taxable earnings

Total taxable earnings less total allowable deductions (see below) **are net taxable earnings of a tax year.** Deductions cannot usually create a loss; they can only reduce the net taxable earnings to nil. If there is more than one employment in the tax year, separate calculations are required for each employment.

3 Allowable deductions

FAST FORWARD

Deductions for expenses are extremely limited. Relief is available for the costs that employees are obliged to incur in travelling in the performance of their duties or in travelling to the place they have to attend in performance of their duties. Relief is **not** available for normal commuting costs.

3.1 The general rules

Deductions for expenses are extremely limited and are notoriously hard to obtain. Although there are some specific deductions, which are covered below, the general rule is that relief is limited to:

(a) **Qualifying travel expenses**

(b) **Other expenses the employee is obliged to incur and pay as holder of the employment which are incurred wholly, exclusively and necessarily in the performance of the duties of the employment**

3.2 Travel expenses

3.2.1 Qualifying travel expenses

Tax relief is not available for an employee's normal commuting costs. This means relief is not available for any costs employees incur in getting from home to their normal place of work. However, **employees are entitled to relief for travel expenses that they are obliged to incur and pay in travelling in the performance of their duties or travelling to or from a place which they have to attend in the performance of their duties (other than a permanent workplace).**

Question
Relief for travelling costs (1)

Judi is an accountant. She often travels to meetings at the firm's offices in Scotland, returning to her office in Leeds after the meetings. What tax relief is available for Judi's travel costs?

Answer

Relief is available for the full cost of these journeys as the travel is undertaken in the performance of Judi's duties.

Question
Relief for travelling costs (2)

Zoe lives in Wycombe and normally works in Chiswick. Occasionally she visits a client in Wimbledon and travels direct from home. Distances are shown in the diagram below:

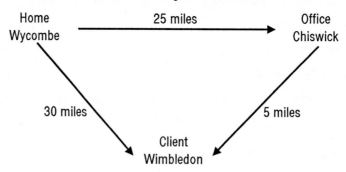

What tax relief is available for Zoe's travel costs?

Answer

Zoe is not entitled to tax relief for the costs incurred in travelling between Wycombe and Chiswick since these are normal commuting costs. However, relief is available for all costs (30 miles) that Zoe incurs when she travels from Wycombe to Wimbledon to visit her client.

To prevent manipulation of the basic rule normal commuting will not become a business journey just because the employee stops during the journey to perform a business task (eg to send an email). Nor will relief be available if the journey is essentially the same as the employee's normal journey to work.

Question
Relief for travelling costs (3)

Jeremy is based in an office in Birmingham City Centre. One day he is required to attend a 9.00 am meeting with a client whose premises are around the corner from his Birmingham office. Jeremy travels from home directly to the meeting. What tax relief is available for Jeremy's travel costs?

Since the journey is substantially the same as Jeremy's ordinary journey to work, tax relief is not available.

3.2.2 Site based employees

Site based employees (eg construction workers, management consultants etc) **who do not have a permanent workplace, are entitled to relief for the costs of all journeys made from home to wherever they are working.** This is because these employees do not have an ordinary commuting journey or any normal commuting costs.

3.2.3 Temporary workplace

If an employee is seconded to work at another location for some considerable time, then the question arises as to whether the journey from home to that workplace can become normal commuting. There is a 24-month rule.

Tax relief is available for travel, accommodation and subsistence expenses incurred by an employee who is working at a temporary workplace on a secondment expected to last up to 24 months. If a secondment is initially expected not to exceed 24 months, but it is extended, relief ceases to be due from the date the employee becomes aware of the change.

When looking at how long a secondment is expected to last, HMRC will consider not only the terms of the written contract but also any verbal agreement by the employer and other factors such as whether the employee buys a house etc.

Question

Relief for travelling costs (4)

Philip works for Vastbank at its Newcastle City Centre branch. Philip is sent to work full-time at another branch in Morpeth for 20 months, at the end of which he will return to the Newcastle branch. Morpeth is about 20 miles north of Newcastle. What tax relief is available for Philip's travel costs?

Answer

Although Philip is spending all of his time at the Morpeth branch it will not be treated as his normal work place because his period of attendance will be less than 24 months. Thus Philip can claim relief in full for the costs of travel from his home to the Morpeth branch.

3.3 Other expenses

Relief is given for other expenses incurred **wholly, exclusively and necessarily in the performance of the duties** of the employment. The word 'exclusively' strictly implies that the expenditure must **give no private benefit at all.** If it does, none of it is deductible. In practice, HMRC may ignore a small element of private benefit or make an apportionment between business and private use.

Whether an expense is 'necessary' is not determined by what the employer requires. The test is **whether the duties of the employment could not be performed without the outlay.**

The following cases illustrate how the requirements are interpreted. Remember you are not expected to know the case names, they are given for information only.

(a) *Sanderson v Durbridge 1955*

The cost of evening meals taken when attending late meetings was not deductible because it was not incurred in the performance of the duties.

(b)   *Blackwell v Mills 1945*

As a condition of his employment, an employee was required to attend evening classes. The cost of his text books and travel was not deductible because it was not incurred in the performance of the duties.

(c)   *Lupton v Potts 1969*

Examination fees incurred by a solicitor's articled clerk were not deductible because they were incurred neither wholly nor exclusively in the performance of the duties, but in furthering the clerk's ambition to become a solicitor.

(d)   *Brown v Bullock 1961*

The expense of joining a club that was virtually a condition of an employment was not deductible because it would have been possible to carry on the employment without the club membership, so the expense was not necessary.

(e)   *Elwood v Utitz 1965*

A managing director's subscriptions to two residential London clubs were claimed by him as an expense on the grounds that they were cheaper than hotels.

The expenditure was deductible as it was necessary in that it would be impossible for the employee to carry out his London duties without being provided with appropriate accommodation. The residential facilities (which were cheaper than hotel accommodation) were given to club members only.

(f)   *Lucas v Cattell 1972*

The cost of business telephone calls on a private telephone is deductible, but **no part of the line or telephone rental charges is deductible**.

(g)   *Fitzpatrick v IRC 1994; Smith v Abbott 1994*

Journalists could not claim a deduction for the cost of buying newspapers which they read to keep themselves informed, since they were merely preparing themselves to perform their duties.

The cost of clothes for work is not deductible, except for certain trades requiring protective clothing where there are annual deductions on a set scale.

An employee required to work at home may be able to claim a deduction for the additional costs of working from home, such as an appropriate proportion of expenditure on lighting and heating. Employers can pay up to £4 per week (or £18 per month for monthly paid employees) without the need for supporting evidence of the costs incurred by the employee. Payments above the £4 (or £18) limit require evidence of the employee's actual costs.

3.4 Other deductions   9/16, 6/17

Some expenditure is specifically deductible in computing net taxable earnings:

(a)   **Contributions to registered occupational pension schemes**

(b)   **Subscriptions to professional bodies** on the list of bodies issued by the HMRC (which includes most UK professional bodies such as the ACCA), if relevant to the duties of the employment

(c)   Payments for certain liabilities relating to the employment and for insurance against them (see below)

Employees may also claim capital allowances on plant and machinery (other than cars or other vehicles) necessarily provided for use in the performance of those duties. The computation of capital allowances is discussed later in this Study Text.

3.5 Liabilities and insurance

If a director or employee incurs a liability related to their employment or pays for insurance against such a liability, the cost is a deductible expense. If the employer pays such amounts, there is no taxable benefit.

A liability relating to employment is one which is imposed in respect of the employee's acts or omissions as employee. Thus, for example, liability for negligence would be covered. Related costs, for example the costs of legal proceedings, are included.

For insurance premiums to qualify, the insurance policy:

(a) Must cover only liabilities relating to employment, vicarious liability in respect of liabilities of another person's employment, related costs and payments to the employee's own employees in respect of their employment liabilities relating to employment and related costs

(b) Must not last for more than two years (although it may be renewed for up to two years at a time), and the insured person must not be required to renew it

4 Statutory approved mileage allowances 9/16, 6/17

FAST FORWARD

Employers may pay a mileage allowance to employees who use their own car on business journeys. Payments up to the statutory limits are tax free, any excess is taxable, and a deduction can be claimed if the payment is lower.

A single approved mileage allowance for business journeys in an employee's own vehicle applies to all cars and vans. There is no income tax on payments up to this allowance and employers do not have to report mileage allowances up to this amount. The allowance for 2017/18 is **45p per mile on the first 10,000 miles** in the tax year with **each additional mile over 10,000 miles at 25p per mile**.

The authorised mileage allowance for **employees using their own motor cycle is 24p per mile**. For **employees using their own pedal cycle it is 20p per mile**.

If employers pay less than the statutory approved mileage allowance, employees can claim tax relief up to that level.

The statutory approved mileage allowance does not prevent employers from paying higher rates, but any excess will be subject to income tax. There is a similar (but slightly different) system for NICs, covered later in this Study Text.

Employers can make income tax and NIC free payments of up to 5p per mile for each fellow employee making the same business trip who is carried as a passenger. If the employer does not pay the employee for carrying business passengers, the employee cannot claim any tax relief.

Question   Mileage allowance

Sophie uses her own car for business travel. During 2017/18, Sophie drove 15,400 miles in the performance of her duties. Sophie's employer paid her a mileage allowance. How is the mileage allowance treated for tax purposes assuming that the rate paid is:

(a) 40p a mile?
(b) 25p a mile?

Answer

(a)

	£
Mileage allowance received (15,400 × 40p)	6,160
Less tax free [(10,000 × 45p) + (5,400 × 25p)]	(5,850)
Taxable benefit	310

£5,850 is tax free and the excess amount received of £310 is a taxable benefit.

(b)

	£
Mileage allowance received (15,400 × 25p)	3,850
Less tax free amount [(10,000 × 45p) + (5,400 × 25p)]	(5,850)
Allowable deduction	(2,000)

There is no taxable benefit and Sophie can claim a deduction from her employment income of £2,000.

5 Charitable donations under the payroll deduction scheme

FAST FORWARD

Employees can make tax deductible donations to charity under the payroll deduction scheme. The amount paid is deducted from gross pay.

Employees can make charitable donations under the payroll deduction scheme by asking their employer to make deductions from their gross earnings. The deductions are then passed to a charitable agency which will either distribute the funds to the employees' chosen charities on receipt of their instructions, or provide the employee with vouchers that can be redeemed by the recipient charities.

The donation is an allowable deduction from the employee's earnings for tax purposes. Tax relief is given at source as the employer must deduct the donation from gross pay before calculating PAYE.

Exam focus point

Make sure you understand the difference between how tax relief is given for gift aid donations and how tax relief is given through the payroll deduction scheme.

Chapter Roundup

- Employment involves a contract of service whereas self employment involves a contract for services. The distinction between employment and self employment is decided by looking at all the facts of the engagement.

- General earnings are taxed in the year of receipt. Money earnings are generally received on the earlier of the time payment is made and the time entitlement to payment arises.

- Deductions for expenses are extremely limited. Relief is available for the costs that employees are obliged to incur in travelling in the performance of their duties or in travelling to the place they have to attend in performance of their duties. Relief is **not** available for normal commuting costs.

- Employers may pay a mileage allowance to employees who use their own car on business journeys. Payments up to the statutory limits are tax free, any excess is taxable, and a deduction can be claimed if the payment is lower.

- Employees can make tax deductible donations to charity under the payroll deduction scheme. The amount paid is deducted from gross pay.

Quick Quiz

1 On what basis are earnings taxed?

2 In order for general expenses of employment to be deductible, they must be incurred _____, _____ and _____ in the performance of the duties of the employment. Fill in the blanks.

3 In what circumstances can the cost of home to workplace travel be a qualifying travel expense?

4 What relief can Karen claim if she is paid 40p for each mile that she drives her own car on company business and she drives 5,000 miles in 2017/18?

   A £250
   B £1,750
   C £2,000
   D £2,250

5 Could Karen claim any extra relief if she was accompanied by a work colleague for 1,000 of those miles?

Answers to Quick Quiz

1   Earnings are taxed on a receipts basis.

2   In order for general expenses of employment to be deductible, they must be incurred **wholly, exclusively** and **necessarily** in the performance of the duties of the employment.

3   Home to workplace travel will be a qualifying travel expense if the employee travels to a temporary workplace on a secondment expected to last up to 24 months.

4   A. Karen could claim relief of 5,000 × (45 − 40)p = £250. The 40p per mile received would not be taxable.

5   Karen could not claim any extra relief if she was accompanied by a work colleague for 1,000 of those miles. If her employer had made extra payments of up to 5p per mile for those journeys the extra payment would have been tax free.

Now try the questions below from the Practice Question Bank

Number	Type	Marks	Time
Q12	Section A	2	4 mins
Q13	Section A	2	4 mins
Q14	Section A	2	4 mins
Q15	Section B	2	4 mins
Q16	Section B	2	4 mins
Q17	Section B	2	4 mins
Q18	Section B	2	4 mins
Q19	Section B	2	4 mins

Taxable and exempt benefits. The PAYE system

Topic list	Syllabus reference
1 Taxable benefits	B2(g)
2 Exempt benefits	B2(g)
3 The PAYE system	B2(f), (h)

Introduction

In the previous chapter we discussed when workers were employees and when they were self employed. We then considered the taxation of salaries and wages and the deduction of expenses and charitable donations.

In this chapter we look at benefits provided to employees. Benefits are an integral part of many remuneration packages, but the tax cost of receiving a benefit must not be overlooked. Special rules apply to fix the taxable value of certain benefits.

Finally, we look at how tax is deducted from employment income under the Pay As You Earn (PAYE) system. Tax is deducted on cash payments and some benefits. Other benefits are dealt with through the PAYE code.

In the next chapter we look at how taxpayers can save for their retirement through pension provision and the tax reliefs available.

Study guide

		Intellectual level
B2	**Income from employment**	
(f)	Explain the PAYE system, how benefits can be payrolled, and the purpose of form P11D.	1
(g)	Explain and compute the amount of benefits assessable.	2
(h)	Recognise the circumstances in which real time reporting late filing penalties will be imposed on an employer and the amount of penalty which is charged.	2

Exam guide

Benefits are a very important part of employment income and you are likely to come across them in your exam in any of Sections A, B or Section C, in a 15 mark question or a 10 mark question. If you come across exempt benefits in a Section C question, note this in your answer to show that you have considered each item.

The Pay As You Earn (PAYE) system is a system of deduction of tax at source. You should be able to explain how it collects tax. The forms for the PAYE system are important, as are the dates for submission.

Exam focus point

ACCA's article Benefits, written by a member of the Taxation (TX – UK) examining team, states that benefits feature regularly in the Taxation (TX – UK) exam, and this article mainly covers those **aspects of benefits** that have been **examined in previous sittings** of Taxation (TX – UK).

1 Taxable benefits

FAST FORWARD
Employees are taxed on benefits under the benefits code.

1.1 Vouchers

If an employee:

- Receives cash vouchers (vouchers exchangeable for cash)
- Uses a credit token (such as a credit card) to obtain money, goods or services, or
- Receives exchangeable vouchers (such as book tokens), also called non-cash vouchers

the employee is taxed on the **cost to the employer of providing the benefit**, less any amount the employee pays the employer for providing the benefit.

1.2 Accommodation

FAST FORWARD
The benefit in respect of accommodation is its annual value. There is an additional benefit if the property cost over £75,000.

1.2.1 Annual value charge

The taxable value of accommodation provided to an employee is the rent that would have been payable if the premises had been let at their annual value (sometimes called 'rateable value'). **If the premises are rented** rather than owned by the employer, then **the taxable benefit is the higher of the rent actually paid and the annual value.**

1.2.2 Additional benefit charge

If a property was bought by the employer for a cost of more than £75,000, an additional amount is chargeable as follows:

(Cost of providing the living accommodation – £75,000) × the official rate of interest at the start of the tax year.

Exam focus point

The official rate of interest at the start of the 2017/18 tax year is 2.5%. This percentage will be given to you in the Tax Rates and Allowances section of the exam paper.

Thus with an official rate of 2.5%, the total benefit for accommodation costing £95,000 and with an annual value of £2,000 would be £2,000 + £(95,000 – 75,000) × 2.5% = £2,500.

The **'cost of providing' the living accommodation is the total of the cost of purchase and the cost of any improvements made before the start of the tax year** for which the benefit is being computed. It is therefore not possible to avoid the charge by buying an inexpensive property requiring substantial repairs and improving it.

Where the property was acquired more than six years before first being provided to the employee, the **market value when first so provided plus the cost of subsequent improvements** is used as the **cost of providing the living accommodation.** However, unless the actual cost plus improvements up to the start of the tax year in question exceeds £75,000, the additional charge cannot be imposed, however high the market value.

1.2.3 Job related accommodation

There is no taxable benefit in respect of job related accommodation. Accommodation is job related if:

(a)   Residence in the accommodation is necessary for **the proper performance of the employee's duties (as with a caretaker)**; or

(b)   The accommodation is provided **for the better performance of the employee's duties** and the employment is of a kind in which it is customary for accommodation to be provided (as with a policeman); or

(c)   The **accommodation is provided as part of arrangements in force because of a special threat to the employee's security**.

Directors can only claim exemptions (a) or (b) if:

- They have no **material interest** ('material' means over 5%) in the company.
- Either they are **full time working directors** or the company is **non-profit making or is a charity**.

1.2.4 Contribution by employee

Any contribution paid by the employee is deducted from the annual value of the property and then from the additional benefit.

| Question | Accommodation |

Quinton was provided with a company flat in January 2017. The rateable value of the flat is £1,200. The property cost his employer £125,000, but was valued at £150,000 in January 2017. Quinton paid rent of £500 in each tax year.

What is the taxable benefit for 2017/18 assuming:

(a)   His employer purchased the property in 2015?

(b)   His employer purchased the property in 2009?

(c)   Quinton was required to live in the flat as he was employed as the caretaker for the company premises (of which the flat was part)?

Part B Income tax and national insurance contributions | **4: Taxable and exempt benefits. The PAYE system**   61

(b) **The price (including fitting) of all optional accessories provided when the car was first provided** to the employee, excluding mobile telephones and equipment needed by a disabled employee. The extra cost of adapting or manufacturing a car to run on road fuel gases is not included.

(c) **The price (including fitting) of all optional accessories fitted later** and costing at least £100 each, excluding mobile telephones and equipment needed by a disabled employee. Such accessories affect the taxable benefit from and including the tax year in which they are fitted. However, accessories which are merely replacing existing accessories and are not superior to the ones replaced are ignored. Replacement accessories which *are* superior are taken into account, but the cost of the old accessory is then deducted.

There is a special rule for **classic cars**. If the car is at least 15 years old (from the time of first registration) at the end of the tax year, and its market value at the end of the year (or, if earlier, when it ceased to be available to the employee) is over £15,000 and greater than the price found under the above rules, that market value is used instead of the price. The market value takes account of all accessories (except mobile telephones and equipment needed by a disabled employee).

Capital contributions made by the employee in that and previous tax years up to a maximum of £5,000 are deducted from the list price. Capital contributions are payments by the employee in respect of the price of the car or accessories for the same car. Contributions beyond the maximum are ignored.

 Question _____ Car benefit (1)

Nigel is provided with a diesel car which had a list price of £22,000 when it was first registered. The car has CO_2 emissions of 143g/km.

You are required to calculate Nigel's car benefit for 2017/18.

Answer

Car benefit £22,000 × 30% (18% + (140 − 95)/5 + 3%) = £6,600

Note that 143 is rounded down to 140 to be exactly divisible by 5.

 Question _____ Car benefit (2)

Robyn is provided with a petrol car which had a list price of £18,000 when it was first registered. The car has CO_2 emissions of 90 g/km.

You are required to calculate Robyn's car benefit for 2017/18.

Answer

Car benefit £18,000 × 17% = £3,060

1.4.4 Reductions in the benefit

The benefit is reduced on a time basis where a car is first made available or ceases to be made available during the tax year or is incapable of being used for a continuous period of not less than 30 days (for example because it is being repaired).

The benefit is reduced by any payment the user must make for the private use of the car (as distinct from a capital contribution to the cost of the car). The benefit cannot become negative to create a deduction from the employee's income.

Vicky starts her employment on 6 January 2018 and is immediately provided with a new petrol car with a list price of £25,000. The car was more expensive than her employer would have provided and she therefore made a capital contribution of £6,200. The employer was able to buy the car at a discount and paid only £23,000. Vicky contributed £100 a month for being able to use the car privately. CO_2 emissions are 218g/km.

You are required to calculate her car benefit for 2017/18.

Answer

	£
List price *	25,000
Less capital contribution (maximum)	(5,000)
	20,000

	£
£20,000 × 37%** × 3/12 ***	1,850
Less contribution to running costs (£100 × 3)	(300)
Car benefit	1,550

*   The discounted price is not relevant
**   18% + (215 – 95) × 1/5 = 42% restricted to 37% max
*** Only available for three months in 2017/18

1.4.5 Pool cars

Pool cars are exempt. A car is a pool car if **all** the following conditions are satisfied:

(a)   It is used by more than one employee and is not ordinarily used by any one of them to the exclusion of the others.

(b)   Any private use is merely incidental to business use.

(c)   It is not normally kept overnight at or near the residence of an employee.

1.4.6 Ancillary benefits

There are many ancillary benefits associated with the provision of cars, such as insurance, repairs, vehicle licences and a parking space at or near work. No extra taxable benefit arises as a result of these, with the exception of the cost of providing a driver.

1.5 Fuel for cars   12/16

1.5.1 Introduction

Where fuel is provided there is a further benefit in addition to the car benefit.

No taxable benefit arises where either

(a)   **All the fuel provided was made available only for business travel; or**

(b)   **The employee is required to make good** (ie reimburse the employer), **and has made good, the whole of the cost of any fuel provided for their private use.**

Unlike most benefits, a reimbursement of only part of the cost of the fuel available for private use does not reduce the benefit.

1.5.2 Taxable benefit

The taxable benefit is a percentage of a base figure. The base figure for 2017/18 is £22,600. The percentage is the same percentage as is used to calculate the car benefit (see above).

Exam focus point

The fuel base figure will be given to you in the Tax Rates and Allowances section of the exam paper.

1.5.3 Reductions in the benefit

The fuel benefit is reduced in the same way as the car benefit **if the car is not available for 30 days or more.**

The fuel benefit is also reduced if private fuel is not available for part of a tax year. However, if private fuel later becomes available in the same tax year, the reduction is not made. If, for example, fuel is provided from 6 April 2017 to 30 June 2017, then the fuel benefit for 2017/18 will be restricted to just three months. This is because the provision of fuel has permanently ceased. However, if fuel is provided from 6 April 2017 to 30 June 2017, and then again from 1 September 2017 to 5 April 2018, then the fuel benefit will not be reduced since the cessation was only temporary.

Question
Car and fuel benefit

Brian was provided by his employer with a new car with a list price of £15,000 on 6 April 2017. The car emits 131g/km of CO_2. During 2017/18 the employer spent £900 on insurance, repairs and a vehicle licence. The firm paid for all petrol, costing £1,500, without reimbursement. Brian paid the firm £270 for the private use of the car. Calculate the taxable benefits for private use of the car and private fuel.

Answer

Round CO_2 emissions figure down to the nearest 5, ie 130g/km.

Amount by which CO_2 emissions exceed the baseline:

(130 – 95) = 35g/km

Divide by 5 = 7

Taxable percentage = 18% + 7% = 25%

	£
Car benefit £15,000 × 25%	3,750
Less contribution towards use of car	(270)
	3,480
Fuel benefit £22,600 × 25%	5,650
Total benefits	9,130

If the contribution of £270 had been towards the petrol the benefit would have been £(3,750 + 5,650) = £9,400 since partial reimbursement of private use fuel does not reduce the fuel benefit.

Note there is no additional benefit for the insurance, repairs and licence costs. The car benefit is deemed to cover all these expenses incurred by the employer.

1.6 Vans and heavier commercial vehicles

If a van (of normal maximum laden weight up to 3,500 kg) **is made available for an employee's private use, there is an annual scale charge of £3,230.** The scale charge covers ancillary benefits such as insurance and servicing. The benefit is scaled down if the van is not available for the full year (as for cars) and is reduced by any payment made by the employee for private use.

There is, however, **no taxable benefit where an employee takes a van home** (ie uses the van for home to work travel) but is not allowed any other private use.

Where private fuel is provided, there is an additional charge of £610. If the van is unavailable for part of the year, or fuel for private use is only provided for part of the year, the benefit is scaled down.

If a commercial vehicle of normal maximum laden weight over 3,500 kg is made available for an employee's private use, but the employee's use of the vehicle is not wholly or mainly private, no taxable benefit arises except in respect of the provision of a driver.

1.7 Beneficial loans

> Cheap loans are charged to tax on the difference between the official rate of interest and any interest paid by the employee.

1.7.1 Taxable benefit

Employment related loans to employees and their relatives give rise to a benefit equal to:

(a)   **Any amounts written off** (unless the employee has died)

(b)   The excess of the interest based on an official rate prescribed by the Treasury, over any interest actually charged ('taxable cheap loan'). Interest payable during the tax year but paid after the end of the tax year is taken into account.

The following loans are normally not treated as taxable cheap loans for calculation of the interest benefits (but are taxable for the purposes of the charge on loans written off).

(a)   A loan on normal commercial terms made in the ordinary course of the employer's money-lending business.

(b)   A loan made by an individual in the ordinary course of the lender's domestic, family or personal arrangements.

1.7.2 Calculating the interest benefit

There are two alternative methods of calculating the taxable benefit. The simpler **'average' method** automatically applies unless the taxpayer or HM Revenues & Customs (HMRC) elect for the alternative **'strict' method. The taxpayer should make the election for the 'strict' method** if this results in a **lower taxable benefit,** as this will give a **lower charge to income tax. HMRC normally only make the election** where it appears that the **'average' method** is **being deliberately exploited.** In both methods, the benefit is the interest at the official rate minus the interest payable.

<table>
<tr><td>Exam focus
point</td><td>For the purposes of the Taxation (TX – UK) exam, the official rate of interest is assumed to be 2.5% throughout 2017/18. This percentage will be given to you in the Tax Rates and Allowances section of the exam paper.</td></tr>
</table>

The 'average' method averages the balances at the beginning and end of the tax year (or the dates on which the loan was made and/or repaid if it was not in existence throughout the tax year) and applies the official rate of interest to this average. If the loan was not in existence throughout the tax year only the number of complete tax months (from the sixth of the month) for which it existed are taken into account.

The 'strict' method is to compute interest at the official rate on the actual amount outstanding on a daily basis. However, for exam purposes, it is acceptable to work on a monthly basis.

   Question   Loan benefit

Carole is employed by B plc at a salary of £50,000 a year. B plc made a taxable cheap loan of £40,000 to Carole in January 2017. At 6 April 2017 the whole of the loan was outstanding. Carole repaid £18,000 of the loan on 6 December 2017. The remaining balance of £22,000 was outstanding at 5 April 2018. Carole paid interest to B plc of £350 on the loan during 2017/18. What is Carole's taxable benefit under both the 'average' and the 'strict' methods for 2017/18?

Answer

Average method

$$2.5\% \times \frac{40,000 + 22,000}{2}$$

	£
	775
Less interest paid	(350)
Benefit	425

Strict method

	£
$£40,000 \times \dfrac{8}{12}$ (6 April – 5 December) $\times 2.5\%$	667
$£22,000 \times \dfrac{4}{12}$ (6 December – 5 April) $\times 2.5\%$	183
	850
Less interest paid	(350)
Benefit	500

HMRC could elect for the 'strict' method, although this is unlikely given the difference between the methods is relatively small and it does not appear that the 'average' method is being deliberately exploited.

Note. You must always show the workings for the average method. If it appears likely that the taxpayer should or HMRC might elect for the 'strict' method you will need to show those workings as well.

1.7.3 The de minimis test

The interest benefit is not taxable if the total of all non-qualifying loans to the employee did not exceed £10,000 at any time in the tax year.

A qualifying loan is one on which all or part of any interest paid would qualify for tax relief (see further below).

When the £10,000 threshold is exceeded, a benefit arises on interest on the whole loan, not just on the excess of the loan over £10,000.

1.7.4 Qualifying loans

If the whole of the interest payable on a qualifying loan is eligible for tax relief as qualifying interest (as seen earlier in this Study Text), then no taxable benefit arises. If the interest is only partly eligible for tax relief, then the employee is treated as receiving earnings because the actual rate of interest is below the official rate. They are also treated as paying interest equal to those earnings. This **deemed interest paid may qualify as a business expense or as qualifying interest in addition to any interest actually paid.**

Question	Beneficial loans

Anna has an annual salary of £30,000, and two loans from her employer:

*   A season ticket loan of £8,300 at no interest; and
*   A loan, 90% of which was used to buy a partnership interest, of £54,000 at 0.5% interest.

What is Anna's tax liability for 2017/18?

	£
Salary	30,000
Season ticket loan (non-qualifying): not over £10,000	0
Loan to buy partnership interest (qualifying): £54,000 × (2.5 − 0.5 = 2%)	1,080
Earnings/Total income	31,080
Less qualifying interest deemed paid (£54,000 × 2.5% × 90%)	(1,215)
Net income	29,865
Less personal allowance	(11,500)
Taxable income	18,365

Income tax

Tax liability £18,365 × 20%	3,673

1.8 Private use of other assets   9/16, 12/16

> 20% of the value of assets made available for private use is taxable.

When assets are made available for private use to employees or members of their family or household, the taxable benefit is the higher of 20% of the market value when first provided as a benefit to any employee and the rent paid by the employer. The 20% charge is time-apportioned when the asset is provided for only part of the year. The charge after any time apportionment is reduced by any contribution made by the employee.

There is an additional taxable benefit of any other amounts that the employer pays during the tax year relating to the provision of the asset such as running costs.

Bicycles provided for journeys to work, as well as being available for private use, are exempt from the private use benefit rules.

If an asset made available is subsequently acquired by the employee, **the taxable benefit on the acquisition is the greater of:**

- The **current market value minus the price paid by the employee**; and

- The **market value when first provided minus any amounts already taxed (ignoring contributions by the employee) minus the price paid by the employee.**

This rule prevents tax free benefits arising on rapidly depreciating items through the employee purchasing them at their low second-hand value.

There is an exception to this rule for bicycles which have previously been provided as exempt benefits (see later in this chapter) and for car benefit cars. The taxable benefit on acquisition is restricted to current market value, minus the price paid by the employee.

1.9 Example: Assets made available for private use

A suit costing £400 is purchased by an employer for use by an employee on 6 April 2016. On 6 April 2017 the suit is purchased by the employee for £30, its market value then being £50.

The benefit in 2016/17 is £400 × 20% = £80.

The benefit in 2017/18 is £290, being the *greater* of:

		£
(a)	Market value at acquisition by employee	50
	Less price paid	(30)
		20
(b)	Original market value	400
	Less taxed in respect of use	(80)
		320
	Less price paid	(30)
		290

Question | Bicycles

Rupert is provided with a new bicycle by his employer on 6 April 2017. The bicycle is available for private use as well as commuting to work. It cost the employer £1,500 when new. On 6 October 2017 the employer transfers ownership of the bicycle to Rupert when it is worth £800. Rupert does not pay anything for the bicycle. What is the total taxable benefit on Rupert for 2017/18 in respect of the bicycle?

Answer

Use benefit	*Exempt*
Transfer benefit (use MV at acquisition by employee only)	
MV at transfer	£800

1.10 Scholarships

If scholarships are given to members of an employee's family, the **employee is taxable on the cost** unless the scholarship fund's or scheme's payments by reason of people's employments are not more than 25% of its total payments.

1.11 Childcare

FAST FORWARD

> Workplace childcare is an exempt benefit. Employer-supported childcare and childcare vouchers are exempt up to £55 per week. Maximum tax relief is limited to £11 per week (the equivalent of £55 × 20%).

The cost of running a **workplace nursery or playscheme is an exempt benefit (without limit)**.

Otherwise a certain amount of childcare is tax free if the employer contracts with an approved childcarer or provides childcare vouchers to pay an approved childcarer. The childcare must usually be available to all employees and the childcare must either be registered or approved home-childcare.

A **£55 per week limit applies to basic rate employees** who use employer-supported childcare schemes or receive childcare vouchers. The amount of tax relief for a basic rate taxpayer is therefore £55 × 20% = £11 per week.

Higher rate and additional rate employees have their tax relief restricted so that it is the equivalent of that received by a basic rate taxpayer. Higher and additional rate employees can therefore receive vouchers tax-free up to £28 per week and £25 per week respectively, each giving £11 of tax relief which is the same amount a basic rate taxpayer would receive.

Exam focus point

> Whether an employee is considered basic rate, higher rate or additional rate for these purposes is determined by the level of their earnings only (and not other income). However, the examining team has stated that in an exam question involving childcare, it will be quite clear at what rate a taxpayer is paying tax.

70 **4: Taxable and exempt benefits. The PAYE system** | Part B Income tax and national insurance contributions

BPP LEARNING MEDIA

Archie is employed by M plc and is paid a salary of £80,000 in 2017/18. He receives childcare vouchers from M plc worth £50 per week for his daughter for 44 weeks during 2017/18. What is Archie's employment income for 2017/18?

Answer

	£
Salary (higher rate employee)	80,000
Childcare vouchers £(50 – 28) × 44 weeks	968
Employment income 2017/18	80,968

Exam focus point

A new tax free childcare scheme for working families has been introduced. This scheme will eventually replace the existing tax relief on employer-supported childcare. However, since the existing arrangements will continue to be available until April 2018, the new tax free childcare scheme is **not examinable** in Taxation (TX – UK) for the exams in June 2018, September 2018, December 2018 and March 2019.

1.12 Other benefits

FAST FORWARD
There is a residual charge for other benefits, usually equal to the cost to the employer of the benefits.

We have seen above how certain specific benefits are taxed. **There is a sweeping up charge for all other benefits. Under this rule the taxable value of a benefit is the cost of the benefit less any part of that cost made good by the employee to the persons providing the benefit.**

The residual charge applies to any benefit provided for an employee or a member of their family or household, by reason of the employment. There is an exception where the employer is an individual and the provision of the benefit is made in the normal course of the employer's domestic, family or personal relationships.

1.13 Example: Other benefits

A private school offers free places to the children of its staff. The actual cost to the school of providing the place is £2,000 in a tax year, although the fees charged to other pupils is £5,000 in a tax year.

The taxable value of the benefit to the staff is the actual cost of £2,000 per pupil, not the full £5,000 charged to other pupils.

2 Exempt benefits   12/16

FAST FORWARD
There are a number of exempt benefits including removal expenses, sporting facilities, and workplace parking.

Various benefits are exempt from tax. These include:

(a) **Reimbursed expenses** (see earlier in this chapter)

(b) **Entertainment provided to employees by genuine third parties** (eg seats at sporting/cultural events), even if it is provided by giving the employee a voucher

(c) **Gifts of goods** (or vouchers exchangeable for goods) from third parties (ie not provided by the employer or a person connected to the employer) if the total cost (including VAT) of all gifts by the

same donor to the same employee in the tax year is £250 or less. If the £250 limit is exceeded, the full amount is taxable, not just the excess

(d) **Non-cash awards for long service** if the period of service was at least 20 years, no similar award was made to the employee in the past 10 years and the cost is not more than £50 per year of service

(e) **Awards under staff suggestion schemes** if:

    (i)   There is a formal scheme, open to all employees on equal terms.

    (ii)   The suggestion is outside the scope of the employee's normal duties.

    (iii)   Either the award is not more than £25, or the award is only made after a decision is taken to implement the suggestion.

    (iv)   Awards over £25 reflect the financial importance of the suggestion to the business, and either do not exceed 50% of the expected net financial benefit during the first year of implementation or do not exceed 10% of the expected net financial benefit over a period of up to five years.

    (v)   Awards of over £25 are shared on a reasonable basis between two or more employees putting forward the same suggestion.

If an award exceeds £5,000, the excess is always taxable.

(f) **The first £8,000 of removal expenses** if:

    (i)   The employee does not already live within a reasonable daily travelling distance of their new place of employment, but will do so after moving.

    (ii)   The expenses are incurred or the benefits provided by the end of the tax year following the tax year of the start of employment at the new location.

(g) **Some childcare** (see earlier in this chapter)

(h) **Sporting or recreational facilities available to employees generally and not to the general public**, unless they are provided on domestic premises, or they consist of an interest in or the use of any mechanically propelled vehicle or any overnight accommodation. Vouchers only exchangeable for such facilities are also exempt, but membership fees for sports clubs are taxable

(i) **Assets or services used in performing the duties of employment** provided any private use of the item concerned is insignificant. This exempts, for example, the benefit arising on the private use of employer-provided tools

(j) **Welfare counselling** and similar minor benefits if the benefit concerned is available to employees generally

(k) **Bicycles or cycling safety equipment** provided to enable employees to get to and from work or to travel between one workplace and another; the equipment must be available to the employer's employees generally. Also, it must be used mainly for the aforementioned journeys

(l) **Workplace parking**

(m) **Up to £15,480 a year paid to an employee who is on a full-time course lasting at least a year**, with average full-time attendance of at least 20 weeks a year. If the £15,480 limit is exceeded, the whole amount is taxable

(n) **Work related training** and related costs; this includes the costs of training material and assets either made during training or incorporated into something so made

(o) **Air miles** or car fuel coupons obtained as a result of business expenditure but used for private purposes

(p) **The cost of work buses and minibuses or subsidies to public bus services**

A works bus must have a seating capacity of 12 or more and a works minibus a seating capacity of nine or more but not more than 12 and be available generally to employees of the employer concerned. The bus or minibus must mainly be used by employees for journeys to and from work and for journeys between workplaces.

(q) **Transport/overnight costs where public transport is disrupted by industrial action,** late night taxis and travel costs incurred where car sharing arrangements unavoidably breakdown

(r) The private use of one **mobile phone, which can be a smartphone.** Top up vouchers for exempt mobile phones are also tax free. If more than one mobile phone is provided to an employee for private use only the second or subsequent phone is a taxable benefit valued using the rules for assets made available to employees

(s) **Employer provided uniforms** which employees must wear as part of their duties

(t) The cost of **staff parties** which are open to staff generally provided that the **cost per head per year (including VAT) is £150 or less**; the £150 limit may be split between several parties

(u) **Private medical insurance premiums paid to cover treatment when the employee is outside the UK in the performance of their duties.** Other medical insurance premiums are taxable as is the cost of medical diagnosis and treatment except for routine check ups; eye tests and glasses for employees using Visual Display Units (VDUs) are exempt

(v) **Cheap loans that do not exceed £10,000** at any time in the tax year (see above)

(w) **Job related accommodation** (see above)

(x) **Employer contributions towards additional household costs incurred by an employee who works wholly or partly at home.** Payments up to £4 a week (£18 per month for monthly paid employees) may be made without supporting evidence (see earlier in this Study Text)

(y) **Personal incidental expenses** (see earlier in this Study Text)

(z) **Recommended medical treatment** costing up to £500 per employee per tax year paid for by an employer. The treatment must be recommended in writing by a health professional (eg doctor, nurse) and the purpose of the treatment must be to assist the employee to return to work after a period of injury or ill-health lasting at least 28 days. If the payments exceed £500 in a tax year, they are wholly taxable

(aa) **Trivial benefits costing up to £50 per employee per tax year** provided these are not in the form of cash or a cash voucher. Examples of exempt trivial benefits include providing an employee with a Christmas or birthday present and sending flowers to an employee on the birth of a baby

Where a voucher is provided for a benefit which is exempt from income tax the provision of the voucher itself is also exempt.

3 The PAYE system

FAST FORWARD

Most tax in respect of employment income is deducted under the PAYE system. The objective of the PAYE system is to collect the correct amount of tax over the year. An employee's PAYE code is designed to ensure that allowances etc are given evenly over the year.

3.1 Introduction

3.1.1 Cash payments

The objective of the PAYE system is to deduct the correct amount of income tax and national insurance contributions from employees over the year. Its scope is very wide. It applies to most cash payments, other than reimbursed business expenses, and to certain non cash payments.

In addition to wages and salaries, PAYE applies to round sum expense allowances and payments instead of benefits. It also applies to any readily convertible asset.

A readily convertible asset is any asset which can effectively be exchanged for cash. The amount subject to PAYE is the amount that would be taxed as employment income. This is usually the cost to the employer of providing the asset.

Tips paid direct to an employee are normally outside the PAYE system (although still assessable as employment income).

Employers have a duty to deduct income tax and national insurance contributions from the pay of their employees, whether or not they have been directed to do so by HMRC. **If they fail to do this they** (or sometimes the employee) **must pay over the tax which the employer should have deducted and the employer may be subject to penalties.**

3.1.2 Benefits

PAYE must be applied to a taxable non-cash voucher if at the time it is provided:

- The voucher is capable of being exchanged for readily convertible assets; or
- The voucher can itself be sold, realised or traded.

PAYE must normally be operated on cash vouchers and on each occasion when a director/employee uses a credit-token (eg a credit card) to obtain money or goods which are readily convertible assets. However, a cash voucher or credit token which is used to pay expenses is not subject to PAYE.

Other taxable benefits may be included within the payroll if the employer chooses to do so. Otherwise they will be reported on Form P11D (see later in this chapter) and the employee's PAYE code will be adjusted to collect the income tax due on these benefits.

3.2 How PAYE works

Employers must report PAYE information to HMRC under the Real Time Information (RTI) system.

Under RTI, **an employer is required to submit information to HMRC electronically.** This can be done by:

(a) Using commercial payroll software

(b) Using HMRC's Basic PAYE Tools software (designed for use by an employer who has up to nine employees)

(c) Using a payroll provider (such as an accountant or payroll bureau) to do the reporting on behalf of the employer

The employer reports payroll information electronically to HMRC, on or before any day when the employer pays someone (ie in 'real time'). This report will normally be carried out by the payroll software (or the payroll provider) at the same time that the payments are calculated and is called **a Full Payment Submission (FPS)**. The FPS includes details of:

- The amounts paid to employees;
- Deductions made under PAYE such as income tax and national insurance contributions; and
- Details of employees who have started employment or left employment since the last FPS.

The software works out the amount of PAYE tax to deduct on any particular pay day by using the employees' code numbers (see below). Tax is normally worked out on a cumulative basis. This means that with each payment of earnings the running total of tax paid is compared with tax due on total earnings to that date. The difference between the tax due and the tax paid is the tax to be deducted on that particular payday.

NICs are also calculated by the software in relation to the earnings period (see later in this Study Text).

3.3 Payment under the PAYE system

Under PAYE, income tax and national insurance is normally paid over to HMRC monthly, 17 days after the end of the tax month (if paid electronically) or 14 days after the end of the tax month (if paid by cheque). Large employers (with 250 or more employees) must make electronic payments. **A tax month runs from 6th of one calendar month to the 5th of the following calendar month.** For example, for the tax month from 6 June 2017 to 5 July 2017, payment must be made by 22 July 2017 (electronically) or 19 July 2017 (cheque).

If an employer's average monthly payments under the PAYE system are less than £1,500, the employer may choose to pay quarterly, within 17 or 14 days (depending on the method of payment) **of the end of each tax quarter.** Tax quarters end on 5 July, 5 October, 5 January and 5 April. Payments can continue to be made quarterly during a tax year even if the monthly average reaches or exceeds £1,500, but a new estimate must be made and a new decision taken to pay quarterly at the start of each tax year.

3.4 PAYE codes

An employee is normally entitled to various allowances. Under the PAYE system an amount reflecting the effect of a proportion of these allowances is set against their pay each pay day. To determine the amount to set against their pay the allowances are expressed in the form of a code.

An employee's code may be any one of the following:

L   Tax code for people entitled to the full personal allowance
M   Tax code for people who are receiving £1,150 of personal allowance from a spouse or civil partner
N   Tax code for people who are giving £1,150 of personal allowance to a spouse or civil partner

The codes BR, DO and OT are generally used where there is a second source of income and all allowances have been used in a tax code which is applied to the main source of income. The BR code means that basic rate tax will be deducted without any allowances.

Generally, a tax code number is arrived at by deleting the last digit in the sum representing the employee's tax free allowances. Every individual is entitled to a personal tax free allowance of £11,500. The code number for an individual who is entitled to this but no other allowance is 1150L.

The code number may also reflect other items. For example, **it will be restricted to reflect benefits, small amounts of untaxed income** and **unpaid tax on income from earlier years**. If an amount of tax is in point, it is necessary to gross up the tax in the code using the taxpayer's estimated marginal rate of income tax.

 Question PAYE codes

Adrian is entitled to the full personal allowance (code letter L) and earns £15,000 each tax year. He has benefits of £1,160 and his unpaid tax for 2015/16 was £58. Adrian is a basic rate taxpayer. What is Adrian's PAYE code for 2017/18?

Answer

	£
Personal allowance	11,500
Benefits	(1,160)
Unpaid tax £58 × 100/20	(290)
Available allowances	10,050

Adrian's PAYE code is 1005L.

Codes are determined and amended by HMRC. They are normally notified to the employer on a code list. The employer must act on the code until amended instructions are received from HMRC, even if the employee has appealed against the code.

When the payroll is run, an employee is generally given 1/52nd or 1/12th of their tax free allowances against each week's/month's pay. However, because of the cumulative nature of PAYE, if an employee is first paid in, say, September, that month they will receive six months' allowances against their gross pay. In cases where the employee's previous PAYE history is not known, this could lead to under-deduction of tax. To avoid this, codes for the employees concerned have to be operated on a 'week 1/month 1' basis, so that only 1/52nd or 1/12th of the employee's allowances are available each week/month.

3.5 PAYE forms   12/16

FAST FORWARD ⟩

Employers must complete forms P60, P11D and P45 as appropriate. Form P60 is a year end return. A P45 is needed when an employee leaves. Form P11D records details of benefits.

At the end of each tax year, the employer must provide each employee with a form P60. This shows total taxable earnings for the year, tax deducted, code number, NI number and the employer's name and address. **The P60 must be provided by 31 May following the year of assessment.**

Following the end of each tax year, the employer must submit to HMRC by 6 July:

- **Forms P11D** (benefits which are not payrolled)
- **Forms P11D(b)** (return of Class 1A NICs (see later in this Study Text))

A copy of the form P11D must also be provided to the employee by 6 July. The details shown on the P11D include the full cash equivalent of all taxable benefits (other than those which are payrolled), so that the employee may enter the details on his self-assessment tax return.

When an employee leaves, a form P45 (particulars of Employee Leaving) must be prepared. This form shows the employee's code and details of his income and tax paid to date and is handed to the employee. One of the parts is the employee's personal copy. If the employee takes up a new employment, he must hand another part of the form P45 to the new employer. The details on the form are used by the new employer to calculate income tax due under PAYE when the payroll is next run.

Exam focus point

> This topic was tested in Question 32, Array Ltd, in the December 2016 exam. Candidates were required to state how employers are required to report details of employees' taxable benefits to HMRC following the end of the tax year and the deadline for submitting this information. The examining team commented that many candidates appreciated that reporting is done using form P11D, but the submission deadline was often not known. Less well-prepared candidates often discussed (at length) submission details for self-assessment tax returns.

3.6 Interest and penalties

Daily interest is charged on late payments of income tax and NICs under PAYE by taking the number of days by which a payment is late and applying the relevant late payment interest rate. HMRC make the charge after the end of the tax year.

Late payment penalties may be charged on PAYE amounts that are not paid in full and on time. Employers are not charged a penalty for the first late PAYE payment in a tax year, unless that payment is over six months late. The amounts of the penalties on subsequent late payments in the tax year depend on how much is late each time and the number of times payments are late in a tax year. The maximum penalty is 4% of the amount that is late in the relevant tax month and applies to the 11th (or more) late payment that tax year. **Where the tax remains unpaid at six months, the further penalty is 5% of tax unpaid**, with a further 5% if tax remains unpaid at 12 months, even if there is only one late payment in the year.

There are also penalties for making late returns under RTI which are imposed on a monthly basis. The first late submission of the tax year is ignored. Further late submissions will attract penalties based on the number of employees as follows:

Number of employees	Monthly penalty
1 to 9	£100
10 to 49	£200
50 to 249	£300
250 or more	£400

If the return is **more than three months late**, there is an **additional penalty** due of 5% of the tax and NIC due.

Exam focus point

HMRC allows a return to be up to three days late before imposing a penalty. However, the examining team has specifically stated this aspect is **not examinable** in Taxation (TX – UK). There are also various other relaxations to the penalty rules which may apply but you should assume that the rules set out in above apply when answering a Taxation (TX – UK) examination question.

Penalties for inaccurate returns are subject to the common penalty regime for errors (see later in this Study Text).

3.7 PAYE settlement agreements

PAYE settlement agreements (PSAs) are arrangements under which employers can make single payments to settle their employees' income tax liabilities on expense payments and benefits which are minor, irregular or where it would be impractical to operate PAYE.

Chapter Roundup

- Employees are taxed on benefits under the benefits code.

- The benefit in respect of accommodation is its annual value. There is an additional benefit if the property cost over £75,000.

- Employees who have a company car are taxed on a % of the car's list price which depends on the level of the car's CO_2 emissions. The same % multiplied by £22,600 determines the benefit where private fuel is also provided.

- Cheap loans are charged to tax on the difference between the official rate of interest and any interest paid by the employee.

- 20% of the value of assets made available for private use is taxable.

- Workplace childcare is an exempt benefit. Employer-supported childcare and childcare vouchers are exempt up to £55 per week. Maximum tax relief is limited to £11 per week (the equivalent of £55 × 20%).

- There is a residual charge for other benefits, usually equal to the cost to the employer of the benefits.

- There are a number of exempt benefits including removal expenses, sporting facilities, and workplace parking.

- Most tax in respect of employment income is deducted under the PAYE system. The objective of the PAYE system is to collect the correct amount of tax over the year. An employee's PAYE code is designed to ensure that allowances etc are given evenly over the year.

- Employers must complete forms P60, P11D and P45 as appropriate. Form P60 is a year end return. A P45 is needed when an employee leaves. Form P11D records details of benefits.

Quick Quiz

1   What accommodation does not give rise to a taxable benefit?

2   Mike is provided with a petrol-engined car by his employer throughout 2017/18. The car has a list price of £15,000 (although the employer actually paid £13,500 for it) and has CO_2 emissions of 105g/km. Mike's taxable car benefit is:

    A   £2,700
    B   £3,000
    C   £3,450
    D   £5,850

3   When may an employee who is provided with fuel by their employer avoid a fuel benefit?

4   To what extent are qualifying removal expenses paid for by an employer taxable?

5   Give an example of a PAYE code.

Answers to Quick Quiz

1   Job related accommodation

2   B. Amount by which CO_2 emissions exceed the baseline is $(105 - 95)$ $= 10/5 = 2 + 18\%$

                                                        $= 20\% \times £15,000$

                                                        $= £3,000$

3   There is no fuel benefit if:

- All the fuel provided was made available only for business travel; or
- The full cost of any fuel provided for private use was completely reimbursed by the employee.

4   The first £8,000 of qualifying removal expenses are exempt. Any excess is taxable.

5   1150L.

Now try the questions below from the Practice Question Bank			
Number	**Type**	**Marks**	**Time**
Q20	Section A	2	4 mins
Q21	Section A	2	4 mins
Q22	Section A	2	4 mins
Q23	Section B	2	4 mins
Q24	Section B	2	4 mins
Q25	Section B	2	4 mins
Q26	Section B	2	4 mins
Q27	Section B	2	4 mins
Q28	Section C	10	18 mins

Pensions

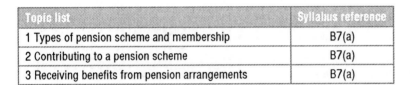

Topic list	Syllabus reference
1 Types of pension scheme and membership	B7(a)
2 Contributing to a pension scheme	B7(a)
3 Receiving benefits from pension arrangements	B7(a)

Introduction

In the previous two chapters we have discussed the taxation of employment income. Most employers are now required to make pension contributions for most of their employees, often using an occupational pension scheme to which employees also contribute. Employees may choose instead (by opting out), or in addition, to take out a personal pension scheme run by a financial institution such as a bank or building society.

Self-employed or non-working individuals can only make provision for a pension using a personal pension scheme.

Whichever type of scheme is chosen the amount of tax relief available is the same. However, the method for giving the relief can be different; contributions to occupational schemes are usually deducted from gross pay before Pay As You Earn (PAYE) is calculated whilst contributions to personal pensions are paid net of basic rate tax and further tax relief is given through the personal tax computation. We cover both methods of giving tax relief in detail in this chapter.

Study guide

		Intellectual level
B7	**The use of exemptions and reliefs in deferring and minimising income tax liabilities**	
(a)	Explain and compute the relief given for contributions to personal pension schemes and to occupational pension schemes.	2

Exam guide

Pension contributions can be paid by all individuals and you may come across them as part of an income tax question in Section C. In Section C you may also be required to discuss the types of pension schemes available and the limits on the tax relief due, or you may have to deal with them in an income tax computation. Pensions may be tested in a 15 mark question or a 10 mark question. Section A or B questions might test a specific aspect of pensions such as the amount of the annual allowance.

You must be sure that you know how to deal with the two ways of giving relief – contributions to occupational schemes are deducted from earnings whilst contributions to personal pensions are paid net of basic rate tax and further tax relief is given by increasing the basic rate and higher rate limits.

1 Types of pension scheme and membership

FAST FORWARD

An employee may be a member of their employer's occupational pension scheme. Any individual whether a member of an occupational pension scheme or not, can take out a 'personal pension' plan with a financial institution such as an insurance company, bank or building society.

1.1 Introduction

Individuals are encouraged by the government to make financial provision to cover their needs when they reach a certain age. There are state pension arrangements which provide some financial support, but the government are keen for individuals to make their own pension provision to supplement their state pensions.

Automatic enrolment is being introduced so that employers must automatically enrol most employees into a workplace pension scheme (although employees can then opt out of the scheme). Under automatic enrolment, **there are minimum contributions to the workplace pension scheme required by law** (up to 5 April 2018 usually equal to 2% of earnings of which a minimum amount equal to 1% of earnings must be contributed by the employer).

Alternatively, individuals (employees, self-employed and those who are not working) may make their own pension provision through a personal pension provider such as an insurance company.

Tax relief is given for both employer pension provision and personal pension provision. This includes both relief for contributions paid into pension schemes during an individual's working life and an exemption from tax on income and gains arising in the pension fund itself.

1.2 Pension arrangements

An individual may make pension provision in a number of ways.

1.2.1 Occupational pension scheme

> Employers may set up an **occupational pension scheme**. The employer may use the services of an insurance company (an insured scheme) or may set up a totally self administered pension fund.

There are two kinds of occupational pension scheme – earnings-related (**defined benefits arrangements**) and investment-related (**money purchase arrangements**). In a **defined benefits arrangements** the pension is generally based on employees' earnings either at retirement (a **final salary** scheme) or throughout their employment (a **career average** scheme) and linked to the number of years they have worked for the employer.

A **money purchase pension** – also known as a **defined contribution scheme** – does not provide any guarantee regarding the level of pension which will be available. The individual invests in the pension scheme and the amount invested is used to build up a pension.

1.2.2 Personal pensions

> **Personal pensions** are money purchase schemes, which are provided by banks, insurance companies and other financial institutions.

Stakeholder pensions are a particular type of personal pension scheme. They must satisfy certain rules, such as a maximum level of charges, ease of transfer and so on.

Any individual (whether employed or not) may join a personal pension scheme.

1.2.3 More than one pension arrangement

An individual may make a number of different pension arrangements depending on their circumstances. For example, they may be a member of an occupational pension scheme and also make pension arrangements independently with a financial provider. If the individual has more than one pension arrangement, the rules we will be looking at in detail later apply to all the pension arrangements they make. For example, **there is a limit on the amount of contributions that the individual can make in a tax year. This limit applies to all the pension arrangements that they make, not each of them.**

The rules below apply to registered pension schemes, ie those registered with HM Revenue & Customs (HMRC).

2 Contributing to a pension scheme

> Anyone can contribute to a personal pension scheme, even if they are not earning, subject to the contributions threshold of £3,600 (gross).

2.1 Contributions by a scheme member

Any individual **under the age of 75 can make tax relievable pension contributions** in a tax year.

The maximum amount of contributions attracting tax relief made by an individual in a tax year is the higher of:

- **The individual's relevant UK earnings chargeable to income tax in the year; or**
- **The basic amount (set at £3,600 for 2017/18).**

These figures are gross contributions (see further below) and apply whether the individual pays into an occupational scheme, a personal pension scheme or both.

Relevant UK earnings are broadly employment income, trading income and income from furnished holiday lettings (see later in this Study Text).

If the individual does not have any UK earnings in a tax year, the maximum pension contribution they can obtain tax relief on is £3,600.

Where an individual contributes to more than one pension scheme, the aggregate of their contributions will be used to give the total amount of tax relief.

2.2 Methods of giving tax relief

Contributions to personal pension plans are paid net of basic rate tax. Higher/additional rate relief is given through the personal tax computation. Contributions to occupational pension schemes are usually paid under the net pay scheme.

2.2.1 Pension tax relief given at source   9/16, 12/16

This method will be used where an individual makes a contribution to a pension scheme run by a personal pension provider such as an insurance company.

Relief is given at source by the contributions being deemed to be made net of basic rate tax. This applies whether the individual is an employee, self-employed or not employed at all and whether or not they have taxable income. HMRC then pay an amount of basic rate tax to the pension provider.

Further tax relief is given if the individual is a higher rate or additional rate taxpayer. The relief is given by increasing the basic rate limit and the higher rate limit for the year by the gross amount of contributions for which the taxpayer is entitled to relief. You will recognise this method as the same way in which relief is given for gift aid donations.

Exam focus point

Make sure your workings show clearly how you have increased the basic rate and higher rate limits. Note the difference between this method and that used for net pay arrangements (see below).

Question   Pension tax relief given at source

Joe has earnings of £60,000 in 2017/18. He pays a personal pension contribution of £7,200 (net). He has no other taxable income.

Show Joe's tax liability for 2017/18.

Answer

	Non-savings Income £
Earnings/Net income	60,000
Less PA	(11,500)
Taxable income	48,500

Tax

	£
£42,500 (W) × 20%	8,500
£6,000 × 40%	2,400
£48,500	10,900

Working: Basic rate limit £33,500 + (£7,200 × 100/80) = £42,500

Remember that **gross personal pension contributions** are also used to compute **adjusted net income** and that **the restriction on the personal allowance** is calculated in relation to adjusted net income.

2.2.2 Net pay arrangements

9/16

An occupational scheme will normally operate net pay arrangements.

In this case, the employer will deduct gross pension contributions from the individual's earnings before operating PAYE. The individual therefore obtains tax relief at their marginal rate of tax automatically.

Question   Net pay arrangements

Maxine has taxable earnings of £60,000 in 2017/18. Her employer deducts a pension contribution of £9,000 from these earnings before operating PAYE. She has no other taxable income.

Show Maxine's tax liability for 2017/18.

Answer

	Non-savings Income £
Earnings/Total income	60,000
Less pension contribution	(9,000)
Net income	51,000
Less PA	(11,500)
Taxable income	39,500

Tax

	£
£33,500 × 20%	6,700
£6,000 × 40%	2,400
£39,500	9,100

This is the same result as Joe in the previous example. Joe had received basic rate tax relief of £(9,000 – 7,200) = £1,800 at source, so his overall tax position was £(10,900 – 1,800) = £9,100.

2.3 Contributions not attracting tax relief

An individual can also make contributions to their pension arrangements which do not attract tax relief, for example out of capital. The member must notify the scheme administrator if they make contributions in excess of the higher of their UK relevant earnings and the basic amount.

Such contributions do not count towards the annual allowance limit (discussed below) but will affect the value of the pension fund for the lifetime allowance.

2.4 Employer pension contributions

6/17

Where the active scheme member is an employee, their **employer will often make contributions to their pension scheme** and under automatic enrolment are required by law to make at least minimum

contributions to a workplace pension scheme. Employer pension contributions to any type of pension scheme are **exempt benefits** for the employee.

There is **no limit** on the amount of the contributions that may be made by an employer but **they always count towards the annual allowance** and will also affect the value of the pension fund for the lifetime allowance (see further below).

All contributions made by an employer are made gross and the employer will usually obtain tax relief for the contribution by deducting it as an expense in calculating trading profits for the period of account in which the payment is made.

2.5 Annual allowance   9/16, 12/16

There is an overriding limit on the amount that can be paid into an individual's pension scheme for each tax year. This is called the annual allowance. The annual allowance is reduced if an individual has adjusted income in excess of £150,000. Unused annual allowance can be carried forward for up to three years.

2.5.1 Introduction

The annual allowance effectively restricts the amount of tax relievable contributions that can be paid into an individual's pension scheme each year. The annual allowance is £40,000.

Exam focus point

> This amount will be shown in the Tax Rates and Allowances in the exam. There were some complex transitional rules which meant that for 2015/16 the annual allowance could have been more than £40,000 for some individuals depending on when contributions were made in the year. These transitional rules were **not examinable** in Taxation (TX – UK) and you should assume that in any exam question involving pensions the timing of the contributions means that only an annual allowance of £40,000 was available for 2015/16. This assumption also applies in relation to carry forward of unused annual allowance to future years.

2.5.2 Reduced annual allowance

From the tax year 2016/17, **individuals who have adjusted income in excess of £150,000 have a reduced annual allowance.**

The annual allowance is reduced by £1 for every £2 that the individual's adjusted income exceeds £150,000, subject to a **minimum annual allowance of £10,000.** The minimum annual allowance will apply where the individual has adjusted income of £210,000 or more since £(40,000 – [210,000 – 150,000]/2) = £10,000.

Adjusted income for the self-employed is the same as net income (ie total income less loss relief against general income and qualifying interest). This is because the individual will only have made pension contributions with tax relief by deduction at source (see Section 2.2.1) which does not affect the computation of net income.

Adjusted income for employees is net income plus employee pension contributions to occupational pension schemes under net pay arrangements (see Section 2.2.2) (as these will have been deducted in computing net income) **plus employer contributions to occupational pension schemes and/or personal pension schemes**. If the employee has made personal pension contributions with tax relief by deduction at source, these are not relevant in computing adjusted income.

Exam focus point

> There is a threshold level of income below which tapering does not apply but this is **not examinable** in Taxation (TX – UK).

In the tax year 2017/18, Bella was a member of a partnership and had a partnership trading profit of £168,000. During the tax year, Bella paid qualifying interest of £5,000 on a loan to invest in the partnership. She also had property business income of £13,500 for 2017/18. What is Bella's reduced annual allowance for 2017/18?

Answer

First work out Bella's adjusted income. This will be equal to her net income since she is self-employed and so has made pension contributions with tax relief by deduction at source.

	Non-savings income £
Trading income from partnership	168,000
Property business income	13,500
Total income	181,500
Less qualifying interest paid	(5,000)
Net income = adjusted income	176,500

Then compute the reduced annual allowance:

	£
Adjusted income	176,500
Less income limit	(150,000)
Excess	26,500
Annual allowance	40,000
Less half excess £26,500 × ½	(13,250)
Reduced annual allowance	26,750

2.5.3 Carry forward of unused annual allowance 6/17

Where **an individual is a member of a registered pension scheme** but **does not make contributions of at least the annual allowance in a tax year**, the individual can **carry forward the unused amount of the annual allowance for up to three years**. In any year for which the individual is not a member of a pension scheme, the annual allowance does not apply and so there can be no carry forward.

The annual allowance in the current tax year is treated as being used first, then any unused annual allowance is brought forward from earlier years, using the earliest tax year first. Where the annual allowance has been reduced as described in Section 2.5.2, the reduced amount will be carried forward to later years.

Question

Carry forward of annual allowance

Ted is a sole trader. His gross contributions to his personal pension scheme have been as follows:

2014/15	£16,000
2015/16	£36,000
2016/17	£25,000

In 2017/18 Ted will have taxable trading profits of about £100,000 and wishes to make a large pension contribution in January 2018. He has no other sources of income.

(a) What is the maximum gross tax relievable pension contribution Ted can make in January 2018, taking into account any brought forward annual allowance?

(b)   If Ted makes a gross personal pension contribution of £43,000 in January 2018, what are the unused annual allowances he can carry forward to 2018/19?

Answer

(a)

	£
Annual allowance 2017/18	40,000
Annual allowance unused in 2014/15 £(40,000 – 16,000)	24,000
Annual allowance unused in 2015/16 £(40,000 – 36,000)	4,000
Annual allowance unused in 2016/17 £(40,000 – 25,000)	15,000
Maximum gross pension contribution in 2017/18	83,000

(b)

	£
Annual allowance 2017/18 used in 2017/18	40,000
Annual allowance unused in 2014/15 used in 2017/18	3,000
Contribution in 2017/18	43,000

The remaining £(24,000 – 3,000) = £21,000 of the 2014/15 annual allowance cannot be carried forward to 2018/19 since this is more than three years after 2014/15. The unused annual allowances are therefore £4,000 from 2015/16 and £15,000 from 2016/17 and these are carried forward to 2018/19.

2.5.4 Contributions in excess of annual allowance

FAST FORWARD

An annual allowance charge arises if tax-relievable contributions exceed the available annual allowance.

If tax-relievable pension contributions exceed the annual allowance, there is a charge to income tax based on the individual's taxable income. This will occur if the taxpayer has relevant earnings in excess of the available annual allowance and makes a contribution in excess of the available annual allowance (including any brought forward annual allowance). **The taxpayer is primarily liable for the tax on the excess contribution.**

The annual allowance charge is calculated by taxing the excess contribution as an extra amount of income received by the taxpayer. The calculation therefore claws back the tax relief given on the pension contribution.

Question   Annual allowance charge

Jaida had employment income of £240,000 in 2017/18. She made a gross personal pension contribution of £70,000 in December 2017. She does not have any unused annual allowance brought forward. What is Jaida's income tax liability for 2017/18?

Answer

	Non-savings income £
Taxable income (no personal allowance available)	240,000

Tax

	£
£103,500 (W1) × 20%	20,700
£116,500 × 40%	46,600
£220,000 (W2)	
£20,000 × 45%	9,000
£240,000	
£60,000 (W3) × 45%	27,000
Tax liability	103,300

Workings

1. Basic rate limit £33,500 + £70,000 = £103,500
2. Higher rate limit £150,000 + £70,000 = £220,000
3. Excess pension contribution £(70,000 − 10,000 minimum as adjusted income exceeds £210,000) = £60,000

3 Receiving benefits from pension arrangements

One of the competencies you require to fulfil Performance Objective 17 Tax planning and advice of the PER is to assess the tax implications of proposed activities or plans of an individual or entity with reference to relevant and up to date legislation. You can apply the knowledge you obtain from this section of the Study Text to help to demonstrate this competence.

3.1 Pension benefits

FAST FORWARD ❯❯

An individual can start to receive pension benefits from the age of 55. Under flexi-access drawdown, a tax-free lump sum of 25% of the pension fund can be taken and the remainder reinvested to give taxable pension income as required.

After reaching the minimum pension age of 55, an individual can start to receive pension benefits with complete flexibility to access their personal pensions.

There are a number of common ways in which an individual can receive benefits from personal pension schemes. One is **flexi-access drawdown** where the individual usually takes a **tax-free lump sum of 25%** of the pension fund. The **rest of the pension fund** is then reinvested to provide **taxable pension income** as required by the individual. Previously individuals usually had to buy an annuity with the balance (which is still an option).

Exam focus point

There is an anti-avoidance annual allowance limit which applies when an individual starts to receive pension benefits flexibly but is also entitled to make further contributions to the pension fund. This annual allowance limit is **not examinable** in Taxation (TX – UK).

3.2 The lifetime allowance

FAST FORWARD ❯❯

An individual is not allowed to build up an indefinitely large pension fund. There is a maximum value for a pension fund called the lifetime allowance.

The amount of the **lifetime allowance for 2017/18 is £1,000,000**. This limit applies to the total funds built up in an individual's pension funds.

If the pension fund exceeds the lifetime allowance, this will give rise to an income tax charge on the excess value of the fund when the individual receives pension benefits from the fund. The rate of the charge is 55% if the excess value is taken as a lump sum, or 25% if the funds are used to provide a pension income.

Chapter Roundup

- An employee may be a member of their employer's occupational pension scheme. Any individual whether a member of an occupational pension scheme or not, can take out a 'personal pension' plan with a financial institution such as an insurance company, bank or building society.

- Anyone can contribute to a personal pension scheme, even if they are not earning, subject to the contributions threshold of £3,600 (gross).

- Contributions to personal pension plans are paid net of basic rate tax. Higher/additional rate relief is given through the personal tax computation. Contributions to occupational pension schemes are usually paid under the net pay scheme.

- There is an overriding limit on the amount that can be paid into an individual's pension scheme for each tax year. This is called the annual allowance. The annual allowance is reduced if an individual has adjusted income in excess of £150,000. Unused annual allowance can be carried forward for up to three years.

- An annual allowance charge arises if tax-relievable contributions exceed the available annual allowance.

- An individual can start to receive pension benefits from the age of 55. Under flexi-access drawdown, a tax-free lump sum of 25% of the pension fund can be taken and the remainder reinvested to give taxable pension income as required.

- An individual is not allowed to build up an indefinitely large pension fund. There is a maximum value for a pension fund called the lifetime allowance.

Quick Quiz

1   Martha has UK earnings of £3,000 in 2017/18. What is the maximum actual amount of pension contribution she can pay in 2017/18 to a personal pension?

    A   £2,400
    B   £2,880
    C   £3,000
    D   £3,600

2   Fern joined a registered pension scheme in 2015/16 and made a gross contribution of £14,000. She had not been a member of registered pension scheme before this time. She did not make any contribution in 2016/17. Fern has relevant earnings of £125,000 in 2017/18 and no other sources of income. What is the maximum gross pension contribution Fern can make in 2017/18 without incurring an annual allowance charge, taking into account any brought forward annual allowance?

3   Jim became a member of a pension scheme for the first time in 2017/18. His only income in 2017/18 is trading income of £163,000. What is Jim's annual allowance for 2017/18?

4   What are the consequences of the total of employee and employer pension contributions exceeding the annual allowance?

5   What are the consequences of exceeding the lifetime allowance?

1   B. The maximum gross contribution that Martha can pay is the higher of her relevant earnings (£3,000) and the basic amount (£3,600). She will actually pay £3,600 × 80% = £2,880 to the pension provider.

2   Fern will not be able to use any unused personal allowance from 2014/15 as she was not a member of a registered pension scheme in this year. She has £(40,000 – 14,000) = £26,000 unused from 2015/16 and £40,000 from 2016/17. Her total maximum contribution for 2017/18 without incurring an annual allowance charge is therefore £(26,000 + 40,000 + 40,000) = £106,000.

3

	£
Adjusted income = net income	163,000
Less threshold	(150,000)
Excess	13,000
Annual allowance	40,000
Less half excess £13,000 × ½	(6,500)
Reduced annual allowance	33,500

4   The excess is subject to the annual allowance charge primarily chargeable on the employee.

5   If the lifetime allowance is exceeded the excess is charged at 55% (if taken as a lump sum) or 25% (if taken as a pension).

Now try the questions below from the Practice Question Bank

Number	Type	Marks	Time
Q29	Section A	2	4 mins
Q30	Section A	2	4 mins
Q31	Section A	2	4 mins
Q32	Section B	2	4 mins
Q33	Section B	2	4 mins
Q34	Section B	2	4 mins
Q35	Section B	2	4 mins
Q36	Section B	2	4 mins

Property income

Topic list	Syllabus reference
1 Property business income	B4(a), B4(e)
2 Furnished holiday lettings	B4(b)
3 Rent a room relief	B4(c)
4 Premiums on leases	B4(d)
5 Property business losses	B4(f)

Introduction

We have finished looking at an individual's employment income and can turn our attention to other income to be slotted into the tax computation.

We are now going to look at the computation and taxation of the profits of a property letting business. First we see how to work out the profit (you may like to return to this section once you have studied Chapters 7 and 8). There is a special rule about finance costs for individuals.

Next we look at the special conditions which must be satisfied if a letting is to be treated as a furnished holiday let and at the extra tax reliefs available if it is.

We then consider the special relief available to taxpayers who let out rooms in their own homes, rent a room relief.

Finally we see how part of a premium for granting a short lease is taxed as income, and briefly consider how to deal with property business losses.

In the following chapters we shall turn our attention to the profits of traders.

Study guide

		Intellectual level
B4	**Property and investment income**	
(a)	Compute property business profits.	2
(b)	Explain the treatment of furnished holiday lettings.	1
(c)	Understand rent-a-room relief.	1
(d)	Compute the amount assessable when a premium is received for the grant of a short lease.	2
(e)	Understand and apply the restriction on property income finance costs.	2
(f)	Understand how relief for a property business loss is given.	2

Exam guide

You are likely to be required to compute property income as part of a 10 or 15 mark question in Section C. You may find it in the context of income tax or corporation tax – the basic computational rules are mainly the same (apart from interest paid, which is not included as an expense when computing property income for corporation tax purposes, and the restriction on property income finance costs which is not relevant for corporation tax purposes). Specific aspects of property income such as lease premiums may be tested in Section A or Section B questions. Rent a room relief is an important relief for individuals (it does not apply to companies), and the special rules for furnished holiday lettings will only be examined in an income tax context. Remember that property income is non-savings income even though a property portfolio is usually regarded as an investment.

1 Property business income

FAST FORWARD

> Property business profits and losses are calculated for a tax year on an accruals basis. There is a special rule about finance costs for individuals.

1.1 Profits and losses of a property business

Income from land and buildings in the UK is taxed as non-savings income. The profits of the UK property business are **computed for tax years**. Each tax year's profit is taxed in that year. A loss from a UK property business is carried forward to set against the **first future profits from the UK property business** (see later in this chapter).

1.2 Computation of profits and losses 6/17

1.2.1 General principles

A taxpayer with UK rental income is treated as running a business, their 'UK property business'. All the rents and expenses for all properties are pooled, to give a single profit or loss. Profits and losses are generally computed in the same way as trading profits and losses are computed for tax purposes, on an **accruals basis** (we will study trading income in greater detail later in this Study Text).

Allowable expenses include **repairs** to the property, **agent's fees**, **insurance**, and **rent payable** where a landlord is renting the property which they in turn let to others. Relief is available for **irrecoverable rent** as an **impairment loss**. **Capital expenditure** (for example mortgage capital repayments, construction of an extension or boundary wall) **is not allowable**.

1.2.2 Finance costs for individuals

New

A special rule is being introduced from 2017/18 relating to **interest and other finance costs** (including incidental costs incurred in obtaining loans such as fees or commission payments) for **property businesses carried on by individuals** (not companies). The effect of the rule is to **restrict tax relief on these costs to the basic rate.** The tax liability of basic rate taxpayers will not be affected by the introduction of the rule but higher and additional rate taxpayers will have an increased tax liability.

The rule applies to **loans taken out for a residential property business.** It is not necessary for the loan to be for the purchase of the property, for example it could be taken out to pay for repairs to the property. Loans relating to commercial properties or for furnished holiday letting business (see later in this chapter) do not fall within the rule.

The rule is being phased in over four tax years. In 2017/18, 75% of the finance costs are allowable in the computation of property business income in the same way as other expenses. **The remaining 25%, multiplied by the basic rate of tax, is a tax reducer.**

Exam focus point

> **The 25% finance costs restriction** will be given to you in the Tax Rates and Allowances in the exam.

Question

Finance costs

Millicent lets out a house throughout the tax year 2017/18 at a monthly rental of £1,500. She has a mortgage loan on the house and in 2017/18 she makes capital repayments of £1,000 and pays interest of £4,000. Millicent has other expenses (all allowable) of £2,500 for 2017/18. Millicent has other taxable income (after deduction of her personal allowance) of £60,000 in 2017/18.

Compute Millicent's income tax liability in respect of her property business income for the tax year 2017/18.

Answer

	£
Rental income £1,500 × 12	18,000
Less expenses	
finance costs £4,000 × 75%	(3,000)
other allowable expenses	(2,500)
Property business income	12,500

Note that the mortgage capital repayments are not allowable.

Income tax on property business income	£
£12,500 × 40% (higher rate taxpayer)	5,000
Less property business finance costs tax reducer	
£4,000 × 25% × 20%	(200)
Property business income tax liability	4,800

1.3 Capital allowances

FAST FORWARD

> Capital allowances are not normally available for residential property.

In principle, **capital allowances** are **available on plant and machinery used in the UK property business** in the same way as for a trading business with an accounting date of 5 April (we will study capital allowances in greater detail later in this Study Text).

However, **capital allowances are not normally available on plant or machinery used in residential property.**

FAST FORWARD

> If a residential property is let furnished, replacement of domestic items relief can be claimed.

No relief is given for the **initial cost** of providing domestic items. **Relief is given** if a domestic item is **replaced**.

Domestic items are defined as furniture, furnishings, household appliances and kitchenware. Examples include beds, televisions, fridges, freezers, washing machines, carpets and other floor coverings, curtains, crockery and cutlery. It does not include fixtures which become part of the property including boilers and radiators.

The **amount of the relief** is the **expenditure on the new replacement asset less any proceeds** from selling the old asset which has been replaced. If the **new asset is not the same, or substantially the same, as the old asset, only the cost of an equivalent asset is given relief.**

Question
Property business income with replacement domestic items relief

Over the last few years, Peter has purchased several properties in Manchester as 'buy to let' investments.

5 Whitby Ave is let out furnished at £500 per month. A tenant moved in on 1 March 2017 but left unexpectedly on 1 May 2018 having paid rent only up to 31 December 2017. The tenant left no forwarding address.

17 Bolton Rd has been let furnished to the same tenant for a number of years at £800 per month.

A recent purchase, 27 Turner Close has been let unfurnished since 1 August 2017 at £750 per month. Before then it was empty whilst Peter redecorated it after its purchase in March 2017.

Peter's expenses during 2017/18 are:

	No 5 £	No 17 £	No 27 £
Insurance	250	250	200
Letting agency fees	–	–	100
Repairs	300	40	–
Redecoration	–	–	500
Curtains	130	–	–
Washer-dryer	–	600	–
Dining table and chairs	–	350	–

No 27 was in a fit state to let when Peter bought it but he wanted to redecorate the property as he felt this would allow him to achieve a better rental income.

The new curtains for No 5 were replacements for old curtains. Peter sold the old curtains for £15.

The washer-dryer for No 17 was a replacement for a washing machine without a dryer. If Peter had bought a new washing machine without a dryer, similar to the old machine, it would have cost him £475. The old washing machine was scrapped with no proceeds. Peter had not previously provided a dining table and chairs in No 17.

Peter made a UK property business loss in 2016/17 of £300.

What is Peter's taxable property income for 2017/18?

Answer

	No 5 £	No 17 £	No 27 £
2017/18			
Accrued income			
12 × £500	6,000		
12 × £800		9,600	
8 × £750			6,000

BPP
LEARNING MEDIA

	No 5 £	No 17 £	No 27 £
Less:			
Insurance	(250)	(250)	(200)
Letting agency fees			(100)
Impairment loss (irrecoverable rent)			
3 × £500	(1,500)		
Repairs	(300)	(40)	
Redecoration (N)			(500)
Replacement domestic items relief			
Curtains £(130 -15)	(115)		
Washer dryer (limited to cost of washing machine without dryer)		(475)	
Dining table and chairs (no relief for initial expenditure)		(0)	
Property Income	3,835	8,835	5,200

	£
Total property income	17,870
Less loss b/fwd	(300)
Taxable property income for 2017/18	17,570

Note. The redecoration of No.27 is an allowable expense. This is an example of the application of the case of *Odeon Associated Theatres Ltd v Jones 1971* (covered in more detail later in this Study Text) which showed that the cost of initial repairs to remedy normal wear and tear of a recently acquired asset was an allowable expense. This contrasts with the case of *Law Shipping v CIR 1921* where the cost of initial repairs to improve an asset recently acquired to make it fit to earn profits was disallowable capital expenditure. The key point in relation to No. 27 is that it was in a fit state to let when acquired.

2 Furnished holiday lettings (FHLs)

FAST FORWARD

Special rules apply to income from furnished holiday lettings (FHLs). Whilst the income is taxed as normal as property business income, the letting is treated as if it were a trade. Finance costs are not restricted, capital allowances are available on the furniture and the income is relevant earnings for pension purposes. However, only carry forward trade loss relief is available.

2.1 Introduction

There are special rules for FHLs. The letting is treated as if it were a trade. This means that, although the income is taxed as income from a property business, the provisions which apply to actual trades also apply to furnished holiday lettings and so there are the **following differences between normal property businesses and furnished holiday lettings**:

(a)   **Finance costs for individuals are not restricted** (see earlier in this chapter).

(b)   **Capital allowances are available on furniture instead of replacement domestic items relief** (see earlier in this chapter).

(c)   The income qualifies as **relevant earnings for pension relief** (see earlier in this Study Text).

(d)   **Capital gains tax rollover relief, entrepreneurs' relief and relief for gifts of business assets are available** (see later in this Study Text).

However, losses from FHLs are not treated as trade losses for relief against general income, early years loss relief and terminal loss relief. If a loss arises on a FHL, the only trade loss relief available is carry forward loss relief by deduction from the first available future profits of the same FHL business. Trading loss reliefs are dealt with later in this Study Text.

2.2 Conditions

Exam focus point

A FHL must be situated in the UK or in another state within the European Economic Area. However, **only FHLs situated within the UK are within the Taxation (TX – UK) syllabus.**

The letting must be of furnished accommodation made on a **commercial basis with a view to the realisation of profit**. The property must also satisfy the following three conditions.

(a)   **The availability condition** – the accommodation is available for commercial let as holiday accommodation to the public generally, for **at least 210 days during the year**.

(b)   **The letting condition** – the accommodation is commercially let as holiday accommodation to members of the public for **at least 105 days during the year**.

If the **landlord has more than one FHL**, at least one of which satisfies the 105 day rule ('qualifying holiday accommodation') and at least one of which does not, ('the underused accommodation'), they may elect to **average the occupation of the qualifying holiday accommodation and any or all of the underused accommodation**. If the average of occupation is at least 105 days, the underused accommodation will be treated as qualifying holiday accommodation.

Exam focus point

It is possible to make an election so that a rental property continues to qualify as a FHL for up to two years after the 105 day test ceases to be met. This election is **not examinable** in Taxation (TX – UK).

(c)   **The pattern of occupation condition – not more than 155 days in the year** fall during periods of longer term occupation. Longer term occupation is defined as a **continuous period of more than 31 days during which the accommodation is in the same occupation** unless there are abnormal circumstances.

If someone has FHLs and other lettings, **draw up two income statements as if they had two separate property businesses**. This is so that the profits and losses can be identified for the special rules which apply to FHLs.

3 Rent-a-room relief   12/16, 6/17

FAST FORWARD

Rents received from letting a room in the taxpayer's home may be tax free under the rent-a-room scheme.

3.1 The exemption

If an individual lets a room or rooms, furnished, in their main residence as living accommodation, then a special exemption may apply under the rent a room scheme.

The limit on the exemption is gross rents (before any expenses or capital allowances) of £7,500 in a tax year (2017/18). This limit is halved if any other person (eg spouse/civil partner) also received income from renting accommodation in the property.

If gross rents are not more than the limit, the rents are wholly exempt from income tax and expenses are ignored. However, the taxpayer may claim to ignore the exemption, for example to generate a loss by taking into account both rent and expenses.

Exam focus point

If you are asked to calculate property income in an exam don't overlook rent-a-room relief, but be sure to state whether the relief applies.

3.2 Alternative basis

If gross rents exceed the limit, the taxpayer will be taxed in the ordinary way, ignoring the rent a room scheme, unless they elect for the 'alternative basis'. If they so elect, they will be taxable on gross receipts less £7,500 (or £3,750 if the limit is halved), with no deductions for expenses.

3.3 Election

An election to ignore the exemption (if gross rents are below £7,500), or an election for the alternative basis (if gross rents exceed £7,500) must be made by the 31 January which is 22 months from the end of the tax year concerned. An election to ignore the exemption applies only for the tax year for which it is made, but an election for the alternative basis remains in force until it is withdrawn or until a year in which gross rents do not exceed the limit.

Question
Rent-a-room relief

Sylvia owns a house near the sea in Norfolk. She has a spare bedroom and during 2017/18 this was let to a lodger for £148 per week which includes the cost of heating and electricity.

Sylvia estimates that her lodger costs her an extra £150 on gas, £125 on electricity, and £50 on buildings insurance each year. What is Sylvia's property income for 2017/18 assuming that she makes any beneficial election?

Answer

Sylvia's gross rents are above the rent-a-room limit. Therefore she has the following choices:

(1) Under the normal method (no election needed), she can be taxed on her actual profit:

	£
Rental income £148 × 52	7,696
Less expenses (150 + 125 + 50)	(325)
	7,371

(2) Under the 'alternative basis' (elect for rent a room relief):

Total rental income of £7,696 exceeds £7,500 limit, so taxable income is £196 (ie 7,696 – 7,500) if rent a room relief claimed.

Sylvia should elect for rent-a-room relief and so be taxed on the 'alternative basis'.

4 Premiums on leases

FAST FORWARD

A premium received on the grant of a lease may be partly taxable as property income.

When a premium or similar consideration is received on the grant (that is, by a landlord to a tenant) of a short lease (50 years or less), part of the premium is treated as property income received in the year of grant.

The premium taxed as property income is the whole premium, less 2% of the premium for each complete year of the lease, except the first year.

This rule does not apply on the **assignment** of a lease (one tenant selling their entire interest in the property to another).

4.1 Example: Income element of premium

Janet granted a lease to Jack on 1 March 2018 for a period of 40 years. Jack paid a premium of £16,000. How much of the premium received by Janet is taxed as property income?

	£
Premium received	16,000
Less 2% × (40 −1) × £16,000	(12,480)
Taxable as property income	3,520

Note that if Janet **owned a 40 year lease and assigned it to Jack**, no part of the amount received would be taxed as property income.

4.2 Premiums paid by traders

If the premium is paid by a trader, a deduction can be made in computing taxable trading profits.

Where a trader pays a premium for a lease they may deduct an amount when computing their taxable trading profits in each year of the lease. The amount deductible is the figure taxed as property income on the landlord divided by the number of years of the lease.

You may want to look at this point again once you have studied trade profits later in this Study Text.

4.3 Example: Deduction for premium paid by trader

On 1 July 2017 Bryony, a trader, pays Scott, the landlord, a premium of £30,000 for a 10-year lease on a shop. Bryony makes up accounts to 31 December each year.

Scott is taxable on property income in 2017/18 of £30,000 − (£30,000 × (10 − 1) × 2%) = £24,600.

Bryony can therefore deduct £24,600/10 = £2,460 in each of the 10 years of the lease. She starts with the accounts year in which the lease starts (year ended 31 December 2017) and apportions the relief to the nearest month. Her deduction for 2017/18 is therefore:

1 July 2017 to 31 December 2017: 6/12 × £2,460   £1,230

5 Property business losses

A loss on a property letting business is carried forward to set against future property business profits.

A loss from a UK property business is carried forward to set against the **first future profits from the UK property business**. It may be carried forward until the UK property business ends, but it must be used as soon as possible.

As explained above, however, FHL losses are dealt with under special rules so that **losses from a FHL business must be kept separate and can only be used against profits of the same FHL business.**

Chapter Roundup

- Property business profits and losses are calculated for a tax year on an accruals basis. There is a special rule about finance costs for individuals.

- Capital allowances are not normally available for residential property.

- If residential property is let furnished replacement of domestic items relief can be claimed.

- Special rules apply to income from furnished holiday lettings (FHLs). Whilst the income is taxed as normal as property business income, the letting is treated as if it were a trade. Finance costs are not restricted, capital allowances are available on the furniture and the income is relevant earnings for pension purposes. However, only carry forward trade loss relief is available.

- Rents received from letting a room in the taxpayer's home may be tax free under the rent a room scheme.

- A premium received on the grant of a lease may be partly taxable as property income.

- If the premium is paid by a trader, a deduction can be made in computing taxable trading profits.

- A loss on a property letting business is carried forward to set against future property business profits.

Quick Quiz

1   For what period is property business income computed?

2   Frank lets out a residential property (not a furnished holiday letting) throughout the tax years 2017/18 and incurs finance costs in that year. How will these costs be given tax relief?

3   How is capital expenditure relieved for furnished lettings?

4   In order for property to be a furnished holiday letting it must be:

    (a)   Available for letting for at least _____ days during the year

    (b)   Actually let for at least _____ days during the year

    (c)   Not let as longer term accommodation for more than _____ days in the year (longer term occupation is a continuous period of more than _____ days in the same occupation)

    Fill in the blanks.

5   How much income per annum is tax free under the rent a room scheme?

    A   £3,750
    B   £7,500
    C   £10,000
    D   £11,000

6   Laura owns a property which qualifies as a FHL on which she made a profit in 2016/17 and a loss in 2017/18. She also lets out another property, which is not a FHL, on which she has a profit in 2017/18. How can Laura relieve the loss on the FHL?

    A   Against the other property profit of 2017/18
    B   Carry forward against all future property business income
    C   Carry back against the FHL profit of 2016/17
    D   Carry forward against profits of the same FHL business

1   Property business income is computed for tax years (6 April to 5 April).

2   75% of the finance costs can be deducted in computing property business income and so will be given tax relief at Frank's marginal rate of tax. The remaining 25% of the finance costs will be given tax relief at the basic rate through a tax reducer.

3   Except for FHLs where capital allowances are available for the cost of furniture, capital expenditure on furnishings is relieved through replacement of domestic items relief.

4   In order for property to be a furnished holiday letting it must be:

   (a)   Available for letting for at least **210** days during the year

   (b)   Actually let for at least **105** days during the year

   (c)   Not let as longer term accommodation for more than **155** days in the year (longer term occupation is a continuous period of more than **31** days in the same occupation)

5   B. £7,500

6   D. Carry forward against profits of the same FHL business

Now try the questions below from the Practice Question Bank

Number	Type	Marks	Time
Q37	Section A	2	4 mins
Q38	Section A	2	4 mins
Q39	Section A	2	4 mins
Q40	Section C	10	18 mins

Computing trading income

Topic list	Syllabus reference
1 The badges of trade	B3(b)
2 The adjustment of profits	B3(c)
3 Cash basis of accounting for small businesses	B3(d)
4 Pre-trading expenditure	B3(e)

Introduction

The final figure to slot into the income tax computation is income from self employment (trading income).

We are therefore going to look at the computation of profits of unincorporated businesses. We work out a business's profit as if it were a separate entity (the separate entity concept familiar to you from basic bookkeeping) but, as an unincorporated business has no legal existence apart from its trader, we cannot tax it separately. We have to feed its profit into the owner's personal tax computation.

Later chapters will consider capital allowances, which are allowed as an expense in the computation of profits, the taxation of business profits, and how trading losses can be relieved. We will then extend our study to partnerships, ie to groups of two or more individuals trading together.

Study guide

		Intellectual level
B3	**Income from self-employment**	
(b)	Describe and apply the badges of trade.	2
(c)	Recognise the expenditure that is allowable in calculating the tax-adjusted trading profit.	2
(d)	Explain and compute the assessable profits using the cash basis for small businesses.	2
(e)	Recognise the relief that can be obtained for pre-trading expenditure.	2

Exam guide

Section A questions on computing taxable trading income may test two or three particular adjustments such as the restriction for motor cars with high carbon dioxide (CO_2) emissions. You may also be required to deal with a number of adjustments in a Section B question. You may be required to compute trading profits in a Section C question. The computation may be for an individual, a partnership or a company. In each case the same principles are applied. You must however watch out for the adjustments which only apply to individuals, such as private use expenses. You may also be asked to explain the badges of trade in a Section C question. These topics may be tested as part of a 15 mark or a 10 mark question.

1 The badges of trade

FAST FORWARD

The badges of trade are used to decide whether or not a trade exists. If one does exist, the accounts profits need to be adjusted in order to establish the taxable profits.

Key term

A trade is defined in Income Tax Act 2007 only as any venture in the nature of trade. Further guidance about the scope of this definition is found in a number of cases which have been decided by the courts. This guidance is summarised in a collection of principles known as the **'badges of trade'**. These are set out below. They apply to both corporate and unincorporated businesses.

Exam focus point

You are not expected to know case names – we have included these below for your information only.

1.1 The subject matter

Whether a person is trading or not may sometimes be decided by examining the subject matter of the transaction. Some assets are commonly held as investments for their intrinsic value: an individual buying some shares or a painting may do so in order to enjoy the income from the shares or to enjoy the work of art. A subsequent disposal may produce a gain of a capital nature rather than a trading profit. But **where the subject matter of a transaction is such as would not be held as an investment** (for example, 34,000,000 yards of aircraft linen (*Martin v Lowry 1927*) or 1,000,000 rolls of toilet paper (*Rutledge v CIR 1929*)), **it is presumed that any profit on resale is a trading profit.**

1.2 The frequency of transactions

Transactions which may, in isolation, be of a capital nature will be interpreted as **trading transactions where their frequency indicates the carrying on of a trade.** It was decided that whereas normally the purchase of a mill-owning company and the subsequent stripping of its assets might be a capital transaction, where the taxpayer was embarking on the same exercise for the fourth time he must be carrying on a trade (*Pickford v Quirke 1927*).

1.3 Existence of similar trading transactions or interests

If there is an **existing trade**, then a **similarity to the transaction which is being considered** may point to that transaction having a trading character. For example, a builder who builds and sells a number of houses may be held to be trading even if he retains one or more houses for longer than usual and claims that they were held as an investment (*Harvey v Caulcott 1952*).

1.4 The length of ownership

The courts may infer a venture in the nature of trade where **items purchased are sold soon afterwards**.

1.5 The organisation of the activity as a trade

The courts may infer that a trade is being carried on if the transactions are **carried out in the same manner as someone who is unquestionably trading**. For example, an individual who bought a consignment of whiskey and then sold it through an agent, in the same way as others who were carrying on a trade, was also held to be trading (*CIR v Fraser 1942*). On the other hand, if an **asset has to be sold in order to raise funds in an emergency, this is less likely to be treated as trading.**

1.6 Supplementary work and marketing

When work is done to make an asset more marketable, or **marketing steps are taken to find purchasers**, the courts will be more ready to ascribe a trading motive. When a group of accountants bought, blended and recasked a quantity of brandy, they were held to be taxable on a trading profit when the brandy was later sold (*Cape Brandy Syndicate v CIR 1921*).

1.7 A profit motive

The absence of a profit motive will not necessarily preclude a tax charge as trading income, but its presence is a strong indication that a person is trading. The purchase and resale of £20,000 worth of silver bullion by the comedian Norman Wisdom, as a hedge against devaluation, was held to be a trading transaction (*Wisdom v Chamberlain 1969*).

1.8 The way in which the asset sold was acquired

If goods are acquired deliberately, trading may be indicated. If goods are acquired unintentionally, for example by gift or inheritance, their later sale is unlikely to be trading.

1.9 Method of finance

If the **purchaser has to borrow money to buy an asset such that they have to sell that asset quickly to repay the loan**, it may be inferred that trading was taking place. This was a factor in the *Wisdom v Chamberlain* case as Mr Wisdom financed his purchases by loans at a high rate of interest. It was clear that he had to sell the silver bullion quickly in order to repay the loan and prevent the interest charges becoming too onerous. On the other hand, taking out a long term loan to buy an asset (such as a mortgage on a house) would not usually indicate that trading is being carried on.

1.10 The taxpayer's intentions

Where a transaction is clearly trading on objective criteria, **the taxpayer's intentions are irrelevant**. If, however, a transaction has (objectively) a dual purpose, the taxpayer's intentions may be taken into account. An example of a transaction with a dual purpose is the acquisition of a site partly as premises from which to conduct another trade, and partly with a view to the possible development and resale of the site.

This test is not one of the traditional badges of trade, but it may be just as important.

2 The adjustment of profits

Exam focus point

> ACCA's article **Adjustment of profit,** written by a member of the Taxation (TX – UK) examining team, gives advice on attempting exam questions on adjustment of profit, with a working example of a question in a recent Taxation (TX – UK) exam.

FAST FORWARD

> The net profit in the statement of profit or loss must be adjusted to find the taxable trading profit.

2.1 Illustrative adjustment

Exam focus point

> The rules relating to profits from trades apply equally to profits from all professions and vocations.

Although the **net profit** shown in the statement of profit or loss is the starting point in computing the taxable trade profits, many adjustments may be required to calculate the taxable amount.

Exam focus point

> Only international accounting standard terminology is used when presenting accounting information contained within an examination question. This applies for companies, sole traders and partnerships.

Here is an illustrative adjustment of a statement of profit or loss:

	£	£
Net profit		140,000
Add: Expenditure charged in the accounts which is not deductible from trading profits	50,000	
Income taxable as trading profits which has not been included in the accounts	30,000	
		80,000
		220,000
Less: Profits included in the accounts but which are not taxable as trading profits	40,000	
Expenditure which is deductible from trading profits but has not been charged in the accounts (eg capital allowances)	20,000	
		(60,000)
Adjusted taxable trading profit		160,000

You may refer to deductible and non-deductible expenditure as allowable and disallowable expenditure respectively. The two sets of terms are interchangeable.

Exam focus point

> An examination question requiring adjustment to profit will direct you to start the adjustment with the net profit of £XXXX and to deal with all the items listed, indicating with a zero (0) any items which do not require adjustment. Marks will not be given for relevant items unless this approach is used. Therefore students who attempt to rewrite the statement of profit or loss will be penalised.

2.2 Accounting policies

The fundamental concept is that the profits of the business must be calculated in accordance with generally accepted accounting principles. These profits are subject to any adjustment specifically required for income tax purposes.

2.3 Deductible and non-deductible expenditure

FAST FORWARD

> Disallowable (ie non-deductible) expenditure must be added back to the net profit in the computation of the taxable trading profit. Any item not deducted wholly and exclusively for trade purposes is disallowable expenditure. Certain other items, such as depreciation, are specifically disallowable.

BPP
LEARNING MEDIA

2.3.1 Introduction

Certain expenses are specifically disallowed by the legislation. These are covered below. If, however, a deduction is specifically permitted this overrides the disallowance.

2.3.2 Payments contrary to public policy and illegal payments

Fines and penalties are not deductible. However, **HMRC usually allow employees' parking fines incurred in parking their employer's cars while on their employer's business. Fines relating to traders, however, are never allowed.**

A payment is not deductible if making it constitutes an offence by the payer. This covers protection money paid to terrorists, and also bribes. Statute also prevents any deduction for payments made in response to blackmail or extortion.

2.3.3 Capital expenditure

Capital expenditure is not deductible. This means that depreciation is non-deductible.

Profits and losses on the sale of non-current assets must be deducted or added back respectively. Chargeable gains or allowable losses may be dealt with under capital gains tax (see later in this Study Text).

The most contentious items of expenditure will often be repairs (revenue expenditure) **and improvements** (capital expenditure). Examples include:

(a) **The cost of restoration of an asset by, for instance, replacing a subsidiary part of the asset is revenue expenditure.** Expenditure on a new factory chimney replacement was allowable since the chimney was a subsidiary part of the factory (*Samuel Jones & Co (Devondale) Ltd v CIR 1951*). However, in another case a football club demolished a spectators' stand and replaced it with a modern equivalent. This was held not to be repair, since repair is the restoration by renewal or replacement of subsidiary parts of a larger entity, and the stand formed a distinct and *separate* part of the club (*Brown v Burnley Football and Athletic Co Ltd 1980*).

(b) **The cost of initial repairs to improve an asset recently acquired to make it fit to earn profits is disallowable capital expenditure.** In *Law Shipping Co Ltd v CIR 1923* the taxpayer failed to obtain relief for expenditure on making a newly bought ship seaworthy prior to using it.

(c) **The cost of initial repairs to remedy normal wear and tear of recently acquired assets is allowable revenue expenditure.** *Odeon Associated Theatres Ltd v Jones 1971* can be contrasted with the *Law Shipping* judgement. Odeon were allowed to charge expenditure incurred on improving the state of recently acquired cinemas.

Capital allowances may, however, be available as a deduction for capital expenditure from trading profits (see later in this Study Text).

Two exceptions to the 'capital' rule are worth noting:

(a) **The costs of registering patents and trade marks are deductible.**

(b) **Incidental costs of obtaining loan finance,** or of attempting to obtain or redeeming it, are deductible, other than a discount on issue or a premium on redemption (which are really alternatives to paying interest).

2.3.4 Expenditure not wholly and exclusively for the purposes of the trade

Expenditure is not deductible if it is not for trade purposes (the remoteness test), or if it reflects more than one purpose (the duality test). The private proportion of payments for motoring expenses, rent, heat and light and telephone expenses of a trader is non-deductible. If an exact apportionment is possible, relief is given on the business element. Where the payments are to or on behalf of employees, the full amounts are deductible but the employees are taxed under the benefits code (see earlier in this Study Text).

The remoteness test is illustrated by the following cases.

(a)   *Strong & Co of Romsey Ltd v Woodifield 1906*
A customer injured by a falling chimney when sleeping in an inn owned by a brewery claimed compensation from the company. The compensation was not deductible as it did not relate to the trade of inn-keeping.

(b)   *Bamford v ATA Advertising Ltd 1972*
A director misappropriated £15,000. The loss was not allowable as it did not relate to the trade.

(c)   Expenditure which is wholly and exclusively to benefit the trades of several companies (for example in a group) but is not wholly and exclusively to benefit the trade of one specific company is not deductible *(Vodafone Cellular Ltd and others v Shaw 1995).*

(d)   *McKnight (HMIT) v Sheppard (1999)* concerned expenses incurred by a stockbroker in defending allegations of infringements of Stock Exchange regulations. It was found that the expenditure was incurred to prevent the destruction of the taxpayer's business and that as the expenditure was incurred for business purposes it was deductible. It was also found that although the expenditure had the effect of preserving the taxpayer's reputation, that was not its purpose, so there was no duality of purpose.

The **duality test** is illustrated by the following cases.

(a)   *Caillebotte v Quinn 1975*
A self-employed carpenter spent an average of 40p per day when obliged to buy lunch away from home but just 10p when he lunched at home. He claimed the excess 30p. It was decided that the payment had a dual purpose and was not deductible.

(b)   *Mallalieu v Drummond 1983*
Expenditure by a lady barrister on black clothing to be worn in court (and on its cleaning and repair) was not deductible. The expenditure was for the dual purpose of enabling the barrister to be warmly and properly clad as well as meeting her professional requirements.

(c)   *McLaren v Mumford 1996*
A publican traded from a public house which had residential accommodation above it. He was obliged to live at the public house but he also had another house which he visited regularly. It was held that the private element of the expenditure incurred at the public house on electricity, rent, gas, etc was not incurred for the purpose of earning profits, but for serving the non-business purpose of satisfying the publican's ordinary human needs. The expenditure, therefore, had a dual purpose and was disallowed.

However, the cost of overnight accommodation when on a business trip may be deductible and reasonable expenditure on an evening meal and breakfast in conjunction with such accommodation is then also deductible.

2.3.5 Impairment losses (bad debts)

Only impairment losses where the liability was incurred wholly and exclusively for the purposes of the trade are deductible for taxation purposes. For example, **loans to employees written off are not deductible** unless the business is that of making loans, or it can be shown that the writing-off of the loan was earnings paid out for the benefit of the trade.

Under generally accepted accounting principles, a review of all trade receivables should be carried out to assess their fair value at the balance sheet date and any impairment losses written off. **The tax treatment follows the accounting treatment so no adjustment is required for tax purposes.** General provisions (ie those calculated as a percentage of total trade receivables, without reference to specific receivables) will now rarely be seen. In the event that they do arise, increases or decreases in a general provision are not allowable/taxable and an adjustment will need to be made.

Where a tax deduction has been taken for an impairment loss, but the relevant debt is later recovered, the recovery is taxable so no adjustment is required to the amount of the recovery shown in the statement of profit or loss.

When this topic was tested in a Taxation (TX – UK) examination, the examining team commented that there was a consistent problem with the revenue received in respect of a previously written-off impairment loss. Most candidates did not appreciate that no adjustment was necessary.

Think carefully about this point – an impairment loss equal to the receipt had been deducted in a previous accounting period, but this amount has now been received. This is part of the current period trading profit. Since this is how the receipt is shown in the statement of profit or loss, no adjustment needs to be made.

2.3.6 Unpaid remuneration and employee benefit contributions

If earnings for employees are charged in the accounts but are not paid within nine months of the end of the period of account, the cost is only deductible for the period of account in which the earnings are paid. When a tax computation is made within the nine-month period, it is initially assumed that unpaid earnings will not be paid within that period. The computation is adjusted if they are so paid.

Earnings are treated as paid at the same time as they are treated as received for employment income purposes.

Similar rules apply to employee benefit contributions.

2.3.7 Entertaining and gifts

The general rule is that expenditure on entertaining and gifts is non-deductible. This applies to amounts reimbursed to employees for specific entertaining expenses and gifts, and to round sum allowances which are exclusively for meeting such expenses. There is no distinction between UK and overseas customer entertaining for income tax and corporation tax purposes (you will find out later in this Study Text that a different rule applies for value added tax).

There are specific exceptions to the general rule:

- **Entertaining for and gifts to employees are normally deductible** although where gifts are made, or the entertainment is excessive, a charge to tax may arise on the employee under the benefits legislation.

- Gifts to customers not costing more than £50 per donee per year are allowed if they carry a conspicuous advertisement for the business and are not food, drink, tobacco or vouchers exchangeable for goods.

- **Gifts to charities may also be allowed** although many will fall foul of the 'wholly and exclusively' rule above (see further later in this chapter). If a gift aid declaration is made by an individual in respect of a gift, tax relief will be given under the gift aid scheme, not as a trading expense. If a qualifying charitable donation is made by a company, it will be given tax relief by deduction from total profits (we deal with companies later in this Study Text).

2.3.8 Lease charges for cars with CO_2 emissions exceeding 130g/km

ACCA's article Motor cars, written by a member of the Taxation (TX – UK) examining team, explains the implications of acquiring, running, or having the use of a motor car for income tax, corporation tax, value added tax (VAT) and national insurance contributions (NIC).

There is a restriction on the leasing costs of a car with CO_2 emissions exceeding 130 g/km. 15% of the leasing costs will be disallowed in the adjustment of profits calculation.

Question

Mandy is a sole trader. In May 2017 she leased a car for use in her business. The leasing costs for 2017/18 were £4,000. The car had CO_2 emissions of 141g/km.

What is the amount of the leasing costs that will be disallowed in the adjustment of profits calculation?

Answer

Since the car has CO_2 emissions exceeding 130 g/km, 15% of the leasing costs will be disallowed ie £4,000 × 15% = <u>£600</u>. This disallowed amount will be added back to the net profit assuming the full leasing cost of £4,000 has originally been deducted in calculating the net profit. If the leasing cost has not been deducted in calculating the net profit, then the allowable 85% of the leasing cost can be deducted.

2.3.9 Patent royalties and copyright royalties

Patent royalties and copyright royalties paid in connection with an individual's trade are deductible as trading expenses.

2.3.10 National insurance contributions (NICs)

No deduction is allowed for any (NICs) **except for employer's contributions**. For your exam, these are Class 1 employer's contributions and Class 1A contributions (see later in this Study Text).

2.3.11 Penalties and interest on tax

Penalties and interest on late paid tax are not allowed as a trading expense. For the purpose of your exam, tax includes income tax, capital gains tax, corporation tax (for companies), and VAT.

2.3.12 Appropriations

Salary or interest on capital paid to a trader are not deductible. A salary paid to a member of the trader's family is allowed as long as it is not excessive in respect of the work performed by that family member.

The private proportion of payments for motoring expenses, rent, heat and light and telephone expenses of a trader is not deductible. Where the payments are to or on behalf of employees, the full amounts are deductible but are taxed on the employees as benefits for income tax.

Payments of the trader's income tax and national insurance contributions are not deductible.

Here is the statement of profit or loss of John, a trader.

STATEMENT OF PROFIT OR LOSS FOR YEAR ENDED 31 MAY 2017

	£	£
Gross profit		79,500
Other income		
Bank interest received		500
Expenses		
Wages and salaries (Note 1)	47,000	
Rent and rates	12,000	
Depreciation	1,500	
Motor expenses – cars owned by business (Note 2)	5,000	
Motor expenses – cost of leased car CO_2 emissions 150g/km (Note 4)	500	
Entertainment expenses – customers	750	
Office expenses	1,350	
		(68,100)
Finance costs		
Interest payable on overdraft		(1,500)
Net profit		10,400

Notes

1   Salaries include £10,000 paid to John's wife, Julie, who works part time in the business. If John had employed another person to do this work, John would have had to pay at least this amount.

2   Motor expenses on cars owned by the business are £3,000 for John's car used 20% privately and £2,000 for his part-time salesman's car used 40% privately.

3   Capital allowances are £860.

4   The lease of the car started on 1 May 2017. No private use on the leased car.

Compute the adjusted taxable trade profit for the year ended 31 May 2017. You should start with the net profit figure of £10,400 and indicate by the use of zero any items which do not require adjustment.

Answer

JOHN – ADJUSTED TAXABLE TRADING PROFIT FOR YEAR ENDED 31 MAY 2017

		£	£
Net profit			10,400
Add:	Wages and salaries	0	
	Rents and rates	0	
	Depreciation	1,500	
	Trader private motor expenses (£3,000 × 20%)	600	
	Salesman's car	0	
	Leased car cost disallowed (£500 × 15%)	75	
	Entertainment expenses customers	750	
	Office expenses	0	
	Interest payable on overdraft	0	
			2,925
			13,325
Deduct:	Bank interest received	(500)	
	Capital allowances	(860)	
			(1,360)
Profit adjusted for tax purposes			11,965

Note. The employee's private motor expenses are allowable for the trader but the provision of the car will be taxed on the employee as an income tax benefit. The salary paid to Julie is allowed as it is reasonable remuneration for the work actually done.

2.3.13 Subscriptions and donations

The general 'wholly and exclusively' rule determines the deductibility of expenses. Subscriptions and donations are not deductible unless the expenditure is for the benefit of the trade. The following are the main types of subscriptions and donations you may meet and their correct treatments.

- Trade subscriptions (such as to a professional or trade association) are generally deductible.

- Charitable donations are generally deductible only if they are small and to local charities.

- Political subscriptions and donations are generally not deductible.

- When a business makes a gift of equipment manufactured, sold or used in the course of its trade to an educational establishment or for a charitable purpose, nothing need be brought into account as a trading receipt.

2.3.14 Legal and professional charges

Legal and professional charges relating to capital or non-trading items are not deductible. These include charges incurred in acquiring new capital assets or legal rights, issuing shares, drawing up partnership agreements and litigating disputes over the terms of a partnership agreement.

Professional charges are deductible if they relate directly to trading. Deductible items include:

- Legal and professional charges incurred defending the taxpayer's title to non-current assets
- Charges connected with an action for breach of contract
- Expenses of the **renewal** (not the original grant) of a lease for less than 50 years
- Charges for trade debt collection
- Normal charges for preparing accounts/assisting with the self assessment of tax liabilities

Accountancy expenses arising out of an enquiry into the accounts information in a particular year's return are not allowed where the enquiry reveals discrepancies and additional liabilities for the year of enquiry, or any earlier year, which arise as a result of negligent or fraudulent conduct.

Where, however, the enquiry results in no addition to profits, or an adjustment to the profits for the year of enquiry only and that assessment does not arise as a result of negligent or fraudulent conduct, the additional accountancy expenses are allowable.

2.3.15 Interest

Interest paid by an individual on borrowings for trade purposes is deductible as a trading expense on an accruals basis, so no adjustment to the accounts figure is needed.

Individuals cannot deduct interest on overdue tax.

2.3.16 Miscellaneous deductions

Below is a list of various other items that you may meet.

Item	Treatment	Comment
Educational courses for staff	Allow	
Educational courses for trader	Allow	If to update existing knowledge or skills, not if to acquire new knowledge or skills
Removal expenses (to new business premises)	Allow	Only if not an expansionary move

Item	Treatment	Comment
Travelling expenses to the trader's place of business	Disallow	*Ricketts v Colquhoun 1925*: unless an itinerant trader (*Horton v Young 1971*)
Counselling services for employees leaving employment	Allow	If qualify for exemption from employment income charge on employees
Pension contributions (to schemes for employees and company directors)	Allow	If paid, not if only provided for; special contributions may be spread over the year of payment and future years
Premiums for insurance: • Against an employee's death or illness • To cover locum costs or fixed overheads whilst the policyholder is ill	Allow	Receipts are taxable
Damages paid	Allow	If not too remote from trade: *Strong and Co v Woodifield 1906*
Improving an individual's personal security	Allow	Provision of a car, ship or dwelling is excluded

2.4 Income taxable as trading income but excluded from the accounts

The usual example is when a trader takes goods for their own use. In such circumstances the selling price of the goods if sold in the open market is added to the accounting profit. If the trader pays anything for the goods, this is left out of the account. In other words, the trader is treated for tax purposes as having made a sale to themselves.

This rule does not apply to supplies of services, which are treated as sold for the amount (if any) actually paid (but the cost of services to the trader or their household is not deductible).

2.5 Accounting profits not taxable as trading income

Receipts not taxable as trading profit must be deducted from the net profit. For example, rental income and interest received are not taxable as trading profit. The rental income is taxed instead as property business income, whilst the interest is taxed as savings income.

There are three types of receipts which may be found in the accounting profits but which must be excluded from the taxable trading profit computation. These are:

(a) **Capital receipts**
(b) **Income taxed in another way** (at source or as another type of income)
(c) **Income specifically exempt from tax**

However, compensation received in one lump sum for the loss of income is likely to be treated as income (*Donald Fisher (Ealing) Ltd v Spencer 1989*).

Income taxed as another type of income, for example rental income, is excluded from the computation of taxable trading profits but it is brought back into the income tax computation further down as property business income. Similarly capital receipts are excluded from the computation of taxable trading profits but they may be included in the computation of chargeable gains (see later in this Study Text).

2.6 Deductible expenditure not charged in the accounts

Amounts not charged in the accounts that are deductible from trading profits must be deducted when computing the taxable trading income. An example is capital allowances.

Capital allowances (see the next chapter) are an example of deductible expenditure not charged in the accounts.

A second example is **an annual sum which can be deducted by a trader that has paid a lease premium to a landlord who is taxable on the premium as property business income** (see earlier in this Study Text). Normally, the amortisation of the lease will have been deducted in the accounts and must be added back as an appropriation of profit.

Question	Adjustment of profits

Here is the statement of profit or loss of Steven, a trader, for the year ended 5 April 2018.

	£	£
Gross profit		90,000
Other income		
Bank interest received		860
c/f		90,860

	£	£
c/f		90,860
Expenses		
Wages and salaries	59,000	
Rent and rates	8,000	
Depreciation	1,500	
Impairment losses (trade)	150	
Entertainment expenses for customers	750	
Patent royalties paid	3,200	
Legal expenses on acquisition of new factory	250	
		(72,850)
Finance costs		
Bank interest paid		(300)
Net profit		17,710

Salaries include £15,000 paid to Steven's wife, Melanie, who works full time in the business.

Compute the adjusted taxable trade profit. You should start with the net profit figure of £17,710 and indicate by the use of zero (0) any items which do not require adjustment.

Answer

STEVEN
ADJUSTED TAXABLE TRADING PROFIT FOR THE YEAR ENDED 5 APRIL 2018

	£	£
Net profit		17,710
Add: Wages and salaries (Melanie's salary not excessive for full-time work)	0	
Rent and rates	0	
Depreciation	1,500	
Impairment losses (trade)	0	
Entertainment expenses for customers	750	
Patent royalties	0	
Legal expenses (capital)	250	
Bank interest paid	0	
		2,500
		20,210
Less: Bank interest received		(860)
Profit adjusted for tax purposes		19,350

3 Cash basis of accounting for small businesses

3.1 Introduction

An election can be made for an unincorporated business to calculate trading profits on the cash basis (instead of in accordance with generally accepted accounting principles) in certain circumstances.

Usually, **businesses prepare accounts using generally accepted accounting principles for tax purposes.** In particular, this means that **income and expenses are dealt with on an accruals basis.** This is referred to as **'accruals accounting'** in this section.

Certain small unincorporated businesses may elect to use cash accounting (known as 'the cash basis') rather than accruals accounting for the purposes of calculating their taxable trading income.

Exam focus point

The detailed cash basis rules are quite complex. These more complex aspects are **not examinable** in Taxation (TX – UK). In any examination question involving an unincorporated business, **it should be assumed that the cash basis is not relevant unless it is specifically mentioned.**

3.2 Which businesses can use the cash basis?

The cash basis can only be used by **unincorporated businesses** (sole traders and partnerships) **whose receipts for the tax year do not exceed £150,000** (this limit is given in the Tax rates and Allowances available in the exam).

An election must be made for the cash basis to apply. The election is generally effective for the tax year for which it is made and all subsequent tax years.

However, **a business must cease to use the cash basis** if:

(a)   (i)   **Receipts in the previous tax year exceeded twice the limit (ie £300,000)**; and

       (ii)   **Receipts for the current year exceed £150,000**; or

(b)   Its **'commercial circumstances' change** such that the **cash basis is no longer appropriate** and **an election is made to use accruals accounting.**

3.3 Calculation of taxable profits under the cash basis

3.3.1 Introduction

The taxable trading profits under the cash basis are calculated as:

- **Cash receipts; less**
- **Deductible business expenses actually paid in the period.**

3.3.2 Cash receipts

Cash receipts include all amounts received relating to the business including cash and card receipts. They include **amounts received from the sale of plant and machinery, other than on the sale of motor cars.** We look at the definition of plant and machinery when we look at capital allowances later in this Study Text.

Receipts from the sale of motor cars and capital assets which are not classed as plant and machinery (eg land) are not taxable receipts.

3.3.3 Deductible business expenses

Under the cash basis, business expenses are deductible when they are paid.

Business expenses for the cash basis of accounting include capital expenditure on plant and machinery (except motor cars). Other capital expenses are not business expenses eg purchase of land, motor cars, and legal fees on such purchases.

The majority of the specific tax rules covered earlier in this chapter concerning the deductibility of business expenses also apply when the cash basis is used. It should be remembered, in particular, that only business expenses are tax deductible so that any private element must be disallowed. **Fixed rate expenses** for private use of motor cars and business premises used for private purposes may be used instead (see further below).

3.3.4 Fixed rate expenses

FAST FORWARD

Fixed rate expenses can be used in relation to expenditure on motor cars and business premises partly used as the trader's home.

Exam focus point

Although the **use of fixed rate expenses is optional**, in **any examination question involving the cash basis**, it should be assumed that, where relevant, **expenses are claimed on this basis**.

The option of claiming expenses on a fixed rate basis is also available to unincorporated businesses generally, but it will **only be examined in Taxation (TX – UK) within the context of the cash basis**.

Where a business elects to use the cash basis, for Taxation (TX – UK) purposes, it will be assumed to use **fixed rate expenses** rather than make deductions on the usual basis of actual expenditure incurred.

For Taxation (TX – UK) purposes, fixed rate expenses relate to:

- **Expenditure on motor cars**
- **Business premises partly used as the trader's home**

These are dealt with in detail in the following two subsections.

3.3.5 Fixed rate mileage expense (FRM)

The fixed rate mileage (FRM) expense can be claimed in respect of **motor cars** which are **owned or leased by the business** and which are **used for business purposes by the sole trader/partner or an employee of the business**.

The FRM expense is calculated as the business mileage times the appropriate rate per mile. The appropriate mileage rates for motor cars are **45p per mile for the first 10,000 miles**, then **25p per mile thereafter**.

Exam focus point

These rates are the **same as the authorised mileage rates for employment income** given in the Tax rates and Allowances available in the exam.

3.3.6 Business premises used partly as trader's home

A fixed rate monthly adjustment can be made where a sole trader/partner uses part of the business premises as their home eg where a sole trader runs a small hotel or guesthouse and also lives in it. The adjustment is deducted from the actual allowable business premises costs to reflect the private portion of household costs, including food, and utilities (eg heat and light). It does not include mortgage interest, rent, council tax or rates: apportionment of these expenses must be made based on the extent of the private occupation of the premises.

The deductible fixed rate amount depends on **how many people use the business premises each month as a private home**:

Number relevant occupants	Non-business use amount
1	£350
2	£500
3 or more	£650

Exam focus point

These rates will be **given in the examination question**, if relevant.

Be careful when using these amounts – they are **not the deductible expense itself but the disallowable amount**.

3.4 Example

Larry started trading as an interior designer on 6 April 2017. The following information is relevant for the year to 5 April 2018:

(a) Revenue was £65,000 of which £8,000 was owed as receivables at 5 April 2018.

(b) A motor car was acquired on 6 April 2017 for £15,000. Larry drove 10,000 miles in the car during the year to 5 April 2018 of which 3,000 miles were for private journeys. The car qualifies for a capital allowance of £1,890, after taking account of private use. The motoring costs were £2,000. The fixed rate mileage expense for motoring is 45p per mile for the first 10,000 miles, then 25p per mile after that.

(c) Machinery was acquired on 1 May 2017 for £4,000. The machinery qualifies for a capital allowance of £4,000.

Other allowable expenses were £12,000 of which £1,000 was owed as payables at 5 April 2018.

If Larry uses the accruals accounting basis and does not use fixed rate expenses, his trading profit will be calculated as follows:

	£	£
Revenue (accruals)		65,000
Less: Capital allowance on motor car	1,890	
Business motoring expenses £2,000 × 7,000/10,000	1,400	
Capital allowance on machinery	4,000	
Other allowable expenses (accruals)	12,000	
		(19,290)
Taxable trading profit		45,710

If Larry uses the cash basis of accounting and fixed rate expenses, his trading profit will be calculated as follows:

	£	£
Revenue (cash received £65,000 – £8,000)		57,000
Less: FRM on car 7,000 × 45p	3,150	
Cost of machinery	4,000	
Other allowable expenses (cash paid £12,000 – £1,000)	11,000	
		(18,150)
Taxable trading profit		38,850

3.5 Basis of assessment

A trader using the cash basis can, like any other trader, prepare their accounts to any date in the year. The basis of assessment rules which determine in which tax year the profits of an accounting period are taxed apply in the same way for accruals accounting and cash basis traders (see later in this Study Text).

3.6 Losses

A net cash deficit (ie a loss) can normally only be relieved against future cash surpluses (ie future trading profits). Cash basis traders cannot offset a loss against other income or gains. Trading losses for the accruals accounting traders are dealt with in detail later in this Study Text.

4 Pre-trading expenditure

FAST FORWARD

Pre-trading expenditure incurred within the seven years prior to the commencement of trade is allowable if it would have been allowable had the trade already started.

Expenditure incurred before the commencement of trade is deductible, if it is incurred within seven years of the start of trade and it is of a type that would have been deductible had the trade already started. **It is treated as a trading expense incurred on the first day of trading.**

Chapter Roundup

- The badges of trade are used to decide whether or not a trade exists. If one does exist, the accounts profits need to be adjusted in order to establish the taxable profits.

- The net profit in the statement of profit or loss must be adjusted to find the taxable trading profit.

- Disallowable (ie non-deductible) expenditure must be added back to the net profit in the computation of the taxable trading profit. Any item not deducted wholly and exclusively for trade purposes is disallowable expenditure. Certain other items, such as depreciation, are specifically disallowable.

- Receipts not taxable as trading profit must be deducted from the net profit. For example, rental income and interest received are not taxable as trading profit. The rental income is taxed instead as property business income, whilst the interest is taxed as savings income.

- Amounts not charged in the accounts that are deductible from trading profits must be deducted when computing the taxable trading income. An example is capital allowances.

- An election can be made for an unincorporated business to calculate trading profits on the cash basis (instead of in accordance with generally accepted accounting principles) in certain circumstances.

- Fixed rate expenses can be used in relation to expenditure on motor cars and business premises partly used as the trader's home.

- Pre-trading expenditure incurred within the seven years prior to the commencement of trade is allowable if it would have been allowable had the trade already started.

Quick Quiz

1 List the traditional badges of trade.

2 What are the remoteness and duality tests?

3 No adjustment for taxation is required to the accounts for deduction of a trader's salary. True/False?

4 Sid is a sole trader. Included in his most recent statement of profit or loss are the following deductions:

£3,000 legal fees for acquiring a new 15-year lease of his business premises.

£180 car parking fines incurred by Sid whilst on business trips.

£40 interest for late payment of Sid's previous year's income tax.

How much must be added back to the net profit figure when calculating the tax adjusted profit figure?

A £3,180
B £3,220
C £220
D £3,040

5 Which ONE of the following items of expenditure will Leila, a fashion designer, be allowed to deduct in calculating her tax adjusted trading profit?

A The cost of building a new wall in front of her retail shop

B The cost of installing air conditioning in her workshop

C The cost of initial repairs to a recently acquired second-hand office building which was not usable until the repairs were carried out

D The cost of redecorating her retail shop

6 Which ONE of the following is an allowable trading expense for a sole trader?

A Gift of fleece jackets to customers with trade logo costing £60 each
B A subscription to a political party
C Legal fees in respect of employment contracts
D A Gift Aid donation

7 Which businesses can elect to use the cash basis of accounting?

8 Pre-trading expenditure is deductible if it is incurred within ____ years of the start of trade and is of a type that would have been deductible if the trade had already started. Fill in the blank.

1   The subject matter
    The frequency of transactions
    Existence of similar trading transactions or interests
    The length of ownership
    The organisation of the activity as a trade
    Supplementary work and marketing
    Method of finance
    A profit motive
    The way in which the goods were acquired

2   Expenditure is not deductible if it is not for trade purposes (the remoteness test) or if it reflects more than one purpose (the duality test).

3   False. The trader's salary must be added back as it is an appropriation of profit.

4   B. All three items are disallowed and must be added back.

5   D. The cost of redecoration is an allowable expense in calculating trading profit. The other expenditure is capital expenditure and so is not allowable.

6   C. Legal fees on employment contracts are an allowable income expense.

7   Unincorporated businesses (sole traders and partnerships) whose receipts for the tax year do not exceed £150,000 can elect to use the cash basis of accounting.

8   Pre-trading expenditure is deductible if it is incurred within **seven** years of the start of the trade and is of a type that would have been deductible if the trade had already started.

Now try the questions below from the Practice Question Bank

Number	Type	Marks	Time
Q41	Section A	2	4 mins
Q42	Section A	2	4 mins
Q43	Section A	2	4 mins
Q44	Section B	2	4 mins
Q45	Section B	2	4 mins
Q46	Section B	2	4 mins
Q47	Section B	2	4 mins
Q48	Section B	2	4 mins
Q49	Section C	15	27 mins

Capital allowances

Topic list	Syllabus reference
1 Capital allowances in general	B3(h)
2 Plant and machinery – qualifying expenditure	B3(h)(i)
3 The main pool	B3(h)(ii), (iii), (iv)
4 Special rate pool	B3(h)(ii), (iii), (vi)
5 Private use assets	B3(h)(ii), (iv)
6 Motor cars	B3(h)(iii)
7 Short life assets	B3(h)(v)

Introduction

We saw in the last chapter that depreciation cannot be deducted in computing taxable trade profits and that capital allowances may be given instead. In this chapter, we look at the rules for calculating capital allowances, starting with plant and machinery.

Our study of plant and machinery falls into three parts. First, we look at what qualifies for allowances: many business assets obtain no allowances at all.

Secondly, we see how to compute the allowances on the main pool and the special rate pool.

Lastly, we look at the special rules for assets with private use, motor cars and assets with short lives.

You may wish to return to this chapter while you are studying Chapter 19 on companies.

Study guide

		Intellectual level
B3	**Income from self-employment**	
(h)	Capital allowances	
(h)(i)	Define plant and machinery for capital allowances purposes.	1
(h)(ii)	Compute writing down allowances, first year allowances and the annual investment allowance.	2
(h)(iii)	Compute capital allowances for motor cars.	2
(h)(iv)	Compute balancing allowances and balancing charges.	2
(h)(v)	Recognise the treatment of short life assets.	2
(h)(vi)	Recognise the treatment of assets included in the special rate pool.	2

Exam guide

Section A questions on capital allowances may focus on one particular type of asset such as a motor car. You may also be asked to compute capital allowances on a variety of assets in a Section B question. In Section C, you may have to answer a whole question on capital allowances or a capital allowances computation may be included as a working in a computation of taxable trading profits. This may be as part of a 15 mark question or a 10 mark question. The computations may be for either income tax or corporation tax purposes; the principles are basically the same. Look out for private use assets; only restrict the capital allowances if there is private use by **traders**, never restrict capital allowances for private use by **employees**. This means that when you calculate capital allowances for a company there will never be any private use adjustments. Also watch out for the length of the period of account; you may need to scale writing down allowances (WDAs) and the annual investment allowance (AIA) up (income tax only) or down (income tax or corporation tax).

1 Capital allowances in general

FAST FORWARD

Capital allowances are available to give tax relief for certain capital expenditure.

Capital expenditure is not deducted in computing taxable trade profits when using the accruals method of accounting, but it *may* attract capital allowances. Capital allowances are treated as a trading expense and are deducted in arriving at taxable trade profits. Balancing charges, effectively negative allowances, are added in arriving at those profits.

Capital expenditure on plant and machinery qualifies for capital allowances. Both unincorporated businesses (sole traders and partnerships) and companies are entitled to capital allowances. For completeness, in this chapter we will look at the rules for companies alongside those for unincorporated businesses. We will look at companies in more detail later in this Study Text.

For the purposes of the Taxation (TX – UK) exam, if an unincorporated business uses the cash basis of accounting (as seen in the previous chapter), **capital allowances are not available.**

For unincorporated businesses, capital allowances are calculated for periods of account. These are simply the periods for which the trader chooses to prepare accounts. For companies, capital allowances are calculated for accounting periods (see later in this Study Text).

For capital allowances purposes, expenditure is generally deemed to be incurred when the obligation to pay becomes unconditional. This will often be the date of delivery, even if payment is actually required later than this date. For example, the sales contract may require payment to be made within four weeks of delivery but the obligation to pay still becomes unconditional on the delivery date. However, amounts due more than four months after the obligation becomes unconditional are deemed to be incurred when they fall due. Pre-trading expenditure is treated for capital allowances purposes as if it had been incurred on the first day on which the business is carried on.

2 Plant and machinery – qualifying expenditure

FAST FORWARD

There are various statutory rules on what does or does not qualify as plant.

2.1 Definition of plant and machinery

Capital expenditure on plant and machinery qualifies for capital allowances if the plant or machinery is used for a qualifying activity, such as a trade. 'Plant' is not fully defined by the legislation, although some specific exclusions and inclusions are given. The word 'machinery' may be taken to have its normal everyday meaning.

2.2 The statutory exclusions

2.2.1 Buildings

Expenditure on a building and on any asset which is incorporated in a building or is of a kind normally incorporated into buildings does not usually qualify as expenditure on plant. (There are exceptions to this (see Section 2.2.3 below) and also certain 'integral features' (see later in this chapter) are specifically treated as plant).

In addition to complete buildings, **the following assets count as 'buildings', and are therefore not plant (except if they qualify as 'integral features')**.

- Walls, floors, ceilings, doors, gates, shutters, windows and stairs
- Mains services, and systems, of water, electricity and gas
- Waste disposal, sewerage and drainage systems
- Shafts or other structures for lifts etc

2.2.2 Structures

Expenditure on structures and on works involving the alteration of land **does not qualify as expenditure on plant**, but see below for exceptions.

A 'structure' is a fixed structure of any kind, other than a building. An example is a bridge.

2.2.3 Exceptions

Over the years, a large body of case law has been built up under which plant and machinery allowances have been given on certain types of expenditure which might be thought to be expenditure on a building or structure. Statute therefore gives a list of various assets which **may** still be plant. These include:

- Any machinery not within any other item in this list
- Gas and sewerage systems:
    - Provided mainly to meet the particular requirements of the trade; or
    - Provided mainly to serve particular machinery or plant used for the purposes of the trade
- Manufacturing or processing equipment, storage equipment, including cold rooms, display equipment, and counters, checkouts and similar equipment
- Cookers, washing machines, refrigeration or cooling equipment, sanitary ware and furniture and furnishings
- Hoists
- Sound insulation provided mainly to meet the particular requirements of the trade
- Refrigeration or cooling equipment

- Computer, telecommunication and surveillance systems
- Sprinkler equipment, fire alarm and burglar alarm systems
- Partition walls, where movable and intended to be moved
- Decorative assets provided for the enjoyment of the public in the hotel, restaurant or similar trades; advertising hoardings
- Movable buildings intended to be moved in the course of the trade
- Expenditure on altering land for the purpose only of installing machinery or plant

Items falling within the above list of exclusions will only qualify as plant if they fall within the meaning of plant as established by case law. This is discussed below.

2.2.4 Land

Land or an interest in land does not qualify as plant and machinery. For this purpose 'land' excludes buildings, structures and assets which are installed or fixed to land in such a way as to become part of the land for general legal purposes.

2.2.5 Integral features

The following **integral features of a building or structure** qualify for capital allowances as plant (in the special rate pool, see later in this chapter):

- Electrical systems (including lighting systems)
- Cold water system
- Space or water heating system, a powered system of ventilation, air cooling or air purification, and any floor or ceiling comprised in such a system
- Lift, an escalator or a moving walkway
- External solar shading

When a building is sold, the vendor and purchaser can make a joint election to determine how the sale proceeds are apportioned between the building and its integral features.

2.2.6 Computer software

Capital expenditure on computer software (both programs and data) **normally qualifies as expenditure on plant and machinery.**

2.3 Case law

FAST FORWARD

There are also cases on the definition of plant. To help you to absorb them, try to see the function/setting theme running through them.

Exam focus point

In this chapter we mention the names of cases where it was decided what was or wasn't 'plant'. You are **not** expected to know the names of cases for your examination. We have included them for your information only.

Plant was originally defined to be apparatus used by taxpayers to carry on their businesses, other than inventory *(Yarmouth v France 1887)*.

Subsequent cases have refined the original definition and have largely been concerned with the **distinction between plant actively used in the business (qualifying) and the setting in which the business is carried on (non-qualifying). This is the 'functional' test.** Some of the decisions have now been enacted as part of statute law, but they are still relevant as examples of the principles involved.

A barrister succeeded in his claim for his law library (*Munby v Furlong 1977*).

Office partitioning was allowed. Because it was movable, it was not regarded as part of the setting in which the business was carried on (*Jarrold v John Good and Sons Ltd 1963*) (actual item now covered by statute).

At a motorway service station, false ceilings contained conduits, ducts and lighting apparatus. **They did not qualify because they did not perform a function in the business. They were merely part of the setting in which the business was conducted** (*Hampton v Fortes Autogrill Ltd 1979*).

Similarly, it has been held that when an attractive floor is provided in a restaurant, the fact that the floor performs the function of making the restaurant attractive to customers is not enough to make it plant. It functions as premises, and the cost therefore does not qualify for capital allowances (*Wimpy International Ltd v Warland 1988*).

Conversely, light fittings, decor and murals can be plant. A company carried on business as hoteliers and operators of licensed premises. The function of the items was the creation of an atmosphere conducive to the comfort and well being of its customers (*CIR v Scottish and Newcastle Breweries Ltd 1982*) (decorative assets used in hotels etc, now covered by statute).

General lighting in a department store was held not to be plant, as it was merely setting. Special display lighting, however, could be plant *(Cole Brothers Ltd v Phillips 1982)*. Note that changes in legislation mean that it is now possible to claim allowances on lighting as an integral feature (see earlier in this chapter), but the case is still a useful example of the distinction between setting and function.

3 The main pool

FAST FORWARD

With capital allowances computations, the main thing is to get the layout right. Having done that, you will find that the figures tend to drop into place.

3.1 Main pool expenditure

Most expenditure on plant and machinery, including expenditure on cars with CO_2 emissions of 130g/km or less, is put into a pool of expenditure (the main pool) on which capital allowances may be claimed. An addition increases the pool whilst a disposal decreases it.

Exceptionally the following items are not put into the main pool:

- Assets dealt with in the special rate pool
- Assets with private use by the trader
- Short life assets where an election has been made

These exceptions are dealt with later in this chapter.

Expenditure on plant and machinery by a person about to begin a trade is treated as incurred on the first day of trading. Assets previously owned by a trader and then brought into the trade (at the start of trading or later) are treated as bought for their market values at the times when they are brought in.

3.2 Annual investment allowance (AIA) 9/16

One of the competencies you require to fulfil Performance Objective 17 Tax planning and advice of the PER is to identify when to refer matters to someone with more specialist knowledge. You can apply the knowledge you obtain from this section of the Study Text to help to demonstrate this competence.

FAST FORWARD

Businesses are entitled to an annual investment allowance (AIA) of £200,000 for a 12-month period of account.

Businesses can claim an **AIA on the first £200,000 spent each year on plant or machinery**, including assets in the main pool, but not including motor cars. Expenditure on motorcycles does qualify for the AIA.

Where the period of account is more or less than a year, the maximum allowance is proportionately increased or reduced.

After claiming the AIA, the balance of expenditure on main pool assets is transferred to the main pool immediately and is eligible for writing down allowances in the same period.

3.3 First year allowance for low emission cars

FAST FORWARD

A first year allowance (FYA) at the rate of 100% is available on new low emission cars. The FYA is not pro-rated in short or long periods of account.

Key term

A **low emission car** is one which has CO_2 emissions of 75g/km or less.

A 100% first year allowance (FYA) is available for expenditure incurred on new (ie unused and not second hand) **low emission motor cars.**

If the FYA is not claimed in full (for example if the trader does not want to create a loss – see later in this Study Text), the balance of expenditure is transferred to the main pool after any writing down allowance has been calculated on the main pool.

The FYA is not adjusted pro-rata in a short or long period of account, unlike the AIA and writing down allowances.

3.4 Writing down allowances (WDAs)

FAST FORWARD

Expenditure on plant and machinery in the main pool qualifies for a WDA at 18% every 12 months.

Key term

A **writing down allowance (WDA)** is given on main pool expenditure **at the rate of 18% a year** (on a reducing balance basis). The WDA is calculated on the tax written down value (TWDV) of pooled plant, after adding the current period's additions and taking out the current period's disposals.

When plant is sold, proceeds, limited to a maximum of the original cost, are taken out of the pool. Provided that the trade is still being carried on, the pool balance remaining is written down in the future by WDAs, even if there are no assets left.

3.5 Example

Elizabeth has tax written down value on her main pool of plant and machinery of £16,000 on 6 April 2017. In the year to 5 April 2018 she bought a car with CO_2 emissions of 110g/km for £8,000 (no non-business use) and she disposed of plant, which originally cost £4,000, for £6,000. The maximum capital allowances claim for the year is as follows.

	Main pool £	Allowances £
TWDV b/f	16,000	
Addition (not qualifying for AIA)	8,000	
Less disposal (limited to cost)	(4,000)	
	20,000	
WDA @ 18%	(3,600)	3,600
TWDV c/f	16,400	
Maximum capital allowances claim		3,600

Julia is a sole trader preparing accounts to 5 April each year. At 5 April 2017, the tax written down value on her main pool is £12,500.

In the year to 5 April 2018, Julia bought the following assets:

1 June 2017	Machinery	£190,000
12 November 2017	Van	£17,500
10 February 2018	Car for salesman (CO_2 emissions 120g/km)	£9,000

She disposed of plant on 15 December 2017 for £12,000 (original cost £16,000).

Calculate the maximum capital allowances claim that Julia can make for the year ended 5 April 2018.

Answer

	AIA £	Main pool £	Allowances £
y/e 5 April 2018			
TWDV b/f		12,500	
Additions qualifying for AIA			
1.6.17 Machinery	190,000		
12.11.17 Van	17,500		
	207,500		
AIA	(200,000)		200,000
	7,500		
Transfer balance to pool	(7,500)	7,500	
Additions not qualifying for AIA			
10.2.18 Car		9,000	
Disposal			
15.12.17 Plant		(12,000)	
		17,000	
WDA @ 18%		(3,060)	3,060
TWDV c/f		13,940	
Maximum capital allowances			203,060

3.6 Short and long periods of account

WDAs are 18% × number of months/12:

(a)   For unincorporated businesses where the period of account is longer or shorter than 12 months. For individuals, capital allowances computations are computed for periods of account not tax years.

(b)   For companies where the accounting period is shorter than 12 months (a company's accounting period for tax purposes is never longer than 12 months), or where the trade concerned started in the accounting period and was therefore carried on for fewer than 12 months. For companies, capital allowances computations are computed for accounting periods (we will be studying companies in detail later in this Study Text).

 Question

Venus is a sole trader and has prepared accounts to 30 April each year. At 30 April 2017, the tax written down value of her main pool was £66,667. She decides to prepare her next set of accounts to 31 December 2017.

In the period to 31 December 2017, the following acquisitions were made:

1 May 2017	Plant	£146,666
10 July 2017	Car (CO_2 emissions 110 g/km)	£9,000
3 August 2017	Car (CO_2 emissions 65 g/km) – new	£11,000

Venus disposed of plant on 1 November 2017 for £20,000 (original cost £28,000).

Calculate the maximum capital allowances that Venus can claim for the period ending 31 December 2017.

Answer

	AIA £	FYA £	Main pool £	Allowances £
p/e 31 December 2017				
TWDV b/f			66,667	
Additions qualifying for AIA				
1.5.17 Plant	146,666			
AIA £200,000 × 8/12	(133,333)			133,333
	13,333			
Transfer balance to pool	(13,333)		13,333	
Additions qualifying for FYA				
3.8.17 Car (new – low emission)		11,000		
Less: 100% FYA		(11,000)		11,000
Additions not qualifying for AIA or FYA				
10.7.17 Car			9,000	
Disposals				
1.11.17 Plant			(20,000)	
			69,000	
WDA @ 18% × 8/12			(8,280)	8,280
TWDVs c/f			60,720	
Maximum allowances claim				152,613

Note that the annual investment allowance and the writing down allowance are reduced for the short period of account, but the first year allowance is given in full.

 Question

Oscar started trading on 1 July 2017 and prepared his first set of accounts to 31 December 2018. He bought the following assets:

10 July 2017	Plant	£130,000
1 October 2017	Car for business use only (CO_2 emissions 120g/km)	£11,000
12 February 2018	Plant	£235,000

Calculate the maximum capital allowances claim that Oscar can make for the period ended 31 December 2018. Assume that the rates of capital allowances in 2017/18 also apply in 2018/19.

	AIA £	Main pool £	Allowances £
p/e 31 December 2018			
Additions qualifying for AIA			
10.7.17 Plant	130,000		
12.2.18 Plant	235,000		
	365,000		
AIA £200,000 × 18/12	(300,000)		300,000
	65,000		
Transfer balance to main pool	(65,000)	65,000	
Additions not qualifying for AIA			
1.10.17 Car		11,000	
		76,000	
WDA @ 18% × 18/12		(20,520)	20,520
TWDV c/f		55,480	
Maximum capital allowances			320,520

Note that the annual investment allowance and the writing down allowance are increased for the long period of account.

3.7 Small balance on main pool

A writing down allowance equal to unrelieved expenditure in the main pool (after adjusting for current period acquisitions and disposals) can be claimed where this is **£1,000 or less for a 12-month period of account** (pro-rated for long or short period of account). If the maximum WDA is claimed, the main pool will then have a nil balance carried forward.

Small balance on main pool

Alan has traded for many years, preparing accounts to 5 April each year. At 5 April 2017, the tax written down value of his main pool was £15,000. On 1 October 2017, he sold some plant and machinery for £14,200 (original cost £16,000).

Calculate the maximum capital allowances claim that Alan can make for the year ending 5 April 2018.

	Main pool £	Allowances £
y/e 5 April 2018		
TWDV b/f	15,000	
Disposal	(14,200)	
	800	
WDA (small pool)	(800)	800
TWDV c/f	nil	
Maximum capital allowances		800

Note the tax planning opportunities available. If plant is bought just before an accounting date, allowances become available as soon as possible. Alternatively, it may be desirable to claim less than the maximum allowances to even out annual taxable profits and avoid a higher rate of tax in later years. However, in the exam you should always claim the maximum available capital allowances unless you are told otherwise.

3.8 Balancing charges and allowances

Balancing charges occur when the disposal value deducted exceeds the balance remaining in the pool. The charge equals the excess and is effectively a negative capital allowance, increasing profits. Most commonly this happens when the trade ceases and the remaining assets are sold. It may also occur, however, whilst the trade is still in progress.

Balancing allowances on the main and special pools of expenditure arise only when the trade ceases. The balancing allowance is equal to the remaining unrelieved expenditure after deducting the disposal value of all the assets. Balancing allowances may also arise on single pool items (see later in this chapter) whenever those items are disposed of.

3.9 Interaction with value added tax (VAT)

We deal with value added tax (VAT) in Chapters 24 and 25. You may want to make a note to re-read this section when you study VAT.

Qualifying expenditure includes irrecoverable VAT. The VAT may be irrecoverable because the trader is not VAT registered, or because it is type of expenditure on which the VAT is not recoverable (eg the acquisition of a car not used wholly for business purposes).

If the trader is VAT registered and can reclaim VAT on a purchase, only the expenditure net of VAT will be qualifying expenditure. Similarly, on a disposal of an asset on which capital allowances have been claimed, if VAT is charged by the trader on the disposal, **only the disposal proceeds net of VAT will be deducted**.

Not all capital allowances questions will require you to consider VAT. Take care, if the question mentions VAT inclusive or exclusive amounts or states that the trader is VAT-registered, that you make the appropriate VAT adjustments when performing capital allowances calculations.

3.10 Example

Frank is registered for VAT. He had the following transactions in capital assets during the year ended 5 April 2018:

Purchases:

12 May 2017	Plant for £42,000 (including VAT of £7,000)
4 October 2017	A car with CO_2 emissions of 115 g/km for £15,000 (including VAT of £2,500), 20% private use by one of Frank's employees.

Disposal:

30 September 2017	Machinery, which had originally cost £24,000 (including VAT of £4,000), was sold for £21,000 (including VAT of £3,500)

The tax written down value of Frank's main pool on 6 April 2017 was £70,000.

The maximum capital allowances that Frank can claim for the year ended 5 April 2018 are:

	AIA £	Main pool £	Allowances £
y/e 5 April 2018			
TWDV b/f		70,000	
Addition qualifying for AIA			
12.5.17 Plant			
£(42,000 – 7,000)	35,000		
AIA	(35,000)		35,000
Addition not qualifying for AIA			
4.10.17 Car (N)		15,000	
Disposal			
30.9.17 Machinery			
£(21,000 – 3,500)		(17,500)	
		67,500	
WDA @ 18%		(12,150)	12,150
TWDV c/f		55,350	
Maximum capital allowances			47,150

Note. The VAT on the car is irrecoverable because an employee uses it partly for private purposes (see Chapter 24). Whilst private use by the employee does not restrict the rate of capital allowances (as private use by Frank would), for VAT purposes **any** private use prevents the recovery of VAT.

3.11 Cessation of trade

For plant and machinery, **when a business ceases to trade, no AIAs, FYAs or WDAs are given in the final period of account** (unincorporated businesses) or accounting period (companies – see later in this Study Text). Each asset is deemed to be disposed of on the date the trade ceased (usually at the then market value). Additions (if any) in the relevant period are brought in and then the disposal proceeds (limited to cost) are deducted from the balance of qualifying expenditure. If the proceeds exceed the balance then a balancing charge arises. If the balance of qualifying expenditure exceeds the proceeds then a balancing allowance is given.

4 Special rate pool

FAST FORWARD

The special rate pool contains expenditure on thermal insulation, long life assets, features integral to a building and cars with CO_2 emissions over 130g/km. The AIA can be used against such expenditure except cars. The WDA is 8%.

4.1 Operation of the special rate pool

Expenditure on thermal insulation, long life assets, features integral to a building (see earlier in this chapter), **solar panels, and cars with CO_2 emissions over 130g/km is not dealt with in the main pool but in a special rate pool.**

The annual investment allowance can apply to expenditure on such assets except on cars. The taxpayer can decide how to allocate the AIA. It will be more tax efficient to set the allowance against special rate pool expenditure in priority to main pool expenditure where there is expenditure on assets in both pools in the period. Expenditure in excess of the AIA is added to the special rate pool and will be eligible for writing down allowance in the same period in which the expenditure is incurred.

The writing down allowance for the special rate pool is 8% for a 12-month period. As with the writing down allowance on the main pool, this is adjusted for short and long periods of account.

Where the **unrelieved expenditure in the special rate pool** (after adjusting for current period acquisitions and disposals) **is £1,000 or less for a 12-month period**, a writing down allowance can be claimed of up to

£1,000. This amount is pro-rated for long and short periods. This is in addition to any similar claim in relation to the main pool (see earlier in this chapter).

4.2 Long life assets

> **Long life assets** are assets with an expected working life of 25 years or more.

The **long life asset rules only apply to businesses whose total expenditure on assets with an expected working life of 25 years or more in a chargeable period is more than £100,000.** If the expenditure exceeds £100,000, the whole of the expenditure enters the special rate pool, not just the excess over £100,000. If the expenditure is £100,000 or less, the long life asset rules do not apply and the expenditure will be added to the main pool in the normal way. For this purpose all expenditure incurred under a contract is treated as incurred in the first chargeable period to which that contract relates.

The £100,000 limit is reduced or increased proportionately in the case of a chargeable period of less or more than 12 months.

The following are **not** treated as long life assets:

- **Plant and machinery in dwelling houses, retail shops, showrooms, hotels and offices**
- **Cars**

4.3 Example

Lucy has been trading for many years, preparing accounts to 5 April each year. The tax written down value of her main pool at 5 April 2017 was £110,000. In the year to 5 April 2018, Lucy had the following expenditure:

10 June 2017	General plant costing £45,000
12 December 2017	Lighting system in shop £50,000
15 January 2018	Car for business use only (CO_2 emissions 155 g/km) £25,000
26 January 2018	Delivery van £15,000
4 March 2018	Lifts £152,500

The maximum capital allowances claim that Lucy can make for the year to 5 April 2018 is as follows.

		AIA £	Main pool £	Special rate pool £	Allowances £
y/e 5 April 2018					
TWDV b/f			110,000		
Additions for AIA (best use)					
12.12.17	Lighting	50,000			
4.3.18	Lifts	152,500			
		202,500			
AIA		(200,000)			200,000
		2,500			
Transfer balance to special rate pool		(2,500)		2,500	
Additions not given AIA					
10.6.17	Plant		45,000		
26.1.18	Van		15,000		
Additions not qualifying for AIA					
15.1.18	Car			25,000	
			170,000	27,500	
WDA @ 18%			(30,600)		30,600
WDA @ 8%				(2,200)	2,200
TWDVs c/f			139,400	25,300	
Allowances					232,800

5 Private use assets

FAST FORWARD An asset which is used privately by a trader is dealt with in a single asset pool and the capital allowances are restricted.

An asset which is used partly for private purposes by a sole trader or a partner is put into its own pool (single asset pool).

Capital allowances are calculated on the full cost. However, only the business use proportion of the allowances is allowed as a deduction from trading profits. This restriction applies to the AIA, FYAs, WDAs, balancing allowances and balancing charges.

An asset with some private use by an employee (not the owner of the business) suffers no such restriction. The employee may be taxed under the benefits code (see earlier in this Study Text) so the business receives capital allowances on the full cost of the asset.

Exam focus point

Capital allowances on assets with some private use is a common exam topic. Check carefully whether the private use is by the owner of the business or by an employee.

Question — Capital allowances on private use asset

Jacinth has been in business as a sole trader for many years, preparing accounts to 31 March. On 1 November 2017 she bought computer equipment for £2,700 which she uses 75% in her business and 25% privately. She has already used the AIA against other expenditure in the year to 31 March 2018.

Calculate the maximum capital allowance that Jacinth can claim in respect to the computer equipment in the year to 31 March 2018.

Answer

	Computer equipment £	Allowances @ 75% £
y/e 31 March 2018		
Acquisition	2,700	
WDA @ 18%	(486)	365
TWDV c/f	2,214	
Maximum capital allowance on computer equipment		365

6 Motor cars   9/16

Exam focus point

ACCA's article Motor cars, written by a member of the Taxation (TX – UK) examining team, explains the implications of acquiring, running, or having the use of a motor car for income tax, corporation tax, value added tax (VAT) and national insurance contribution (NIC).

FAST FORWARD Motor cars are generally dealt with in the main pool or the special rate pool (cars emitting over 130g/km), unless there is private use by the trader in which case the car is held in a single asset pool.

As we have already seen, motor cars are categorised in accordance with their CO_2 emissions:

(a)   **Cars emitting over 130g/km**: expenditure is added to the special rate pool

(b)   **Cars emitting between 76 and 130 g/km**: expenditure is added to the main pool

(c) **Cars emitting 75 g/km or less:** expenditure on new cars eligible for 100% first year allowance, if allowance not claimed in full, excess added to main pool; expenditure on second hand cars is added to main pool

Cars with an element of private use are kept separate from the main and special pools and are dealt with in single asset pools. Such cars are entitled to a WDA of 18% (car with CO_2 emissions between 76 and 130 g/km) or 8% (car with CO_2 emissions over 130 g/km).

Question
Capital allowances on private use car

Quodos started to trade on 1 July 2017, preparing accounts to 31 December 2017 and each 31 December thereafter. On 1 August 2017 he bought a car for £17,000 with CO_2 emissions of 110 g/km. The private use proportion is 10%. The car was sold in July 2020 for £4,000. Quodos has no other assets which qualify for capital allowances.

Calculate the capital allowances, assuming:

(a) The car was used by an employee; or
(b) The car was used by Quodos

and that the capital allowances rates in 2017/18 apply throughout.

Answer

(a)

	Main pool £	Allowances £
1.7.17–31.12.17		
Purchase price	17,000	
WDA 18% × 6/12 × £17,000	(1,530)	1,530
	15,470	
1.1.18–31.12.18		
WDA 18% × £15,470	(2,785)	2,785
	12,685	
1.1.19–31.12.19		
WDA 18% × £12,685	(2,283)	2,283
	10,402	
1.1.20–31.12.20		
Proceeds	(4,000)	
	6,402	
WDA 18% × £6,402	(1,152)	1,152
TWDV c/f	5,250	

The private use of the car by the employee has no effect on the capital allowances due to Quodos. The car will be placed in the main pool. No balancing allowance is available on the main pool until trade ceases even though the car has been sold.

(b)

	Car	Allowances 90%
	£	£
1.7.17–31.12.17		
Purchase price	17,000	
WDA 18% × 6/12 × £17,000	(1,530)	1,377
	15,470	
1.1.18–31.12.18		
WDA 18% × £15,470	(2,785)	2,507
	12,685	
1.1.19–31.12.19		
WDA 18% × £12,685	(2,283)	2,055
	10,402	
1.1.20–31.12.20		
Proceeds	(4,000)	
Balancing allowance	6,402	5,762

The car is placed in a single asset pool because of the private use by the trader, Quodos. Only 90% of the WDAs and balancing allowance are available as a result of this private use.

7 Short life assets

 FAST FORWARD

Short life asset elections can bring forward the allowances due on an asset.

A trader can elect that specific items of plant, which are expected to have a short working life, be kept separately from the main pool.

Key term

> Any asset subject to this election is known as a **'short life asset'**, and the election is known as a 'de-pooling election'.

The election is irrevocable. For an unincorporated business, the time limit for electing is the 31 January which is 22 months after the end of the tax year in which the period of account of the expenditure ends. (For a company, it is two years after the end of the accounting period of the expenditure.) **Short life asset treatment cannot be claimed for any motor cars, or plant used partly for non-trade purposes.**

The short life asset is kept in a single asset pool. Provided that the short life asset is disposed of **within eight years of the end of the accounting period** in which it was bought, a balancing charge or allowance arises on its disposal.

If the asset is not disposed of within this time period, its tax written down value is added to the main pool at the beginning of the next period of account (accounting period for companies). This will be after allowances have been claimed nine times on the asset; once in the period of acquisition and then each year for the following eight years.

The election should therefore be made for assets likely to be sold for less than their tax written down values within eight years. It should not usually be made for assets likely to be sold within eight years for more than their tax written down values. There is no requirement to show from the outset that the asset will actually have a 'short life', so it is a matter of judgment whether the election should be made.

The annual investment allowance can be set against short life assets. The taxpayer can decide how to allocate the AIA. It will be more tax efficient to set the allowance against main pool expenditure in priority to short life asset expenditure.

Caithlin bought a machine for business use on 1 May 2017 for £9,000 and elected for de-pooling. She did not claim the AIA in respect of this asset. Her accounting year end is 30 April.

Calculate the capital allowances due if:

(a) The asset is scrapped for £300 in August 2025
(b) The asset is scrapped for £200 in August 2026

and assuming that the capital allowances rates in 2017/18 apply throughout.

Answer

		£
(a)	*Year to 30.4.18*	
	Cost	9,000
	WDA 18%	(1,620)
		7,380
	Year to 30.4.19	
	WDA 18%	(1,328)
		6,052
	Year to 30.4.20	
	WDA 18%	(1,089)
		4,963
	Year to 30.4.21	
	WDA 18%	(893)
		4,070
	Year to 30.4.22	
	WDA 18%	(733)
		3,337
	Year to 30.4.23	
	WDA 18%	(601)
		2,736
	Year to 30.4.24	
	WDA 18%	(492)
		2,244
	Year to 30.4.25	
	WDA 18%	(404)
		1,840
	Year to 30.4.26	
	Disposal proceeds	(300)
	Balancing allowance	1,540

(b) If the asset is still in use at 30 April 2025, WDAs up to 30.4.25 will be as above. In the year to 30.4.26, a WDA can be claimed of 18% × £1,840 = £331. The tax written down value of £1,840 − £331 = £1,509 will be added to the main pool at the beginning of the next period of account. The disposal proceeds of £200 will be deducted from the main pool in that period's capital allowances computation. No balancing allowance will arise and the main pool will continue.

Chapter Roundup

- Capital allowances are available to give tax relief for certain capital expenditure.

- There are various statutory rules on what does or does not qualify as plant.

- There are also cases on the definition of plant. To help you to absorb them, try to see the function/setting theme running through them.

- With capital allowances computations, the main thing is to get the layout right. Having done that, you will find that the figures tend to drop into place.

- Businesses are entitled to an annual investment allowance (AIA) of £200,000 for a 12-month period of account.

- A first year allowance (FYA) at the rate of 100% is available on new low emission cars. The FYA is not pro-rated in short or long periods of account.

- Expenditure on plant and machinery in the main pool qualifies for a writing down allowance (WDA) at 18% every 12 months.

- The special rate pool contains expenditure on thermal insulation, long life assets, features integral to a building and cars with CO_2 emissions over 130g/km. The AIA can be used against such expenditure except cars. The WDA is 8%.

- An asset which is used privately by a trader is dealt with in a single asset pool and the capital allowances are restricted.

- Motor cars are generally dealt with in the main pool or the special rate pool (cars emitting over 130g/km), unless there is private use by the trader in which case the car is held in a single asset pool.

- Short life asset elections can bring forward the allowances due on an asset.

Quick Quiz

1 WDAs are pro-rated in a six-month period of account. True/False?

2 Lucas makes up accounts for a 15-month period to 30 June 2017. What AIA is he entitled to?

  A £50,000
  B £150,000
  C £200,000
  D £250,000

3 Is a FYA on a low emission car pro-rated in a six-month period of account?

4 When may balancing allowances arise?

5 An asset must be disposed of within ____ years of the end of the accounting period (or period of account) in which it was acquired in order for it to be advantageous to treat it as a short life asset. Fill in the blank.

6 Paula makes up accounts to 5 April each year. She buys a car in August 2017 costing £20,000 for use in her business. Her private use of the car is 30%. The CO_2 emissions of the car are 150g/km.

  What WDA is available on the car for the year ended 5 April 2018?

  A £1,120
  B £1,600
  C £2,520
  D £3,600

Answers to Quick Quiz

1   True. In a six-month period, WDA are pro-rated by multiplying by 6/12.

2   D. £200,000 × 15/12 = £250,000.

3   No. A FYA is given in full in a short period of account.

4   Balancing allowances may arise in respect of main or special rate pool expenditure only when the trade ceases. Balancing allowances may arise on single pool assets whenever those assets are disposed of.

5   An asset must be disposed of within **eight** years of the end of the accounting period (or period of account) in which it was acquired in order for it to be advantageous to treat it as a short life asset.

6   A. £20,000 × 8% (CO_2 emissions of the car exceed 130g/km) = £1,600. WDA is £1,600 × 70% = £1,120.

Now try the questions below from the Practice Question Bank

Number	Type	Marks	Time
Q50	Section A	2	4 mins
Q51	Section A	2	4 mins
Q52	Section A	2	4 mins
Q53	Section B	2	4 mins
Q54	Section B	2	4 mins
Q55	Section B	2	4 mins
Q56	Section B	2	4 mins
Q57	Section B	2	4 mins
Q58	Section C	15	27 mins

BPP
LEARNING MEDIA

Assessable trading income

Topic list	Syllabus reference
1 Recognise the basis of assessment	B3(a)
2 Commencement and cessation	B3(f)
3 The choice of an accounting date	B3(g)

Introduction

In the previous two chapters we have seen how to calculate the taxable trading profits after capital allowances. We are now going to look at how these are taxed in the owner's hands.

Businesses do not normally prepare accounts for tax years so we look at the basis of assessment which is the method by which the taxable trading profits of periods of account are allocated to tax years. As well as the normal rules for a continuing business we need special rules for the opening years of a trade, and again in the closing years.

A business may choose its accounting date and this may have an effect on when the tax is payable on profits.

In the next chapter we will look at the tax reliefs available should the business make a loss.

Study guide

		Intellectual level
B3	**Income from self-employment**	
(a)	Recognise the basis of assessment for self-employment income.	2
(f)	Compute the assessable profits on commencement and on cessation.	2
(g)	Recognise the factors that will influence the choice of accounting date.	2

Exam guide

You are likely to have to deal with a tax computation for an unincorporated business in any of Sections A, B or C. It may be a simple computation for a continuing business, or you may have to deal with a business in its opening or closing years, including computing taxable trading profits and allocating them to tax years. You must be totally familiar with the rules and be able to apply them in the exam. These topics may be tested in a 15 mark question or a 10 mark question in Section C. A specific point, such as computing an amount of overlap profits, may be tested in Sections A or B.

1 Recognise the basis of assessment

FAST FORWARD

> Basis periods are used to link periods of account to tax years. Broadly, the profits of a 12-month period of account ending in a tax year are taxed in that year (current year basis).

1.1 Basis periods and tax years

A tax year runs from 6 April to 5 April, but most businesses do not have periods of account ending on 5 April. **Thus there must be a link between a period of account of a business and a tax year.** The procedure is to **find a period to act as the basis period for a tax year. The profits for a basis period are taxed in the corresponding tax year.** If a basis period is not identical to a period of account, the profits of periods of account are time-apportioned as required on the assumption that profits accrue evenly over a period of account. We will apportion to the nearest month for exam purposes.

The same rules apply to link periods of account to tax years regardless of whether the normal accruals method of accounting or the cash basis is used.

The general rule is that **the basis period is the year of account ending in the tax year**. This is known as the **current year basis of assessment**. For example, if a trader prepares accounts to 31 December each year, the profits of the year to 31 December 2017 will be taxed in the tax year 2017/18.

This general rule does not apply in the opening or closing years of a business. This is because in the first few years the business has not normally established a pattern of annual accounts, and very few businesses cease trading on the annual accounting date.

Apart from the first tax year of trade and the last tax year of trade, HM Revenue & Customs (HMRC) will expect to see 12 months of profits showing in the income tax computation each year. As the periods of account may not be 12 months long in the opening and closing years, the current year basis may be impossible to apply, therefore special rules need to be applied to establish which 12 months should be allocated to which tax year.

2 Commencement and cessation

FAST FORWARD

In the first tax year of trade actual profits of the tax year are taxed. In the second tax year, the basis period is either the first 12 months, the 12 months to the accounting date ending in year two or the actual profits from April to April. Profits of the 12 months to the accounting date are taxed in year three.

2.1 The first tax year

The first tax year is the year during which the trade commences. For example, if a trade commences on 1 June 2017 the first tax year is 2017/18.

The **basis period for the first tax year runs from the date the trade starts to the next 5 April** (or to the date of cessation if the trade does not last until the end of the tax year).

So continuing the above example a trader commencing in business on 1 June 2017 will be taxed on profits arising from 1 June 2017 to 5 April 2018 in 2017/18, the first tax year.

2.2 The second tax year

(a)   **If the accounting date falling in the second tax year is at least 12 months after the start of trading, the basis period is the 12 months to that accounting date.**

(b)   **If the accounting date falling in the second tax year is less than 12 months after the start of trading, the basis period is the first 12 months of trading.**

(c)   **If there is no accounting date falling in the second tax year, because the first period of account is a very long one which does not end until a date in the third tax year, the basis period for the second tax year is the year itself (from 6 April to 5 April).**

The following flowchart may help you determine the basis period for the second tax year.

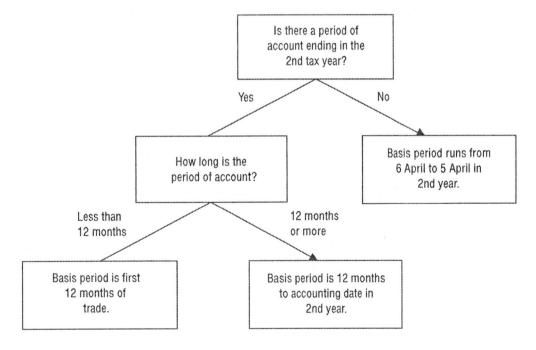

2.3 Example: Period of 12 months or more ending in second year

John starts to trade on 1 January 2018 preparing accounts to 31 December 2018.

1st tax year: 2017/18 – tax profits 1 January 2018 to 5 April 2018, ie 3/12 × year ended 31 December 2018

2nd tax year: 2018/19

(a)   Is there a period of account ending in 2018/19?

        Yes – year ended 31 December 2018 ends in 2018/19.

(b)   How long is the period of account?

        12 months or more, ie 12 months (exactly) to 31 December 2018.

(c)   So in 2018/19 tax profits of 12 months to 31 December 2018.

2.4 Example: Short period ending in second year

Janet starts to trade on 1 January 2018 preparing accounts as follows:

- Six months to 30 June 2018
- 12 months to 30 June 2019

1st tax year: 2017/18 – tax profits 1 January 2018 to 5 April 2018, ie 3/6 × 6 months ended 30 June 2018

2nd tax year: 2018/19

(a)   Is there a period of account ending in 2018/19?

        Yes – period ended 30 June 2018 ends in 2018/19.

(b)   How long is the period of account?

        Less than 12 months

(c)   So in 2018/19 tax profits of first 12 months of trade ie 1 January 2018 to 31 December 2018, ie
        six-month period ended 30 June 2018 profits plus 6/12 of year ended 30 June 2019 profits.

(d)   You may notice that profits between 1 January 2018 to 5 April 2018 have been taxed in both
        2017/18 and 2018/19 because the basis periods for these tax years overlap. These profits are
        therefore called 'overlap profits'. Relief for overlap profits is usually given when the trade ceases.
        The treatment of overlap profits is dealt with in more detail in Section 2.11.

2.5 Example: No period ending in second year

Jodie starts to trade on 1 March 2018 preparing a 14 month set of accounts to 30 April 2019.

1st tax year: 2017/18 – tax profits 1 March 2018 to 5 April 2018, ie 1/14 × 14 months ended 30 April 2019

2nd tax year: 2018/19

(a)   Is there a period of account ending in 2018/19?

        No – period ended 30 April 2019 ends in 2019/20.

(b)   So in 2018/19 tax profits of 6 April 2018 to 5 April 2019, ie 12/14 × 14 months ended 30 April
        2019.

2.6 The third tax year

(a)   **If there is an accounting date falling in the second tax year, the basis period for the third tax
        year is the 12 month period of account ending in the third tax year (current year basis).**

(b)   If there is no accounting date falling in the second tax year, the basis period for the third tax year is
        the 12 months to the accounting date falling in the third tax year.

2.7 Example: Accounting date in second year

Wilma starts to trade on 1 October 2017. She made taxable profits of £9,000 for the first nine months to 30 June 2018 and £30,000 for the year to 30 June 2019.

The taxable profits for the first three tax years are as follows:

Year	Basis period	Working	Taxable profits £
2017/18	1.10.17–5.4.18	£9,000 × 6/9	6,000
2018/19	1.10.17–30.9.18	£9,000 + £30,000 × 3/12	16,500
2019/20	1.7.18–30.6.19 (period of account ending in 3rd year)		30,000

2.8 Example: No accounting date in the second year

Thelma starts to trade on 1 March 2018. Her first accounts, covering the 16 months to 30 June 2019 show a profit of £36,000. The taxable profits for the first three tax years are as follows.

Year	Basis period	Working	Taxable profits £
2017/18	1.3.18–5.4.18	£36,000 × 1/16	2,250
2018/19	6.4.18–5.4.19	£36,000 × 12/16	27,000
2019/20	1.7.18–30.6.19 (12 months to the accounting date in 3rd year)	£36,000 × 12/16	27,000

2.9 Later tax years

For later tax years, except the year in which the trade ceases, the normal current year basis of assessment applies, ie the basis period is the 12-month period of account ending in the tax year (see above).

Question   Basis periods

Peter commenced trading on 1 September 2013 preparing accounts to 30 April each year with the following results.

Period	Profit £
1.9.13 – 30.4.14	8,000
1.5.14 – 30.4.15	15,000
1.5.15 – 30.4.16	9,000
1.5.16 – 30.4.17	10,500

Show the profits to be taxed in each year from 2013/14 to 2017/18.

Answer

Year	Basis period	Working	Taxable Profits £
2013/14	1.9.13–5.4.14	£8,000 × 7/8	7,000
2014/15	1.9.13–31.8.14	£8,000 + (£15,000 × 4/12)	13,000
2015/16	1.5.14–30.4.15		15,000
2016/17	1.5.15–30.4.16		9,000
2017/18	1.5.16–30.4.17		10,500

2.10 The final year

FAST FORWARD

On a cessation the basis period runs from the end of the basis period for the previous tax year.

(a)   If a trade starts and ceases in the same tax year, the basis period for that year is the whole lifespan of the trade.

(b)   If the final year is the second year, the basis period runs from 6 April at the start of the second year to the date of cessation. This rule overrides the rules that normally apply for the second year.

(c)   If the final year is the third year or a later year, **the basis period runs from the end of the basis period for the previous year to the date of cessation**. This rule overrides the rules that normally apply in the third and later years.

Question

Ceasing to trade

Harriet, who has been trading since 2002, ceases her trade on 31 March 2018.

Her results for recent years were:

Year ended 31 December	£
2015	10,000
2016	14,000
2017	21,000
Period ended 31 March 2018	4,000

Show the taxable trade profits for the last three tax years of trading.

Answer

Trade ceases in 2017/18.

Year	Basis period	Working	Assessment £
2015/16	Y/e 31.12.15		10,000
2016/17	Y/e 31.12.16		14,000
2017/18	1.1.17–31.3.18	Y/e 31.12.17 plus p/e 31.3.18	25,000

2.11 Overlap profits

Key term

Profits which have been taxed more than once are called **overlap profits**.

When a business starts, some profits may be taxed twice because the basis period for the second year includes some or all of the period of trading in the first year or because the basis period for the third year overlaps with that for the second year, or both.

Overlap profits are relieved when the trade ceases by being deducted from the final year's taxable profits. Any deduction of overlap profits may create or increase a loss. The usual loss reliefs (covered later in this Study Text) are then available.

Exam focus point

A business with a 31 March year end will have no overlap profits as its accounting year coincides with the tax year. A business with a 31 December year end, for example, will have three months of overlap profit as its accounting year ends three months before the end of the tax year. Use this rule of thumb to check your calculation of overlap profits.

2.12 Examples: Overlap profits

(a) John starts to trade on 1 January 2018 preparing accounts to 31 December 2018. Show the overlap period.

Tax year	Basis period
2017/18	1.1.18–5.4.18
2018/19	1.1.18–31.12.18
2019/20	1.1.19–31.12.19

Overlap period: 1.1.18 – 5.4.18 (three months)

(b) Janet starts to trade on 1 January 2018 preparing accounts as follows:

6m to 30 June 2018
12m to 30 June 2019

Show the overlap period.

Tax year	Basis period
2017/18	1.1.18–5.4.18
2018/19	1.1.18–31.12.18
2019/20	1.7.18–30.6.19

Overlap period: 1.1.18–5.4.18 plus 1.7.18–31.12.18 (nine months)

(c) Jodie starts to trade on 1 March 2018 preparing a 14 month set of accounts to 30 April 2019. Show the overlap period.

Tax year	Basis period
2017/18	1.3.18–5.4.18
2018/19	6.4.18–5.4.19
2019/20	1.5.18–30.4.19

Overlap period: 1.5.18 – 5.4.19 (11 months)

Question	Ceasing to trade and overlap profits

Jenny trades from 1 July 2012 to 31 December 2017, with the following results.

Period	Profit £
1.7.12–31.8.13	7,000
1.9.13–31.8.14	12,000
1.9.14–31.8.15	15,000
1.9.15–31.8.16	21,000
1.9.16–31.8.17	18,000
1.9.17–31.12.17	5,600
	78,600

Calculate the taxable trade profits to be taxed from 2012/13 to 2017/18, the overlap profits and state when these overlap profits can be relieved.

The profits to be taxed in each tax year from 2012/13 to 2017/18 and the total of these taxable profits are calculated as follows.

Year	Basis period	Working	Taxable profit £
2012/13	1.7.12–5.4.13	£7,000 × 9/14	4,500
2013/14	1.9.12–31.8.13	£7,000 × 12/14	6,000
2014/15	1.9.13–31.8.14		12,000
2015/16	1.9.14–31.8.15		15,000
2016/17	1.9.15–31.8.16		21,000
2017/18	1.9.16–31.12.17	£(18,000 + 5,600 − 3,500)	20,100
			78,600

The overlap profits are those in the period 1 September 2012 to 5 April 2013, a period of seven months. They are £7,000 × 7/14 = £3,500. Overlap profits are deducted from the final year's taxable profit when the business ceases.

Exam focus point

Over the life of the business, the total taxable profits equal the total actual profits.

3 The choice of an accounting date 9/16

FAST FORWARD

The choice of an accounting date may affect when tax is payable on trading profits. It may also create overlap profits and help or hinder tax planning.

A new trader should consider which accounting date would be best. There are **a number of factors to consider** from the point of view of taxation.

(a) **If profits are expected to rise, a date early in the tax year** (such as 30 April) will delay the time when rising accounts profits feed through into rising taxable profits, whereas a date late in the tax year (such as 31 March) will accelerate the taxation of rising profits. This is because with an accounting date of 30 April, the taxable profits for each tax year are mainly the profits earned in the previous tax year. With an accounting date of 31 March the taxable profits are almost entirely profits earned in the current year.

(b) If the accounting date in the second tax year is less than 12 months after the start of trading, the taxable profits for that year will be the profits earned in the first 12 months. If the accounting date is at least 12 months from the start of trading, they will be the profits earned in the 12 months to that date. **Different profits may thus be taxed twice**, and if profits are fluctuating this can make a considerable difference to the taxable profits in the first few years.

(c) **The choice of an accounting date affects the profits shown in each set of accounts**, and this may affect the taxable profits.

(d) **An accounting date of 30 April gives the maximum interval between earning profits and paying the related tax liability.** For example if a trader prepares accounts to 30 April 2018, this falls into the tax year 2018/19 with payments on account being due on 31 January 2019 and 31 July 2019, and a balancing payment due on 31 January 2020 (details of payment of income tax are dealt with later in this Study Text). If the trader prepares accounts to 31 March 2018, this falls in the tax year 2017/18 and the payments will be due one year earlier (ie on 31 January 2018, 31 July 2018 and 31 January 2019).

(e) **Knowing profits well in advance of the end of the tax year makes tax planning much easier.** For example, if a trader wants to make personal pension contributions and prepares accounts to 30 April 2018 (2018/19), they can make contributions up to 5 April 2019 based on those relevant earnings. If they prepare accounts to 31 March 2018, they will probably not know the amount of their relevant earnings until after the end of the tax year 2017/18, too late to adjust their pension contributions for 2017/18.

(f) **However, a 31 March or 5 April accounting date means that the application of the basis period rules is more straightforward and there will be no overlap profits.** This may be appropriate for small traders.

(g) **With an accounting date of 30 April, the assessment for the year of cessation could be based on up to 23 months of profits.** For example, if a trader who has prepared accounts to 30 April ceases trading on 31 March 2018 (2017/18), the basis period for 2017/18 will run from 1 May 2016 to 31 March 2018. This could lead to larger than normal trading profits being assessable in the year of cessation. However, this could be avoided by carrying on the trade for another month so that a cessation arises on 30 April 2018 so that the profits from 1 May 2016 to 30 April 2017 are taxable in 2017/18 and those from 1 May 2017 to 30 April 2018 are taxable in 2018/19. Each case must be looked at in relation to all relevant factors, such as other income which the taxpayer may have and loss relief – there is no one rule which applies in all cases.

Exam focus point

This topic was tested in Question 32, Ashura, in the September 2016 exam. The requirement was to state two advantages of the taxpayer choosing 5 April as an accounting date rather than a date early in the tax year such as 30 April. The examining team commented that there were three obvious advantages, and many candidates correctly explained that the application of the basis period rules is more straightforward and that there will be no overlap profits. Less well-prepared candidates instead covered the advantages of a 30 April accounting date, so not surprisingly did not achieve high marks.

Question   The choice of an accounting date

Christine starts to trade on 1 December 2015. Her monthly profits are £1,000 for the first seven months, and £2,000 thereafter. Show the taxable profits for the first three tax years with each of the following accounting dates (in all cases starting with a period of account of less than 12 months).

(a) 31 March
(b) 30 April
(c) 31 December

Answer

(a) *31 March*

Period of account	Working	Profits £
1.12.15–31.3.16	£1,000 × 4	4,000
1.4.16–31.3.17	£1,000 × 3 + £2,000 × 9	21,000
1.4.17–31.3.18	£2,000 × 12	24,000

Year	Basis period	Taxable profits £
2015/16	1.12.15–5.4.16	4,000
2016/17	1.4.16–31.3.17	21,000
2017/18	1.4.17–31.3.18	24,000

(b)   30 April

Period of account	Working	Profits £
1.12.15–30.4.16	£1,000 × 5	5,000
1.5.16–30.4.17	£1,000 × 2 + £2,000 ×10	22,000

Year	Basis period	Working	Taxable profits £
2015/16	1.12.15–5.4.16	£5,000 × 4/5	4,000
2016/17	1.12.15–30.11.16	£5,000 + £22,000 × 7/12	17,833
2017/18	1.5.16–30.4.17		22,000

(c)   31 December

Period of account	Working	Profits £
1.12.15–31.12.15	£1,000 × 1	1,000
1.1.16–31.12.16	£1,000 × 6 + £2,000 × 6	18,000
1.1.17–31.12.17	£2,000 × 12	24,000

Year	Basis period	Working	Taxable profits £
2015/16	1.12.15–5.4.16	£1,000 + £18,000 × 3/12	5,500
2016/17	1.1.16–31.12.16		18,000
2017/18	1.1.17–31.12.17		24,000

Chapter Roundup

- Basis periods are used to link periods of account to tax years. Broadly, the profits of a 12-month period of account ending in a tax year are taxed in that year (current year basis).

- In the first tax year of trade actual profits of the tax year are taxed. In the second tax year, the basis period is either the first 12 months, the 12 months to the accounting date ending in year two or the actual profits from April to April. Profits of the 12 months to the accounting date are taxed in year three.

- On a cessation the basis period runs from the end of the basis period for the previous tax year.

- The choice of an accounting date may affect when tax is payable on trading profits. It may also create overlap profits and help or hinder tax planning.

Quick Quiz

1   What is the normal basis of assessment?

2   Isabella started trading on 1 September 2017. She prepares her first set of accounts to 31 December 2018. The basis period for the year of commencement is:

    A   1 September 2017 to 31 December 2017
    B   1 September 2017 to 5 April 2018
    C   1 September 2017 to 31 August 2018
    D   1 September 2017 to 31 December 2018

3   Ernie started trading on 1 January 2017. He decided to prepare accounts to 31 October each year. His taxable trading profits is as follows:

p/e 31.10.17	£3,000
y/e 31.10.18	£23,760

What are Ernie's overlap profits?

    A   £900
    B   £2,880
    C   £3,960
    D   £4,860

4   Gita ceased trading on 31 March 2018. Her taxable trading profits were:

y/e 31.12.17	£5,600
p/e 31.3.18	£4,500

Gita had £2,300 of unused overlap profits.

What is her taxable trading profit for 2017/18?

    A   £10,100
    B   £7,800
    C   £6,400
    D   £2,200

5   How are overlap profits relieved?

1   The normal basis of assessment is that the profits for a tax year are those of the 12-month accounting period ending in the tax year.

2   B. 1 September 2017 to 5 April 2018 ie the actual tax year.

3   D £4,860

> *First tax year (2016/17)*
> Actual basis
> Basis period 1.1.17 to 5.4.17
>
> *Second tax year (2017/18)*
> Period of account in 2nd year less than 12 months
> Basis period 1.1.17 to 31.12.17
>
> *Third tax year (2018/19)*
> Current year basis
> Basis period 1.11.17 to 31.10.18
>
> *Overlap profits*
> Period of overlap 1.1.17 to 5.4.17 and 1.11.17 to 31.12.17
>
> Overlap profits

	£
3/10 × £3,000	900
2/12 × £23,760	3,960
	4,860

4   B £7,800

> Last tax year (2017/18) Basis period 1.1.17 to 31.3.18

	£
y/e 31.12.17	5,600
p/e 31.3.18	4,500
	10,100
Less overlap profits	(2,300)
	7,800

5   On the cessation of a business by deduction from the final year's taxable profits.

Now try the questions below from the Practice Question Bank

Number	Type	Marks	Time
Q59	Section A	2	4 mins
Q60	Section A	2	4 mins
Q61	Section A	2	4 mins
Q62	Section C	15	27 mins
Q63	Section C	15	27 mins

10

Trading losses

Topic list	Syllabus reference
1 Losses	B3(i)
2 Carry forward trade loss relief	B3(i)(i)
3 Trade loss relief against general income	B3(i)(ii), (i)(v)
4 Losses in the early years of a trade	B3(i)(iii)
5 Terminal trade loss relief	B3(i)(iv)

Introduction

We have seen how to calculate taxable trading profits and how to allocate them to tax years so that they can be slotted into the income tax computation.

Traders sometimes make losses rather than profits. In this chapter we consider the reliefs available for losses. A loss does not in itself lead to getting tax back from HM Revenue & Customs (HMRC). Relief is obtained by setting a loss against trading profits, against general income or against capital gains (which are covered later in this Study Text), so that tax need not be paid on them. There are restrictions on how much loss relief can be claimed in a tax year.

An important consideration is the choice between different reliefs. The aim is to use a loss to save as much tax as possible, as quickly as possible.

In the next chapter we will see how the rules on trading profits and losses for sole traders are extended to those trading in partnership.

Study guide

		Intellectual level
B3	**Income from self-employment**	
(i)	Relief for trading losses	
(i)(i)	Understand how trading losses can be carried forward.	2
(i)(ii)	Understand how trading losses can be claimed against total income and chargeable gains, and the restriction that can apply.	2
(i)(iii)	Explain and compute the relief for trading losses in the early years of a trade.	1
(i)(iv)	Explain and compute terminal loss relief.	1
(i)(v)	Recognise the factors that will influence the choice of loss relief claim.	2

Exam guide

Section A questions on loss relief may deal with a specific aspect such as the cap on loss relief against general income. You may also have to deal with a number of aspects of loss relief in a Section B question. Section C could have a detailed computational question involving the carry back and carry forward of losses for a sole trader. Ensure you know the rules for ongoing trades and the additional relief in the early years of trading. On cessation, terminal loss relief may be used. Once you have established the reliefs available look to see which is most beneficial.

One of the competencies you require to fulfil Performance Objective 17 Tax planning and advice of the PER is to mitigate and/or defer tax liabilities through the use of standard reliefs, exemptions and incentives. You can apply the knowledge you obtain from this chapter of the Study Text to help to demonstrate this competence.

1 Losses

Trading losses may be relieved against future profits of the same trade, against general income and against capital gains.

1.1 Introduction

When computing taxable trade profits, profits may turn out to be negative, meaning a loss has been made in the basis period. **A loss is computed in exactly the same way as a profit**, making the same adjustments to the accounts profit or loss.

If there is a loss in a basis period, the taxable trade profits for the tax year based on that basis period are nil.

This chapter considers how losses are calculated and how a loss-suffering taxpayer can use a loss to reduce their tax liability.

The rules in this chapter apply only to individuals, trading alone or in partnership. They do not apply to a business using the cash basis. Loss reliefs for companies are completely different and are covered later in this Study Text.

1.2 The computation of the loss

The trade loss for a tax year is the trade loss in the basis period for that tax year.

1.3 Example: Computation of trade loss

Here is an example of a trader with a 31 December year end who has been trading for many years.

Period of account	Loss £
Y/e 31.12.17	9,000
Y/e 31.12.18	24,000

Tax year	Basis period	Trade loss for the tax year £
2017/18	Y/e 31.12.17	9,000
2018/19	Y/e 31.12.18	24,000

1.4 How loss relief is given

Loss relief is given by deducting the loss from total income to calculate net income. Carry forward loss relief and terminal loss relief can only be set against the trading profits of the same trade. Other loss reliefs may be set against general income (ie any component of total income).

2 Carry forward trade loss relief

FAST FORWARD

Trading losses may be relieved against future profits of the same trade. The relief is against the first available profits of the same trade.

2.1 The relief

A trade loss not relieved in any other way will be **carried forward to set against the first available trade profits of the same trade** in the calculation of net trading income. Losses may be carried forward for any number of years unless they have been entirely used up.

Carry forward trade loss relief is the only trade loss relief which applies to furnished holiday lettings (see earlier in this Study Text).

2.2 Example: Carrying forward losses

Brian has the following results.

Year ending	£
31 December 2015	(6,000)
31 December 2016	5,000
31 December 2017	11,000

Brian's net trading income, assuming that he uses carry forward loss relief only are:

	2015/16 £		2016/17 £		2017/18 £
Trade profits	0		5,000		11,000
Less carry forward loss relief	(0)	(i)	(5,000)	(ii)	(1,000)
Net trading income	0		0		10,000

Loss memorandum			£
Trading loss, y/e 31.12.15			6,000
Less: Claim in y/e 31.12.16 (16/17)		(i)	(5,000)
Claim in y/e 31.12.17 (balance of loss) (17/18)		(ii)	(1,000)
			0

FAST FORWARD

A trading loss may be set against general income in the year of the loss and/or the preceding year. Personal allowances may be lost as a result of a claim. Once a claim has been made in any year, the remaining loss can be set against net chargeable gains.

3.1 The relief

Instead of carrying a trade loss forward against future trade profits, a claim may be made to relieve it against general income.

3.2 Relieving the loss

Relief is against the income of the tax year in which the loss arose. **In addition or instead,** relief may be claimed **against the income of the preceding year.**

If there are losses in two successive years, and relief is claimed against the first year's income both for the first year's loss and for the second year's loss, relief is given for the first year's loss before the second year's loss.

A claim for a loss must be made by the 31 January which is 22 months after the end of the tax year of the loss: thus by 31 January 2020 for a loss in 2017/18.

The taxpayer cannot choose the amount of loss to relieve: thus the loss may have to be set against income part of which would have been covered by the personal allowance or taxed at 0% in the savings income nil rate band or the dividend nil rate band. However, the taxpayer can choose whether to claim full relief in the current year and then relief in the preceding year for any remaining loss, or the other way round.

When calculating the income tax liability, the **loss is usually set against non-savings income, then against savings income and finally against dividend income.**

Exam focus point

There are some situations where this order of set off will not be the most beneficial but such a scenario will **not be examined** in Taxation (TX – UK).

Question   Loss relief against general income

Janet has a loss in her period of account ending 31 December 2017 of £37,500. Her other income is dividend income of £30,500 a year, and she wishes to claim loss relief against general income for the year of loss and then for the preceding year. Her trading income in the previous year was £1,500. Show her taxable income for each year, and comment on the effectiveness of the loss relief. Assume that tax rates and allowances for 2017/18 have always applied.

Answer

The loss-making period ends in 2017/18, so the year of the loss is 2017/18.

	2016/17 £	2017/18 £
Total income £(30,500 + 1,500)/£30,500	32,000	30,500
Less loss relief against general income	(7,000)	(30,500)
Net income	25,000	0
Less personal allowance	(11,500)	(11,500)
Taxable income	13,500	0

In 2017/18, £(11,500 + 5,000) = £16,500 of the loss has been wasted because that amount of income would have been covered by the personal allowance and the dividend nil rate band. If Janet just claims loss relief against general income, there is nothing she can do about this waste of loss relief.

3.3 Capital allowances

The trader may adjust the size of the loss relief claim by not claiming all the capital allowances they are entitled to: a reduced claim will increase the balance carried forward to the next year's capital allowances computation. This may be a useful **tax planning point to preserve the personal allowance or where the effective rate of relief for capital allowances in future periods will be greater than the rate of tax relief for the loss relief**.

Question
Capital allowances and loss relief

Mario is a sole trader making up accounts to 31 December each year. In the year to 31 December 2017, he makes a trading loss, before taking capital allowances into account, of £7,000. Mario has a tax written down value on his main pool at 1 January 2017 of £12,000. He does not make any additions or disposals in the year to 31 December 2017 and does not intend to make any additions or disposals in the year to 31 December 2018.

Mario has property income of £19,000 in 2017/18 and wishes to use trade loss relief against general income in 2017/18 only (ie without any carry back to 2016/17). He expects to make a trading profit of £30,000 in the year to 31 December 2018.

What advice would you give Mario?

Answer

Mario should make a reduced capital allowance claim so that the loss relief claim will preserve his personal allowance in 2017/18.

The maximum capital allowances claim that Mario could make in 2017/18 is £12,000 × 18% = £2,160. He should only claim £(19,000 − 7,000 − 11,500) = £500. The tax written down value of the pool at 1 January 2018 will then be £(12,000 − 500) = £11,500 on which Mario can claim the maximum allowance at 18% for relief in 2018/19.

3.4 Trading losses relieved against capital gains

Where relief is claimed against general income of a given year, the taxpayer may include **a further claim to set the loss against their chargeable gains for the year** less any allowable capital losses for the same year or for previous years. This amount of net gains is computed ignoring the annual exempt amount (see later in this Study Text).

The trading loss is first set against general income of the year of the claim, and only any excess loss is set against capital gains. The taxpayer cannot specify the amount to be set against capital gains, so the annual exempt amount may be wasted. We include an example here for completeness. You will study chargeable gains later in this Study Text and we suggest that you come back to this example at that point.

Sibyl had the following results for 2017/18.

	£
Loss available for relief against general income	27,000
Income	19,500
Capital gains less current year capital losses	15,000
Annual exempt amount for capital gains tax purposes	11,300
Capital losses brought forward	9,000

Show how the loss would be relieved against income and gains.

Answer

	£
Income	19,500
Less loss relief against general income	(19,500)
Net income	0
Capital gains	15,000
Less loss relief: lower of £(27,000 − 19,500) = £7,500 (Note 1) and	
£(15,000 − 9,000) = £6,000 (Note 2)	(6,000)
	9,000
Less annual exempt amount (restricted)	(9,000)
	0

Notes

1   This equals the loss left after the loss relief claim against general income.
2   This equals the gains left after losses b/fwd but ignoring the annual exempt amount.

A trading loss of £(7,500 − 6,000) = £1,500 is carried forward. Sibyl's personal allowance and £(11,300 − 9,000) = £2,300 of her capital gains tax annual exempt amount are wasted. Her capital losses brought forward of £9,000 are carried forward to 2018/19. Although we deducted this £9,000 in working out how much trading loss we were allowed to use in the claim, we do not actually need to use any of the £9,000 as the remaining gain is covered by the annual exempt amount.

3.5 Restrictions on trade loss relief against general income

3.5.1 Commercial basis

FAST FORWARD

Loss relief cannot be claimed against general income unless the loss-making business is conducted on a commercial basis.

Relief cannot be claimed against general income unless the loss-making business is conducted on a commercial basis with a view to the realisation of profits throughout the basis period for the tax year.

3.5.2 Relief cap

FAST FORWARD

An individual taxpayer can only deduct the greater of £50,000 and 25% of adjusted total income when making a claim for loss relief against general income.

There is a **restriction on certain deductions which may be made by an individual from total income for a tax year**. For Taxation (TX – UK) purposes, the restricted deduction concerns **trade loss relief against general income, whether claimed for the tax year of the loss or the previous year.**

The total deductions in a tax year cannot exceed the greater of:

- **£50,000**; and
- **25% of the taxpayer's adjusted total income for the tax year.**

Key term

> For Taxation (TX – UK) purposes, **adjusted total income** is total income less the gross amounts of personal pension contributions.

If a claim is made for relief against general income in the previous year, there is no restriction on the amount of loss that can be used against trading income (of the same trade). The restriction only applies to the other income in that year. Any restricted loss can still be carried forward against future profits from the same trade.

The limits apply in each year for which relief is claimed. If a current year and a prior year claim are made, the relief in the current year is restricted to the greater of £50,000 and 25% of the adjusted total income in the current year. The relief in the prior year is restricted to the greater of £50,000 and 25% of the adjusted total income in the prior year.

Question
Restriction on loss relief

Grace has been trading for many years, preparing accounts to 5 April each year. Her recent results have been as follows:

	Profit/(loss) £
Year to 5 April 2017	20,000
Year to 5 April 2018	(210,000)

Grace also owns a number of investment properties and her property business income is £130,000 in 2016/17 and £220,000 in 2017/18.

Show Grace's taxable income for the tax years 2016/17 and 2017/18 assuming that she claims relief for her trading loss against general income in both of those years.

Answer

	2016/17 £	2017/18 £
Trading income	20,000	0
Property business income	130,000	220,000
Total income	150,000	220,000
Less loss relief against general income	(70,000)	(55,000)
Net income	80,000	165,000
Less personal allowance	(11,500)	(0)
Taxable income	68,500	165,000

Loss relief for 2017/18 is capped at £(220,000 × 25%) = £55,000 since this is greater than £50,000. The personal allowance is not available as adjusted net income exceeds £123,000.

In 2016/17, the loss relief claim is not capped against the trading profit of £20,000. Relief against other income is capped at £50,000 since this is greater than £(150,000 × 25%) = £37,500. The total loss relief claim is therefore £(20,000 + 50,000) = £70,000. The balance of the loss is £(210,000 – 55,000 – 70,000) = £85,000 is carried forward against future profits of the same trade.

Note that the restriction on loss relief means that the loss has been relieved at the additional rate in 2017/18 and at the higher rate in 2016/17. The personal allowance has also been restored for 2016/17.

3.6 The choice between loss reliefs

It is important for a trader to choose the right loss relief, so as to save tax at the highest possible rate and so as to obtain relief reasonably quickly.

When a trader has a choice between loss reliefs, they should aim to obtain relief both quickly and at the highest possible tax rate. However, do consider that losses relieved against income which would otherwise be covered by the personal allowance are wasted. Consideration also needs to be given to any restriction on loss relief.

Another consideration is that a trading loss cannot be set against the capital gains of a year unless relief is first claimed against general income of the same year. It may be worth making the claim against income and wasting the personal allowance in order to avoid a CGT liability.

Question	The choice between loss reliefs

Felicity's trading results are as follows.

Year ended 30 September	Trading profit/(loss) £
2015	3,900
2016	(21,000)
2017	14,000

Her other income (all non-savings income) is as follows.

	£
2015/16	7,300
2016/17	34,000
2017/18	18,500

Show the most efficient use of Felicity's trading loss. Assume that the personal allowance has been £11,500 throughout.

Answer

Relief could be claimed against general income for 2015/16 and/or 2016/17, with any unused loss being carried forward. Relief in 2015/16 would be against general income of £(3,900 + 7,300) = £11,200, all of which would be covered by the personal allowance anyway, so this claim should not be made.

A claim against general income should be made for 2016/17 as this saves tax quicker than carry forward loss relief would in 2017/18.

The final results will be as follows:

	2015/16 £	2016/17 £	2017/18 £
Trading income	3,900	0	14,000
Less carry forward loss relief	(0)	(0)	(0)
	3,900	0	14,000
Other income	7,300	34,000	18,500
	11,200	34,000	32,500
Less loss relief against general income	(0)	(21,000)	(0)
Net income	11,200	13,000	32,500
Less personal allowance	(11,500)	(11,500)	(11,500)
Taxable income	0	1,500	21,000

4 Losses in the early years of a trade 9/16

4.1 The computation of the loss

Under the rules determining the basis period for the first three tax years of trading, there may be periods where the basis periods overlap. If profits arise in these periods, they are taxed twice but are relieved later, usually on cessation. However, a loss in an overlap period can only be relieved once. It must not be double counted.

If basis periods overlap, **a loss in the overlap period is treated as a loss for the earlier tax year only**.

4.2 Example: Losses in early years

Here is an example of a trader who starts to trade on 1 July 2017 and makes losses in opening periods.

Period of account			Loss £
P/e 31.12.17			9,000
Y/e 31.12.18			24,000

Tax year	Basis period	Working	Trade loss for the tax year £
2017/18	1.7.17–5.4.18	£9,000 + (£24,000 × 3/12)	15,000
2018/19	1.1.18–31.12.18	£24,000 less loss already used in 2017/18 (£24,000 × 3/12 = 6,000)	18,000

4.3 Example: Losses and profits in early years

The rule against using losses twice also applies when losses are netted off against profits in the same basis period. Here is an example, with a commencement on 1 July 2017.

Period of account			(Loss)/profit £
1.7.17 – 30.4.18			(10,000)
1.5.18 – 30.4.19			24,000

Tax year	Basis period	Working	Trade (Loss)/Profit £
2017/18	1.7.17 – 5.4.18	£(10,000) × 9/10	(9,000)
2018/19	1.7.17 – 30.6.18	£24,000 × 2/12 + £(10,000) × 1/10	3,000

4.4 Early trade losses relief

FAST FORWARD

In opening years, a special relief involving the carry back of losses against general income is available. Losses arising in the first four tax years of a trade may be set against general income in the three years preceding the loss making year, taking the earliest year first.

Early trade losses relief is available for **trading losses incurred in the first four tax years of a trade**.

Relief is obtained by **setting the allowable loss against general income in the three years preceding the year of loss**, applying the loss to the earliest year first. Thus a loss arising in 2017/18 may be set off against income in 2014/15, 2015/16 and 2016/17 in that order.

A claim for early trade losses relief applies to all three years automatically, provided that the loss is large enough. The taxpayer cannot choose to relieve the loss against just one or two of the years, or to relieve only part of the loss. However, the taxpayer could reduce the size of the loss by not claiming the full capital allowances available to them. This will result in higher capital allowances in future years.

Claims for the relief must be made by the 31 January which is 22 months after the end of the tax year in which the loss is incurred.

Early trade losses relief is an alternative to using trade loss relief against general income or using carry forward loss relief. The advantage of early trade losses relief is that it enables losses to be carried back for three years and so gives relief earlier than the other loss reliefs. Whether that is advantageous or not depends on the particular circumstances of the trader, for example whether the trader has any other income and whether there are different rates of tax in the tax years which might be affected by a particular loss relief claim.

 Question   **Early trade losses relief**

Albert is employed as a part time refuse collector until 1 January 2016. On that date he starts up his own business as a scrap metal merchant, making up his accounts to 30 June each year. His earnings as a refuse collector are:

	£
2012/13	5,000
2013/14	6,000
2014/15	7,000
2015/16 (nine months)	6,000

His trading results as a scrap metal merchant are:

	Profit/ (Loss) £
Six months to 30 June 2016	(3,000)
Year to 30 June 2017	(1,500)
Year to 30 June 2018	(1,200)

Assuming that loss relief is claimed as early as possible, show the net income for each of the years 2012/13 to 2018/19 inclusive.

Answer

Since reliefs are to be claimed as early as possible, early trade loss relief is applied. The losses available for relief are as follows.

	£	£	Years against which relief is available
2015/16 (basis period 1.1.16–5.4.16)			
Three months to 5.4.16 £(3,000) × 3/6		(1,500)	2012/13 to 2014/15
2016/17 (basis period 1.1.16–31.12.16)			
Three months to 30.6.16			
(omit 1.1.16 – 5.4.16: overlap) £(3,000) × 3/6	(1,500)		
Six months to 31.12.16 £(1,500) × 6/12	(750)		
		(2,250)	2013/14 to 2015/16
2017/18 (basis period 1.7.16–30.6.17)			
Six months to 30.6.17			
(omit 1.7.16 – 31.12.16: overlap) £(1,500) × 6/12		(750)	2014/15 to 2016/17
2018/19 (basis period 1.7.17–30.6.18)			
12 months to 30.6.18		(1,200)	2015/16 to 2017/18

The net income is as follows.

	£	£
2012/13		
Original	5,000	
Less 2015/16 loss	(1,500)	
		3,500
2013/14		
Original	6,000	
Less 2016/17 loss	(2,250)	
		3,750
2014/15		
Original	7,000	
Less 2017/18 loss	(750)	
		6,250
2015/16		
Original	6,000	
Less 2018/19 loss	(1,200)	
		4,800

The taxable trade profits for 2015/16 to 2018/19 are zero because there were losses in the basis periods.

5 Terminal trade loss relief

FAST FORWARD

On the cessation of trade, a loss arising in the last 12 months of trading may be set against trade profits of the tax year of cessation and the previous three years, taking the latest year first.

5.1 The relief

Trade loss relief against general income will often be insufficient on its own to deal with a loss incurred in the last months of trading. For this reason there is a special relief, **terminal trade loss relief, which allows a loss on cessation to be carried back for relief against taxable trading profits in previous years**.

5.2 Computing the terminal loss

A terminal loss is **the loss of the last 12 months of trading**.

It is built up as follows.

		£
(a)	The actual trade loss for the tax year of cessation (calculated from 6 April to the date of cessation)	X
(b)	The actual trade loss for the period from 12 months before cessation until the end of the penultimate tax year	X
Total terminal trade loss		X

If the result of either (a) or (b) is a profit rather than a loss, it is treated as zero.

Any unrelieved overlap profits are included within (a) above.

If any loss cannot be included in the terminal loss (eg because it is matched with a profit) it can be relieved instead against general income.

5.3 Relieving the terminal loss

The loss is relieved against trade profits only.

Relief is given in the tax year of cessation and the three preceding years, later years first.

Question	Terminal loss relief

Set out below are the results of a business up to its cessation on 30 September 2017.

	Profit/(loss) £
Year to 31 December 2014	2,000
Year to 31 December 2015	400
Year to 31 December 2016	300
Nine months to 30 September 2017	(1,950)

Unrelieved overlap profits were £450.

Show the available terminal loss relief, and suggest an alternative claim if the trader had had other non-savings income of £14,500 in each of 2016/17 and 2017/18. Assume that 2017/18 tax rates and allowances apply to all years.

Answer

The terminal loss comes in the last 12 months, the period 1 October 2016 to 30 September 2017. This period is split as follows.

2016/17   Six months to 5 April 2017
2017/18   Six months to 30 September 2017

The terminal loss is made up as follows.

Unrelieved trading losses		£	£
2017/18			
6 months to 30.9.17	£(1,950) × 6/9		(1,300)
Overlap relief	£(450)		(450)
2016/17			
3 months to 31.12.16	£300 × 3/12	75	
3 months to 5.4.17	£(1,950) × 3/9	(650)	
			(575)
			(2,325)

Taxable trade profits will be as follows.

Year	Basis period	Profits £	Terminal loss relief £	Final taxable profits £
2014/15	Y/e 31.12.14	2,000	1,625	375
2015/16	Y/e 31.12.15	400	400	0
2016/17	Y/e 31.12.16	300	300	0
2017/18	1.1.17–30.9.17	0	0	0
			2,325	

If the trader had had £14,500 of other income in 2016/17 and 2017/18 we could consider loss relief claims against general income for these two years, using the loss of £(1,950 + 450) = £2,400 for 2017/18.

The final results would be as follows. (We could alternatively claim loss relief in 2017/18, but a claim in either year would save income tax at the same (basic) rate, so the preference is to save tax earlier rather than later.)

	2014/15	2015/16	2016/17	2017/18
	£	£	£	£
Trade profits	2,000	400	300	0
Other income	0	0	14,500	14,500
	2,000	400	14,800	14,500
Less loss relief against general income	0	0	(2,400)	0
Net income	2,000	400	12,400	14,500

Another option would be to make a claim for terminal loss relief (as above) and a claim against general income for the balance of the loss not relieved as a terminal loss £(2,400 – 2,325) = £75 in either 2016/17 or 2017/18.

However, as there is only taxable income (after the personal allowance) in 2016/17 and 2017/18 the terminal loss relief claim in fact saves no tax in earlier years, and the full claim against general income is more tax efficient.

Chapter Roundup

- Trading losses may be relieved against future profits of the same trade, against general income and against capital gains.

- Trading losses may be relieved against future profits of the same trade. The relief is against the first available profits of the same trade.

- A trading loss may be set against general income in the year of the loss and/or the preceding year. Personal allowances may be lost as a result of the claim. Once a claim has been made in any year, the remaining loss can be set against net chargeable gains.

- Loss relief cannot be claimed against general income unless the loss-making business is conducted on a commercial basis.

- An individual taxpayer can only deduct the greater of £50,000 and 25% of adjusted total income when making a claim for loss relief against general income.

- It is important for a trader to choose the right loss relief, so as to save tax at the highest possible rate and so as to obtain relief reasonably quickly.

- In opening years, a special relief involving the carry back of losses against general income is available. Losses arising in the first four tax years of a trade may be set against general income in the three years preceding the loss making year, taking the earliest year first.

- On the cessation of trade, a loss arising in the last 12 months of trading may be set against trade profits of the tax year of cessation and the previous three years, taking the latest year first.

Quick Quiz

1 Against what income can trade losses carried forward be set off?

    A   General income
    B   Non-savings income
    C   Any trading income
    D   Trading income from the same trade

2 When a loss is to be relieved against general income, how are losses linked to particular tax years?

3 Against which years' general income may a loss be relieved, for a continuing business which has traded for many years?

4 Maggie has been trading as a decorator for many years. In 2016/17, she made a trading profit of £10,000. She has savings income of £16,000 each year. She makes no capital gains.

    Maggie makes a loss of £(48,000) in 2017/18 and expects to make either a loss or smaller profits in the foreseeable future. How can Maggie obtain loss relief?

5 Marie has total income of £230,000 in 2017/18, consisting of employment income. She has also carried on a sole trade for many years, preparing accounts to 31 December. For the year to 31 December 2017, the sole trade business made a loss of £80,000. What is the maximum amount of the loss that Marie can relieve in 2017/18 under loss relief against general income?

6 Joe starts trading on 6 April 2017, having previously been employed for many years. He makes a loss in his first year of trading. Against income of which years can he set the loss under early trade loss relief?

7 Terminal loss relief can be given in the year of _____ and then in the _____ preceding years, _____ years first. Fill in the blanks.

Answers to Quick Quiz

1   D. Against trading income from the same trade.

2   The loss for a tax year is the loss in the basis period for that tax year. However, if basis periods overlap, a loss in the overlap period is a loss of the earlier tax year only.

3   The year in which the loss arose and/or the preceding year.

4   Maggie can make a claim to set the loss against general income of £16,000 in 2017/18. She can also claim loss relief against general income of £(10,000 + 16,000) = £26,000 in 2016/17. The remaining £(48,000 − 16,000 − 26,000) = £6,000 will be carried forward and set against the first available trading profits of her decorating trade.

5   Greater of £50,000 and (25% × £230,000) = £57,500.

6   Loss incurred 2017/18: set against general income of 2014/15, 2015/16 and 2016/17 in that order.

7   Terminal loss relief can be given in the year of **cessation** and then in the **three** preceding years, **later** years first.

Now try the questions below from the Practice Question Bank

Number	Type	Marks	Time
Q64	Section A	2	4 mins
Q65	Section A	2	4 mins
Q66	Section A	2	4 mins
Q67	Section C	10	18 mins

10: Trading losses | Part B Income tax and national insurance contributions

Partnerships and limited liability partnerships

Topic list	Syllabus reference
1 Assessment of partnerships to tax	B3(j)(i)
2 Change in profit sharing ratios	B3(j)(ii)
3 Change in membership of partnership	B3(j)(iii)
4 Loss reliefs for partners	B3(j)(iv)

Introduction

We have covered sole traders, learning how to calculate taxable trading profits after capital allowances and allocate them to tax years and how to deal with losses.

We now see how the income tax rules for traders are adapted to deal with business partnerships. On the one hand, a partnership is a single trading entity, making profits as a whole. On the other hand, each partner has a personal tax computation, so the profits must be apportioned to the partners. The general approach is to work out the profits of the partnership, then tax each partner as if they were a sole trader running a business equal to their slice of the partnership (for example 25% of the partnership).

This chapter concludes our study of the income tax computation. In the next chapter we will turn our attention to national insurance.

Study guide

		Intellectual level
B3	**Income from self-employment**	
(j)	Partnerships and limited liability partnerships	
(j)(i)	Explain and compute how a partnership is assessed to tax.	2
(j)(ii)	Explain and compute the assessable profits for each partner following a change in the profit sharing ratio.	2
(j)(iii)	Explain and compute the assessable profits for each partner following a change in the membership of the partnership.	2
(j)(iv)	Describe the alternative loss relief claims that are available to partners.	1

Exam guide

Section A questions on partnerships may involve allocation of profits to partners, possibly involving salaries and/or interest on capital. You may also have to deal with a number of partners in a Section B question. A Section C question, which may be for 15 marks or 10 marks, may involve changes in partnerships such as a partner joining or leaving. As long as you remember to allocate the profits between the partners according to their profit sharing arrangements for the period of account, you should be able to cope with any aspect of partnership tax. Remember that each partner is taxed as a sole trader, and you should apply the opening and closing year rules and loss reliefs as appropriate to that partner.

1 Assessment of partnerships to tax

FAST FORWARD

A partnership is simply treated as a source of profits and losses for trades being carried on by the individual partners.

1.1 Introduction

A partnership is **a group of individuals who are trading together**. They will agree amongst themselves how the business should be run and how profits and losses should be shared. Most partnerships have **unlimited liability** for the partners for the debts of the partnership. A **partnership** is **not treated as a separate entity from the partners for tax purposes** (in contrast to a company).

It is possible to set up a **limited liability partnership** (LLP) where the liability of the partners for debts of the partnership is limited. A LLP is a legal person in its own right (similar to a company). However, LLPs and their partners are generally taxed on the same basis as unlimited partnerships, as described in the rest of this chapter.

1.2 Computing partnership profits

A **business partnership is treated like a sole trader for the purposes of computing its profits.** Partners' salaries and interest on capital are not deductible expenses and must be added back in computing profits, because they are a form of drawings.

Where the partners own assets (such as their cars) individually, capital allowances must be calculated in respect of such assets (not forgetting any adjustment for private use). **The capital allowances must go into the partnership's tax computation as they must be claimed by the partnership, not by the individual partner.**

Question

Gustav and Melanie have been in partnership for many years, preparing accounts to 31 March each year. They share profits in the ratio 3:2. In the year to 31 March 2018, the partnership's trading profit is £60,000. The partnership does not own any assets which qualify for capital allowances but Gustav owns a car (which he acquired for £22,000 in May 2017) which he uses 75% for the business of the partnership. The car has CO_2 emissions of 150 g/km.

Show the trade profits allocated to each partner for the period of account to 31 March 2018, assuming that the partnership makes the maximum capital allowances claim.

Answer

	Total £	Gustav £	Melanie £
Partnership profit	60,000		
Less capital allowance on car £22,000 × 8% × 75%	(1,320)		
Trade profits allocated to partners (3:2)	58,680	35,208	23,472

1.3 Allocating partnership profits between partners

FAST FORWARD

Divide profits or losses between the partners according to the profit sharing arrangements in the period of account concerned. If any of the partners are entitled to a salary or interest on capital, apportion this first, not forgetting to pro-rate in periods of less than 12 months.

Once the partnership's profits for a period of account have been computed, they are shared between the partners according to the profit sharing arrangements for that period of account.

Question — Allocating profits

Steve and Tanya have been in partnership for many years, preparing accounts to 31 October each year. For the year ended 31 October 2017, taxable trading profits were £70,000. Steve is allocated an annual salary of £12,000 and Tanya's salary is £28,000. The profit sharing ratio is 2:1.

Show the trade profits allocated to each partner for the period of account ended 31 October 2017.

Answer

Allocate the profits for the period of account ended 31 October 2017.

	Total £	Steve £	Tanya £
Profit	70,000		
Salaries	40,000	12,000	28,000
Balance (2:1)	30,000	20,000	10,000
Trade profits allocated to partners	70,000	32,000	38,000

1.4 The tax positions of individual partners

Each partner is taxed like a sole trader who runs a business which:

- Starts when they join the partnership
- Finishes when they leave the partnership
- Has the same periods of account as the partnership (except that a partner who joins or leaves during a period will have a period which starts and/or ends part way through the partnership's period)
- Makes profits or losses equal to the partner's share of the partnership's profits or losses

Exam focus point

Partners are effectively taxed in the same way as sole traders with just one difference. Before you tax the partner you need to take each set of accounts (as adjusted for tax purposes) and divide the trade profit (or loss) between each partner.

Then carry on as normal for a sole trader – each partner is treated in the same way as a sole trader in respect of their trade profits for each period of account.

Question
Taxing partnership profits

Ursula and Victor have been in partnership for many years, preparing accounts to 30 April each year. For the year ended 30 April 2017, taxable trading profits were £45,000. Victor is allocated an annual salary of £5,000 and the remaining profits are then shared between Ursula and Victor in the ratio 3:1. Neither Ursula nor Victor have any other sources of income.

Compute the taxable income for Ursula and Victor for the tax year 2017/18.

Answer

First, allocate the profits for the period of account ended 30 April 2017.

	Total £	Ursula £	Victor £
Profit	45,000		
Salary to Victor	5,000	0	5,000
Balance (3:1)	40,000	30,000	10,000
Trade profits allocated to partners	45,000	30,000	15,000

Then compute the taxable income for the tax year 2017/18. The current year basis of assessment applies so the partnership income is the share of profits for each partner for the period of account ended 30 April 2017. It is important to note that Victor's 'salary' is not taxable as employment income but is part of his trading income.

	Ursula £	Victor £
Trading income	30,000	15,000
Less personal allowance	(11,500)	(11,500)
Taxable income	18,500	3,500

2 Change in profit sharing ratios

If the **profit sharing arrangements change part way through the period of account**, the **profits, salaries and interest** for the period of account must be **pro-rated** accordingly.

Question

Sue and Tim have been in partnership for many years, preparing accounts to 31 December each year. For the year ended 31 December 2017, taxable trading profits were £50,000. Sue is allocated an annual salary of £10,000 and Tim's salary is £15,000.

The profit sharing ratio was 1:1 until 31 August 2017 when it changed to 1:2 with no provision for salaries.

Show the trade profits allocated to each partner for the period of account ended 31 December 2017.

Answer

Allocate the profits for the period of account ended 31 December 2017.

	Total £	Sue £	Tim £
Profit	50,000		
1 January – 31 August (8 months)	33,333		
Salaries (8/12 × £10,000/£15,000)	16,667	6,667	10,000
Balance (1:1)	16,666	8,333	8,333
	33,333		
1 September – 31 December (four months)	16,667		
Salaries	Nil	–	–
Balance (1:2)	16,667	5,556	11,111
	16,667		
Trade profits allocated to partners	50,000	20,556	29,444

Note. Since the profit sharing arrangements changed part way through the period of account, the profits and salaries for the period of account must be pro-rated accordingly.

3 Change in membership of partnership

Commencement and cessation rules apply to partners individually when they join or leave.

When a trade continues but partners join or leave (including cases when a sole trader takes in partners or a partnership breaks up leaving only one partner as a sole trader), **the special rules for basis periods in opening and closing years do not apply to the people who were carrying on the trade both before and after the change. They carry on using the period of account ending in each tax year as the basis period for the tax year (ie the current year basis). The commencement rules only affect joiners, and the cessation rules only affect leavers.**

Question   Partner joining partnership

Daniel and Ashley have been in partnership for many years preparing accounts to 31 December each year and sharing profits in the ratio 2:1.

On 1 June 2017, Kate joined the partnership. From that date, profits were shared Daniel 50% and Ashley and Kate 25% each.

The partnership profits for the year ended 31 December 2017 were £72,000 and for the year ended 31 December 2018 were £90,000.

Compute the partnership profits taxable on Daniel, Ashley and Kate for 2017/18 and 2018/19 and the overlap profits for Kate on commencement.

Allocation of partnership profits

	Total £	Daniel £	Ashley £	Kate £
y/e 31.12.17				
1.1.17 – 31.5.17				
Profits (5/12) 2:1	30,000	20,000	10,000	n/a
1.6.17 – 31.2.17				
Profits (7/12) 50:25:25	42,000	21,000	10,500	10,500
Profit allocation	72,000	41,000	20,500	10,500
y/e 31.12.18				
Profits 50:25:25	90,000	45,000	22,500	22,500

Taxable partnership profits for 2017/18 and 2018/19

	Daniel £	Ashley £	Kate £
2017/18			
CYB y/e 31.12.17	41,000	20,500	
First year – actual basis			
1.6.17 – 31.12.17			10,500
1.1.18 – 5.4.18			
3/12 × £22,500			5,625
			16,125
2018/19			
CYB y/e 31.12.18	45,000	22,500	
Second year – 12 months to 31.12.18			22,500

Overlap profits

Kate has overlap profits for the period 1.1.18 to 5.4.18 of £5,625.

Question   **Partner leaving partnership**

Maxwell, Laura and Wesley traded in partnership for many years, preparing accounts to 30 September.

Each partner was entitled to 5% interest per annum on capital introduced into the partnership. Each partner had introduced £60,000 of capital on the commencement of the partnership. From that date, profits were shared in the ratio 50% to Maxwell, 30% to Laura and 20% to Wesley.

On 1 May 2017, Wesley left the partnership. From that date profits were shared equally between the two remaining partners and no interest was paid on capital. The partnership taxable trading income for the year to 30 September 2017 was £120,000. Wesley had overlap profits on commencement of £5,000.

Compute the partnership profits taxable on Maxwell, Laura and Wesley for 2017/18.

Answer

Allocation of partnership profits

	Total £	Maxwell £	Laura £	Wesley £
1.10.16 – 30.4.17				
Interest 7/12 × £60,000 × 5% each	5,250	1,750	1,750	1,750
Profits (7/12) 50:30:20	64,750	32,375	19,425	12,950
	70,000	34,125	21,175	14,700
1.5.17 – 30.9.17				
Profits (5/12) 1:1	50,000	25,000	25,000	n/a
Profits allocated for year	120,000	59,125	46,175	14,700

Taxable partnership profits for 2017/18

	Maxwell £	Laura £	Wesley £
2017/18			
CYB y/e 30.9.17	59,125	46,175	
Final year			
1.10.16 – 30.4.17			14,700
Less: overlap relief			(5,000)
			9,700

When no-one carries on the trade both before and after the change, as when a partnership transfers its trade to a completely new owner or set of owners, the **cessation rules apply to the old owners** and the **commencement rules apply to the new owners**.

4 Loss reliefs for partners

FAST FORWARD

Partners are individually entitled to loss relief in the same way as sole traders.

4.1 Entitlement to loss relief

Partners are entitled to the same loss reliefs as sole traders. The reliefs are:

(a) **Carry forward against future trading profits.**

(b) **Set off against general income of the same and/or preceding year.** This claim can be extended to set off against capital gains. The restriction on loss relief (see earlier in this Study Text) applies.

(c) **For a new partner, losses in the first four tax years of trade can be set off against general income of the three preceding years.** This is so even if the actual trade commenced many years before the partner joined.

(d) **For a ceasing partner, terminal loss relief is available** when they are treated as ceasing to trade. This is so even if the partnership continues to trade after they leave.

Different partners may claim loss reliefs in different ways.

Question   Partnership losses

Mary and Natalie have been trading for many years sharing profits equally. On 1 January 2018 Mary retired and Oliver joined the partnership. Natalie and Oliver share profits in the ratio of 2:1. Although the partnership had previously been profitable it made a loss of £24,000 for the year to 31 March 2018. The partnership is expected to be profitable in the future.

Calculate the loss accruing to each partner for 2017/18 and explain what reliefs are available.

Answer

We must first share the loss for the period of account between the partners.

	Total £	Mary £	Natalie £	Oliver £
y/e 31.3.18				
1.4.17– 31.12.17				
Total £24,000 × 9/12	(18,000)	(9,000)	(9,000)	
1.1.18 – 31.3.18				
Total £24,000 × 3/12	(6,000)		(4,000)	(2,000)
Total for y/e 31.03.18	(24,000)	(9,000)	(13,000)	(2,000)

Mary

For 2017/18, Mary has a loss of £9,000. She may claim relief against general income of 2017/18 and/or 2016/17 and may extend the claim to capital gains.

Mary has ceased trading and may instead claim terminal loss relief. The terminal loss will be £9,000 (a profit arose in the period 1.1.17–31.3.17 which would be treated as zero) and this may be set against her taxable trade profits for 2017/18 (£nil), 2016/17, 2015/16 and 2014/15.

Natalie

For 2017/18, Natalie has a loss of £13,000. She may claim relief against general income of 2017/18 and/or 2016/17 and may extend the claim to capital gains. Any loss remaining unrelieved may be carried forward against future income from the same trade.

Oliver

Oliver's loss for 2017/18 is £2,000. He may claim relief for the loss against general income (and gains) of 2017/18 and/or 2016/17. As he has just started to trade he may claim relief for the loss against general income of 2014/15, 2015/16 and 2016/17. Any loss remaining unrelieved may be carried forward against future income from the same trade.

Chapter Roundup

- A partnership is simply treated as a source of profits and losses for trades being carried on by the individual partners.

- Divide profits or losses between the partners according to the profit sharing arrangements in the period of account concerned. If any of the partners are entitled to a salary or interest on capital, apportion this first, not forgetting to pro-rate in periods of less than 12 months.

- Commencement and cessation rules apply to partners individually when they join or leave.

- Partners are individually entitled to loss relief in the same way as sole traders.

Quick Quiz

1 How are partnership trading profits divided between the individual partners?

2 Janet and John are partners sharing profits 60:40. For the years ended 30 June 2017 and 2018 the partnership made profits of £100,000 and £150,000 respectively. John's taxable trading profits in 2017/18 are:

    A   £30,000
    B   £40,000
    C   £50,000
    D   £60,000

3 Yolanda and Yan are in partnership sharing profits 80:20. For the year ended 31 December 2017 the business makes a loss of £40,000. Yan decides to use his share of the loss against general income.

Yolanda must also use her share of the loss against general income. True/False?

4 Pete and Doug have been partners for many years, sharing profits equally. On 1 January 2017 Dave joins the partnership and it is agreed to share profits 40:40:20. For the year ended 30 June 2017 profits are £100,000.

Doug's share of these profits is:

    A   £42,500
    B   £45,000
    C   £47,500
    D   £50,000

5 What loss reliefs are partners entitled to?

1   Profits are divided in accordance with the profit sharing arrangements that existed during the period of account in which the profits arose.

2   B. £40,000.

2017/18: y/e 30 June 2017

£100,000 × 40% = £40,000.

3   False. Yolanda has a choice of loss reliefs:

Loss relief against general income or carry forward loss relief.

Her loss relief claim is unaffected by Yan's.

4   B. £45,000

	Pete £	Doug £	Dave £
Y/e 30 June 2017			
1.7.16–31.12.16			
6m × £100,000			
£50,000 50:50	25,000	25,000	
1.1.17–30.6.17			
6m × £100,000			
£50,000 40:40:20	20,000	20,000	10,000
	45,000	45,000	10,000

5   Partners are entitled to the same loss reliefs as sole traders. These are loss relief against general income, early years trade loss relief, carry forward loss relief and terminal loss relief.

Now try the questions below from the Practice Question Bank

Number	Type	Marks	Time
Q68	Section A	2	4 mins
Q69	Section A	2	4 mins
Q70	Section A	2	4 mins
Q71	Section B	2	4 mins
Q72	Section B	2	4 mins
Q73	Section B	2	4 mins
Q74	Section B	2	4 mins
Q75	Section B	2	4 mins

National insurance contributions

Topic list	Syllabus reference
1 Scope of national insurance contributions (NICs)	B6
2 Class 1 and Class 1A NICs for employed persons	B6(a)(i), (b)
3 Class 2 and Class 4 NICs for self-employed persons	B6(a)(ii)

Introduction

In the previous chapters we have covered income tax for employees and for the self-employed.

We look at the national insurance contributions payable under Classes 1 and 1A in respect of employment and under Classes 2 and 4 in respect of self-employment.

In the next chapter we will turn our attention to the taxation of chargeable gains.

		Intellectual level
	ional insurance contributions for employed and self-employed ons	
(a)	Explain and compute national insurance contributions payable	
(a)(i)	Class 1 and Class 1A NIC.	2
(a)(ii)	Class 2 and Class 4 NIC.	2
(b)	Understand the annual employment allowance.	2

Exam guide

National insurance contributions may be tested in Sections A or B or as part of a 15 mark or 10 mark question in Section C. You must be absolutely clear who is liable for which class of contributions; only employers, for example, pay Class 1A.

1 Scope of national insurance contributions (NICs)

Four main classes of national insurance contribution (NIC) exist, as set out below.

(a) **Class 1**. This is divided into:

    (i) **Employee's Class 1**, paid by employees

    (ii) **Employer's Class 1, Class 1A** and **Class 1B** paid by employers

(b) **Class 2**. Paid by the self-employed

(c) **Class 3**. Voluntary contributions (paid to maintain rights to certain state benefits)

(d) **Class 4**. Paid by the self-employed

Exam focus point

> Class 1B and Class 3 contributions are outside the scope of your syllabus.

The National Insurance Contributions Office (NICO), which is part of HM Revenue & Customs (HMRC), examines employers' records and procedures to ensure that the correct amounts of NICs are collected.

2 Class 1 and Class 1A NICs for employed persons

2.1 Class 1 NICs

6/17

FAST FORWARD

> Class 1 NICs are payable by employees and employers on earnings.

Both **employees** and **employers pay NICs** related to the employee's earnings. NICs are not deductible from an employee's gross salary for income tax purposes. However, employers' contributions are deductible trade expenses.

2.1.1 Earnings

'Earnings' broadly comprise gross pay, excluding benefits which cannot be turned into cash by surrender (eg holidays). Earnings also include payments for use of the employee's own car on business over the approved amount of 45p per mile (irrespective of total mileage). Therefore, where an employer reimburses an employee using their own car for business mileage, the earnings element is the excess of the mileage rate paid over 45 per mile. This applies even where business mileage exceeds 10,000 miles in a tax year.

Certain payments are exempt. In general the income tax and NIC exemptions mirror one another. For example, payment of personal incidental expenses covered by the £5/£10 a night income tax *de minimis* exemption are excluded from NIC earnings. Relocation expenses of a type exempt from income tax are also excluded from NIC earnings but without the income tax £8,000 upper limit (although expenses exceeding £8,000 are subject to Class 1A NICs as described below).

An expense with a business purpose is not treated as earnings. For example, if an employee is reimbursed for business travel or for staying in a hotel on the employer's business this is not normally 'earnings'. Again the NIC rules for travel expenses follow the income tax rules.

One commonly met expenses payment is telephone calls. If an employee is reimbursed for their own telephone charges the reimbursed cost of private calls (and all reimbursed rental) is earnings.

In general, non cash vouchers are subject to Class 1 NICs. However, the following are exempt.

- Childcare vouchers up to the amount exempt from income tax (see earlier in this Study Text)
- Any other voucher which is exempt from income tax

An employer's contribution to an employee's occupational or private registered pension scheme is excluded from the definition of 'earnings'.

2.1.2 Rates of Class 1 NICs

The rates of contribution for 2017/18, and the income bands to which they apply, are set out in the Tax Rates and Allowance Tables in this Study Text.

Employees pay main employee's contributions of 12% of earnings between the employee's threshold of £8,164 and the upper earnings limit (UEL) of £45,000 or the equivalent monthly or weekly limit (see below). They also pay additional employee's contributions of 2% on earnings above the upper earnings limit.

Where the employee is aged 21 or over, employers pay employer's contributions of 13.8% on earnings above the employer's threshold of £8,164, or the equivalent monthly or weekly limit. There is no upper limit.

Exam focus point

There are different rules for employer's contributions if the employee is aged under 21 and for apprentices aged under 25. These rules are **not examinable** in Taxation (TX – UK). You should therefore assume that all employees are aged 25 or over in questions.

If an individual has more than one job then NIC is calculated on the earnings from each job separately and independently. However, there is an overall annual maximum amount of Class 1 NIC any individual will be due to pay. If the total NIC paid from those different jobs exceeds the maximum that individual can claim a refund of the excess.

2.1.3 Earnings period

NICs are calculated in relation to an earnings period. This is the period to which earnings paid to an employee are deemed to relate. Where earnings are paid at regular intervals, the earnings period will generally be equated with the payment interval, for example a week or a month. An earnings period cannot usually be less than seven days long.

Exam focus point

In the exam NICs will generally be calculated on an annual basis.

Question — Class 1 contributions

Sally works for Red plc. She is paid £4,250 per month.

Show Sally's employee's Class 1 contributions and the employer's Class 1 contributions paid by Red plc for 2017/18. Ignore the employment allowance (see Section 2.1.4 later in this chapter).

Employee's threshold £8,164
Employer's threshold £8,164
Upper earnings limit £45,000
Annual salary £4,250 × 12 = £51,000

Sally

	£
Employee's contributions	
£(45,000 − 8,164) = £36,836 × 12% (main)	4,420
£(51,000 − 45,000) = £6,000 × 2% (additional)	120
Total employee's contributions	4,540

	£
Red plc	
Employer's contributions	
£(51,000 − 8,164) = £42,836 × 13.8%	5,911

Special rules apply to company directors, regardless of whether they are paid at regular intervals or not. Where a person is a director at the beginning of the tax year, their earnings period is the tax year, even if they cease to be director during the year. **The annual limits as shown in the Tax Tables apply.**

Question Employees and directors

Bill and Ben work for Weed Ltd. Bill is a monthly paid employee. Ben, who is a director of Weed Ltd, is also paid monthly. Each is paid an annual salary of £42,000 in 2017/18 and each also received a bonus of £4,000 in December 2017.

Show the employee's and employer's contributions for both Bill and Ben, using a monthly earnings period for Bill. Ignore the employment allowance (see Section 2.1.4 later in this chapter).

Answer

Bill
Employee's threshold £8,164/12 = £680
Employer's threshold £8,164/12 = £680
Upper earnings limit £45,000/12 = £3,750
Regular monthly earnings £42,000/12 = £3,500

Employee's contributions

	£
11 months	
£(3,500 − 680) = £2,820 × 12% × 11 (main only)	3,722
1 month (December)	
£(3,750 − 680) = £3,070 × 12% (main)	368
£(3,500 + 4,000 − 3,750) = £3,750 × 2% (additional)	75
Total employee's contributions	4,165

Employer's contributions

	£
11 months	
£(3,500 − 680) = £2,820 × 13.8% × 11	4,281
1 month (December)	
£(3,500 + 4,000 − 680) = £6,820 × 13.8%	941
Total employer's contributions	5,222

Ben
Total earnings £(42,000 + 4,000) = £46,000

Employee's contributions

	£
Total earnings exceed UEL	
£(45,000 – 8,164) = £36,836 × 12% (main)	4,420
£(46,000 – 45,000) = £1,000 × 2% (additional)	20
Total employee's contributions	4,440

Employer's contributions

	£
£(46,000 – 8,164) = £37,836 × 13.8%	5,221

Because Ben is a director an annual earnings period applies. The effect of this is that increased employee's contributions are due.

2.1.4 Employment allowance

FAST FORWARD
The employment allowance enables an employer to reduce its total Class 1 employer's contributions by up to £3,000 per tax year.

An employer can make a claim to **reduce its total Class 1 employer's contributions** by an **employment allowance equal to those contributions**, subject to a **maximum allowance of £3,000 per tax year.**

Some employers are **excluded employers** for the purposes of the employment allowance. These include **companies** where the **only employed earner for whom the company pays Class 1 employer's contributions is a director of the company,** employers who employ **employees for personal, household or domestic work, public authorities** and employers who **carry out functions either wholly or mainly of a public nature** such as provision of National Health Service services.

Question   Employment allowance

Blue plc is a trading company which has two employees, one who earns £25,000 per year and the other who earns £20,000 per year. Each employee is paid in equal monthly amounts and so an annual computation of Class 1 computation can be made.

Calculate the Class 1 employer's contributions payable by Blue plc for 2017/18.

Answer

	£
Employee 1: £(25,000 – 8,164) = 16,836 × 13.8%	2,323
Employee 2: £(20,000 – 8,164) = 11,836 × 13.8%	1,633
	3,956
Less employment allowance (maximum)	(3,000)
Employer's contributions 2017/18	956

Exam focus point

ACCA's article **Motor cars,** written by a member of the Taxation (TX – UK) examining team explains the implications of acquiring, running, or having the use of a motor car for income tax, corporation tax, value added tax (VAT) and NIC.

FAST FORWARD

Class 1A NICs are payable by employers on benefits provided for employees.

Employers must pay Class 1A NIC at 13.8% in respect of most taxable benefits. Taxable benefits are calculated in accordance with income tax rules. There is no Class 1A in respect of any benefits already treated as earnings for Class 1 purposes (eg non cash vouchers). Tax exempt benefits are not liable to Class 1A NIC.

Question
Class 1A NIC

James has the following benefits for income tax purposes:

	£
Company car	5,200
Living accommodation	10,000
Medical insurance	800

Calculate the Class 1A NICs that the employer will have to pay.

Answer

Total benefits are £16,000 (£10,000 + £5,200 + £800)

Class 1A NICs:

13.8% × £16,000 = £2,208

2.3 Miscellaneous points

Class 1 contributions are collected under the PAYE system described earlier in this Study Text.

Class 1A contributions are collected annually in arrears. If the payment is made electronically, payment must reach HMRC's bank account no later than 22 July following the end of the tax year. Payment by cheque must reach HMRC no later than 19 July following the end of the tax year.

It is important to note that Class 1 and 1A contributions broadly apply to amounts which are taxable as employment income. They do not apply to dividends paid to directors and employees who are also shareholders in the company. This means that it may be more tax-efficient for an employee/shareholder to receive payment from a company in the form of dividends. We look at this situation when we consider the company's liability to corporation tax later in this Study Text.

3 Class 2 and Class 4 NICs for self-employed persons

FAST FORWARD

The self-employed pay Class 2 and Class 4 NICs. Class 2 NICs are paid at a flat weekly rate. Class 4 NICs are based on the level of the individual's profits.

3.1 Class 2 contributions

The self-employed (sole traders and partners) pay NICs in two ways.

Class 2 contributions are payable at a flat rate. The Class 2 rate for 2017/18 is £2.85 a week. No Class 2 contributions are payable if the individual's taxable trading profits are less than the small profits threshold which is £6,025 (2017/18).

Class 2 NICs are payable under the self assessment system but payments on account are not required. For 2017/18, Class 2 NICs are payable by 31 January 2019.

3.2 Class 4 contributions   9/16, 12/16

Additionally, **the self-employed pay Class 4 NICs,** based on the level of the individual's taxable trading profits.

Main rate Class 4 NICs are calculated by applying a fixed percentage (9% for 2017/18) to the individual's profits between the lower profits limit (£8,164 for 2017/18) and the upper profits limit (£45,000 for 2017/18). Additional rate contributions are 2% (for 2017/18) on profits above that limit.

3.3 Example: Class 4 contributions

If a sole trader had profits of £17,020 for 2017/18 their Class 4 NIC liability would be as follows.

	£
Profits	17,020
Less lower profits limit	(8,164)
	8,856

Class 4 NICs = 9% × £8,856 = £797 (main only)

3.4 Example: Additional Class 4 contributions

If an individual's profits are £49,000, additional Class 4 NICs are due on the excess over the upper profits limit. Thus the amount payable in 2017/18 is as follows.

	£
Profits (upper limit)	45,000
Less lower limit	(8,164)
	36,836
Main rate Class 4 NICs 9% × £36,836	3,315
Additional rate Class 4 NICs £(49,000 – 45,000) = £4,000 × 2%	80
	3,395

Class 4 NICs are collected by HMRC through the self assessment system. They are paid at the same time as the associated income tax liability and so are part of payments on account and balancing payments. We look at the self assessment system in detail later in this Study Text.

Chapter Roundup

- Class 1 national insurance contributions (NICs) are payable by employees and employers on earnings.

- The employment allowance enables an employer to reduce its total Class 1 employer's contributions by up to £3,000 per tax year.

- Class 1A NICs are payable by employers on benefits provided for employees.

- The self-employed pay Class 2 and Class 4 NICs. Class 2 NICs are paid at a flat weekly rate. Class 4 NICs are based on the level of the individual's profits.

Quick Quiz

1   What NICs are payable by employers and employees?

2   Purple Ltd has one employee, Frank, who is also a director of the company. In 2017/18, Purple Ltd pays Frank an annual salary of £37,000. What are the Class 1 employer's contributions payable by Purple Ltd for 2017/18?

    A   £979
    B   £5,106
    C   £3,979
    D   £2,106

3   On what are Class 1A NICs based?

4   Class 2 NICs are paid by an employer. True/False?

5   How are Class 4 NICs calculated?

Answers to Quick Quiz

1   Employees –   Class 1 employee's contributions

    Employers –   Class 1 employer's contributions
                  Class 1A contributions

2   C. £(37,000 – 8,164) = 28,836 × 13.8% = £3,979. The employment allowance is not available Frank is the sole employed earner and a director of Purple Ltd.

3   Class 1A NICs are based on taxable benefits paid to employees.

4   False. Class 2 contributions are paid by the self-employed.

5   The main rate is a fixed percentage (9% in 2017/18) of an individual's tax profits between an upper profits limit and lower profits limit. The additional rate (2%) applies above the upper profits limit.

Now try the questions below from the Practice Question Bank

Number	Type	Marks	Time
Q76	Section A	2	4 mins
Q77	Section A	2	4 mins
Q78	Section A	2	4 mins
Q79	Section B	2	4 mins
Q80	Section B	2	4 mins
Q81	Section B	2	4 mins
Q82	Section B	2	4 mins
Q83	Section B	2	4 mins
Q84	Section C	15	27 mins

Chargeable gains for individuals

13

Computing chargeable gains

Topic list	Syllabus reference
1 Chargeable persons, disposals and assets	C1(a), (b)
2 Computing a gain or loss	C2(a), (b)
3 The annual exempt amount	C5(a)
4 Capital losses	C2(b)
5 Capital gains tax payable by individuals	C5(a), C6(b)
6 Transfers between spouses/civil partners	C2(c), C6(b)
7 Part disposals	C2(d)
8 The damage, loss or destruction of an asset	C2(e)

Introduction

Now that we have completed our study of the income tax and national insurance liabilities, we turn our attention to the capital gains tax computation. We deal with individuals in this chapter. Chargeable gains for companies are dealt with later in this Study Text.

We look at the circumstances in which a chargeable gain or allowable loss may arise. Then we look at the detailed calculation of the gain or loss on a disposal of an asset.

We then consider the annual exempt amount and look at the relief for capital losses, including the interaction between capital losses brought forward and the annual exempt amount. This enables us to compute capital gains tax (CGT) payable by individuals.

Following on from this, we start to identify the different types of disposals you may be presented with in the exam. We look first at part disposals. If only part of an asset has been disposed of we need to know how to allocate the cost between the part disposed of and the part retained.

Finally, for this chapter we consider the damage or destruction of an asset and the receipt of compensation or insurance proceeds, and look at the reliefs available where the proceeds are applied in restoring or replacing the asset.

In the following chapters we look at further rules, including those for disposals of shares, and various CGT reliefs that may be available.

Study guide

		Intellectual level
C1	**The scope of the taxation of capital gains**	
(a)	Describe the scope of capital gains tax.	2
(b)	Recognise those assets which are exempt.	1
C2	**The basic principles of computing gains and losses**	
(a)	Compute and explain the treatment of capital gains.	2
(b)	Compute and explain the treatment of capital losses.	2
(c)	Understand the treatment of transfers between a husband and wife or between a couple in a civil partnership.	2
(d)	Understand the amount of allowable expenditure for a part disposal.	2
(e)	Recognise the treatment where an asset is damaged, lost or destroyed, and the implications of receiving insurance proceeds and reinvesting such proceeds.	2
C5	**The computation of capital gains tax**	
(a)	Compute the amount of capital gains tax payable.	2
C6	**The use of exemptions and reliefs in deferring and minimising tax liabilities arising on the disposal of capital assets**	
(b)	Basic capital gains tax planning.	2

Exam guide

Section A questions on the topics in this chapter may include dealing with losses or computing the amount of capital gains tax payable. You may have to deal with a number of disposals in a Section B question. You might have to prepare a detailed capital gains computation for either an individual or company in Section C. Learn the basic layout, so that slotting in the figures becomes automatic. Then in the exam you will be able to turn your attention to the particular points raised in the question. The A/(A+B) formula for part disposals must be learnt.

Exam focus point

ACCA's article **Chargeable gains,** written by a member of the Taxation (TX – UK) examining team, in Part 1 looks at **chargeable gains** in either a **personal or corporate context**. Part 2 focuses on **shares, reliefs,** and the way in which **gains made by limited companies are taxed.**

1 Chargeable persons, disposals and assets

FAST FORWARD

A gain is chargeable if there is a chargeable disposal of a chargeable asset by a chargeable person.

Key term

For a chargeable gain to arise there must be:

- A **chargeable person**; and
- A **chargeable disposal**; and
- A **chargeable asset**

otherwise no charge to tax occurs.

1.1 Chargeable persons

Capital gains are chargeable on individuals and companies.

The following are chargeable persons.

- **Individuals**
- **Companies**

UK resident individuals are chargeable persons in relation to the disposal of assets situated anywhere in the world. Residence is defined for capital gains tax (CGT) in the same way as for income tax (see Section 1.1 in Chapter 2).

The computation of capital gains arising on overseas assets is **not examinable** in Taxation (TX – UK).

We will look at the taxation of chargeable gains on companies later in this Study Text. Note that individuals pay CGT on capital gains, whilst companies bring chargeable gains into their corporation tax computation and pay corporation tax on them.

1.2 Chargeable disposals

The following are chargeable disposals.

- **Sales of assets or parts of assets**
- **Gifts of assets or parts of assets**
- **The loss or destruction of assets**

A chargeable disposal occurs on the date of the contract (where there is one, whether written or oral), or the date of a conditional contract becoming unconditional. This may differ from the date of transfer of the asset. However, when a capital sum is received for example on the loss or destruction of an asset, the disposal takes place on the day the sum is received.

Where a disposal involves an acquisition by someone else, the date of acquisition for that person is the same as the date of disposal.

Transfers of assets on death are exempt disposals.

1.3 Chargeable assets

All forms of property, wherever in the world they are situated, are chargeable assets unless they are specifically designated as exempt (see further below).

1.4 Exempt assets

The following are exempt assets.

- **Motor vehicles** suitable for private use
- **National Savings and Investments certificates** and **premium bonds**
- **Gilt-edged securities (treasury stock)**
- **Qualifying corporate bonds (QCBs)**
- **Certain chattels**
- **Investments held in individual savings accounts (ISAs)**
- Foreign currency bank accounts held by individuals
- Decorations for bravery where awarded, not purchased
- Damages for personal or professional injury
- Debts (except debts on a security)

If an asset is an exempt asset any gain is not chargeable and any loss is not allowable.

In the exam, if you think that an asset is exempt just state this – don't waste time working out a gain or loss.

2 Computing a gain or loss

A gain or loss is computed by taking the proceeds and deducting the cost. Incidental costs of acquisition and disposal are deducted together with any enhancement expenditure reflected in the state and nature of the asset at the date of disposal.

2.1 Basic calculation

A gain (or an allowable loss) is generally calculated as follows.

	£
Disposal consideration	45,000
Less incidental costs of disposal	(400)
Net proceeds	44,600
Less allowable costs	(21,000)
Gain	23,600

Usually the disposal consideration is the proceeds of sale of the asset, but a disposal is deemed to take place at market value:

- Where the disposal is not a bargain at arm's length
- Where the disposal is made for a consideration which cannot be valued
- Where the disposal is by way of a gift

Special valuation rules apply for shares (see later in this Study Text).

Incidental costs of disposal may include:

- Valuation fees
- Estate agency fees
- Advertising costs
- Legal costs

Allowable costs include:

- The original cost of acquisition
- Incidental costs of acquisition
- Capital expenditure incurred in enhancing the asset

Enhancement expenditure is capital expenditure which enhances the value of the asset and is reflected in the state or nature of the asset at the time of disposal, or expenditure incurred in establishing, preserving or defending title to, or a right over, the asset. Excluded from this category are:

- Costs of repairs and maintenance
- Costs of insurance
- Any expenditure deductible from trading profits
- Any expenditure met by public funds (for example council grants)

Question   Calculating the gain

Joanne bought a piece of land as an investment for £20,000. The legal costs of purchase were £250. Joanne spent £2,000 on installing drainage pipes on the land which enhanced its value.

Joanne sold the land on 12 December 2017 for £35,000. She incurred estate agency fees of £700 and legal costs of £500 on the sale.

Calculate Joanne's gain on sale.

	£
Proceeds of sale	35,000
Less: Costs of disposal £(700 + 500)	(1,200)
	33,800
Less: Costs of acquisition £(20,000 + 250)	(20,250)
Costs of enhancement	(2,000)
Gain	11,550

3 The annual exempt amount

FAST FORWARD ▶ An individual is entitled to an annual exempt amount for each tax year.

There is an annual exempt amount for each tax year. For each individual for 2017/18 it is £11,300.

The annual exempt amount is deducted from the **chargeable gains** for the year after the deduction of losses and other reliefs. The resulting amount is the individual's **taxable gains**.

An individual who has gains taxable at more than one rate of tax may deduct the annual exempt amount for that year in the way that produces the lowest possible tax charge.

4 Capital losses

FAST FORWARD ▶ Losses are set off against gains of the same year and any excess carried forward. Brought forward losses are only set off to reduce net gains down to the amount of the annual exempt amount.

4.1 Allowable losses of the same year

Allowable capital losses arising in a tax year are deducted from gains arising in the same tax year.

An individual who has gains taxable at more than one rate of tax may deduct any allowable losses in the way that produces the lowest possible tax charge.

Any loss which cannot be set off is carried forward to set against future gains. Losses must be used as soon as possible (but see below).

4.2 Allowable losses brought forward

Allowable losses brought forward are only set off to reduce net current year gains to the annual exempt amount. No set-off is made if net chargeable gains for the current year do not exceed the annual exempt amount.

Net current year gains are current year gains less current year allowable losses. Note that if a claim is made to set trading losses against capital gains in any tax year (as we saw earlier in this Study Text), they will be set off before capital losses brought forward. Unlike capital losses brought forward, trading losses cannot be restricted to preserve the annual exempt amount.

4.3 Example: The use of losses

(a) George has gains for 2017/18 of £13,000 and allowable losses of £6,000. As the losses are **current year losses** they must be fully relieved against the £13,000 of gains to produce net gains of £7,000 despite the fact that net gains are below the annual exempt amount.

(b)   Bob has gains of £15,200 for 2017/18 and allowable losses brought forward of £6,000. Bob restricts his loss relief to £3,900 so as to leave net gains of £(15,200 – 3,900) = £11,300, which will be exactly covered by his annual exempt amount for 2017/18. The remaining £2,100 of losses will be carried forward to 2018/19.

(c)   Tom has gains of £10,500 for 2017/18 and losses brought forward from 2016/17 of £4,000. He will not use any of his brought forward losses in 2017/18 and instead will carry forward all of his losses to 2018/19. His gains of £10,500 are covered by his annual exempt amount for 2017/18.

5 Capital gains tax payable by individuals   9/16

FAST FORWARD

Capital gains tax (CGT) is usually payable at the rate of 10% or 20% depending on the individual's taxable income.

PER alert

One of the competencies you require to fulfil Performance Objective 15 Tax computations and assessments of the PER is to prepare or contribute to the computation or assessment of tax computations for individuals. You can apply the knowledge you obtain from this section of the Study Text to help to demonstrate this competence.

5.1 Rates of tax on most taxable gains

Taxable gains on gains, other than those on residential property, are usually chargeable to capital gains tax at a rate depending on the individual's taxable income. The basic rate band is treated as being used first by income. Gains are taxed at 20% if the individual's taxable income exceeds the basic rate limit (ie they are a higher rate or additional rate taxpayer). If the individual's taxable income falls below the basic rate limit (ie they are a basic rate taxpayer), gains are taxed at 10% up to the basic rate limit and 20% above the limit.

The following diagram shows you how to apply these rules:

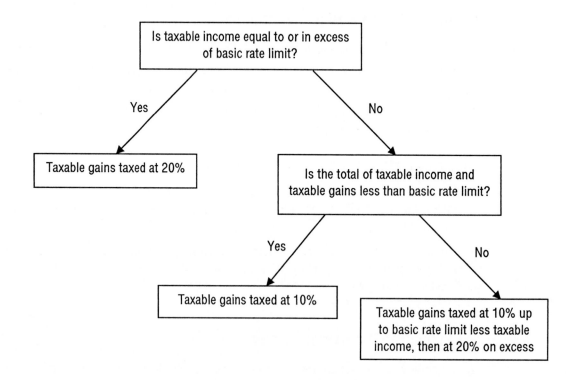

Remember that the basic rate band limit will usually be £33,500 for 2017/18 but the limit will be increased by the gross amount of gift aid donations and personal pension contributions.

Mo has taxable income of £24,130 in 2017/18. He made personal pension contributions of £242 (net) per month during 2017/18. In December 2017, he makes a chargeable gain of £29,200 on the disposal of some shares. The gain does not qualify for entrepreneurs' relief (see later in this Study Text).

Calculate the CGT payable by Mo for 2017/18.

Answer

	£
Chargeable gain	29,200
Less annual exempt amount	(11,300)
Taxable gain	17,900
Basic rate limit	33,500
Add personal pension contributions £(242 × 12) = £2,904 × 100/80	3,630
Increased basic rate limit	37,130
CGT	
£(37,130 – 24,130) = £13,000 @ 10%	1,300
£(17,900 – 13,000) = £4,900 @ 20%	980
Total CGT payable	2,280

5.2 Rates of tax on residential property gains

FAST FORWARD

Capital gains tax is payable at the rate of 18% or 28% on residential property gains depending on the individual's taxable income.

Residential property includes an interest in a dwelling such as a house or flat. It also includes an interest in a contract acquired 'off-plan' where the property has not yet been constructed.

Taxable gains on residential property which are not fully exempt under principal private residence relief (see later in this Study Text) **are chargeable to capital gains tax at the rate of 18% or 28% depending on the individual's taxable income for the tax year.** Residential property gains within the basic rate band are taxed at 18% and those in excess of the basic rate limit (adjusted as described in the previous section) are taxed at 28%.

If an individual has a mixture of residential property gains and gains on other assets (other than those qualifying for entrepreneurs' relief – see later in this Study Text), **the annual exempt amount and allowable losses should be deducted first from residential property gains and secondly from gains on other assets.**

Where the individual has unused basic rate band, it does not matter whether the residential property gains or the other gains are taxed first. This is because the differential between the rates in both cases is 10%.

Fran has taxable income of £24,500 in 2017/18. In August 2017, she makes a chargeable gain of £15,500 on the sale of some shares. In March 2018, she makes a chargeable gain of £19,200 on the disposal of a residential property which is not covered by principal private residence relief. Calculate the CGT payable by Fran for 2017/18.

Answer

	Other gain £	Residential property £
Shares	15,500	
Residential property		19,200
Less annual exempt amount (best use)		(11,300)
Taxable gains	15,500	7,900
CGT		
If tax residential property gain first		
£7,900 @ 18%		1,422
£1,100 (33, 500 – 24,500 – 7,900) @ 10%		110
£14,400 (15,500 – 1,100) @ 20%		2,880
Total CGT		4,412
If tax other gain first		
£9,000 (33,500 – 24,500) @ 10%		900
£6,500 (15,500 – 9,000) @ 20%		1,300
£7,900 @ 28%		2,212
Total CGT		4,412

Exam focus point

In the exam, **you only need to compute the CGT payable in one way** eg residential property gains then other gains. It is **not necessary** to show that the same amount of CGT is payable if the gains are taxed the other way around.

5.3 CGT on entrepreneurs' relief gains

There is also a special 10% rate of tax for gains for which the taxpayer claims entrepreneurs' relief. We will look at this situation later in this Study Text.

5.4 Payment date for CGT   12/16

Capital gains tax is payable by 31 January following the end of the tax year (ie by 31 January 2019 for the tax year 2017/18). We look at payment of capital gains tax in more detail later in this Study Text.

5.5 Basic CGT planning   12/16

FAST FORWARD

Basic CGT planning involves maximising the use of the annual exempt amount, ensuring the lowest rate of tax applies and timing of payment of tax.

Basic CGT planning usually involves three considerations.

The first consideration is that an individual should make use of the annual exempt amount. For example, if there is a gain which already uses the annual exempt amount in the tax year, it may be advisable to delay making another gain until the next tax year.

The second consideration is the rate of tax in relation to the individual's taxable income. Where possible, gains should be made in the tax year in which the individual has the lowest amount of taxable income, in particular where they have part of the basic rate band unused.

The third consideration is the timing of the payment of CGT. It may be better to make a gain early in a tax year rather than late in a tax year to give the longest gap between receiving the proceeds and paying the tax due.

6 Transfers between spouses/civil partners 9/16

FAST FORWARD

Disposals between spouses or members of a civil partnership are made on a no gain no loss basis and do not give rise to a chargeable gain or allowable loss.

Spouses/civil partners are taxed as two separate people. Each has an annual exempt amount, and losses of one spouse/civil partner cannot be set against gains of the other.

Disposals between spouses/civil partners living together give rise to no gain or loss, whatever actual price (if any) was charged by the transferor. **This means that there is no chargeable gain or allowable loss, and the transferee takes over the transferor's cost.** This is not the same as the disposal being exempt from CGT.

Since transfers between spouses/civil partners are on a no gain no loss basis, it may be beneficial to transfer the whole or part of an asset to the spouse/civil partner with an unused annual exempt amount or with taxable income below the basic rate limit.

Question

Inter spouse transfer

Harry is a higher rate taxpayer who always makes gains of at least £20,000 each year on disposals of investments. His wife, Margaret, has taxable income of £3,630 each year and has no chargeable assets.

Harry bought a plot of land for £150,000 in 2013. He gave it to Margaret when it was worth £180,000 on 10 May 2016. Margaret sold it on 27 August 2017 for £190,000. The land does not qualify for entrepreneurs' relief and is not residential property.

Calculate any chargeable gains arising to Harry and Margaret and show the tax saving arising from the transfer between Harry and Margaret, followed by the disposal by Margaret, instead of a disposal in August 2017 by Harry.

Answer

The disposal from Harry to Margaret in May 2016 is a no gain no loss disposal. Harry has no chargeable gain, and the cost for Margaret is Harry's original cost.

The gain on the sale by Margaret in August 2017 is:

	£
Proceeds of sale	190,000
Less cost	(150,000)
Gain	40,000

If Harry had made the disposal in August 2017, the whole of the gain would have been taxed at 20%.

Margaret's gain will be reduced by her annual exempt amount, saving tax at 20% on that amount compared with the situation where Harry makes the disposal.

Margaret also has £(33,500 − 3,630) = £29,870 of her basic rate band remaining. She will be taxed at 10% on the gain within the basic rate band, instead of 20% if Harry makes the disposal.

The tax saving is therefore:

	£
Tax saved on annual exempt amount £11,300 @ 20%	2,260
Tax saved at basic rate £(40,000 – 11,300) = £28,700 @ (20 – 10)%	2,870
Tax saving on disposal by Margaret instead of Harry	5,130

7 Part disposals

On a part disposal, the cost must be apportioned between the part disposed of and the part retained.

The disposal of part of a chargeable asset is a chargeable event. The chargeable gain (or allowable loss) is computed by deducting a fraction of the original cost of the whole asset from the disposal value. The balance of the cost is carried forward until the eventual disposal of the remaining part of the asset.

Exam formula

The fraction is:

$$\text{Cost} \times \frac{A}{A+B} = \frac{\text{Value of the part disposed of}}{\text{Value of the part disposed of} + \text{Market value of the remainder}}$$

In this fraction, A is the proceeds **before** deducting incidental costs of disposal.

The part disposal fraction should not be applied indiscriminately. Any expenditure incurred wholly in respect of a particular part of an asset should be treated as an allowable deduction in full for that part and not apportioned. An example of this is incidental selling expenses, which are wholly attributable to the part disposed of.

Question

Part disposal

Hedley owns a four hectare plot of land which originally cost him £150,000. He sold one hectare in July 2017 for £60,000. The incidental costs of sale were £3,000. The market value of the three hectares remaining is estimated to be £180,000. What is the gain on the sale of the one hectare?

Answer

The amount of the cost attributable to the part sold is:

$$\frac{60,000}{60,000+180,000} \times £150,000 = £37,500$$

	£
Proceeds	60,000
Less disposal cost	(3,000)
Net proceeds of sale	57,000
Less cost (see above)	(37,500)
Gain	19,500

8 The damage, loss or destruction of an asset

The gain which would otherwise arise on the receipt of insurance proceeds may, subject to certain conditions, be deferred.

8.1 Destruction or loss of an asset

If an asset is destroyed any compensation or insurance monies received will normally be brought into an ordinary CGT disposal computation as proceeds.

If all the proceeds are applied for the replacement of the asset within 12 months, any gain can be deducted from the cost of the replacement asset. The replacement asset should have a similar function to the destroyed asset and be a similar type of asset.

If only part of the proceeds are used, the gain immediately chargeable can be limited to the amount not used. The rest of the gain is then deducted from the cost of the replacement.

Question   Asset destroyed

Fiona bought a painting for £25,000. It was destroyed in July 2017. Insurance proceeds were £34,000, and Fiona spent £30,500 on a replacement painting in January 2018. Compute the gain immediately chargeable and the base cost of the new painting.

Answer

	£
Proceeds	34,000
Less cost	(25,000)
Gain	9,000
Gain immediately chargeable £(34,000 – 30,500)	(3,500)
Deduction from base cost	5,500

The base cost of the new painting is £(30,500 – 5,500) = £25,000.

8.2 Damage to an asset   12/16

If an asset is damaged then the receipt of any compensation or insurance monies received will normally be treated as a part disposal.

If all the proceeds are applied in restoring the asset the taxpayer can elect to disregard the part disposal. The proceeds will instead be deducted from the cost of the asset.

Question   Asset damaged

Frank bought an investment property for £100,000 in May 2017. It was damaged two and a half months later. Insurance proceeds of £20,000 were received in November 2017, and Frank spent a total of £25,000 on restoring the property. Prior to restoration the property was worth £120,000. Compute the gain immediately chargeable, if any, and the base cost of the restored property assuming Frank elects for there to be no part disposal.

How would your answer differ if no election were made?

As the proceeds have been applied in restoring the property Frank has elected to disregard the part disposal.

The base cost of the restored property is £(100,000 – 20,000 + 25,000) = £105,000.

If no election were made, the receipt of the proceeds would be a part disposal in November 2017:

	£
Proceeds	20,000
Less cost £100,000 × 20,000/(20,000 + 120,000)	(14,286)
Gain	5,714

The base cost of the restored asset is £(100,000 – 14,286 + 25,000) = £110,714.

Assuming this is Frank's only disposal in the tax year, the gain is covered by the annual exempt amount. It may therefore be preferable not to make the election.

Chapter Roundup

- A gain is chargeable if there is a chargeable disposal of a chargeable asset by a chargeable person.

- Capital gains are chargeable on individuals and companies.

- A gain or loss is computed by taking the proceeds and deducting the cost. Incidental costs of acquisition and disposal are deducted together with any enhancement expenditure reflected in the state and nature of the asset at the date of disposal.

- An individual is entitled to an annual exempt amount for each tax year.

- Losses are set off against gains of the same year and any excess carried forward. Brought forward losses are only set off to reduce net gains down to the amount of the annual exempt amount.

- Capital gains tax (CGT) is usually payable at the rate of 10% or 20% depending on the individual's taxable income.

- CGT is payable at the rate of 18% or 28% on residential property gains depending on the individual's taxable income.

- Basic CGT planning involves maximising the use of the annual exempt amount, ensuring the lowest rate of tax applies and timing of payment of tax.

- Disposals between spouses or members of a civil partnership are made on a no gain no loss basis and do not give rise to a chargeable gain or allowable loss.

- On a part disposal, the cost must be apportioned between the part disposed of and the part retained.

- The gain which would otherwise arise on the receipt of insurance proceeds may, subject to certain conditions, be deferred.

Quick Quiz

1   Give some examples of chargeable disposals.

2   On what assets does a UK resident pay CGT?

3   What is enhancement expenditure?

4   To what extent must allowable losses be set against chargeable gains?

5   At what rate or rates do individuals pay CGT on gains which are not residential property gains and do not qualify for entrepreneurs' relief?

6   Ten acres of land are sold for £15,000 out of 25 acres. Original cost for the 25 acres was £9,000. Costs of sale are £2,000. Rest of land valued at £30,000. What is the total amount deductible from proceeds?

    A   £2,000
    B   £2,872
    C   £5,000
    D   £5,600

7   Emma drops and destroys a vase. She receives compensation for £2,000 from her insurance company. How can she avoid a charge to CGT arising?

1   The following are chargeable disposals:

    - Sales of assets or parts of assets
    - Gifts of assets or parts of assets
    - Receipts of capital sums following the loss or destruction of an asset

2   All assets, whether situated in the UK or abroad, unless specifically exempt.

3   Enhancement expenditure is capital expenditure enhancing the value of the asset and reflected in the state/nature of the asset at disposal, or expenditure incurred in establishing, preserving or defending title to asset.

4   Current year losses must be set off against gains in full, even if this reduces net gains below the annual exempt amount. Losses brought forward are set off to bring down gains to the level of the annual exempt amount.

5   Individuals pay CGT at the rate of 10% or 20% on most taxable gains depending on their taxable income.

6   C. $\dfrac{15,000}{15,000+30,000} \times £9,000 = £3,000 + £2,000$ (costs of disposal) = £5,000

7   Emma can avoid a charge to CGT on receipt of the compensation by investing at least £2,000 in a replacement asset within 12 months.

Now try the questions below from the Practice Question Bank

Number	Type	Marks	Time
Q85	Section A	2	4 mins
Q86	Section A	2	4 mins
Q87	Section A	2	4 mins
Q88	Section C	10	18 mins

Chattels and the principal private residence exemption

Topic list	Syllabus reference
1 Chattels	C3(a), (b)
2 Wasting assets	C3(a), (b)
3 Private residences	C3(c), C6(b)

Introduction

In the previous chapter we have considered the basic rules for the capital gains computation and the calculation of capital gains tax (CGT) payable by an individual, together with the rules for part disposals and assets damaged or destroyed.

We now turn our attention to specific assets, starting with chattels. Where there is a disposal of low value assets, the chattels rules may apply to restrict the gain or allowable loss. The gain may even be exempt in certain circumstances. We look at the detailed rules.

The highest value item that an individual is likely to sell is his home. We look at the rules to see when the gain may be wholly or partly exempt.

In the next chapter we will consider the reliefs specifically available on business assets, and later we will turn our attention to the special rules for shares.

Study guide

		Intellectual level
C3	**Gains and losses on the disposal of movable and immovable property**	
(a)	Identify when chattels and wasting assets are exempt.	1
(b)	Compute the chargeable gain when a chattel or a wasting asset is disposed of.	2
(c)	Calculate the chargeable gain when a principal private residence is disposed of.	2
C6	**The use of exemptions and reliefs in deferring and minimising tax liabilities arising on the disposal of capital assets**	
(b)	Basic capital gains tax planning	2

Exam guide

You are quite likely to come across a question on either chattels or the reliefs available on the disposal of a principal private residence in any of Sections A, B or C.

With chattels always look for the exemption for wasting chattels, a restriction of the gain if proceeds exceed £6,000, or a restriction of loss relief if proceeds are less than £6,000. The rules for chattels apply to companies as well as individuals, but watch out for assets on which capital allowances have been given.

On the disposal of a principal private residence if there has been any non-occupation or business use make a schedule of the relevant dates before you start to calculate the gain in case it turns out to be wholly exempt.

1 Chattels

1.1 What is a chattel?

Key terms

A **chattel** is tangible moveable property.

A **wasting asset** is an asset with an estimated remaining useful life of 50 years or less.

Plant and machinery, whose predictable useful life is always deemed to be less than 50 years, is an example of a wasting chattel (unless it is immoveable, in which case it will be wasting but not a chattel). Machinery includes, in addition to its ordinary meaning, motor vehicles (unless exempt as cars), railway and traction engines, engine-powered boats and clocks.

1.2 Wasting chattels

 FAST FORWARD

Gains on most wasting chattels are exempt and losses are not allowable.

Wasting chattels are exempt (so that there are no chargeable gains and no allowable losses).

There is one exception to this: assets used for the purpose of a trade, profession or vocation in respect of which capital allowances have been or could have been claimed. This means that items of plant and machinery used in a trade are not exempt merely on the grounds that they are wasting (see below). However, cars are always exempt.

1.3 Gains on non-wasting chattels

When a non-wasting chattel is sold for less than £6,000, any gain is exempt. There is marginal relief for gains where sale proceeds exceed £6,000.

If a chattel is not exempt under the wasting chattels rule, any gain arising on its disposal will still be exempt if the asset is sold for gross proceeds of £6,000 or less, even if capital allowances were claimed on it.

If sale proceeds exceed £6,000, any gain is limited to a maximum of 5/3 × (gross proceeds – £6,000).

Question
Chattels: gains

Adam purchased a Chippendale chair for £1,800. On 10 October 2017 he sold the chair at auction for £6,300 (which was net of the auctioneer's 10% commission). What is the gain?

Answer

	£
Proceeds (£6,300 × 100/90)	7,000
Less incidental costs of sale	(700)
Net proceeds	6,300
Less cost	(1,800)
Gain	4,500

The maximum gain is 5/3 × £(7,000 – 6,000) = £1,667.

The chargeable gain is the lower of £4,500 and £1,667, so it is £1,667.

1.4 Losses on non-wasting chattels

A loss on the sale of a non-wasting chattel is restricted where proceeds are less than £6,000.

Where a chattel which is not exempt under the wasting chattels rule is sold for less than £6,000 and a loss arises, the allowable loss is restricted by assuming that the chattel was sold for gross proceeds of £6,000. This rule cannot turn a loss into a gain, only reduce the loss, perhaps to zero.

Question
Chattels: losses

Eve purchased a rare first edition for £8,000 which she sold in October 2017 at auction for £2,700 (which was net of 10% commission). Compute the gain or loss.

Answer

	£
Proceeds (assumed)	6,000
Less incidental costs of disposal (£2,700 × 10/90)	(300)
	5,700
Less cost	(8,000)
Allowable loss	(2,300)

1.5 Chattels and capital allowances

> The CGT rules are modified for assets eligible for capital allowances.

The wasting chattels exemption does not apply to chattels on which capital allowances have been claimed or could have been claimed. The chattels rules based on £6,000 do apply.

Where a chattel on which capital allowances have been obtained is sold at a loss, the allowable cost for chargeable gains purposes is reduced by the lower of the loss and the net amount of allowances given (taking into account any balancing allowances or charges). **The result is no gain and no loss.** This is because relief for the loss has already been given through the capital allowances computation.

If the chattel is sold at a gain the cost is not adjusted for capital allowances. This is because the capital allowances will have been clawed back through the balancing charge.

2 Wasting assets   12/16

> When a wasting asset is disposed of its cost must be depreciated over its estimated useful life.

2.1 Introduction

A wasting asset is one which has an estimated remaining useful life of 50 years or less and whose original value will depreciate over time. Examples of such assets are copyrights and registered designs.

2.2 The computation

The normal capital gains computation is amended to reflect the anticipated depreciation over the life of the asset.

The cost is written down on a straight line basis, and it is this depreciated cost which is deducted in the computation.

Thus if a taxpayer acquires a wasting asset with a remaining life of 40 years and disposes of it after 15 years, so that 25 years of useful life remain, only 25/40 of the cost is deducted in the computation.

Any enhancement expenditure must be separately depreciated.

2.3 Example: Wasting asset

Harry bought a copyright on 1 July 2013 for £20,000. The copyright is due to expire in July 2033. He sold it on 1 July 2017 for £22,000.

Harry's gain is:

	£
Proceeds of sale	22,000
Less depreciated cost £20,000 × 16/20	(16,000)
Gain	6,000

2.4 Capital allowances

If capital allowances have been given on a wasting asset its cost is not depreciated over time.

BPP
LEARNING MEDIA

3.1 General principles

A gain arising on the sale of an individual's only or main private residence (sometimes called their **principal private residence or PPR) is exempt from CGT.** The exemption covers total grounds, including the house, of up to half a hectare. The total grounds can exceed half a hectare if the house is large enough to warrant it, but if not, the gain on the excess grounds is taxable.

For the exemption to be available the taxpayer must have occupied the property as a residence rather than just as temporary accommodation.

3.2 Occupation

The gain is wholly exempt where the owner has occupied the whole of the residence throughout their period of ownership. Where occupation has been for only part of the period, the proportion of the gain exempted is

$$\text{Total gain} \times \frac{\text{Period of occupation}}{\text{Total period of ownership}}$$

The **last 18 months of ownership are always** treated as **a period of occupation**, if at some time the residence has been the taxpayer's main residence, even if within those last 18 months the taxpayer also has another house which is their actual principal private residence.

Where a loss arises and all, or a proportion of, any gain would have been exempt, all or the same proportion of the loss is not allowable.

3.3 Deemed occupation

The **period of occupation is also deemed to include certain periods of absence, provided the individual had no other exempt residence at the time and the period of absence was at some time both preceded and followed by a period of actual occupation.** The last 18 months rule (see above) takes precedence over this rule.

These periods of **deemed occupation** are:

(a)   **Any period** (or periods taken together) of absence, **for any reason, up to three years**; and

(b)   **Any periods** during which the owner was **required by their employment** (ie employed taxpayer) **to live abroad**; and

(c)   **Any period** (or periods taken together) **up to four years** during which the owner was **required to live elsewhere due to their work** (ie both employed and self employed taxpayer) so that they could not occupy their private residence.

It does not matter if the residence is let during the absence.

Exempt periods of absence must normally be preceded and followed by periods of actual occupation. This rule is relaxed where an individual who has been required to work abroad or elsewhere (ie (b) and (c) above) is unable to resume residence in their home because the terms of their employment require them to work elsewhere.

Abel purchased a house on 1 April 1992 for £88,200. He lived in the house until 31 December 1993. He then worked abroad for two years before returning to the UK to live in the house again on 1 January 1996. He stayed in the house until 30 June 2012 before retiring and moving out to live with friends in Spain until the house was sold on 31 December 2017 for £175,000.

Calculate Abel's capital gains tax payable for 2017/18, assuming that this is the only disposal that he makes in the tax year and that he is a higher rate taxpayer.

Answer

	£
Proceeds	175,000
Less cost	(88,200)
Gain before PPR exemption	86,800
Less PPR exemption (working)	
$\dfrac{261}{309} \times £86,800$	(73,317)
Chargeable gain	13,483
Less annual exempt amount	(11,300)
Taxable gain	2,183
CGT on £2,183 @ 28% (residential property rate)	611

Working

Exempt and chargeable periods

Period	Total months	Exempt months	Chargeable Months
(i) April 1992 – December 1993 (occupied)	21	21	0
(ii) January 1994 – December 1995 (working abroad)	24	24	0
(iii) January 1996 – June 2012 (occupied)	198	198	0
(iv) July 2012 – June 2016 (see below)	48	0	48
(v) July 2016 – December 2017 (last 18 months)	18	18	0
	309	261	48

No part of the period from July 2012 to June 2016 can be covered by the exemption for three years of absence for any reason because it is not followed at any time by actual occupation.

Exam focus point

> To help you to answer questions such as that above it is useful to draw up a table showing the period of ownership, exempt months (actual/deemed occupation) and chargeable months (non-occupation) similar to that in the working.

3.4 Business use

Where part of a residence is used exclusively for business purposes throughout the entire period of ownership, the gain attributable to use of that part is taxable. The 'last 18 months always exempt' rule does not apply to that part.

 Question   Business use of PPR

Smail purchased a property for £35,000 on 31 May 2011 and began operating a dental practice from that date in one quarter of the house. He closed the dental practice on 31 December 2017, selling the house on that date for £130,000.

Compute the gain arising.

	£
Proceeds	130,000
Less cost	(35,000)
Gain before PPR exemption	95,000
Less PPR exemption 0.75 × £95,000	(71,250)
Gain	23,750

Exemption is lost on one quarter throughout the period of ownership (including the last 18 months) because of the use of that fraction for business purposes.

If part of a residence was used for business purposes for only part of the period of ownership, the gain is apportioned between chargeable and exempt parts. If the business part was **at some time** used as part of the residence, the gain apportioned to that part **will** qualify for the last 18 months exemption.

3.5 Letting relief

The principal private residence exemption is extended to any gain accruing while the property is let, up to a certain limit. The two main circumstances in which the letting exemption applies are:

(a) When the owner is absent and lets the property, where the absence is not a deemed period of occupation.

(b) When the owner lets part of the property while still occupying the rest of it. The absence from the let part cannot be a deemed period of occupation, because the owner has another residence (the rest of the property). However, the let part will qualify for the last 18 months exemption **if** the let part has **at some time** been part of the only or main residence.

In both cases the letting must be for residential use. **The extra exemption is restricted to the lowest of:**

(a) The amount of the total **gain** which is already **exempt under the PPR provisions**
(b) The gain accruing during the letting period (the **letting part of the gain**)
(c) **£40,000** (maximum)

Letting relief cannot convert a gain into an allowable loss.

If a lodger lives as a member of the owner's family, sharing their living accommodation and eating with them, the **whole** property is regarded as the owner's main residence.

Question   Letting relief (1)

Ovett purchased a house in Truro on 5 October 2003 and sold it on 5 April 2018 making a gain of £290,000.

On 5 July 2006 he had been sent to work in Edinburgh, and he did not return to his own house until 6 January 2016. The property was let out during his absence, and he lived in a flat provided for him by his employer. What is the gain arising?

	£
Gain before PPR exemption	290,000
Less PPR exemption (working)	
£290,000 × 144/174	(240,000)
	50,000

Less letting exemption: Lowest of:

(a) Gain exempt under PPR rules: £240,000

(b) Gain attributable to letting: £290,000 × $\dfrac{30}{174}$ = £50,000

(c) £40,000 (maximum)	(40,000)
Gain	10,000

Working

Period	Notes	Total ownership months	Exempt months	Chargeable Months
5.10.03–4.7.06	Actual occupation	33	33	0
5.7.06–4.7.10	Four years absence working in the UK	48	48	0
5.7.10–4.7.13	Three year of absence for any reason	36	36	0
5.7.13–5.1.16	Absent – let	30	0	30
6.1.16–5.4.18	Occupied (includes last 18 months)	27	27	0
		174	144	30

Question

Celia purchased a house on 31 March 2003 for £90,000. She sold it on 31 August 2017 for £340,000. In 2008 the house was redecorated and Celia began to live on the top floor renting out the balance of the house (constituting 60% of the total house) to tenants between 1 July 2008 and 1 January 2017. On 2 January 2017 Celia put the whole house on the market but continued to live only on the top floor until the house was sold. What is the gain arising?

Answer

	£
Proceeds	340,000
Less: Cost	(90,000)
Gain before PPR exemption	250,000
Less PPR exemption (working)	
£250,000 × $\dfrac{117.8}{173}$	(170,231)
	79,769

Less letting exemption: Lowest of:

(a) Gain exempt under PPR rules: £170,231

(b) Gain attributable to letting: £250,000 × $\dfrac{55.2}{173}$ = £79,769

(c) £40,000 (maximum)	(40,000)
Gain	39,769

Working

Period	Notes	Total ownership months	Exempt months	Chargeable months
1.4.03–30.06.08	100% of house occupied	63	63	0
1.7.08–28.2.16	40% of house occupied	92	36.8	
	60% of house let			55.2
1.3.16–31.8.17	Last 18 months treated as 100% of house occupied	18	18	0
		173	117.8	55.2

Note. The gain on the 40% of the house always occupied by Celia is fully covered by PPR relief. The other 60% of the house has not always been occupied by Celia and thus any gain on this part of the house is taxable where it relates to periods of time when Celia was not actually (or deemed to be) living in it.

Even if Celia reoccupied all floors prior to the sale, she cannot claim exemption for part of the period of letting under the three year absence for any reason rule since during this time she has a main residence which qualifies for relief (ie the rest of the house). However, she can claim exemption for the whole of the house for the last 18 months since the let part was part of her only residence prior to the letting.

Chapter Roundup

- Gains on most wasting chattels are exempt and losses are not allowable.

- When a non-wasting chattel is sold for less than £6,000, any gain is exempt. There is marginal relief for gains where sale proceeds exceed £6,000.

- A loss on the sale of a non-wasting chattel is restricted where proceeds are less than £6,000.

- The capital gains tax (CGT) rules are modified for assets eligible for capital allowances.

- When a wasting asset is disposed of its cost must be depreciated over its estimated useful life.

- There is an exemption for gains on principal private residences, but the exemption may be restricted because of periods of non-occupation or because of business use.

Quick Quiz

1   How are gains on non-wasting chattels sold for more than £6,000 restricted?

2   How are losses on non-wasting chattels sold for less than £6,000 restricted?

3   Leonie bought a copyright on 1 December 2011 for £30,000. The copyright had a life of 25 years when she bought it. She sold the copyright on 1 December 2017. What is her allowable cost for computing the gain on sale?

4   For what periods may an individual be deemed to occupy his principal private residence?

5   The maximum letting exemption is:

    A   £30,000
    B   £40,000
    C   £60,000
    D   £80,000

Answers to Quick Quiz

1   Gain restricted to 5/3 × (gross proceeds – £6,000)

2   Allowable loss restricted by deeming proceeds to be £6,000

3   £30,000 × 19/25 = £22,800. The copyright has a life of 19 years when it is sold.

4   Periods of deemed occupation are:

- Last 18 months of ownership

- Any period of absence up to three years

- Any period during which the owner was required by their employment to work abroad

- Any period up to four years during which the owner was required to live elsewhere due to their work (employed or self employed) so that they could not occupy their private residence

5   B. £40,000

Now try the questions below from the Practice Question Bank

Number	Type	Marks	Time
Q89	Section A	2	4 mins
Q90	Section A	2	4 mins
Q91	Section A	2	4 mins
Q92	Section B	2	4 mins
Q93	Section B	2	4 mins
Q94	Section B	2	4 mins
Q95	Section B	2	4 mins
Q96	Section B	2	4 mins

14: Chattels and the principal private residence exemption | Part C Chargeable gains for individuals

Business reliefs

Introduction

Having discussed the general rules for capital gains we now turn our attention to specific reliefs for businesses.

Entrepreneurs' relief is a very important relief. It applies on the sale of a business and certain trading company shares. The rate of tax payable is 10% on such disposals regardless of the taxpayer's taxable income. Investors' relief is similar to entrepreneurs' relief but applies to trading company shares held by external investors.

Another important relief is rollover relief, which enables a gain on the disposal of a business asset to be rolled over if a new asset is purchased for business use. This enables the payment of tax to be deferred until the business has actually retained the proceeds of sale uninvested so that it can meet the liability. This is the only relief that is available to both individuals and companies.

Finally, we consider the relief for gifts of business assets. This relief allows an entrepreneur to give away their business during their lifetime and pass any gains to the donee.

In the next chapter we will cover the computation of capital gains on the disposal of shares.

Study guide

		Intellectual level
C5	**The computation of capital gains tax**	
(b)	Explain and apply entrepreneurs' relief.	2
C6	**The use of exemptions and reliefs in deferring and minimising tax liabilities arising on the disposal of capital assets**	
(a)	Explain and apply capital gains tax reliefs:	
(a)(i)	Rollover relief.	2
(a)(ii)	Holdover relief for the gift of business assets.	2
(b)	Basic capital gains tax planning.	2

Exam guide

Business reliefs are an important part of the Taxation (TX – UK) exam and may be tested in any of Sections A, B or C. Rollover relief may be met in either an unincorporated business or a company context, and as it is an extremely important relief for all businesses it is likely to be examined. If you are required to compute a gain on a business asset look out for the purchase of a new asset, but carefully check the date and cost of the acquisition. Do not be caught out by the purchase of an investment property. The relief for gifts of assets is only available to individuals, and effectively passes the gain to the donee. Entrepreneurs' relief is only available to individuals but is a particularly valuable relief as it reduces the rate of capital gains tax (CGT) to 10%.

 One of the competencies you require to fulfil Performance Objective 17 Tax planning and advice of the PER is to mitigate and/or defer tax liabilities through the use of standard reliefs, exemptions and incentives. You can apply the knowledge you obtain from this chapter of the Study Text to help to demonstrate this competence.

1 Entrepreneurs' relief

 Entrepreneurs' relief applies on the disposal of a business and certain trading company shares. Gains on assets qualifying for the relief are taxed at 10%.

1.1 Conditions for entrepreneurs' relief   12/16

Entrepreneurs' relief is available where there is a **material disposal of business assets**.

A **material disposal** of business assets is:

- A disposal of the **whole or part of a business** which has been **owned by the individual** throughout the period of **one year** ending with the date of the disposal

- A disposal of **one or more assets in use for the purposes of a business at** the time at which the business **ceases to be carried on** provided that:

    - The business was owned by the individual throughout **the period of one year** ending with the date on which the business ceases to be carried on; **and**

    - The date of cessation is within **three years** ending with the date of the disposal.

- A disposal of **shares or securities of a company where** the company is the individual's **personal company**; the company is either a **trading company** or the **holding company of a trading group**;

BPP
LEARNING MEDIA

the individual is an **officer or employee** of the company (or a group company) and these conditions are met either:

- – Throughout the period of **one year** ending with the date of the disposal; **or**

- – Throughout the period of **one year** ending with the date on which the company (or group) **ceases to be a trading company (or trading group)** and that date is within the period of **three years** ending with the date of the disposal.

For the first category to apply, there has be a **disposal of the whole or part of the business as a going concern**, not just a disposal of individual assets. A business includes one carried on as a partnership of which the individual is a partner. The business must be a **trade, profession or vocation** conducted on a **commercial basis with a view to the realisation of profits**. Note that gains on all business assets on such a disposal are eligible for entrepreneurs' relief, provided the business has been owned for more than a year. This is the case regardless of how long the assets themselves have been owned.

In relation to the third category, a **personal company** in relation to an individual is one where:

- The individual holds **at least 5% of the ordinary share capital**; and

- The individual can exercise **at least 5% of the voting rights in the company** by virtue of that holding of shares.

For both the first and second category, relief is only available on **relevant business assets**. These are assets **used for the purposes of the business** and **cannot include shares and securities** or **assets held as investments**.

1.2 The operation of the relief   9/16

Where there is a material disposal of business assets which results in both gains and losses, losses are netted off against gains to give a single chargeable gain on the disposal of the business assets.

The rate of tax on this chargeable gain is 10% regardless of the level of the individual's taxable income.

An individual may use losses on assets not qualifying for entrepreneurs' relief and the annual exempt amount in the most beneficial way. This will be achieved if these amounts are set off in the following order:

(1)   **Residential property gains**
(2)   **Other gains not qualifying for entrepreneurs' relief**
(3)   **Entrepreneurs' relief gains**

The chargeable gain qualifying for entrepreneurs' relief is always treated as the lowest part of the amount on which an individual is chargeable to capital gains tax. This means chargeable gains qualifying for entrepreneurs' relief will use up any unused basic rate band before those gains that do not qualify for the relief. Although this does not affect the tax on the gain qualifying for entrepreneurs' relief (which is always at 10%), it may have an effect on the rate of tax on other taxable gains.

1.3 Example

Simon sells his business, all the assets of which qualify for entrepreneurs' relief, in September 2017. The chargeable gain arising is £10,000.

Simon also made a chargeable gain of £25,200 in December 2017 on an asset which did not qualify for entrepreneurs' relief and is not residential property.

Simon has taxable income of £16,500 in 2017/18.

The CGT payable for 2017/18 is calculated as follows:

	Gains £	CGT £
Gain qualifying for entrepreneurs' relief		
Taxable gain	10,000	
CGT @ 10%		1,000
Gain not qualifying for entrepreneurs' relief		
Gain	25,200	
Less annual exempt amount (best use)	(11,300)	
Taxable gain	13,900	
CGT on £(33,500 − 16,500 − 10,000)		
= 7,000 @ 10%		700
CGT on £(13,900 − 7,000) = 6,900 @ 20%		1,380
CGT 2017/18		3,080

Note that the £10,000 gain qualifying for entrepreneurs' relief is deducted from the basic rate limit for the purposes of computing the rate of tax on the gain not qualifying for entrepreneurs' relief.

1.4 Lifetime limit

There is a lifetime limit of £10 million of gains on which entrepreneurs' relief can be claimed.

Question — Limit on entrepreneurs' relief

Maureen sells a shareholding in January 2018 realising a gain of £9,300,000. The conditions for entrepreneurs' relief are satisfied for this disposal and Maureen makes a claim for the relief to apply. Maureen had already made a claim for entrepreneurs' relief in an earlier tax year in respect of gains totalling £900,000. Maureen also makes an allowable loss of £(20,000) in 2017/18 on an asset not qualifying for entrepreneurs' relief. Her taxable income for 2017/18 is £200,000.

Calculate the CGT payable by Maureen for 2017/18.

Answer

	Gains £	CGT £
Gain qualifying for entrepreneurs' relief		
£(10,000,000 − 900,000)	9,100,000	
CGT @ 10% on £9,100,000		910,000
Gain not qualifying for entrepreneurs' relief		
£(9,300,000 − 9,100,000)	200,000	
Less allowable loss (best use)	(20,000)	
Net gain	180,000	
Less annual exempt amount (best use)	(11,300)	
Taxable gain	168,700	
CGT @ 20% on £168,700		33,740
Total CGT due		943,740

Exam focus point

The entrepreneurs' relief lifetime limit of £10,000,000 and rate of tax of 10% will be given in the Tax Rates and Allowances section of the examination paper.

1.5 Claim

One of the competencies you require to fulfil Performance Objective 16 Tax compliance and verification of the PER is to identify available claims, or the need to object to/appeal an assessment, ensuring that they are submitted within the required time limits. You can apply the knowledge you obtain from this section of the Study Text to help to demonstrate this competence.

An individual must claim entrepreneurs' relief; it is not automatic. The claim deadline is the first anniversary of 31 January following the end of the tax year of disposal. For a 2017/18 disposal, the taxpayer must claim by 31 January 2020.

1.6 Investors' relief

FAST FORWARD

Investors' relief will apply from 2019/20 for disposals of qualifying shares in unlisted trading companies of which the investor is not usually an officer or employee. The rate of tax on gains qualifying for investors' relief will be 10%.

Investors' relief is a similar relief; to entrepreneurs' relief. It will apply to gains on qualifying shares from 2019/20.

Qualifying shares must satisfy the following conditions:

(a) They must be **new ordinary shares** in an **unlisted trading company** (or unlisted holding company of a trading group) which have been **subscribed for** by the **individual making the disposal**.

(b) The shares must have **been issued by the company on or after 17 March 2016 and held continuously** by that individual usually for **at least three years** from **the date of the issue of the shares** until **the date of disposal**. However, where the shares were issued between 17 March 2016 and 5 April 2016, the three-year period is extended by the period between the issue of the shares and 5 April 2016.

There is **no minimum shareholding** requirement.

The individual (and connected persons) **must not usually be an officer or employee of the company** (nor any connected company).

The **rate of tax** on investors' relief gains **will be 10%**. There will be a **£10 million lifetime limit of gains on which investors' relief can be claimed** separate from the limit for entrepreneurs' relief.

Exam focus point

As a result of this three-year holding period, investors' relief will not be available on disposals until the tax year 2019/20. You need to be aware of the tax advantages of investors' relief and the qualifying conditions. However, computational aspects will **not be examined** in Taxation (TX – UK) until such time as the relief is available on disposals.

2 The replacement of business assets (rollover relief)

FAST FORWARD

Rollover relief is available to all businesses that reinvest in qualifying assets in the period commencing one year before and ending 36 months after the disposal concerned.

2.1 Conditions

A gain may be 'rolled over' (deferred) where the proceeds received on the disposal of a business asset are spent on a replacement business asset. This is **rollover relief**. A claim cannot specify that only part of a gain is to be rolled over.

All of the following conditions must be met:

(a) **The old asset sold and the new asset bought are both used only in the trade** or trades carried on **by the person claiming rollover relief.** Where part of a building is in non-trade use for all or a substantial part of the period of ownership, the building (and the land on which it stands) is treated as two separate assets, the trade part (qualifying) and the non-trade part (non-qualifying). This split cannot be made for other assets.

(b) **The old asset and the new asset both fall within one** (but not necessarily the same one) **of the following classes:**

   (i) Land and buildings (including parts of buildings) occupied as well as used only for the purpose of the trade

   (ii) Fixed (that is, immovable) plant and machinery

   (iii) Goodwill

(c) **Reinvestment of the proceeds received on the disposal of the old asset** takes place in a period beginning one year before and ending three years after the date of the disposal.

(d) **The new asset is brought into use in the trade on its acquisition** (not necessarily immediately, but not after any significant and unnecessary delay).

The new asset can be used in a different trade from the old asset.

A claim for the relief must be made by the later of four years of the end of the tax year in which the disposal of the old asset takes place and four years of the end of the tax year in which the new asset is acquired.

2.2 Operation of relief

> **FAST FORWARD**
>
> A rolled over gain is deducted from the base cost of the replacement asset acquired.

Deferral is obtained by deducting the chargeable gain from the cost of the new asset. For full relief, the whole of the proceeds must be reinvested. Where only part is reinvested, a gain equal to the amount not reinvested or the full gain, if lower, will be chargeable to tax immediately.

The new asset will have a base cost for chargeable gains purposes of its purchase price less the gain rolled over.

Question
Rollover relief

A freehold factory was purchased by Zoë for business use in August 2008. It was sold in December 2017 for £70,000, giving rise to a gain of £17,950. A replacement factory was purchased in June 2018 for £60,000. Compute the base cost of the replacement factory, taking into account any possible rollover of the gain from the disposal in December 2017.

Answer

	£
Gain	17,950
Less rollover relief (balancing figure)	(7,950)
Chargeable gain: Amount not reinvested £(70,000 – 60,000)	10,000
Cost of new factory	60,000
Less rolled over gain	(7,950)
Base cost of new factory	52,050

222   **15: Business reliefs** | Part C Chargeable gains for individuals

BPP
LEARNING MEDIA

2.3 Non-business use

Where the old asset has not been used in the trade for a fraction of its period of ownership, the amount of the gain that can be rolled over is reduced by the same fraction. When considering proceeds not reinvested the restriction on rollover relief is based on the proportion of proceeds relating to the part of the asset used in the trade or the proportion relating to the period of trade use.

Question — Assets with non-business use

John bought a factory for £150,000 on 11 January 2013, for use in his business. From 11 January 2014, he let the factory out for a period of two years. He then used the factory for his own business again, until he sold it on 10 July 2017 for £225,000. On 13 January 2018, he purchased another factory for use in his business. This second factory cost £100,000.

Calculate the chargeable gain on the sale of the first factory and the base cost of the second factory.

Answer

Gain on first factory

	Non-business £	Business £
Proceeds of sale (24:30) (W1)	100,000	125,000
Less cost (24:30)	(66,667)	(83,333)
Gain	33,333	41,667
Less rollover relief		(16,667)
Chargeable gain (W2)	33,333	25,000

Base cost of second factory

	£
Cost	100,000
Less gain rolled over	(16,667)
Base cost c/f	83,333

Workings

1   Use of factory

Total ownership period:

11.1.13 – 10.07.17 = 54 months

Attributable to non business use:

11.1.14 – 10.1.16 = 24 months

Attributable to business use (balance: 54m – 24m) = 30 months

2   Proceeds not reinvested

	£
Proceeds of business element	125,000
Less cost of new factory	(100,000)
Not reinvested	25,000

2.4 Depreciating assets

When the replacement asset is a depreciating asset, the gain on the old asset is 'frozen' rather than rolled over.

Where the replacement asset is a depreciating asset, the gain is not rolled over by reducing the cost of the replacement asset. Rather it is deferred until it crystallises on the earliest of:

(a) The disposal of the replacement asset

(b) The date the replacement asset ceases to be used in the trade (but the gain does not crystallise on the taxpayer's death)

(c) Ten years after the acquisition of the replacement asset (maximum)

Key term

An asset is a **depreciating asset** if it is, or within the next ten years will become, a wasting asset. Thus, any asset with an expected life of 60 years or less is covered by this definition. Plant and machinery is always treated as depreciating.

Question
Gain deferred into depreciating asset

Norma bought a freehold shop for use in her business in June 2016 for £125,000. She sold it for £140,000 on 1 August 2017. On 10 July 2017, Norma bought some fixed plant and machinery to use in her business, costing £150,000. She then sells the plant and machinery for £167,000 on 19 November 2019. Show Norma's gains in relation to these transactions.

Answer

2017/18 – Gain deferred

	£
Proceeds of shop	140,000
Less cost	(125,000)
Gain	15,000

This gain is deferred in relation to the purchase of the plant and machinery as all the proceeds have been reinvested.

2019/20 – Sale of plant and machinery

	£
Proceeds	167,000
Less cost	(150,000)
Gain	17,000

Total gain chargeable on sale in 2019/20 (gain on plant and machinery plus deferred gain)
£(15,000 + 17,000) = £32,000

Where a gain on disposal is deferred against a replacement depreciating asset it is possible to transfer the deferred gain to a non-depreciating asset provided the non-depreciating asset is bought before the deferred gain has crystallised.

3 Gift relief (holdover relief)

FAST FORWARD

Gift relief can be claimed on gifts of business assets.

3.1 The relief

If an individual gives away a qualifying asset, the transferor and the transferee can jointly claim within four years of the end of the tax year of the transfer, that the transferor's gain be reduced to nil. The transferee is then deemed to acquire the asset for market value at the date of transfer less the transferor's deferred gain.

If a disposal involves actual consideration rather than being an outright gift, but is still not a bargain made at arm's length (so that the proceeds are deemed to be the market value of the asset), this is known as a sale at undervalue. **Any excess of actual consideration over actual cost is chargeable immediately and only the balance of the gain is deferred.** The amount chargeable immediately is limited to the full gain.

Exam focus point

> The asset need only be a business asset in the hands of the donor. It is immaterial if the donee does not use it for business purposes.

3.2 Qualifying assets

Gift relief can be claimed on gifts or sales at undervalue on transfers of **business assets.** The definition of a business asset for gift relief is **not** the same as for entrepreneurs' relief.

Business assets are:

(a)   Assets used in a trade, profession or vocation carried on:

     (i)   By the donor

     (ii)   By the donor's personal company (ie one where the individual holds at least 5% of the voting rights)

If the asset was used for the purposes of the trade, profession or vocation for only part of its period of ownership, the gain to be held over is the gain otherwise eligible × period of such use/total period of ownership.

If the asset was a building or structure only partly used for trade, professional or vocational purposes, only the **part of the gain attributable to the part so used is eligible for gift relief.**

(b)   **Shares and securities in trading companies**

     (i)   The shares or securities are **not listed on a recognised stock exchange** (but they may be on the AIM); or

     (ii)   If the donor is an individual, the company concerned is their **personal company** (defined as above).

If the company has chargeable non-business assets at the time of the gift, and point (b)(ii) above applied at any time in the last 12 months, **the gain to be held over is:**

Exam formula

> $$\text{Gain} \times \frac{\text{The market value of the chargeable business assets (CBA)}}{\text{The market value of the chargeable assets (CA)}}$$

Question

On 6 May 2017 Angelo sold to his son Michael a freehold shop valued at £200,000 for £50,000, and claimed gift relief. Angelo had originally purchased the shop from which he had run his business for £30,000. Michael continued to run a business from the shop premises but decided to sell the shop in March 2018 for £195,000. Compute any chargeable gains arising.

Answer

(a)   *Angelo's gain*

	£
Proceeds (market value)	200,000
Less cost	(30,000)
Gain	170,000
Less gain deferred (balance)	(150,000)
Chargeable gain £(50,000 – 30,000) (actual proceeds less actual cost)	20,000

(b)   *Michael's gain*

	£
Proceeds	195,000
Less cost £(200,000 – 150,000) (MV less deferred gain)	(50,000)
Gain	145,000

Question   Gift of shares – CBA/CA restriction

Morris gifts shares in his personal company to his son Minor realising a gain of £100,000. The market values of the assets owned by the company at the date of the gift are:

	£
Freehold factory and offices	150,000
Leasehold warehouse	80,000
Investments	120,000
Current assets	200,000

Show the gain qualifying for hold-over relief and the chargeable gain.

Answer

Gain qualifying for hold-over relief:

$$£100,000 \times \frac{\text{Chargeable business assets (CBA)}}{\text{Chargeable assets (CA)}} = £100,000 \times \frac{150+80}{150+80+120}$$

$$= £100,000 \times \frac{230}{350}$$

$$= \underline{£65,714}$$

The gain which is not held-over (ie chargeable in current year) is £100,000 – £65,714 = £34,286

Chapter Roundup

- Entrepreneurs' relief applies on the disposal of a business and certain trading company shares. Gains on assets qualifying for the relief are taxed at 10%.

- Investors' relief will apply from 2019/20 for disposals of qualifying shares in unlisted trading companies of which the investor is not usually an officer or employee. The rate of tax on gains qualifying for investors' relief will be 10%.

- Rollover relief is available to all businesses that reinvest in qualifying assets in the period commencing one year before and ending 36 months after the disposal concerned.

- A rolled over gain is deducted from the base cost of the replacement asset acquired.

- When the replacement asset is a depreciating asset, the gain on the old asset is 'frozen' rather than rolled over.

- Gift relief can be claimed on gifts of business assets.

Quick Quiz

1   Patrick has been running a trading business for five years. In 2017/18 he sold the business to Andrew realising gains of £75,000. Patrick has already used his annual exempt amount for 2017/18 against other gains. He had not made any previous claim for entrepreneurs' relief. What is Patrick's capital gains tax (CGT) liability?

2   On 10 July 2017, Olivia subscribes for 5,000 new ordinary shares in X Ltd, a trading company. She is not an employee or officer of the company. What is the earliest date that Olivia can dispose of her shares and claim investors' relief?

3   Alice sells a factory for £500,000 realising a gain of £100,000. She acquires a factory two months later for £480,000. How much rollover relief is available?

    A   £20,000
    B   £60,000
    C   £80,000
    D   £100,000

4   What deferral relief is available when a business asset is replaced with a depreciating business asset?

5   Which disposals of shares qualify for gift relief?

Answers to Quick Quiz

1 CGT @ 10% on £75,000 £7,500

2 10 July 2020 (three years)

3 C. Amount not reinvested £(500,000 – 480,000) = £20,000. Rollover relief £(100,000 – 20,000) = £80,000.

4 The gain is frozen on the acquisition of a depreciating asset until the earliest of: Disposal of that asset; the date the asset is no longer used in the trade; ten years after the acquisition of replacement asset.

5 Shares which qualify for gift relief are those in trading companies:

- Which are not listed on a recognised stock exchange; or

- Which are in the individual's personal company ie the individual holds at least 5% of the voting rights.

Now try the questions below from the Practice Question Bank

Number	Type	Marks	Time
Q97	Section A	2	4 mins
Q98	Section A	2	4 mins
Q99	Section A	2	4 mins
Q100	Section B	2	4 mins
Q101	Section B	2	4 mins
Q102	Section B	2	4 mins
Q103	Section B	2	4 mins
Q104	Section B	2	4 mins
Q105	Section C	10	18 mins

Shares and securities

16

Topic list	Syllabus reference
1 Valuing quoted shares	C4(a)
2 The matching rules for individuals	C4(b)
3 The share pool	C4(c)
4 Bonus and rights issues	C4(d)
5 Reorganisations and takeovers	C4(d)
6 Gilts and qualifying corporate bonds	C4(e)

Introduction

We have now covered most aspects of the capital gains computation apart from shares and securities.

Shares and securities need special rules because an individual may hold several shares or securities in the same company, bought at different times for different prices but otherwise identical. We need to identify the shares which are disposed to compute the gain or loss.

We also discuss bonus and rights issues, takeovers and reorganisations.

In the next chapter we will conclude our study of personal taxation by considering administration.

Study guide

		Intellectual level
C4	**Gains and losses on the disposal of shares and securities**	
(a)	Recognise the value of quoted shares where they are disposed of by way of a gift.	2
(b)	Explain and apply the identification rules as they apply to individuals including the same day and 30 day matching rules.	2
(c)	Explain and apply the pooling provisions.	2
(d)	Explain and apply the treatment of bonus issues, rights issues, takeovers and reorganisations.	2
(e)	Identify the exemption available for gilt-edged securities and qualifying corporate bonds.	1

Exam guide

The valuation rules for gifts of quoted shares may be tested in either Section A or B. The disposal of shares and securities are likely to form at least part of a question on capital gains in Section C. You must learn the identification rules as they are crucial in calculating the gain correctly. The identification rules for companies are covered later in this Study Text. Takeovers and reorganisations are important; remember to apportion the cost across the new holding.

1 Valuing quoted shares   12/16

FAST FORWARD
> Where quoted shares are disposed of by way of a gift, the market value of the shares is the lower of the two prices shown in the Stock Exchange Daily Official List plus one-half of the difference between those two prices.

Where quoted shares are disposed of by way of a gift, the market value of these shares is needed as **'proceeds'** in order to calculate the chargeable gain or allowable loss.

Quoted shares are valued as the lower of the two prices shown in the Stock Exchange Daily Official List plus one-half of the difference between those two prices.

Question   CGT value of shares

Shares in A plc are quoted at 100–110p. What is the market value for CGT purposes?

Answer

The value is $100 + \frac{1}{2} \times (110 - 100) = 105p$.

2 The matching rules for individuals

FAST FORWARD

There are special rules for matching shares sold with shares purchased. Disposals are matched first with shares acquired on the same day, then within the following 30 days and finally with the share pool.

Quoted and unquoted shares and securities present special problems when attempting to compute gains or losses on disposal. For instance, suppose that Ivy buys some quoted shares in X plc as follows.

Date	Number of shares	Cost £
5 May 2010	220	150
17 August 2017	100	375

On 15 August 2017, Ivy sells 120 of the shares for £1,450. To determine the chargeable gain, we need to be able to work out which shares out of the two original holdings were actually sold.

We therefore need **matching rules**. These **allow us to decide which shares have been sold and so work out what the allowable cost on disposal should be**.

At any one time, we will only be concerned with shares or securities of the same class in the same company. If an individual owns both ordinary shares and preference shares in X plc, we will deal with the two classes of share entirely separately, because they are distinguishable.

Below 'shares' refers to both shares and securities.

For individuals, share disposals are matched with acquisitions in the following order.

(a) **Same day acquisitions**

(b) **Acquisitions within the following 30 days** (known as the 'bed and breakfast rule'); if more than one acquisition, use a 'first in, first out' (FIFO) basis

(c) **Any shares in the share pool (see below)**

The 'bed and breakfast' rule stops shares being sold to crystallise a capital gain or loss, usually to use the annual exempt amount, and then being repurchased a day or so later. Without the rule a gain or loss would arise on the sale, since it would be 'matched' to the original acquisition.

Exam focus point

Learn the 'matching rules' because a crucial first step to getting a shares question right is to correctly match the shares sold to the original shares purchased.

3 The share pool

3.1 Composition of pool

We treat any shares acquired (other than those acquired on the same day or within the next 30 days) as a 'pool' which grows as new shares are acquired and shrinks as they are sold.

In making computations which use the share pool, we must keep track of:

(a) The **number** of shares
(b) The **cost** of the shares

3.2 Disposals from the share pool

In the case of a disposal the cost attributable to the shares disposed of are deducted from the amounts within the share pool. The proportion of the cost to take out of the pool should be computed using the A/(A + B) fraction that is used for any other part disposal. However, we are not usually given the value of the remaining shares (B in the fraction). We just use numbers of shares.

In August 2006 Oliver acquired 4,000 shares in Twist plc at a cost of £10,000. Oliver sold 3,000 shares on 10 July 2017 for £17,000. Compute the gain and the value of the share pool following the disposal.

Answer

The gain is computed as follows:

	£
Proceeds	17,000
Less cost (working)	(7,500)
Gain	9,500

Working – share pool

	No of shares	Cost £
Acquisition – August 2006	4,000	10,000
Disposal – July 2017	(3,000)	
Cost $\dfrac{3,000}{4,000} \times £10,000$		(7,500)
	1,000	2,500

 Question

Anita acquired shares in Kent Ltd as follows:

1 July 1996	1,000 shares for £2,000
11 April 2001	2,500 shares for £7,500
17 July 2017	500 shares for £2,000
10 August 2017	400 shares for £1,680

Anita sold 4,000 shares for £16,400 on 17 July 2017.

Calculate Anita's net gain on sale.

Answer

First match the disposal with the acquisition on the same day:

	£
Proceeds $\dfrac{500}{4,000} \times £16,400$	2,050
Less cost	(2,000)
Gain	50

Next match the disposal with the acquisition in the next thirty days:

	£
Proceeds $\dfrac{400}{4,000} \times £16,400$	1,640
Less cost	(1,680)
Loss	(40)

Finally, match the disposal with the shares in the share pool:

	£
Proceeds $\frac{3,100}{4,000} \times £16,400$	12,710
Less cost (working)	(8,414)
Gain	4,296
Net gain £(50 + 4,296 – 40)	4,306

Working	*No. of shares*	*Cost*
		£
1.7.96 Acquisition	1,000	2,000
11.4.01 Acquisition	2,500	7,500
	3,500	9,500
17.7.17 Disposal	(3,100)	(8,414)
c/f	400	1,086

4 Bonus and rights issues

FAST FORWARD

Bonus shares are shares acquired at no cost. Rights issue shares are acquired for payment.

4.1 Bonus issues

Bonus shares are shares issued by a company in proportion to each shareholder's existing holding. For example, a shareholder may have 1,000 shares. If the company makes a 2 shares for each 1 share held bonus issue (called a '2 for 1 bonus issue'), the shareholder will receive 2 bonus shares for each 1 share held. So the shareholder will end up with 1,000 original shares and 2,000 bonus shares making 3,000 shares in total.

When a company issues bonus shares all that happens is that the size of the original holding is increased. Since bonus shares are issued at no cost there is no need to adjust the original cost.

4.2 Rights issues   9/16, 12/16

In a rights issue the company offers shareholders rights issue shares in proportion to their existing shareholdings.

The difference between a bonus issue and a rights issue is that in a rights issue the new shares are paid for by the shareholder and this results in an adjustment to the original cost.

Question	Rights issue

Simon had the following transactions in S Ltd.

1.10.97	Bought 10,000 shares for £15,000
1.2.10	Took up rights issue 1 for 2 at £2.75 per share
14.10.17	Sold 2,000 shares for £6,000

Compute the gain arising in October 2017.

Share pool

	Number	Cost £
1.10.97 Acquisition	10,000	15,000
1.2.10 Rights issue (1 for 2)	5,000	13,750
	15,000	28,750
14.10.17 Sale	(2,000)	(3,833)
c/f	13,000	24,917

Gain

	£
Proceeds	6,000
Less cost	(3,833)
Gain	2,167

5 Reorganisations and takeovers

 FAST FORWARD

The costs of the original holding are allocated to the new holdings pro rata to their values on a takeover or reorganisation.

5.1 Reorganisations

A reorganisation takes place where new shares or a mixture of new shares and debentures are issued in exchange for the original shareholdings. The new shares take the place of the old shares. The problem is how to apportion the original cost between the different types of capital issued on the reorganisation.

If the new shares and securities are quoted, then the cost is apportioned by reference to the market values of the new types of capital on the first day of quotation after the reorganisation.

 Question   Reorganisations

Devon has an original quoted shareholding of 3,000 shares which is held in a share pool with a cost of £13,250.

In 2017 there is a reorganisation whereby each ordinary share is exchanged for two 'A' ordinary shares (quoted at £2 each) and one preference share (quoted at £1 each). Show how the original cost will be apportioned.

Answer

Share pool

	New holding	MV £	Cost £
Ords 2 new shares	6,000	12,000	10,600 (W)
Prefs 1 new share	3,000	3,000	2,650 (W)
Total		15,000	13,250

Working

$^{12}/_{15} \times £13,250$ = cost of ordinary shares

$^{3}/_{15} \times £13,250$ = cost of preference shares

5.2 Takeovers

A chargeable gain does not arise on a 'paper for paper' takeover. The cost of the original holding is passed on to the new holding which takes the place of the original holding.

The takeover rules apply where the company issuing the new shares ends up with **more than 25%** of the ordinary share capital of the old company or the majority of the voting power in the old company, or the company issuing the new shares makes a general offer to shareholders in the other company which is initially made subject to a condition which, if satisfied, would give the first company control of the second company.

The exchange must take place for bona fide commercial reasons and does not have as its main purpose, or one of its main purposes, the avoidance of CGT or corporation tax.

Question   Takeover (1)

Simon held 20,000 £1 shares in D plc out of a total number of issued shares of one million. They were bought in 2002 for £2 each. In 2017 the board of D plc agreed to a takeover bid by S plc under which shareholders in D plc received three ordinary S plc shares plus one preference share for every four shares held in D plc. Immediately following the takeover, the ordinary shares in S plc were quoted at £5 each and the preferences shares at 90p. Show the base costs of the ordinary shares and the preference shares.

Answer

The total value due to Simon on the takeover is as follows.

		£
Ordinary	20,000 × 3/4 × £5	75,000
Preference	20,000 × 1/4 × 90p	4,500
		79,500

The base costs are therefore:

	£
Ordinary shares: 75,000/79,500 × 20,000 × £2	37,736
Preference shares: 4,500/79,500 × 20,000 × £2	2,264
	40,000

If part of the takeover consideration is cash then a gain must be computed.

Question   Takeover (2)

In May 2005 Rosanna bought 50,000 £1 shares in P plc (a 1% holding) for £2.10 each. In 2017 P plc was taken over by L plc and shareholders in P plc received two ordinary shares in L plc plus £2 in cash for each five shares held in P plc. Immediately following the takeover, the ordinary shares in L plc were quoted at £6 each. Calculate the gain arising on the takeover and show the base cost of the ordinary shares in L plc.

Answer

The total value due to Rosanna on the takeover is as follows.

		£
Ordinary	50,000 × 2/5 × £6	120,000
Cash	50,000 × 1/5 × £2	20,000
		140,000

The cost of the original shares is therefore apportioned between the ordinary shares and the cash as follows.

	£
Ordinary shares: 120,000/140,000 × 50,000 × £2.10	90,000
Cash: 20,000/140,000 × 50,000 × £2.10	15,000
	105,000

The gain on the takeover relates to the cash received.

	£
Proceeds	20,000
Less cost	(15,000)
Gain	5,000

6 Gilts and qualifying corporate bonds

FAST FORWARD

Gilts and qualifying corporate bonds held by individuals are exempt from CGT. You should never waste time computing gains and losses on them.

Key term

Gilts are UK Government securities issued by HM Treasury as shown on the Treasury list. You may assume that the list includes all issues of Treasury Loan, Treasury Stock, Exchequer Loan, Exchequer Stock and War Loan.

Disposals of gilt edged securities (gilts) and qualifying corporate bonds by individuals are exempt from CGT.

Key term

A **qualifying corporate bond (QCB)** is a security (whether or not secured on assets) which satisfies all of the following conditions:

(a) Represents a **'normal commercial loan'**. This excludes any bonds which are convertible into shares (although bonds convertible into other bonds which would be QCBs are not excluded), or which carry the right to excessive interest or interest which depends on the results of the issuer's business.

(b) Is **expressed in sterling** and for which no provision is made for conversion into or redemption in another currency

(c) Was **acquired** by the person now disposing of it **after 13 March 1984**

(d) Does not have a redemption value which depends on a published index of share prices on a stock exchange

Chapter Roundup

- Where quoted shares are disposed of by way of a gift, the market value of the shares is the lower of the two prices shown in the Stock Exchange Daily Official List plus one-half of the difference between those two prices.

- There are special rules for matching shares sold with shares purchased. Disposals are matched first with acquisitions on the same day, then within the following 30 days and finally with the share pool.

- Bonus shares are shares acquired at no cost. Rights issue shares are acquired for payment.

- The costs of the original holding are allocated to the new holdings pro rata to their values on a takeover or reorganisation.

- Gilts and qualifying corporate bonds held by individuals are exempt from CGT. You should never waste time computing gains and losses on them.

Quick Quiz

1   In what order are acquisitions of shares matched with disposals for individuals?

2   In July 2006 Rick acquired 1,000 shares in X plc. He acquired 1,000 more shares on each of 15 January 2008 and 15 January 2018. He sells 1,800 shares on 10 January 2018. How are the shares matched on sale?

3   How are bonus issues dealt with?

4   Sharon acquired 10,000 shares in Z plc in 2007. She takes up a 1 for 2 rights offer in May 2017. How many shares does Sharon have in her share pool after the rights offer?

5   What is a qualifying corporate bond?

BPP LEARNING MEDIA

1   The matching of shares sold is in the following order:

  (a)   Same day acquisitions
  (b)   Acquisitions within the following 30 days
  (c)   Shares in the share pool

2   January 2018 1,000 shares (following 30 days)
     Share pool 800 shares

3   Number of shares increased. No adjustment to cost.

4   10,000 + 5,000 = 15,000 shares

5   A qualifying corporate bond is a security which:

  • Represents a normal commercial loan
  • Is expressed in sterling
  • Was acquired after 13 March 1984
  • Is not redeemable in relation to share prices on a stock exchange

Now try the questions below from the Practice Question Bank

Number	Type	Marks	Time
Q106	Section A	2	4 mins
Q107	Section A	2	4 mins
Q108	Section A	2	4 mins
Q109	Section C	10	18 mins

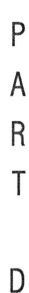

P
A
R
T

D

Tax administration for individuals

Self assessment and payment of tax by individuals

Topic list	Syllabus reference
1 The self assessment system	A3(a)
2 Tax returns and keeping records	A4(a), (d)
3 Self assessment and claims	A4(a)
4 Payment of income tax and capital gains tax	A4(b)
5 HMRC powers	A5(a)
6 Interest and penalties	A6(a)
7 Disputes and appeals	A5(b)

Introduction

In the earlier chapters we have learned how to calculate an individual's liability to income tax, capital gains tax and national insurance.

In this chapter we see how individuals (including partners) must 'self assess' their liability to income tax, capital gains tax and Class 4 national insurance contributions (NICs).

We also look at how HM Revenue & Customs (HMRC) enforces compliance with tax law, including compliance checks and imposing penalties and interest.

In the remaining chapters we will consider the other taxes within the syllabus: inheritance tax, corporation tax and VAT.

Study guide

		Intellectual level
A3	**The systems for self-assessment and the making of returns**	
(a)	Explain and apply the features of the self assessment system as it applies to individuals.	2
A4	**The time limits for the submission of information, claims and payment of tax, including payments on account**	
(a)	Recognise the time limits that apply to the filing of returns and the making of claims.	2
(b)	Recognise the due dates for the payment of tax under the self-assessment system and compute payments on account and balancing payments/repayments for individuals.	2
(d)	List the information and records that taxpayers need to retain for tax purposes.	1
A5	**The procedures relating to compliance checks, appeals and disputes**	
(a)	Explain the circumstances in which HM Revenue & Customs can make a compliance check into a self assessment tax return.	2
(b)	Explain the procedures for dealing with appeals and First and Upper Tier Tribunals.	2
A6	**Penalties for non-compliance**	
(a)	Calculate late payment interest and state the penalties that can be charged.	2

Exam guide

Section A or B questions on the topics in this chapter might relate to the dates for filing returns or the amount of interest or penalties. In Section C you might be asked to explain an aspect of the self assessment system, such as the filing of a return, the payment of tax or compliance checks by HMRC. Your knowledge should include the penalties used to enforce the self assessment system.

1 The self assessment system

One of the competencies you require to fulfil Performance Objective 16 Tax compliance and verification of the PER is to explain tax filing and payment requirements and the consequences of non-compliance to clients. You can apply the knowledge you obtain from this section of the Study Text to help to demonstrate this competence.

1.1 Introduction

The self assessment system relies upon the taxpayer completing and filing a tax return and paying the tax due. The system is enforced by a system of penalties for failure to comply within the set time limits, and by interest for late payment of tax.

Many taxpayers have very simple affairs: receiving a salary under deduction of tax through PAYE, with a small amount of investment income which can be dealt with through the PAYE code. These individuals will not normally have to complete a tax return. Self-employed taxpayers, company directors and individuals with complicated affairs will have to complete a tax return.

Individuals within the self assessment system are required to complete and file a return every year unless HMRC recognise that their affairs have become sufficiently straightforward for no return to be required.

Conversely, individuals whose affairs become more complicated so that they are likely to owe tax must notify HMRC that they should be brought within the self assessment system.

1.2 Notification of liability to income tax and CGT

FAST FORWARD

Individuals who do not receive a tax return must notify their chargeability to income tax or CGT.

Individuals who are chargeable to income tax or CGT for any tax year and who have not received a notice to file a return are required to give notice of chargeability to an Officer of the Revenue and Customs within six months from the end of the year ie by 5 October 2018 for 2017/18.

A person who has no chargeable gains and who is not liable to higher rate tax does not have to give notice of chargeability if all their income:

(a)   Is taken into account under PAYE

(b)   Is from a source of income not subject to tax under a self assessment

(c)   Has had (or is treated as having had) income tax deducted at source, or

(d)   Is savings income and/or dividend income falling within the savings income nil rate band and the dividend nil rate band.

A penalty may be imposed for late notification (see later in this chapter).

2 Tax returns and keeping records

PER alert

One of the competencies you require to fulfil Performance Objective 16 Tax compliance and verification of the PER is to verify and question client submissions and ensure timely submission of all relevant information to the tax authorities by the due date. You can apply the knowledge you obtain from this section of the Study Text to help to demonstrate this competence.

FAST FORWARD

Tax returns must usually be filed by 31 October (paper) or 31 January (electronic) following the end of the tax year.

2.1 Tax returns   9/16

The tax return comprises a basic six-page return form, **together with supplementary pages for particular sources of income**. Taxpayers are sent a return and a number of supplementary pages depending on their known sources of income, together with a Tax Return Guide and various notes relating to the supplementary pages. Taxpayers with new sources of income may have to ask for further supplementary pages. Taxpayers with simple tax returns may be asked to complete a short four-page tax return. If a return for the previous year was filed electronically the taxpayer may be sent a notice to file a return, rather than the official HMRC form.

The taxpayer must sign a declaration that the information given on the tax return and any supplementary pages is **correct and complete to the best of the taxpayer's knowledge and belief** and a statement that the **taxpayer understands** that they may have to **pay financial penalties and face prosecution if they give false information**.

Partnerships must file a separate return which includes a Partnership Statement showing the firm's profits, losses, proceeds from the sale of assets, tax suffered, tax credits, and the division of all these amounts between partners. Each partner must then include their share of partnership profits on their personal tax return.

A partnership return must include a declaration of the name and tax reference of each partner, as well as the usual declaration that the return is correct and complete to the best of the signatory's knowledge. There is a warning on the form that if false information is given or any of the partnership's income or gains is concealed, the partners may be liable to financial penalties and/or HMRC may prosecute them.

2.2 Time limit for submission of tax returns

Key term

> The **latest filing date** for a personal tax return for a tax year (Year 1) is:
>
> - **31 October** in the next tax year (Year 2), for a **non-electronic return** (eg a paper return)
> - **31 January** in Year 2, for an **electronic return** (eg made via the internet)

There are **two exceptions to this general rule**.

The **first exception applies if the notice to file a tax return is issued by HMRC to the taxpayer after 31 July in Year 2, but on or before 31 October in Year 2**. In this case, the **latest filing date is**:

- **The end of three months following the notice, for a non-electronic return.**
- **31 January in Year 2, for an electronic return.**

The second exception applies **if the notice to file the tax return is issued to the taxpayer after 31 October in Year 2**. In this case, **the latest filing date is the end of three months following the notice.**

| Question | Submission of tax returns |

Advise each of the following clients of the latest filing date for her personal tax return for 2017/18 if the return is:

(a) Non-electronic
(b) Electronic

Norma   Notice to file tax return issued by HMRC on 6 April 2018
Melanie   Notice to file tax return issued by HMRC on 10 August 2018
Olga   Notice to file tax return issued by HMRC on 12 December 2018

Answer

	Non-electronic	*Electronic*
Norma	31 October 2018	31 January 2019
Melanie	9 November 2018	31 January 2019
Olga	11 March 2019	11 March 2019

A partnership return may be filed as a non-electronic return or an electronic return. **The general rule and the exceptions to the general rule for personal returns apply also to partnership returns.**

2.3 Keeping records   12/16

All taxpayers must retain all records required to enable them to make and deliver a correct tax return.

Records must be retained until the later of:

(a)   (i)   **Five years after the 31 January following the tax year where the taxpayer is in business** (as a sole trader or partner or letting property). Note that this applies to all of the records, not only the business records; or

      (ii) One **year after the 31 January following the tax year otherwise**; or

(b)   Provided notice to deliver a return is given before the date in (a):

  (i)   **The time after which a compliance check enquiry by HMRC into the return can no longer be commenced; or**

  (ii) **The date any such compliance check enquiry has been completed.**

HMRC can specify a shorter time limit for keeping records where the records are bulky and the information they contain can be provided in another way.

Where a person receives a notice to deliver a tax return after the normal record keeping period has expired, they must keep all records in their possession at that time until no compliance issues can be raised in respect of the return or until such a compliance check enquiry has been completed.

Taxpayers can keep 'information', rather than 'records', but must show that they have prepared a complete and correct tax return. The information must also be able to be provided in a legible form on request. Records can be kept in electronic format.

HMRC can inspect 'in-year' records, ie *before* a return is submitted, if they believe it is reasonably required to check a tax position.

3 Self assessment and claims

FAST FORWARD ⟩⟩ If a paper return is filed the taxpayer can ask HMRC to compute the tax due. Electronic returns have tax calculated automatically.

3.1 Self assessment

Key term

A **self assessment** is a calculation of the amount of taxable income and gains after deducting reliefs and allowances, a calculation of income tax and CGT payable after taking into account tax deducted at source.

If the taxpayer is filing a **paper return (other than a Short Tax Return), they may make the tax calculation on their return or ask HMRC to do so on their behalf.**

If the taxpayer wishes HMRC to make the calculation for Year 1, a paper return must be filed:

- **On or before 31 October in Year 2; or**

- **If the notice to file the tax return is issued after 31 August in Year 2, within two months of the notice**

If the taxpayer is filing an **electronic return, the calculation of tax liability is made automatically when the return is made online.**

3.2 Amending the self assessment

The taxpayer may amend their return (including the tax calculation) for Year 1 within twelve months after the filing date. For this purpose the filing date means:

- **31 January of Year 2; or**

- **Where the notice to file a return was issued after 31 October in Year 2, the last day of the three month period starting with the issue**

A return may be amended by the taxpayer at a time when a compliance check enquiry is in progress into the return. The amendment does not restrict the scope of a compliance check enquiry into the return but may be taken into account in that enquiry. If the amendment is made during a compliance check enquiry to the amount of tax payable, the amendment does not take effect while the compliance check enquiry is in progress.

A return may be amended by HMRC to correct any obvious error or omission in the return (such as errors of principle and arithmetical mistakes) or anything else that an officer has reason to believe is incorrect in the light of information available. The correction must be usually be made within nine months after the day on which the return was actually filed. The taxpayer can object to the correction but must do so within 30 days of receiving notice of it.

3.3 Claims

All claims and elections which can be made in a tax return must be made in this manner if a return has been issued. A claim for any relief, allowance or repayment of tax must be quantified at the time it is made. **In general, the time limit for making a claim is four years from the end of tax year.** Where different time limits apply, these have been mentioned throughout this Study Text.

3.4 Recovery of overpaid tax

If a taxpayer discovers that they have overpaid tax, for example because they have made an error in their tax return, they can make a claim to have the overpaid tax repaid to them. The claim must be made within four years of the end of the tax year to which the overpayment relates.

4 Payment of income tax and capital gains tax

One of the competencies you require to fulfil Performance Objective 16 Tax compliance and verification of the PER is to determine the incidence (timing) of tax liabilities and their impact on cash flow/financing requirements. You can apply the knowledge you obtain from this section of the Study Text to help to demonstrate this competence.

Two payments on account and a final balancing payment of income tax and Class 4 NICs are due. All capital gains tax and Class 2 NICs are due on 31 January following the end of the tax year.

4.1 Payments on account and final payment

4.1.1 Introduction

The self assessment system may result in the taxpayer making three payments of income tax and Class 4 NICs.

Date	Payment
31 January in the tax year	1st payment on account
31 July after the tax year	2nd payment on account
31 January after the tax year	Final payment to settle the remaining liability

HMRC issue payslips/demand notes in a credit card type 'Statement of Account' format, but there is no statutory obligation for it to do so and **the onus is on the taxpayer to pay the correct amount of tax on the due date.**

4.1.2 Payments on account

9/16

Key term

Payments on account are usually required where the income tax and Class 4 NICs due in the previous year exceeded the amount of income tax deducted at source; this excess is known as **'the relevant amount'**. Income tax deducted at source for Taxation (TX – UK) is tax deducted under Pay As You Earn.

The payments on account are each equal to 50% of the relevant amount for the previous year.

Payments on account of Class 2 NICs and capital gains tax are never required.

Question	Payments on account

Sue is employed and paid tax for 2016/17 as follows:

	£
Total amount of income tax charged	11,100
This included: Tax deducted under PAYE	3,200
She also paid: Capital gains tax	4,800

How much are the payments on account for 2017/18 and by what dates are they due?

Answer

	£
Income tax:	
Total income tax charged for 2016/17	11,100
Less tax deducted for 2016/17 under PAYE	(3,200)
'Relevant amount'	7,900
Payments on account for 2017/18:	
31 January 2018 £7,900 × 50%	3,950
31 July 2018 £7,900 × 50%	3,950

There is no requirement to make payments on account of capital gains tax.

Payments on account are not required if the relevant amount falls below a de minimis limit of £1,000. Also, payments on account are not required from taxpayers who paid 80% or more of their tax liability for the previous year through PAYE or other deduction at source arrangements.

4.1.3 Reducing payments on account 6/17

Payments on account are normally fixed by reference to the previous year's tax liability but if a taxpayer expects their liability to be lower than this **they may claim to reduce their payments on account to:**

(a)   **A stated amount; or**
(b)   **Nil**

The claim must state the reason why they believe their tax liability will be lower, or nil.

If the taxpayer's eventual liability is higher than they estimated they will have reduced the payments on account too far. Although the payments on account will not be adjusted, the taxpayer will suffer an interest charge on late payment.

A penalty of the difference between the reduced payment on account and the correct payment on account may be levied if the reduction was claimed fraudulently or negligently.

4.1.4 Balancing payment

The balance of any income tax and Class 4 NICs together with all CGT due for a year, is normally payable on or before the 31 January following the year. Class 2 NICs for 2017/18 will also be payable on or before 31 January 2019.

Giles made payments on account for 2017/18 of £6,500 each on 31 January 2018 and 31 July 2018, based on his 2016/17 liability. He then calculates his total income tax and Class 4 NIC liability for 2017/18 at £15,250. No tax was deducted at source or under PAYE in 2016/17. In addition he calculated that his CGT liability for disposals in 2017/18 is £5,120 and his Class 2 NIC for 2017/18 is £148.

What is the final payment due for 2017/18?

Answer

Income tax and Class 4 NIC: £15,250 – £6,500 – £6,500 = £2,250. CGT = £5,120. Class 2 NIC = £148.

Final payment due on 31 January 2019 for 2017/18: £2,250 + £5,120 + £148 = £7,518

In one case the due date for the final payment is later than 31 January following the end of the year. **If a taxpayer has notified chargeability by 5 October but the notice to file a tax return is not issued before 31 October, then the due date for the payment is three months after the issue of the notice.**

Tax charged in an amended self assessment is usually payable on the later of:

(a)   The normal due date, generally 31 January following the end of the tax year
(b)   The day following 30 days after the making of the revised self assessment

5 HM Revenue & Customs (HMRC) powers

One of the competencies you require to fulfil Performance Objective 16 Tax compliance and verification of the PER is to correspond appropriately and in a professional manner with the relevant parties in relation to both routine and specific matters/enquiries. You can apply the knowledge you obtain from this section of the Study Text to help to demonstrate this competence.

5.1 Compliance check enquiries

FAST FORWARD

A compliance check enquiry into a return, claim or election can be started by an officer of HM Revenue & Customs (HMRC) within a limited period.

5.1.1 Starting compliance check enquiry

HMRC has powers to make compliance check enquiries into returns, claims or elections which have already been submitted.

Some returns, claims or elections are **selected for a compliance check enquiry at random, others for a particular reason**, for example, if HMRC believes that there has been an **underpayment of tax** due to the taxpayer's failure to comply with tax legislation.

An officer of HMRC has a limited period within which to commence a compliance check enquiry on a return or amendment. The officer must give written notice of their intention by:

(a)   **The first anniversary of the actual filing date, if the return was delivered on or before the due filing date; or**

(b)   **The quarter day following the first anniversary of the actual filing date, if the return is filed after the due filing date. The quarter days are 31 January, 30 April, 31 July and 31 October.**

If the taxpayer amends the return after the due filing date, the compliance check enquiry 'window' extends to the quarter day following the first anniversary of the date the amendment was filed. Where the compliance check enquiry was not started within the limit which would have applied had no amendment been filed, the enquiry is restricted to matters contained in the amendment.

The officer does not have to have, or give, any reason for starting a compliance check enquiry. In particular, the taxpayer will not be advised whether they have been selected at random for an audit. Compliance check enquiries may be full enquires, or may be limited to 'aspect' enquiries.

5.1.2 During the compliance check enquiry

In the course of the compliance check enquiry **the officer may require the taxpayer to produce documents, accounts or any other information required. The taxpayer can appeal to the Tax Tribunal against such a requirement.**

5.1.3 Completion of a compliance check enquiry

An officer must issue a notice that the compliance check enquiry is complete.

The officer cannot then make a further compliance check enquiry into that return. HMRC may, in limited circumstances, raise a discovery assessment if they believe that there has been a loss of tax.

5.2 Determinations

If notice has been served on a taxpayer to submit a return but the return is not submitted by the due filing date, an officer of HMRC may make a determination of the amounts liable to income tax and CGT and of the tax due. Such a determination must be made to the best of the officer's information and belief, and is then treated as if it were a self assessment. This enables the officer to seek payment of tax, including payments on account for the following year and to charge interest.

A determination must be made within four years following the end of the relevant tax year.

5.3 Discovery assessments

If an officer of HMRC discovers that profits have been omitted from assessment, that any assessment has become insufficient, or that any relief given is, or has become excessive, an assessment may be raised to recover the tax lost.

If the tax lost results from an error in the taxpayer's return but the return was made in accordance with prevailing practice at the time, no discovery assessment may be made.

A discovery assessment may only be raised where a return has been made if:

(a)   There has been **careless or deliberate understatement** by the taxpayer or their agent; or

(b)   At the time that compliance check enquiries on the return were completed, or could no longer be made, the officer **did not have information** to make them aware of the loss of tax.

Information is treated as available to an officer if it is contained in the taxpayer's return or claim for the year or either of the two preceding years, or it has been provided as a result of a compliance check enquiry covering those years, or it has been specifically provided.

The time limit for raising a discovery assessment is four years from the end of the tax year but this is extended to six years if there has been careless understatement and 20 years if there has been deliberate understatement. The taxpayer may appeal against a discovery assessment within 30 days of issue.

5.4 Dishonest conduct of tax agents

FAST FORWARD

HMRC can investigate dishonest conduct by a tax agent and issue a civil penalty of up to £50,000 where there has been dishonest conduct.

HMRC can investigate whether there has been dishonest conduct by a tax agent (ie an individual who, in the course of business, assists clients with their tax affairs). Dishonest conduct occurs when a tax agent does something dishonest with a view to bringing about a loss of tax.

HMRC can issue a civil penalty of up to £50,000 where there has been **dishonest conduct and the tax agent fails to supply the information or documents that HMRC has requested.**

6 Interest and penalties

One of the competencies you require to fulfil Performance Objective 16 Tax compliance and verification of the PER is to explain tax filing and payment requirements and the consequences of non-compliance to clients. You can apply the knowledge you obtain from this section of the Study Text to help to demonstrate this competence.

6.1 Interest on late paid tax   9/16

FAST FORWARD

Interest is chargeable by HMRC on late payment of tax.

Interest is chargeable on late payment of both payments on account and balancing payments. Late payment interest is charged from the due date for payment until the day before the date on which payment is made.

Exam focus point

For the purpose of Taxation (TX – UK) exams in June 2018, September 2018, December 2018 and March 2019, the **assumed rate of interest on underpaid tax is 2.75%.** You will be given this rate of interest in the Tax Rates and Allowances in the exam.

Interest is charged from 31 January following the tax year (or the normal due date for the balancing payment, in the rare event that this is later), even if this is before the due date for payment on:

(a)   Tax payable following an amendment to a self assessment
(b)   Tax payable in a discovery assessment
(c)   Tax postponed under an appeal, which becomes payable

Since a determination (see above) is treated as if it were a self assessment, interest runs from 31 January following the tax year.

If a taxpayer claims to reduce their payments on account and there is still a balancing payment to be made, interest is normally charged on the payments on account as if each of those payments had been the lower of:

(a)   The reduced amount, plus 50% of the balancing payment
(b)   The amount which would have been payable had no claim for reduction been made

Question   Interest

Herbert's payments on account for 2017/18 based on his income tax liability for 2016/17 were £4,500 each. However when he submitted his 2016/17 income tax return in January 2018 he made a claim to reduce the payments on account for 2017/18 to £3,500 each. The first payment on account was made on 29 January 2018 and the second on 12 August 2018.

Herbert filed his 2017/18 tax return in December 2018. The return showed that his tax liabilities for 2017/18 (before deducting payments on account) were income tax and Class 4 NIC: £10,000, capital gains tax: £2,352, Class 2 NIC: £148. Herbert paid the balance of tax due of £5,500 on 19 February 2019.

For what periods and in respect of what amounts will Herbert be charged interest?

Answer

Herbert made an excessive claim to reduce his payments on account, and will therefore be charged interest on the reduction. The payments on account should have been £4,500 each based on the original 2016/17 liability (not £5,000 each based on the 2017/18 liability). Interest will be charged as follows:

(a)   First payment on account

    (i)   On £3,500 – nil – paid on time
    (ii)   On £1,000 from due date of 31 January 2018 to day before payment date, 18 February 2019

250   **17: Self assessment and payment of tax by individuals** | Part D Tax administration for individuals

BPP
LEARNING MEDIA

(b) Second payment on account

     (i)   On £3,500 from due date of 31 July 2018 to day before payment date, 11 August 2018

     (ii)   On £1,000 from due date of 31 July 2018 to day before payment date, 18 February 2019

(c) Balancing payment (£1,000), capital gains tax (£2,352) and Class 2 NIC (£148) = £3,500

     (i)   On £3,500 from due date of 31 January 2019 to day before payment date, 18 February 2019

Where interest has been charged on late payments on account but the final balancing settlement for the year produces a repayment, all or part of the original interest is repaid.

6.2 Repayment of tax and repayment supplement

Interest (repayment supplement) is payable by HMRC on overpayment of tax.

Tax is repaid when claimed unless a greater payment of tax is due in the following 30 days, in which case it is set-off against that payment.

Interest (repayment supplement) is paid on overpayments of:

(a) **Payments on account**

(b) **Final payments** of income tax and Class 4 NICs and CGT, including tax deducted at source or tax credits on dividends

(c) **Penalties**

Exam focus point

> For the purpose of Taxation (TX – UK) exams in June 2018, September 2018, December 2018 and March 2019, **the assumed rate of interest on overpaid tax is 0.5%.** You will be given this rate of interest in the Tax Rates and Allowances in the exam.

Repayment supplement runs from the original date of payment (even if this was prior to the due date), until the day before the date the repayment is made. Income tax deducted at source and tax credits are treated as if they were paid on the 31 January following the tax year concerned.

Repayment supplement is tax free.

6.3 Penalties for errors

There is a common penalty regime for errors in tax returns, including income tax, NICs, corporation tax and VAT. Penalties range from 30% to 100% of the Potential Lost Revenue. Penalties may be reduced.

A common penalty regime for errors in tax returns for income tax, national insurance contributions, corporation tax and value added tax.

A penalty may be imposed where **a taxpayer makes an inaccurate return** if they have:

- Been **careless** because they have not taken reasonable care in making the return or discovers the error later but does not take reasonable steps to inform HMRC; or

- Made a **deliberate error** but **does not make arrangements to conceal it**; or

- Made a **deliberate error** and **has attempted to conceal it** eg by submitting false evidence in support of an inaccurate figure.

Note that **an error which is made where the taxpayer has taken reasonable care** in making the return and which they **do not discover later, does not result in a penalty**.

In order for a penalty to be charged, the **inaccurate return must result in**:

- **An understatement of the taxpayer's tax liability**; or
- **A false or increased loss for the taxpayer**; or
- **A false or increased repayment of tax to the taxpayer.**

If a return contains more than one error, a penalty can be charged for each error.

The rules also extend to **errors in claims for allowances and reliefs** and in **accounts submitted in relation to a tax liability**.

Penalties for error also apply where **HMRC has issued an assessment estimating a person's liability** where:

- **A return has been issued to that person and has not been returned**; or
- The taxpayer was **required to deliver a return to HMRC but has not delivered it**.

The taxpayer will be charged a penalty where:

- The **assessment understates the taxpayer's liability** to income tax, capital gains tax, corporation tax or VAT; and
- **The taxpayer fails to take reasonable steps within 30 days of the date of the assessment** to tell HMRC that there is an under-assessment.

The amount of **the penalty for error is based on the Potential Lost Revenue (PLR)** to HMRC as a result of the error. For example, if there is an understatement of tax, this understatement will be the PLR.

The maximum amount of the penalty for error depends on the type of error:

Type of error	Maximum penalty payable
Careless	30% of PLR
Deliberate not concealed	70% of PLR
Deliberate and concealed	100% of PLR

Question
Penalty for error

Alex is a sole trader. He files his tax return for 2017/18 on 10 January 2019. The return shows his trading income to be £60,000. In fact, due to carelessness, his trading income should have been stated to be £68,000. State the maximum penalty that could be charged by HMRC on Alex for his error.

Answer

The Potential Lost Revenue as a result of Alex's error is:

£(68,000 − 60,000) = £8,000 × [40% (income tax) + 2% (Class 4 NIC)]   £3,360

Alex's error is careless so the maximum penalty for error is:

£3,360 × 30%   £1,008

A penalty for error may be reduced if the taxpayer tells HMRC about the error – this is called a disclosure. The reduction depends on the **circumstances of** the disclosure and the **help that the taxpayer gives to HMRC in relation to the disclosure.**

An **unprompted disclosure is one made at a time when the taxpayer has no reason to believe HMRC has discovered, or is about to discover, the error**. Otherwise, the disclosure will be a **prompted disclosure.**

The **minimum penalties** that can be imposed are as follows:

Type of error	Unprompted	Prompted
Careless	0% of PLR	15% of PLR
Deliberate not concealed	20% of PLR	35% of PLR
Deliberate and concealed	30% of PLR	50% of PLR

Question

Sue is a sole trader. She files her tax return for 2016/17 on 31 January 2018. The return shows a loss for the year of £(80,000). In fact, Sue has deliberately increased this loss by £(12,000) and has submitted false figures in support of her claim. HMRC initiate a review into Sue's return and in reply Sue then makes a disclosure of the error. Sue is a higher rate taxpayer due to her substantial investment income and she has made a claim to set the loss against general income in 2017/18.

State the maximum and minimum penalties that could be charged by HMRC on Sue for her error.

Answer

The potential lost revenue as a result of Sue's error is:

£12,000 × 40%	£4,800

Sue's error is deliberate and concealed so the maximum penalty for error is:

£4,800 × 100%	£4,800

Sue has made a prompted disclosure so the minimum penalty for error is:

£4,800 × 50%	£2,400

The help that the taxpayer gives to HMRC relates to when, how and to what extent the taxpayer:

- **Tells HMRC about the error,** making full disclosure and explaining how the error was made
- **Gives reasonable help** to HMRC to enable it **to quantify the error**
- **Allows access to business and other records** and other relevant documents

A taxpayer can appeal to the First Tier Tax Tribunal against:

- The **penalty being charged**
- The **amount of the penalty**

6.4 Penalties for late notification of chargeability

FAST FORWARD

A common penalty regime also applies to late notification of chargeability.

A common penalty regime also applies to certain taxes for failures to notify chargeability to, or liability to register for, tax that result in a loss of tax. The taxes affected include income tax, NICs, PAYE, CGT, corporation tax and VAT. Penalties are behaviour related, increasing for more serious failures, and are based on the 'potential lost revenue'.

The minimum and maximum penalties as percentages of PLR are as follows:

Behaviour	Maximum penalty	Minimum penalty with unprompted disclosure		Minimum penalty with prompted disclosure	
Deliberate and concealed	100%	30%		50%	
Deliberate but not concealed	70%	20%		35%	
		≥12m	<12m	≥12m	<12m
Careless	30%	10%	0%	20%	10%

Note that there is no zero penalty for reasonable care (as there is for penalties for errors on returns – see above), although the penalty may be reduced to 0% if the failure is rectified within 12 months through unprompted disclosure. The penalties may also be reduced at HMRC's discretion in 'special circumstances'. However, inability to pay the penalty is not a 'special circumstance'.

The same penalties apply for failure to notify HMRC of a new taxable activity.

Where the taxpayer's failure is not classed as deliberate, there is no penalty if they can show they have a 'reasonable excuse'. Reasonable excuse does not include having insufficient money to pay the penalty. Taxpayers have a right of appeal against penalty decisions to the First Tier Tribunal.

6.5 Penalties for late filing of tax return

FAST FORWARD

A penalty can be charged for late filing of a tax return based on how late the return is and how much tax is payable.

An individual is liable to a penalty where a tax return is filed after the due filing date. The penalty date is the date on which the return will be overdue (ie the date after the due filing date).

The initial penalty for late filing of the return is £100.

If the failure continues after the end of the period of three months starting with the penalty date, HMRC may give the individual notice specifying that a daily penalty of £10 is payable for a maximum of 90 days. The daily penalty runs from a date specified in the notice which may be earlier than the date of the notice but cannot be earlier than the end of the three month period.

If the failure continues after the end of the period of six months starting with the penalty date, a further penalty is payable. This penalty is the greater of:

- **5% of the tax liability** which would have been shown in the return
- **£300**

If the failure continues after the end of the period of 12 months starting with the penalty date, a further penalty is payable. This penalty is determined in accordance with the taxpayer's conduct in withholding information which would enable or assist HMRC in assessing the taxpayer's liability to tax. **The penalty is computed as follows:**

Type of conduct	Penalty
Deliberate and concealed	Greater of: • 100% of tax liability which would have been shown on return • £300
Deliberate not concealed	Greater of: • 70% of tax liability which would have been shown on return • £300

Type of conduct	Penalty
Any other case (eg careless)	Greater of: • 5% of tax liability which would have been shown on return • £300

6.6 Penalty for late payment of tax

FAST FORWARD

A penalty is chargeable where tax is paid after the due date based on the amount of unpaid tax. Up to 15% of that amount is payable where the tax is more than 12 months late.

A penalty is chargeable where tax is paid after the penalty date. The penalty date is 30 days after the due date for the tax. Therefore no penalty arises if the tax is paid within 30 days of the due date.

The penalty chargeable is:

Date of payment	Penalty
Not more than five months after the penalty date	5% of tax which is unpaid at the penalty date.
More than five months after the penalty date but not more than 11 months after the penalty date	5% of tax which is unpaid at the end of the five month period. This is in addition to the 5% penalty above.
More than 11 months after the penalty date	5% of tax which is unpaid at the end of the 11 month period. This is in addition to the two 5% penalties above.

Penalties for late payment of tax apply to:

(a) **Balancing payments of income tax and Class 4 NICs and any CGT under self assessment or a determination**

(b) Tax due on the amendment of a self assessment

(c) Tax due on a discovery assessment

Penalties for late payment do not apply to late payments on account.

6.7 Penalty for failure to keep records

The maximum penalty for each failure to keep and retain records is £3,000 per tax year/accounting period. This penalty can be reduced by HMRC.

7 Disputes and appeals

One of the competencies you require to fulfil Performance Objective 16 Tax compliance and verification of the PER is to identify available claims, or the need to object to/appeal an assessment, ensuring that they are submitted within the required time limits. You can apply the knowledge you obtain from this section of the Study Text to help to demonstrate this competence.

FAST FORWARD

Disputes between taxpayers and HMRC can be dealt with by an HMRC internal review or by a Tribunal hearing.

7.1 Internal reviews

For direct taxes, appeals must first be made to HMRC, which will assign a 'caseworker'.

For indirect taxes, appeals must be sent directly to the Tax Tribunal, although the taxpayer can continue to correspond with their caseworker where, for example, there is new information.

At this stage the taxpayer may be offered, or may ask for, an **'internal review'**, which will be made by an objective HMRC review officer not previously connected with the case. This is a less costly and more effective way to resolve disputes informally, without the need for a Tribunal hearing. An appeal to the Tax Tribunal cannot be made until any review has ended.

The taxpayer must either accept the review offer, or notify an appeal to the Tax Tribunal within 30 days of being offered the review, otherwise the appeal will be treated as settled.

HMRC must usually carry out the review within 45 days, or any longer time as agreed with the taxpayer. The review officer may decide to uphold, vary or withdraw decisions.

After the review conclusion is notified, **the taxpayer has 30 days to appeal to the Tax Tribunal.**

7.2 Tribunal hearings

If there is no internal review, or the taxpayer is unhappy with the result of an internal review, the case may be heard by the Tax Tribunal. The person wishing to make an appeal (the appellant) must send a notice of appeal to the Tax Tribunal. The Tax Tribunal must then give notice of the appeal to the respondent (normally HMRC).

The Tax Tribunal is made up of two 'tiers':

(a)   A First Tier Tribunal
(b)   An Upper Tribunal

The case will be allocated to one of four **case 'tracks':**

(a)   **Complex cases,** which the Tribunal considers will require lengthy or complex evidence or a lengthy hearing, or involve a complex or important principle or issue, or involves a large amount of money. Such cases will usually be heard by the Upper Tribunal.

(b)   **Standard cases, heard by the First Tier Tribunal,** which have detailed case management and are subject to a more formal procedure than basic cases

(c)   **Basic cases, also heard by the First Tier Tribunal,** which will usually be disposed of after a hearing, with minimal exchange of documents before the hearing

(d)   **Paper cases, dealt with by the First Tier Tribunal,** which applies to straightforward matters such as fixed filing penalties and will usually be dealt with in writing, without a hearing

A decision of the First Tier Tribunal may be appealed to the Upper Tribunal.

Decisions of the Upper Tribunal are binding on the Tribunals and any affected public authorities. A decision of the Upper Tribunal may be appealed to the Court of Appeal.

Chapter Roundup

- Individuals who do not receive a tax return must notify their chargeability to income tax or CGT.

- Tax returns must usually be filed by 31 October (paper) or 31 January (electronic) following the end of the tax year.

- If a paper return is filed the taxpayer can ask HMRC to compute the tax due. Electronic returns have tax calculated automatically.

- Two payments on account and a final balancing payment of income tax and Class 4 NICs are due. All capital gains tax and Class 2 NICs are due on 31 January following the end of the tax year.

- A compliance check enquiry into a return, claim or election can be started by an officer of HMRC within a limited period.

- HMRC can investigate dishonest conduct by a tax agent and issue a civil penalty of up to £50,000 where there has been dishonest conduct.

- Interest is chargeable by HMRC on late payment of tax.

- Interest (repayment supplement) is payable by HMRC on overpayment of tax.

- There is a common penalty regime for errors in tax returns, including income tax, NICs, corporation tax and VAT. Penalties range from 30% to 100% of the Potential Lost Revenue. Penalties may be reduced.

- A common penalty regime also applies to late notification of chargeability.

- A penalty can be charged for late filing of a tax return based on how late the return is and how much tax is payable.

- A penalty is chargeable where tax is paid after the due date based on the amount of unpaid tax. Up to 15% of that amount is payable where the tax is more than 12 months late.

- Disputes between taxpayers and HMRC can be dealt with by an HMRC internal review or by a Tribunal hearing.

Quick Quiz

1 A taxpayer who has not received a tax return must give notice of his chargeability to capital gains tax due in 2017/18 by_____. Fill in the blank.

2 By when must a taxpayer normally file a paper tax return for 2017/18?

    A   31 October 2018
    B   31 December 2018
    C   31 January 2019
    D   5 April 2019

3 What are the normal payment dates for income tax?

4 What penalty is due in respect of income tax payments on account that are paid two months after the due date?

5 What is the maximum penalty for failure to keep records?

6 Which body hears tax appeals?

1   A taxpayer who has not received a tax return must give notice of their chargeability to capital gains tax due in 2017/18 by **5 October 2018**.

2   A. 31 October 2018

3   Two payments on account of income tax are due on 31 January in the tax year and on 31 July following. A final balancing payment is due on 31 January following the tax year.

4   None. The penalty for late paid tax does not apply to late payment of payments on account.

5   £3,000

6   The Tax Tribunal which consists of the First Tier Tribunal and the Upper Tribunal.

Now try the questions below from the Practice Question Bank

Number	Type	Marks	Time
Q110	Section A	2	4 mins
Q111	Section A	2	4 mins
Q112	Section A	2	4 mins
Q113	Section B	2	4 mins
Q114	Section B	2	4 mins
Q115	Section B	2	4 mins
Q116	Section B	2	4 mins
Q117	Section B	2	4 mins

Inheritance tax

18

Inheritance tax: scope and transfers of value

Topic list	Syllabus reference
1 Chargeable persons	D1(a)
2 Transfers of value	D1(b), (c)
3 Exemptions	D3(a), D3(b)
4 Calculation of tax on lifetime transfers	D1(d), D2(a), D3(b)
5 Calculation of tax on death estate	D1(d), D2(b), D2(d)
6 Transfer of unused nil rate band	D2(c)
7 Basic inheritance tax planning	D3(b)
8 Payment of inheritance tax	D4(a)

Introduction

In this chapter we introduce inheritance tax (IHT). IHT is primarily a tax on wealth left on death. It also applies to gifts within seven years of death and to certain lifetime transfers of wealth.

The tax is different from income tax and capital gains tax (CGT), where the basic question is: how much has the taxpayer made? With IHT, the basic question is, how much has been given away? We tax the amount which the taxpayer has transferred – the amount by which they are worse off. If the taxpayer pays IHT on a lifetime gift, they are worse off by the amount of the gift plus the tax due, and we have to take that into account. Some transfers are, however, exempt from IHT.

We will see that the first £325,000 of transfers is taxed at 0% (the 'nil rate band'), and is therefore effectively tax-free. To stop people from avoiding IHT by, for example, giving away £1,625,000 in five lots of £325,000, we need to look back seven years every time a transfer is made to decide how much of the nil rate band is available to set against the current transfer.

Next, we will see how to bring together all of a deceased person's assets at death, and compute the tax on the estate. Finally, we look at the administration and payment of IHT.

In the next chapter we will start our study of corporation tax.

Study guide

		Intellectual level
D1	**The basic principles of computing transfers of value**	
(a)	Identify the persons chargeable.	2
(b)	Understand and apply the meaning of transfer of value, chargeable transfer and potentially exempt transfer.	2
(c)	Demonstrate the diminution in value principle.	2
(d)	Demonstrate the seven year accumulation principle taking into account changes in the level of the nil rate band.	2
D2	**The liabilities arising on chargeable lifetime transfers and on the death of an individual**	
(a)	Understand the tax implications of lifetime transfers and compute the relevant liabilities.	2
(b)	Understand and compute the tax liability on a death estate.	2
(c)	Understand and apply the transfer of any unused nil rate band between spouses.	2
(d)	Understand and apply the residence nil rate band available when a residential property is inherited by direct descendents.	2
D3	**The use of exemptions in deferring and minimising inheritance tax liabilities**	
(a)	Understand and apply the following exemptions:	
(i)	Small gifts exemption.	2
(ii)	Annual exemption.	2
(iii)	Normal expenditure out of income.	2
(iv)	Gifts in consideration of marriage.	2
(v)	Gifts between spouses.	2
(b)	Basic inheritance tax planning.	2
D4	**Payment of inheritance tax**	
(a)	Identify who is responsible for the payment of inheritance tax and the due date for payment of inheritance tax.	2

Exam guide

Inheritance tax (IHT) may be the subject of a 10 mark question in Sections B or C and you may also find specific aspects being tested in Section A such as tax on a single transfer of value. You will need to know when IHT is charged: transfers of value (basically gifts) and chargeable persons. The concepts of potentially exempt transfers (PETs), chargeable lifetime transfers (CLTs) and the seven year accumulation principle are all fundamental to an understanding of IHT. Once you have worked out the amount of a transfer of value, you need to be able to work out the IHT liability on it. This could be payable during the donor's lifetime and/or on death for a lifetime transfer and on death for a death estate. There are a number of exemptions which may be used to reduce IHT liability such as gifts between spouses/civil partners. Finally, you need to have an understanding of how IHT is paid and who pays it.

ACCA's article Inheritance tax, written by a member of the Taxation (TX – UK) examining team, in Part 1 considers the **scope of inheritance tax**, **transfers of value**, **rates of tax** and **exemptions**. Part 2 covers the more difficult aspects of **lifetime transfers**, the calculation of the **value of a person's estate**, and the **payment of inheritance tax**.

1 Chargeable persons

IHT is a tax on gifts made by individuals to other individuals or trustees.

Inheritance tax is a tax on gifts or '**transfers of value**' made by **chargeable persons**. This generally involves a transaction as a result of which wealth is transferred by one individual to another, either directly or via a trust.

Individuals are chargeable persons for inheritance tax.

Spouses and civil partners are taxed separately under inheritance tax although there is an exemption for transfers between the couple (dealt with later in this chapter).

The general principle is that all transfers of value of assets made by individuals, whether during lifetime or on death, are within the charge to IHT.

2 Transfers of value

IHT applies to lifetime transfers of value and transfers of value made on death.

2.1 Introduction

There are **two main chargeable occasions** for inheritance tax:

(a)   Transfers of value made in the lifetime of the donor (**lifetime transfers**)
(b)   Transfers of value made on death, for example when property is left in a Will (**death estate**)

An example of a transfer of value is a **gift by an individual** to **another individual**.

Another example of a transfer of value is a **gift by an individual** to **trustees. A trust is a legal structure where one person (the settlor) gives property to one or more people (the trustees) to be held for the benefit of one or more people (the beneficiaries).**

2.2 Transfers of value

2.2.1 What is a transfer of value?

IHT cannot arise unless there is a transfer of value.

A transfer of value is any gratuitous disposition (eg a gift) made by a person which results in them being worse off, that is, they suffer a diminution (ie reduction) in the value of their estate. An individual's estate is basically all the assets which they own.

The examining team has stated that, as far as Taxation (TX – UK) is concerned, the terms 'transfer' and 'gift' can be taken to mean the same thing and that a transfer of value will always be a gift of assets.

2.2.2 Gratuitous intent

Transfers where there is no gratuitous intent are not chargeable to IHT. An example would be selling a painting for £1,000 at auction which later turns out to be worth £100,000 or other poor business deals.

2.2.3 Diminution in value

In many cases the diminution in value of the donor's estate will be the same as the increase in the value of the donee's estate, for example if there is a cash gift or the gift of a house. However, sometimes the two will not be the same. Typically this is the situation where unquoted shares are gifted.

The measure of the transfer for inheritance tax purposes is always the loss to the donor (the diminution in value of their estate), not the amount gained by the donee.

2.2.4 Example

Audrey holds 5,100 of the shares in an unquoted company which has an issued share capital of 10,000 shares. Currently Audrey's majority holding is valued at £15 per share.

Audrey wishes to give 200 shares to her son, Brian. However, the shares are worth only £2.50 each to Brian, since Brian will have only a small minority holding in the company. After the gift Audrey will hold 4,900 shares and these will be worth £10 each. The value per share to Audrey will fall from £15 to £10 per share since she will lose control of the company.

The diminution in value of Audrey's estate is £27,500, as follows.

	£
Before the gift: 5,100 shares × £15	76,500
After the gift: 4,900 shares × £10	(49,000)
Diminution in value	27,500

Brian has only been given shares with a market value of 200 × £2.50 = £500. Remember, a gift is also a deemed disposal at market value for CGT purposes and it is this value that will be used in any CGT computation. IHT, however, uses the principle of diminution in value which can, as in this case, give a much greater value than the market value of the asset transferred.

2.3 Chargeable transfers and potentially exempt transfers

Inheritance tax is chargeable on a **chargeable transfer**. This is any transfer of value which is not an exempt transfer (see later in this Study Text).

Key terms

> A **potentially exempt transfer (PET)** is a **lifetime transfer** (other than an exempt transfer) **made by an individual to another individual**. Any other lifetime transfer by an individual (eg a gift to trustees) which is not an exempt transfer is a **chargeable lifetime transfer (CLT)**.

A **potentially exempt transfer (PET)** is exempt from IHT when made and will remain exempt if the donor survives for at least seven years from making the gift. If the donor dies within seven years of making the PET, the transfer will become chargeable to IHT.

A **chargeable lifetime transfer (CLT)** is immediately chargeable to IHT when made.

On death, an individual is treated as if they had made a transfer of value of the property comprised in their estate immediately before death. This is a **chargeable transfer** to the extent that it is not covered by an exemption.

3 Exemptions

Exemptions may apply to make transfers or parts of transfers non chargeable. Some exemptions only apply on lifetime transfers (annual, normal expenditure out of income, marriage/civil partnership), but the spouse/civil partner exemption applies on both life and death transfers.

> One of the competencies you require to fulfil Performance Objective 17 Tax planning and advice of the PER is to mitigate and/or defer tax liabilities through the use of standard reliefs, exemptions and incentives. You can apply the knowledge you obtain from this section of the Study Text to help to demonstrate this competence.

3.1 Introduction

There are various exemptions available to eliminate or reduce the chargeable amount of a lifetime transfer or property passing on an individual's death.

The lifetime exemptions apply to PETs as well as to CLTs. Only the balance of such gifts after the lifetime exemptions have been taken into account is then potentially exempt.

3.2 Exemptions applying to lifetime transfers only

3.2.1 The small gifts exemptions   12/16

Outright gifts to individuals totalling £250 or less per donee in any one tax year are exempt. If gifts total more than £250 the whole amount is chargeable. A donor can give up to £250 each year to each of as many donees as they wish. The small gifts exemption cannot apply to gifts into trusts.

3.2.2 The annual exemption (AE)   9/16

The first £3,000 of value transferred in a tax year is exempt from IHT. The annual exemption is used only after all other exemptions (such as for transfers to spouses/civil partners (see below)). If several gifts are made in a year, the £3,000 exemption is applied to earlier gifts before later gifts. The annual exemption is used up by PETs as well as CLTs, even though the PETs might never become chargeable.

Exam focus point

> Where CLTs and PETS are made in the same year the CLTs should be made first to use any available annual exemptions. If used up against the PETs the exemption(s) will be wasted if the PET never becomes chargeable.

Any unused portion of the annual exemption is carried forward for one year only. Only use it the following year **after** that year's own annual exemption has been used.

Question   Annual exemptions

Frank has no unused annual exemption brought forward at 6 April 2016.

On 1 August 2016 he makes a transfer of £600 to his son Peter.
On 1 September 2016 he makes a transfer of £2,000 to his nephew Quentin.
On 1 July 2017 he makes a transfer of £3,300 to a trust for his grandchildren.
On 1 June 2018 he makes a transfer of £5,000 to his friend Rowan.

Show the application of the annual exemptions.

	£
2016/17	
1.8.16 Gift to Peter	600
Less AE 2016/17	(600)
	0

	£
1.9.16 Gift to Quentin	2,000
Less AE 2016/17	(2,000)
	0

The unused annual exemption carried forward is £3,000 – £600 – £2,000 = £400.

	£	£
2017/18		
1.7.17 Gift to trust		3,300
Less: AE 2017/18	3,000	
AE 2016/17 b/f	300	
		(3,300)
		0

The unused annual exemption carried forward is zero because the 2017/18 exemption must be used before the 2016/17 exemption brought forward. The balance of £100 of the 2016/17 exemption is lost, because it cannot be carried forward for more than one year.

	£
2018/19	
1.6.18 Gift to Rowan	5,000
Less AE 2018/19	(3,000)
	2,000

3.2.3 Normal expenditure out of income

Inheritance tax is a tax on transfers of capital, not income. A transfer of value is exempt if:

(a) It is made as part of the normal expenditure of the donor
(b) Taking one year with another, it was made out of income
(c) It leaves the donor with sufficient income to maintain their usual standard of living

As well as covering such things as regular presents **this exemption can cover regular payments out of income such as a grandchild's school fees or the payment of life assurance premiums on a policy for someone else.**

3.2.4 Gifts in consideration of marriage/civil partnership

Gifts in consideration of marriage/civil partnership are exempt up to:

(a) **£5,000 if from a parent of a party to the marriage/civil partnership**
(b) **£2,500 if from a remoter ancestor or from one of the parties to the marriage/civil partnership**
(c) **£1,000 if from any other person**

The limits apply to gifts from any one donor for any one marriage/civil partnership. The exemption is available only if the marriage/civil partnership actually takes place.

3.3 Exemption applying to both lifetime transfers and transfers on death

3.3.1 Transfers between spouses/civil partners

Any transfers of value between spouses/civil partners are exempt. The exemption covers lifetime gifts between them and property passing under a will or on intestacy.

Dale made a gift of £153,000 to her son on 17 October 2013 on the son's marriage. Dale gave £100,000 to her spouse on 1 January 2017. Dale gave £70,000 to her daughter on 11 May 2017. The only other gifts Dale made were birthday and Christmas presents of £100 each to her grandchildren. Compute the amount of the transfers of value after exemptions for each of these gifts.

Answer

17 October 2013

	£
Gift to Dale's son	153,000
Less: Marriage Exemption	(5,000)
AE 2013/14	(3,000)
AE 2012/13 b/f	(3,000)
PET	142,000

1 January 2017

	£
Gift to Dale's spouse	100,000
Less spouse exemption	(100,000)
	0

11 May 2017

	£
Gift to Dale's daughter	70,000
Less: AE 2017/18	(3,000)
AE 2016/17 b/f	(3,000)
PET	64,000

The gifts to the grandchildren are covered by the small gifts exemption.

4 Calculation of tax on lifetime transfers

 One of the competencies you require to fulfil Performance Objective 15 Tax computations and assessments of the PER is to prepare or contribute to the computation or assessment of tax computations for individuals. You can apply the knowledge you obtain from this section of the Study Text to help to demonstrate this competence.

FAST FORWARD ▶ The tax on a chargeable transfer is calculated with reference to chargeable transfers in the previous seven years.

There are two aspects of the calculation of tax on lifetime transfers:

(a) Lifetime tax on CLTs

(b) Additional death tax on CLTs and death tax on PETs, in both cases where the donor dies within seven years of making the transfer

Exam focus point

You should always calculate the lifetime tax on any CLTs first, then move on to calculate the death tax on all CLTs and PETs made within seven years of death.

4.1 Lifetime tax

FAST FORWARD

IHT is charged on what a donor loses. If the donor pays the IHT on a lifetime gift they lose both the asset given away and the money with which they paid the tax due on it. Grossing up is required.

4.1.1 Donee pays tax

Lifetime inheritance tax on lifetime transfers is chargeable at two rates of tax: a 0% rate (the 'nil rate') and 20%. The nil rate is chargeable where accumulated transfers do not exceed the nil rate band limit which is £325,000 for 2017/18. The excess is chargeable at 20%.

When a CLT is made and the donee (ie the trustees) pays the lifetime tax, follow these steps to work out the lifetime IHT on it:

Step 1 Look back seven years from the date of the transfer to see if any other CLTs have been made. If so, these transfers use up the nil rate band available for the current transfer. This is called **seven year accumulation**. Work out the value of any nil rate band still available.

Step 2 Compute the gross value of the CLT. You may be given this in the question or you may have to work out the diminution of value or deduct exemptions (such as the annual exemption).

Step 3 Any part of the CLT covered by the nil rate band is taxed at 0%. Any part of the CLT not covered by the nil rate band is charged at 20%.

Exam focus point

The nil rate band and the lifetime rate will be given in the Tax Rates and Allowances in the exam. Where nil rate bands are required for previous years, these will be given in the question.

Question   Donee pays the lifetime tax

Eric makes a gift of £336,000 to a trust on 10 July 2017. The trustees agree to pay the tax due.

Calculate the lifetime tax payable by the trustees if Eric has made:

(a) A lifetime chargeable transfer of value of £100,000 in August 2009
(b) A lifetime chargeable transfer of value of £100,000 in August 2010
(c) A lifetime chargeable transfer of value of £350,000 in August 2010

Answer

(a) **Step 1** No lifetime transfers in seven years before 10 July 2017 (transfers after 10 July 2010). Nil rate band of £325,000 available.

Step 2 Value of CLT is £336,000 less £3,000 (AE 2017/18) and £3,000 (AE 2016/17) = £330,000.

Step 3

	IHT £
£325,000 × 0%	0
£5,000 × 20%	1,000
£330,000	1,000

(b) **Step 1** Lifetime transfer of value of £100,000 in seven years before 10 July 2017 (transfers after 10 July 2010). Nil rate band of £(325,000 – 100,000) = £225,000 available.

Step 2 Value of CLT after exemptions is £330,000.

		IHT £
	£225,000 × 0%	0
	£105,000 × 20%	21,000
	£330,000	21,000

(c) **Step 1** Lifetime transfer of value of £350,000 in seven years before 10 July 2017 (transfers after 10 July 2010). No nil rate band available as all covered by previous transfer.

Step 2 Value of CLT after exemptions is £330,000.

Step 3

	IHT £
£330,000 @ 20%	66,000

4.1.2 Donor pays tax

Where IHT is payable on a CLT, the **primary liability to pay tax is on the donor,** although the donor may agree with the donee (as in the above example) that the donee is to pay the tax instead.

If the donor pays the lifetime IHT due on a CLT, the total reduction in value of their estate is the transfer of value plus the IHT due on it. The transfer is therefore a net transfer and must be grossed up in order to find the gross value of the transfer. **We do this by working out the tax as follows.**

Formula to learn

> Chargeable amount (ie not covered by nil rate band) $\times \dfrac{20\,(\text{rate of tax})}{80\,(100\,\text{minus the rate of tax})}$

When a CLT is made and the donor pays the lifetime tax, follow these steps to work out the lifetime IHT on it:

Step 1 Look back seven years from the date of the transfer to see if any other CLTs have been made. If so, these transfers use up the nil rate band available for the current transfer. Work out the value of any nil rate band still available.

Step 2 Compute the net value of the CLT. You may be given this in the question or may have to work out the diminution of value or deduct exemptions (such as the annual exemption).

Step 3 Any part of the CLT covered by the nil rate band is taxed at 0%. Any part of the CLT not covered by the nil rate band is taxed at 20/80.

Step 4 Work out the gross transfer by adding the net transfer and the tax together. You can check your figure by working out the tax on the gross transfer.

Question Donor pays the lifetime tax

James makes a gift of £336,000 to a trust on 10 July 2017. James will pay the tax due.

Calculate the lifetime tax payable, if James has made:

(a) A lifetime chargeable transfer of value of £100,000 in August 2009
(b) A lifetime chargeable transfer of value of £100,000 in August 2010
(c) A lifetime chargeable transfer of value of £350,000 in August 2010

(a) **Step 1** No lifetime transfers in seven years before 10 July 2017 (transfers after 10 July 2010). Nil rate band of £325,000 available.

Step 2 Net value of CLT is £336,000 less £3,000 (AE 2017/18) and £3,000 (AE 2016/17) = £330,000.

Step 3

	IHT £
£325,000 × 0%	0
£5,000 × 20/80	1,250
£330,000	1,250

Step 4 Gross transfer is £(330,000 + 1,250) = £331,250.

Check: Tax on the gross transfer would be:

	IHT £
£325,000 × 0%	0
£6,250 × 20%	1,250
£331,250	1,250

(b) **Step 1** Lifetime transfer of value of £100,000 in seven years before 10 July 2017 (transfers after 10 July 2010). Nil rate band of £(325,000 – 100,000) = £225,000 available.

Step 2 Net value of CLT is £330,000.

Step 3

	IHT £
£225,000 × 0%	0
£105,000 × 20/80	26,250
£330,000	26,250

Step 4 Gross transfer is £(330,000 + 26,250) = £356,250.

Check: Tax on the gross transfer would be:

	IHT £
£225,000 × 0%	0
£131,250 × 20%	26,250
£356,250	26,250

(c) **Step 1** Lifetime transfer of value of £350,000 in seven years before 10 July 2017 (transfers after 10 July 2010). No nil rate band available as all covered by previous transfer.

Step 2 Net value of CLT is £330,000.

Step 3

	IHT £
£330,000 × 20/80	82,500

Step 4 Gross transfer is £(330,000 + 82,500) = £412,500.

Check: Tax on the gross transfer would be:

	IHT £
£412,500 × 20%	82,500

Trevor made a cash gift to a trust of £300,000 on 9 December 2006. This was his first transfer of value. The nil rate band in 2006/07 was £285,000.

He then made a gift to the trust of shares worth £206,000 on 15 November 2012. The nil rate band in 2012/13 was £325,000.

Trevor paid the lifetime tax due on the December 2006 transfer but the trustees paid the lifetime tax due on the November 2012 transfer.

Compute:

(a)   The lifetime tax payable by Trevor on the lifetime transfer in December 2006
(b)   The lifetime tax payable by the trustees on the lifetime transfer in November 2012

Answer

Lifetime tax on December 2006 transfer

Step 1   No lifetime transfers in seven years before 9 December 2006. Nil rate band of £285,000 available.

Step 2

		£
Gift		300,000
Less: AE 2006/07		(3,000)
AE 2005/06 b/f		(3,000)
Net CLT		294,000

Step 3

	IHT
	£
£285,000 × 0%	0
£9,000 × 20/80	2,250
£294,000	2,250

Step 4   Gross transfer is £(294,000 + 2,250) = £296,250. **Check:** Tax on the gross transfer would be:

	IHT
	£
£285,000 × 0%	0
£11,250 × 20%	2,250
£296,250	2,250

Lifetime tax on November 2012 transfer

Step 1   Lifetime transfer of value of £296,250 in 7 years before 15 November 2012 (transfers after 15 November 2005). Nil rate band of £(325,000 − 296,250) = £28,750 available.

Step 2

		£
Gift		206,000
Less	AE 2012/13	(3,000)
	AE 2011/12 b/f	(3,000)
		200,000

Step 3

	IHT £
£28,750 × 0%	0
£171,250 × 20%	34,250
£200,000	34,250

4.2 Death tax on chargeable lifetime transfers   12/16

FAST FORWARD

Death tax is chargeable on chargeable lifetime transfers if the donor dies within seven years of making the transfer. Taper relief reduces the death tax if the donor survives between three and seven years.

Death inheritance tax on lifetime transfers is chargeable if the donor dies within seven years of making the lifetime transfer. It is chargeable at two rates: 0% and 40%. The nil rate is chargeable where accumulated transfers do not exceed the nil rate band limit at the date of death which is £325,000 for 2017/18. The excess is chargeable at 40%.

The longer the donor survives after making a gift, the lower the death tax. This is because taper relief applies to lower the amount of death tax payable as follows:

Years before death	% reduction
Over three but less than four years	20
Over four but less than five years	40
Over five but less than six years	60
Over six but less than seven years	80

Exam focus point

The taper relief table will be given in the Tax Rates and Allowances in the exam.

Death tax on a lifetime transfer is **always** payable by the donee, so grossing up is not relevant.

Follow these steps to work out the death tax on a CLT:

Step 1 Look back seven years from the **date of the transfer** to see if any other chargeable transfers were made. If so, these transfers use up the nil rate band available for the current transfer. Work out the value of any nil rate band remaining.

Step 2 Compute the value of the CLT. This is the gross value of the transfer that you worked out for computing lifetime tax.

Step 3 Any part of the CLT covered by the nil rate band is taxed at 0%. Any part of the CLT not covered by the nil rate band is charged at 40%.

Step 4 Reduce the death tax by taper relief (if applicable).

Step 5 Deduct any lifetime tax paid. The death tax may be reduced to nil, but there is **no repayment of lifetime tax**.

Exam focus point

The nil rate band and the death rate will be given in the Tax Rates and Allowances in the exam. Where nil rate bands are required for previous years, these will be given in the question.

Look back at the question **Effect of different nil rate bands** in Section 4.1 earlier in this chapter.

Trevor's lifetime chargeable transfers were 9 December 2006 £296,250 and 15 November 2012 £200,000 (lifetime tax paid £34,250).

Trevor died in August 2017. Compute the death tax payable on the lifetime transfer in November 2012.

Answer

Death tax on November 2012 transfer

Step 1   Lifetime transfer of value of £296,250 in 7 years before 15 November 2012 (transfers after 15 November 2005). Nil rate band of £(325,000 [nil rate band in 2017/18] – 296,250) = £28,750 available.

Step 2   Value of CLT is £200,000.

Step 3

		IHT £
£28,750 × 0%		0
£171,250 × 40%		68,500
£200,000		68,500

Step 4   Death more than 4 years but less than 5 years after transfer

	£
Death tax	68,500
Less: taper relief @ 40%	(27,400)
Death tax left in charge	41,100

Step 5   Tax due £(41,100 – 34,250)   6,850

4.3 Death tax on potentially exempt transfers   9/16

FAST FORWARD

Death tax is chargeable on potentially exempt transfers if the donor dies within seven years of making the transfer. Taper relief reduces the death tax if the donor survives between three and seven years. Grossing up is never required on PET because the death tax is payable by the donee.

If the donor dies within seven years of making a PET it will become chargeable to death tax in the same way as a CLT. There will be no lifetime tax paid, so Step 5 above will not apply.

We will now work through an example where there is both a PET and a CLT.

Exam focus point

Calculate lifetime tax on CLTs first. Then move on to death tax, working through all CLTs and PETs in chronological order. Remember: on death, PETs become chargeable so must be taken into account when calculating the death tax on later CLTs.

Louise gave £346,000 to her son on 1 February 2014. This was the first transfer that Louise had made.

On 10 October 2017, Louise gave £376,000 to a trust. The trustees paid the lifetime IHT due.

On 11 January 2018, Louise died.

Compute:

(a)   The lifetime tax payable by the trustees on the lifetime transfer made in 2017
(b)   The death tax payable on the lifetime transfer made in 2014
(c)   The death tax payable on the lifetime transfer made in 2017

Answer

(a)   Lifetime tax – 2017 CLT

Step 1	There are no chargeable lifetime transfers in the seven years before 10 October 2017 because the 2014 transfer is a PET and therefore exempt during Louise's lifetime. Nil rate band of £325,000 available.
Step 2	Value of CLT £376,000 less £3,000 (AE 2017/18) and £3,000 (AE 2016/17) = £370,000.

Step 3

	IHT £
£325,000 × 0%	0
£ 45,000 × 20%	9,000
£370,000	9,000

(b)   Death tax – 2014 PET becomes chargeable

Step 1	No lifetime transfers of value in seven years before 1 February 2014 (transfers after 1 February 2007). Nil rate band (at date of death) of £325,000 available.
Step 2	Value of PET £346,000 less £3,000 (AE 2013/14) and £3,000 (AE 2012/13) = £340,000.

Step 3

	IHT £
£325,000 × 0%	0
£ 15,000 × 40%	6,000
£340,000	6,000

Step 4	Transfer over three but less than four years before death

	£
Death tax	6,000
Less taper relief @ 20%	(1,200)
Death tax due	4,800

(c)   Death tax – 2017 CLT additional tax

Step 1	Lifetime transfer of value of £340,000 in seven years before 10 October 2017 (transfers after 10 October 2010). Note that as the PET becomes chargeable on death, its value is now included in calculating the death tax on the CLT. No nil rate band available.
Step 2	Value of CLT is £370,000 as before

Step 3

		IHT £
	£370,000 @ 40%	148,000
Step 4	Transfer within three years before death so no taper relief.	
Step 5	Tax due £(148,000 – 9,000)	139,000

4.4 Advantages of making lifetime transfers

One of the competencies you require to fulfil Performance Objective 17 Tax planning and advice of the PER is to review the situation of an individual or entity advising on any potential tax risks and/or additional tax minimisation measures. You can apply the knowledge you obtain from this section of the Study Text to help to demonstrate this competence.

There are a number of inheritance tax advantages of making lifetime transfers:

(a) **If the donor makes a potentially exempt transfer and survives seven years, they have reduced their estate for IHT but the transfer is exempt.** No inheritance tax is payable on the transfer and it does not form part of the seven year cumulation for later transfers.

(b) **If the donor makes a chargeable lifetime transfer and survives seven years, they have reduced their estate for IHT and the only inheritance tax payable is that on the lifetime transfer at lifetime rates.** However, note that the chargeable lifetime transfer remains in cumulation and affects the calculation of tax on transfers made in the seven years after it.

(c) If the donor does not survive seven years, IHT is payable on lifetime transfers at death rates at the date of death but **taper relief reduces the death tax if the donor survives between three and seven years.**

(d) **The values of lifetime transfers cannot exceed the transfer of value when made.** Therefore, **it is good tax planning to give away assets which are likely to increase in value such as land and shares.**

However, there are some situations where **it may not be advantageous for the donor to make a lifetime transfer** in terms of overall tax liability. One is where a **gift of an asset would result in a large chargeable gain (either immediately chargeable or deferred under gift relief).** In this case, it may be better for the donor to retain the asset until death as there is a tax-free uplift in value on death for capital gains tax purposes so that the donee will receive the asset at market value at the date of the donor's death. This is particularly relevant if the donor is unlikely to survive three years from the date of a lifetime gift and so death rates without the benefit of taper relief would apply to a lifetime transfer. Another is if the **gift is residential property so the residence nil rate band applies** in calculating tax on the death estate (see Section 5.2).

5 Calculation of tax on death estate

One of the competencies you require to fulfil Performance Objective 15 Tax computations and assessments of the PER is to prepare or contribute to the computation or assessment of tax computations for individuals. You can apply the knowledge you obtain from this section of the Study Text to help to demonstrate this competence.

FAST FORWARD

When someone dies, we must bring together all their assets to find the value of their death estate and then charge inheritance tax on it (to the extent that it is not exempt) taking account of the available residence nil rate band and the available nil rate band after transfers made in the seven years before death.

5.1 Death estate

5.1.1 What is in the death estate? 12/16

An individual's death estate consists of all the property they owned immediately before death (such as land and buildings, shares and other investments, cars and cash) less debts and funeral expenses.

The death estate also includes anything received as a result of death, for example the proceeds of a life assurance policy which pays out on the individual's death. The value of the policy immediately before the death is not relevant.

5.1.2 Debts and funeral expenses 9/16

The rules on debts are as follows.

(a) **Debts incurred by the deceased can be deducted** if they can be **legally enforced** as they are either **imposed by law** or they are a debt for which the deceased received **consideration**. Specific examples of the application of these rules include:

    (i) **Taxes** – deductible as imposed by law

    (ii) **Electricity and gas bills** – deductible as incurred for consideration

    (iii) **Gambling debts** – deductible if relates to legal gambling (eg in a licensed casino or betting shop), not deductible if relates to illegal gambling or any gambling in Northern Ireland as not legally enforceable

    (iv) **Promise to pay an amount to a relative** – not deductible as no consideration received

    (v) **Oral agreement for sale of interest in land** – not deductible as not legally enforceable since contracts for such sales must be evidenced in writing

(b) **Debts incurred by the deceased but payable after the death may be deductible under the above rules,** but the amount should be discounted because of the future date of payment.

(c) **Rent and similar amounts which accrue day by day should be accrued up to the date of death.**

(d) **If a debt is charged on a specific property it is deductible primarily from that property.** For example, a mortgage secured on a house is deductible from the value of that house.

    This does not include endowment mortgages as these are repaid upon death by the life assurance element of the mortgage.

    Repayment mortgages and interest-only mortgages are deductible (although there may be separate life assurance policies which become payable at death and which will effectively cancel out the mortgage).

Reasonable funeral expenses may also be deducted:

(a) What is reasonable depends on the deceased's condition in life.

(b) Reasonable costs of mourning for the family are allowed.

(c) **The cost of a tombstone is deductible.**

Zack died on 19 June 2017.

Zack's assets at the date of his death consisted of the following:
    10,000 shares in A plc valued at £8,525
    Cash in bank £9,280
    House valued at £150,000 subject to a repayment mortgage of £45,000

Zack's debts due at the date of his death were as follows:

    Electricity £150
    Council tax £300

Zack had also told his daughter on 10 June 2017 that he would pay £1,000 towards the cost of her summer holiday and that he would pay her this amount on 1 July 2017.

Zack's executors paid reasonable funeral expenses of £2,000 (including the cost of a tombstone) on 1 September 2017.

Calculate Zack's death estate for IHT purposes.

Answer

	£	£
A plc shares		8,525
Cash in bank		9,280
House	150,000	
Less repayment mortgage	(45,000)	
		105,000
Gross estate		122,805
Less: debts and funeral expenses		
electricity (incurred for consideration)	150	
council tax (imposed by law)	300	
amount towards holiday for daughter (gratuitous promise)	0	
funeral expenses	2,000	
		(2,450)
Death estate		120,355

5.2 Death tax on the death estate   12/16

5.2.1 Residence nil rate band   New

There is an **additional nil rate band on death** called the **residence nil rate band**. This is **used in computing IHT on the death estate** (but not death tax on lifetime transfers, unlike the nil rate band).

The **residence nil rate band** is used where:

- **The deceased person died on or after 6 April 2017**; and

- **The deceased person owned a home** in which they lived (for Taxation (TX – UK) purposes called 'the **main residence**') which is **part of their death estate**; and

- **The main residence passes** (eg under a will) to **one or more direct descendents** of the deceased person (eg children, grandchildren).

The **available residence nil rate band** is the **lower** of:

- **The maximum residence nil rate band** which is:

    – **£100,000** for 2017/18 **plus**

    – **Any transferred residence nil rate band from a spouse or civil partner** (see later in this chapter); and

- **The value of the main residence passing to direct descendent(s)** after deducting any repayment mortgage or interest-only mortgage secured on the property.

Exam focus point

> The residence nil rate band amount of £100,000 will be given in the Tax rates and Allowances in the exam.

If the **value of the main residence passing to direct descendent(s) is equal to or exceeds the maximum residence nil rate band, all of the maximum residence nil rate band is used up.** However, **if the value of the main residence passing to direct descendent(s) is less than the maximum residence nil rate band**, for example because the value of the main residence is the lower amount in computing the available residence nil rate band, or it passes to a spouse or civil partner, or even if there is no main residence, **the unused residence nil rate band may be transferred to the estate of a surviving spouse or civil partner** (see later in this chapter).

Exam focus point

> There are **other aspects** to the residence nil rate band. **None of the following are examinable** in Taxation (TX – UK):
>
> - **Tapering withdrawal** of the residence nil rate band where the net value of an estate exceeds £2 million
>
> - **Protection of the residence nil rate band** where an individual downsizes to a less valuable property or where a property is disposed of
>
> - **Nominating which property should qualify** where there is more than one main residence

5.2.2 Nil rate band

The **available nil rate band for the death estate** is:

- **The maximum nil rate band** which is:

    – **£325,000** for 2017/18 **plus**

    – **Any transferred nil rate band from a spouse or civil partner** (see later in this chapter); **less**

- **Lifetime transfers in the seven years before death** (CLTs and PETs which have become chargeable).

5.2.3 Computing death tax on the death estate   9/16

Inheritance tax on the death estate is chargeable at two rates: 0% and 40%.

In order to calculate the tax on the death estate, use the following steps:

Step 1 Compute the value of the death estate.

Step 2 Deduct any amount covered by the spouse exemption to leave the chargeable death estate.

Step 3 Calculate the amount of the residence nil rate band (see Section 5.2.1).

Step 4 Calculate the amount of the available nil rate band (see Section 5.2.2).

Step 5 Charge the residence nil rate band found in Step 3 at 0%.

Step 6 Charge the nil rate band found in Step 4 at 0%.

Step 7 Charge the remainder of the chargeable death estate (ie the value in Step 2 less the nil rate bands in Steps 3 and 4) at 40%.

Laura dies on 1 August 2017, leaving a death estate valued at £480,000. In her will, Laura left cash of £80,000 to her husband and the remainder of her estate to her son which included her main residence valued at £150,000. Laura had made a gift of £171,000 to her sister on 11 September 2016.

Compute the tax payable on Laura's death estate.

Answer

Death tax

Note. There is no death tax on the September 2016 PET which becomes chargeable as a result of Laura's death, as it is within the nil rate band at her death. However, it will use up part of the nil rate band, as shown in Step 4.

Step 1   Value of death estate is £480,000.

Step 2   Chargeable death estate is £(480,000 – 80,000) = £400,000.

Step 3   Available residence nil rate band is the lower of £100,000 and the value of the main residence which is £150,000 and so is £100,000.

Step 4   Lifetime transfer of value of £171,000 less £3,000 (AE 2016/17) and £3,000 (AE 2015/16 b/f) = £165,000 in seven years before 1 August 2017 (transfers after 1 August 2010). Available nil rate band is £(325,000 – 165,000) = £160,000.

Steps 5–7

	IHT £
£100,000 × 0% (Step 5)	0
£160,000 × 0% (Step 6)	0
£140,000 × 40% (Step 7)	56,000
£400,000	56,000

Exam focus point

> **A question will make it clear if the residence nil rate band is available.** Therefore, you should assume that the **residence nil rate band is not available** if there is **no mention of a main residence**. Note that other residential property, such as buy-to-let property, does not qualify.

6 Transfer of unused nil rate bands

FAST FORWARD

> If one spouse or civil partner does not use up their whole nil rate bands on death, the excesses may be transferred to the surviving spouse/civil partner.

6.1 Transfer of unused nil rate band   9/16, 12/16

If:

- **An individual ('A') dies;** and
- **A had a spouse or civil partner ('B') who died before A;** and
- **A and B were married or in a civil partnership immediately before B's death;** and
- **B had unused nil rate band (wholly or in part) on death**

then **a claim may be made to increase the nil rate band maximum at the date of A's death by B's unused nil rate band in order to calculate the IHT on A's death.**

The revised nil rate band will apply to the calculation of additional death tax on CLTs made by A, PETs made by A and death tax on A's death estate.

6.2 Example

Robert and Claudia were married for many years until the death of Robert on 10 April 2017. In his will, Robert left his death estate valued at £100,000 to his sister. He had made no lifetime transfers.

Claudia died on 12 January 2018 leaving a death estate worth £850,000 to her brother, so the residence nil rate band is not relevant. Claudia had made a chargeable lifetime transfer of £50,000 in 2014.

The inheritance tax payable on the death of Claudia, assuming that a claim is made to transfer Robert's unused nil rate band, is calculated as follows:

Step 1   Value of Claudia's death estate is £850,000.

Step 2   (a)   Lifetime transfer of value of £50,000 in seven years before 12 January 2018 (transfers after 12 January 2011).

(b)   Nil rate band at Claudia's death is £325,000. Nil rate band is increased by claim to transfer Robert's unused nil rate band at death £(325,000 – 100,000) = £225,000. The maximum nil rate band at Claudia's death is therefore £(325,000 + 225,000) = £550,000 and the available nil rate band for working out the IHT on her estate is £(550,000 – 50,000) = £500,000.

Step 3

	IHT
	£
£500,000 × 0%	0
£350,000 × 40%	140,000
£850,000	140,000

6.3 Changes in nil rate band between deaths of spouses/civil partners

If the nil rate band increases between the death of B and the death of A, the amount of B's unused nil rate band must be scaled up so that it represents the same proportion of the nil rate band at A's death as it did at B's death.

For example, if the nil rate band at B's death was £300,000 and B had an unused nil rate band of £90,000, the unused proportion in percentage terms is therefore 90,000/300,000 × 100 = 30%. If A dies when the nil rate band has increased to £325,000, B's unused nil rate band is £325,000 × 30% = £97,500 and this amount is transferred to increase the nil rate band maximum available on A's death.

The increase in the nil rate band maximum cannot exceed the nil rate band maximum at the date of A's death eg if the nil rate band is £325,000, the increase cannot exceed £325,000, giving a total of £650,000.

Question	Transfer of nil rate band

Jenna and Rebecca were civil partners until the death of Jenna on 19 August 2008.

Jenna made no lifetime transfers. Her death estate was £240,000 and she left it to her mother. The nil rate band at Jenna's death was £300,000.

Rebecca died on 24 February 2018. Her death estate was £550,000 and she left her entire estate to her brother, so the residence nil rate band is not relevant. She had made no lifetime transfers.

Calculate the inheritance tax payable on the death of Rebecca, assuming that any beneficial claims are made.

Step 1   Value of Rebecca's death estate is £550,000.

Step 2   (a)   No lifetime transfers of value in seven years before 24 February 2018.

(b)   Nil rate band at Rebecca's death is £325,000. Nil rate band is increased by claim to transfer Jenna's unused nil rate band at death. Unused proportion was £(300,000 – 240,000) = 60,000/300,000 × 100 = 20%. The adjusted unused proportion is therefore £325,000 × 20% = £65,000. The maximum nil rate band at Rebecca's death is therefore £(325,000 + 65,000) = £390,000 and this is also the available nil rate band for her estate.

Step 3

	IHT
	£
£390,000 × 0%	0
£160,000 × 40%	64,000
£550,000	64,000

6.4 Transfer of unused residence nil rate band

The **unused residence nil rate band** can be **transferred to a spouse or civil partner**, in a similar way to the nil rate band, if **A dies on or after 6 April 2017**. It does not matter when B died nor if their estate included a main residence. **If B died before 6 April 2017**, they are **deemed to have had a residence nil rate band of £100,000, all of which is available for transfer.**

Question   Transfer of nil rate bands

Daniel and Lucy were married for many years until the death of Lucy on 2 August 2017. Lucy made no lifetime transfers. In her will, Lucy left shares worth £50,000 to her son and the remainder of her estate to Daniel. Her residence nil rate band was therefore wholly unused.

Daniel died on 19 January 2018. His death estate consisted of his main residence valued at £180,000, on which there was secured an interest-only mortgage of £50,000, and other assets valued at £720,000. In his will, Daniel left his entire estate to his daughter. Daniel had made no lifetime transfers.

Calculate the inheritance tax payable on the death of Daniel, assuming that any beneficial claims are made.

Answer

Step 1   Value of Daniel's death estate is £(180,000 – 50,000) = £130,000 + £720,000 = £850,000.

Step 2   Daniel's own maximum residence nil rate band is £100,000 and Lucy's unused residence nil rate band is £100,000 making a maximum residence nil rate band of £200,000. The available residence nil rate band is the lower of £200,000 and the value of the main residence which is £130,000 and so is £130,000.

Step 3   (a)   No lifetime transfers of value in seven years before 19 January 2018.

(b)   Nil rate band at Daniel's death is £325,000. Nil rate band is increased by claim to transfer Lucy's unused nil rate band at death £(325,000 – 50,000) = £275,000. Maximum nil rate band at Daniel's death is therefore £(325,000 + 275,000) = £600,000, all available as Daniel made no lifetime transfers.

Step 4

IHT

£

£130,000 × 0%		0
£600,000 × 0%		0
£120,000 × 40%		48,000
£850,000		48,000

6.5 Changes in residence nil rate band between deaths of spouses/civil partners

From 2018/19 onwards, if the residence nil rate band increases between the death of B and the death of A, the amount of B's unused residence nil rate band must be scaled up, in the same way as for the nil rate band, so that it represents the same proportion of the residence nil rate band at A's death as it did at B's death. As for the nil rate band, the increase in the residence nil rate band maximum cannot exceed the residence nil rate band maximum at the date of A's death.

6.6 Claims to transfer unused nil rate bands

Claims to transfer the unused nil rate bands are usually made by the personal representatives of A. The time limit for the claims is two years from the end of the month of A's death (or the period of three months after the personal representatives start to act, if later) or such longer period as an officer of HMRC may allow in a particular case.

If the personal representatives do not make a claim, a claim can be made by any other person liable to tax chargeable on A's death within such later period as an officer of HMRC may allow in a particular case.

7 Basic inheritance tax planning   9/16

One of the competencies you require to fulfil Performance Objective 17 Tax planning and advice of the PER is to assess the tax implications of proposed activities or plans of an individual or entity with reference to relevant and up to date legislation. You can apply the knowledge you obtain from this section of the Study Text to help to demonstrate this competence.

FAST FORWARD

Basic planning may reduce or eliminate inheritance tax payable. Where appropriate, donors should use exemptions, make gifts early in life, make use of the nil rate band in relation to gifts to trusts and the residence nil rate band on death, and consider making gifts to grandchildren, rather than children.

7.1 Use exemptions

Donors should ensure that **use is made of exemptions in relation to lifetime gifts**, in particular the **annual exemption**, the **marriage/civil partnership exemption**, the **normal expenditure out of income exemption** and the **spouse/civil partner exemption**.

When considering how to pass on assets in the **death estate**, the **spouse/civil partner exemption may be used to ensure that no inheritance tax is payable when the first spouse/civil partner dies**. Remember that an election can be made to ensure that unused nil rate band of the first spouse/civil partner is available to be used against the estate of the surviving spouse/civil partner.

7.2 Make gifts early in life

The earlier that a gift is made in lifetime which is, or may become, a chargeable transfer, the more likely it is that the donor will survive seven years from making it.

If a **gift is made shortly before death**, there will be **little or no inheritance tax benefit** as the gift will be chargeable on the death of the donor. In addition, if the **gift is of a chargeable asset for capital gains tax** (eg shares, land) there will be a **chargeable disposal at market value which may result in a chargeable gain**, whereas **transfers of chargeable assets on death are exempt disposals**.

7.3 Make use of the nil rate bands

Gifts to trusts are chargeable transfers. If the gift is **within the nil rate band**, however, there will be **no inheritance tax payable when the gift is made. Transfers are only cumulated for seven years** and therefore, after that time has elapsed, a **further gift within the nil rate band can be made to a trust**, again without incurring any immediate payment of inheritance tax.

The **residence nil rate band** can only be used if the **main residence is passed to direct descendents**, not to other family members. Donors should consider **making a will** which **uses the residence nil rate band** by **leaving the main residence to children or grandchildren** and **assets such as cash or shares to other family members such as brothers and sisters**.

7.4 Skip a generation

Donors may consider giving assets to their children, either during lifetime or on death. Such assets may then be passed by those children to their own children, the grandchildren of the donor.

If the **donor's children already have sufficient assets for their financial needs, it may be beneficial to skip a generation** so that **gifts are made to grandchildren, rather than children**. This **avoids a further charge to inheritance tax on the death of the children** so that gifts will then only be taxed once before being inherited by the grandchildren, rather than twice.

8 Payment of inheritance tax 9/16, 12/16

One of the competencies you require to fulfil Performance Objective 16 Tax compliance and verification of the PER is to determine the incidence (timing) of tax liabilities and their impact on cash flow/financing requirements. You can apply the knowledge you obtain from this section of the Study Text to help to demonstrate this competence.

8.1 Liability for IHT

FAST FORWARD

The liability to pay IHT depends on the type of transfer and whether it was made in lifetime or on death.

The donor is primarily liable for the tax due on chargeable lifetime transfers. However the donee (ie the trustees) may agree to pay the tax out of the trust assets.

On death, liability for payment is as follows.

(a) **Tax on the death estate is paid by the deceased's personal representatives (PRs)** out of estate assets.

(b) **Tax on a PET that has become chargeable is paid by the donee.**

(c) **Additional liabilities on a CLT is paid by the donee.**

8.2 Due dates

(a) **For chargeable lifetime transfers the due date is the later of:**

    (i)   **30 April just after the end of the tax year of the transfer**

    (ii)   **Six months after the end of the month of the transfer**

(b) **Tax arising on the death estate: the due date is six months from the end of the month of death.** However, if the personal representatives **submit an account of the death estate** within the six month period, they must **pay the IHT due on the death estate on the submission of the account.**

(c) **Tax arising on death in respect of PETs and CLTs: the due date for additional tax is six months from the end of the month of death.**

Question
Payment of inheritance tax

Lisa gave some shares to a trust on 10 July 2013. She gave a house to her daughter on 12 December 2013. Lisa died on 17 May 2017 leaving her death estate to her son.

For each of these transfers of value, state who is liable to pay any inheritance tax due and the due date for payment.

Answer

10 July 2013

Chargeable lifetime transfer. Lifetime tax payable by Lisa (unless trustees agree to pay tax), due later of 30 April 2014 and 31 January 2014 ie 30 April 2014. Death tax payable by trustees, due 30 November 2017.

12 December 2013

Potentially exempt transfer – no lifetime tax. Death tax payable by daughter, due 30 November 2017.

17 May 2017

Death tax payable by personal representatives out of death estate, due on earlier of submission of account and 30 November 2017.

Chapter Roundup

- IHT is a tax on gifts made by individuals to other individuals or trustees.

- IHT applies to lifetime transfers of value and transfers of value made on death.

- Exemptions may apply to make transfers or parts of transfers non chargeable. Some exemptions only apply on lifetime transfers (annual, normal expenditure out of income, marriage/civil partnership), but the spouse/civil partner exemption applies on both life and death transfers.

- The tax on a chargeable transfer is calculated with reference to chargeable transfers in the previous seven years.

- IHT is charged on what a donor loses. If the donor pays the IHT on a lifetime gift they lose both the asset given away and the money with which they paid the tax due on it. Grossing up is required.

- Death tax is chargeable on chargeable lifetime transfers if the donor dies within seven years of making the transfer. Taper relief reduces the death tax if the donor survives between three and seven years.

- Death tax is chargeable on potentially exempt transfers if the donor dies within seven years of making the transfer. Taper relief reduces the death tax if the donor survives between three and seven years. Grossing up is never required on a PET because the death tax is payable by the donee.

- When someone dies, we must bring together all their assets to find the value of their death estate and then charge inheritance tax on it (to the extent that it is not exempt) taking account of the available residence nil rate band and the available nil rate band after transfers made in the seven years before death.

- If one spouse or civil partner does not use up their whole nil rate bands on death, the excesses may be transferred to the surviving spouse/civil partner.

- Basic planning may reduce or eliminate inheritance tax payable. Where appropriate, donors should use exemptions, make gifts early in life, make use of the nil rate band in relation to gifts to trusts and the residence nil rate band on death, and consider making gifts to grandchildren, rather than children.

- The liability to pay IHT depends on the type of transfer and whether it was made in lifetime or on death.

Quick Quiz

1 What is a transfer of value?

2 What type of transfer by an individual is a potentially exempt transfer?

3 To what extent may an unused annual exemption be carried forward?

4 Don gives some money to his daughter on her marriage. What marriage exemption is applicable?

5 Why must some lifetime transfers be grossed up?

6 What is taper relief?

7 Greg dies leaving the following debts:

    (a)   Grocery bill
    (b)   HM Revenue & Customs – income tax to death
    (c)   Mortgage on house
    (d)   Illegal gambling debt

    Which are deductible against his death estate and why?

8 Mark and Hilary had been married for many years. Mark died on 11 May 2016 leaving his estate to Hilary. He had made a chargeable lifetime transfer of £160,000 in July 2014. The nil rate band in 2016/17 was £325,000. Hilary dies in February 2018. What are the maximum nil rate bands on her death, assuming any beneficial claims are made?

9 When is lifetime inheritance tax on a chargeable lifetime transfer due for payment?

1 A transfer of value is any gratuitous disposition by a person resulting in a diminution of the value of his estate.

2 A potentially exempt transfer is a lifetime transfer made by an individual to another individual.

3 An unused annual exemption can be carried forward one tax year.

4 The marriage exemption for a gift to the donor's child is £5,000.

5 Where the donor pays the lifetime tax due it must be grossed up to calculate the total reduction in value of the estate.

6 Taper relief reduces death tax where a transfer is made between three and seven years before death.

7 (a) Grocery bill – deductible as incurred for consideration
   (b) Income tax to death – deductible as imposed by law
   (c) Mortgage – deductible, will be set against value of house primarily
   (d) Illegal gambling debt – not deductible as not legally enforceable

8 Hilary's own residence nil rate band is £100,000. Mark's unused residence nil rate band is £100,000. The maximum residence nil rate band on Hilary's death is therefore £200,000.

   Hilary's own nil rate band is £325,000. Mark's unused nil rate band is £(325,000 – 160,000) = £165,000. The maximum nil rate band on Hilary's death is therefore £490,000.

9 The due date for lifetime tax on a chargeable lifetime transfer is the later of:

   (a) 30 April just after the end of the tax year of the transfer
   (b) Six months after the end of the month of transfer

Now try the questions below from the Practice Question Bank

Number	Type	Marks	Time
Q118	Section A	2	4 mins
Q119	Section A	2	4 mins
Q120	Section A	2	4 mins
Q121	Section B	2	4 mins
Q122	Section B	2	4 mins
Q123	Section B	2	4 mins
Q124	Section B	2	4 mins
Q125	Section B	2	4 mins
Q126	Section C	10	18 mins

Corporation tax

Computing taxable total profits and the corporation tax liability

Topic list	Syllabus reference
1 The scope of corporation tax	E1(a)–(c)
2 Taxable total profits	E2(j)
3 Trading income	E2(a)–(c)
4 Property business income	E2(d)
5 Loan relationships (interest income)	E2(h)
6 Miscellaneous income	E2(j)
7 Qualifying charitable donations	E2(i)
8 Long periods of account	E2(j)
9 Computing the corporation tax liability	E4(a)
10 Choice of business medium	E4(a)

Introduction

Now that we have completed our study of personal tax we turn our attention to corporation tax, ie the tax that a company must pay on its profits.

First we consider the scope of corporation tax and we see that a company must pay tax for an 'accounting period' which may be different from its period of account.

We then learn how to calculate taxable total profits. This involves first calculating total profits by adding together income from different sources, such as trading income, interest and property income, and capital gains, and then deducting trading and property losses and qualifying charitable donations. You have learnt the general rules for calculating income in your earlier studies, but here we see where there are special rules for companies.

You will then learn how to compute the corporation tax liability on taxable total profits.

Finally, we investigate choice of business medium by comparing the tax effects of trading as a sole trader and through a company.

In the next chapter we will deal with chargeable gains for companies.

Study guide

		Intellectual level
E1	**The scope of corporation tax**	
(a)	Define the terms 'period of account', 'accounting period', and 'financial year'.	1
(b)	Recognise when an accounting period starts and when an accounting period finishes.	1
(c)	Explain how the residence of a company is determined.	2
E2	**Taxable total profits**	
(a)	Recognise the expenditure that is allowable in calculating the tax-adjusted trading profit.	2
(b)	Recognise the relief which can be obtained for pre-trading expenditure.	1
(c)	Compute capital allowances (as for income tax).	2
(d)	Compute property business profits and understand how relief for a property business loss is given.	2
(h)	Recognise and apply the treatment of interest paid and received under the loan relationship rules.	1
(i)	Recognise and apply the treatment of qualifying charitable donations.	2
(j)	Compute taxable total profits.	2
E4	**The comprehensive computation of corporation tax liability**	
(a)	Compute the corporation tax liability	2

Exam guide

One of the 15 mark questions in Section C will focus on corporation tax. Corporation tax may also be tested in 10 mark questions in Sections B or C. You should also expect to see one or more questions on corporation tax in Section A. When dealing with a corporation tax question in Section C you must first be able to identify the accounting period(s) involved; watch out for long periods of account. You must also be able to calculate taxable total profits; learn the standard layout so that you can easily slot in figures from your workings.

1 The scope of corporation tax

Companies pay corporation tax on their taxable total profits.

1.1 Companies

Companies must pay corporation tax on their **taxable total profits** for each **accounting period**. We look at the meaning of these terms below.

Key term

A **company** is any corporate body (limited or unlimited) or unincorporated association, eg sports club.

1.2 Accounting periods

FAST FORWARD

An accounting period cannot exceed 12 months in length so a long period of account must be split into two accounting periods. The first accounting period of a long period of account is always 12 months in length.

Corporation tax is chargeable in respect of accounting periods. It is important to understand the difference between an accounting period and a period of account.

Key term

A **period of account** is any period for which a company prepares accounts; usually this will be 12 months in length but it may be longer or shorter than this.

Key term

An **accounting period** is the period for which corporation tax is charged and cannot exceed 12 months. Special rules determine when an accounting period starts and ends.

An accounting period starts on the earliest of:

- When a company starts to trade
- When the company otherwise becomes liable to corporation tax (eg it opens a bank account which pays interest)
- Immediately after the previous accounting period finishes

An accounting period finishes on the earliest of:

- 12 months after its start
- The end of the company's period of account
- The company starting or ceasing to trade
- The company entering/ceasing to be in administration
- The commencement of the company's winding up
- The company's ceasing to be resident in the UK
- The company's ceasing to be liable to corporation tax

If a company has a period of account exceeding 12 months (a long period of account), it is split into two accounting periods: the first 12 months and the remainder.

Question	Accounting periods

For each of the following companies, identify the accounting period(s).

(a)   J Ltd, which has been trading for many years, prepares accounts for the 12 months to 30 September 2017.

(b)   K plc is incorporated on 1 April 2017. On 1 June 2017, K plc starts to trade and makes up its first set of accounts to 31 August 2017.

(c)   L Ltd, which has been trading for many years preparing accounts to 31 December each year, prepares accounts for the 11 months to 30 November 2017.

(d)   M Plc, which has been trading for many years preparing accounts to 31 July each year, prepares accounts for the 16 months to 30 November 2017.

(a)   1 October 2016 (immediately after previous accounting period finishes) to 30 September 2017 (12 months after start of accounting period and also the end of period of account).

(b)   1 June 2017 (company starts to trade) to 31 August 2017 (end of period of account).

(c)   1 January 2017 (immediately after previous accounting period finishes) to 30 November 2017 (end of period of account).

(d)   First accounting period: 1 August 2016 (immediately after previous accounting period finishes) to 31 July 2017 (12 months after start).

Second accounting period: 1 August 2017 (immediately after previous accounting period finishes) to 30 November 2017 (end of period of account).

1.3 Financial year

FAST FORWARD   Tax rates are set for financial years.

The rates of corporation tax are fixed for financial years.

Key term   A **financial year** runs from 1 April to the following 31 March and is identified by the calendar year in which it begins. For example, the year ended 31 March 2018 is the Financial year 2017 (FY 2017). This should not be confused with a tax year, which runs from 6 April to the following 5 April.

1.4 Residence of companies   12/16

FAST FORWARD   A company is UK resident if it is incorporated in the UK or if it is incorporated overseas and its central management and control are exercised in the UK.

A company incorporated in the UK is resident in the UK. A company incorporated abroad is resident in the UK if its central management and control are exercised here. Central management and control are usually treated as exercised where the board of directors meet.

Question   Residence of a company

Supraville SARL is a company incorporated in France. It has its head office in London where the board of directors meet monthly. It trades throughout the European Union.

Is Supraville SARL resident in the UK?

Answer

Yes, Supraville SARL is resident in the UK.

The central management and control of Supraville SARL is in London (ie the UK) where the board of directors meet.

This topic was tested in Question 33, Wretched Ltd, in the December 2016 exam. Candidates were required to state whether the company that was incorporated in the UK, but whose directors were all non-resident in the United Kingdom and whose board meetings were always held overseas, was resident or not resident in the UK for corporation tax purposes. The examining team commented that this requirement resulted in a very surprising amount of incorrect answers, with at least half the candidates deciding that the company was not resident because of its central management and control being exercised overseas.

2 Taxable total profits   9/16, 6/17

Taxable total profits comprises the company's income and chargeable gains (total profits) less some losses and qualifying charitable donations. It does not include dividends received from other companies.

One of the competencies you require to fulfil Performance Objective 15 Tax computations and assessments of the PER is to extract and analyse data from financial records and filing information relevant to the preparation of tax computations and related supporting documents. You can apply the knowledge you obtain from this section of the Study Text to help to demonstrate this competence.

2.1 Proforma computation

Income includes trading income, property income, income from non-trading loan relationships (interest) and miscellaneous income.

A company may have both income and gains. As a general rule income arises from receipts which are expected to recur regularly (such as the profits from a trade) whereas chargeable gains arise on the sale of capital assets which have been owned for several years (such as the sale of a factory used in the trade).

A company may receive income from various sources. All income received must be classified according to the nature of the income as different computational rules apply to different types of income. The main types of income for a company are:

- Profits of a trade
- Profits of a property business
- Interest income from non-trading loan relationships
- Miscellaneous income

The computation of chargeable gains for a company is dealt with later in this Study Text. At the moment, you will be given a figure for chargeable gains in order to compute taxable total profits. We also deal with losses in detail later in this Study Text so, at the moment, you just need to know that some losses are given tax relief by being deducted from total profits.

A company's taxable total profits are arrived at by aggregating its various sources of income and its chargeable gains and then deducting losses and qualifying charitable donations. Here is a pro forma computation.

	£
Trading profits	X
Property business income	X
Interest income from non-trading loan relationships	X
Miscellaneous income	X
Chargeable gains	X
Total profits	X
Less losses deductible from total profits	(X)
Less qualifying charitable donations	(X)
Taxable total profits for an accounting period	X

It would be of great help in the exam if you could learn the above proforma. When answering a corporation tax question you could immediately reproduce the proforma and insert the appropriate numbers as you are given the information in the question.

Dividends received from other companies (UK resident and non-UK resident), for the purposes of the Taxation (TX – UK) exam, are usually exempt and so not included in taxable total profits.

3 Trading income

3.1 Adjustment of profits   9/16, 6/17

FAST FORWARD

The adjustment of profits computation for companies broadly follows that for computing business profits subject to income tax. There are, however, some minor differences.

The trading income of companies is derived from the profit before taxation figure in the statement of profit or loss, just as for individuals, adjusted as follows.

	£	£
Profit before taxation		X
Add expenditure not allowed for taxation purposes		X
		X
Less: income not taxable as trading income	X	
expenditure not charged in the accounts but allowable for the purposes of taxation	X	
capital allowances	X	
		(X)
Profit adjusted for tax purposes		X

An examination question requiring adjustment to profit will direct you to start the adjustment with the profit before taxation of £XXXX and deal with all the items listed indicating with a zero (0) any items which do not require adjustment. Marks will not be given for relevant items unless this approach is used. Therefore students who attempt to rewrite the statement of profit or loss will be penalised.

The adjustment of profits computation for companies broadly follows that for computing business profits subject to income tax. There are, however, some minor differences. There is no disallowance for 'private use' for companies; instead the director or employee will be taxed on the benefit received.

Qualifying charitable donations are added back in the calculation of adjusted profit. They are treated instead as a deduction from total profits.

Investment income including rents is deducted from profit before taxation in arriving at trading income but brought in again further down in the computation (see below).

When adjusting profits as supplied in a statement of profit or loss confusion can arise as regards whether figures are net or gross. Properly drawn up company accounts should normally include all income gross. However, some examination questions include items 'net'. Read the question carefully.

3.2 Pre-trading expenditure   9/16

Pre-trading expenditure incurred by the company within the seven years before trade commences is treated as an allowable expense incurred on the first day of trading provided it would have been allowable had the company been trading when the expense was actually incurred.

3.3 Capital allowances

The calculation of capital allowances follows income tax principles.

For companies, however, there is never any reduction of allowances to take account of any private use of an asset. The director or employee suffers a taxable benefit instead. As shown above capital allowances must be deducted in arriving at taxable trading income.

A company's accounting period can never exceed 12 months. If the period of account is longer than 12 months it is **divided into two**; one for the first 12 months and one for the balance. **The capital allowances computation must be carried out for each period separately.**

> **Exam focus point**
>
> The calculation of trading income should be undertaken as a first step to the calculation of taxable total profits. However, it is important to realise that these are two distinct aspects when calculating a company's liability to corporation tax and you should not attempt to present them in one calculation.

4 Property business income

Rental income is deducted in arriving at trading income but brought in again further down in the computation as property business income.

The calculation of property business income follows income tax principles. The income tax rules for property businesses were set out earlier in this Study Text. In summary all UK rental activities are treated as a single source of income calculated in the same way as trading income.

However, **interest paid by a company on a loan to buy or improve property is not a property business expense**. The **loan relationship rules apply** instead (see below). The restriction for tax relief on finance costs does not apply to companies.

5 Loan relationships (interest income)

5.1 General principle

If a company borrows or lends money, including issuing or investing in debentures or buying gilts, it has a loan relationship. This can be a creditor relationship (where the company lends or invests money) **or a debtor relationship** (where the company borrows money or issues securities). Loan interest paid or received is dealt with on a receivable (accruals) basis.

5.2 Treatment of trading loan relationships

If the company is a party to a **loan relationship for trade purposes, any debits – ie interest paid or other debt costs – charged through its accounts are allowed as a trading expense** and are therefore deductible in computing trading income. An example of a trading loan relationship is a loan to buy plant and machinery to use in the trade.

Similarly **if any credits – ie interest income or other debt returns – arise on a trading loan these are treated as a trading receipt and are taxable as trading income.** This is not likely to arise unless the trade is one of money lending.

5.3 Treatment of non-trading loan relationships

If a loan relationship is not one to which the company is a party for trade purposes any debits or credits must be pooled. A net credit on the pool is chargeable as interest income. Examples of non trading loan relationships would be cash on deposit at the bank (creditor relationship), or a loan to purchase a property that is rented out (debtor relationship).

Interest charged on underpaid tax is allowable and interest received on overpaid tax is assessable under the rules for non-trading loan relationships.

> **Exam focus point**
>
> You will not be expected to deal with net deficits (ie losses) on non-trading loan relationships in your exam.

5.4 Accounting methods

Debits and credits must be brought into account using the UK generally accepted accounting practice (GAAP) or using the International Accounting Standards (IAS). This will usually be the **accruals basis**.

5.5 Incidental costs of loan finance

Under the loan relationship rules expenses ('debits') are allowed if incurred directly:

(a) To bring a loan relationship into existence
(b) Entering into or giving effect to any related transactions
(c) Making payment under a loan relationship or related transactions or
(d) Taking steps to ensure the receipt of payments under the loan relationship or related transaction

A related transaction means 'any disposal or acquisition (in whole or in part) of rights or liabilities under the relationship, including any arising from a security issue in relation to the money debt in question'.

The above categories of incidental costs are also allowable even if the company does not enter into the loan relationship (ie abortive costs). Costs directly incurred in varying the terms of a loan relationship are also allowed.

5.6 Other matters

It is not only the interest costs of borrowing that are allowable or taxable. Capital costs are treated similarly.

6 Miscellaneous income

Patent royalties received which do not relate to the trade are taxed as miscellaneous income. Patent royalties which relate to the trade are included in trading income normally on an accruals basis.

7 Qualifying charitable donations

FAST FORWARD

Qualifying charitable donations are deducted from total profits when computing taxable total profits.

Qualifying charitable donations are deductible from total profits when computing taxable total profits.

Almost all donations of money to charity by a company can be qualifying charitable donations whether they are single donations or regular donations. There is no need for a claim to be made in order for a payment to be treated as a qualifying charitable donation (compare with gift aid donations where a declaration is required).

Donations to local charities which are incurred wholly and exclusively for the purposes of a trade are deducted in the calculation of the tax adjusted trading profits.

Marlborough Ltd is a UK resident trading company. The company's statement of profit or loss for the year ended 31 March 2018 is as follows:

	£	£
Gross profit		700,000
Other income		
Loan stock interest (note 1)		14,500
Rental income (note 2)		18,000
Expenses		
Salaries	76,000	
Depreciation	37,900	
Loss on sale of non-current asset	1,400	
Impairment losses (all trade)	2,800	
Professional fees (note 3)	12,900	
Repairs and renewals (note 4)	17,100	
Other expenses (note 5)	25,600	
		(173,700)
Finance costs		
Loan interest (note 6)		(12,000)
Profit before taxation		546,800

Notes

1   Loan stock interest

The loan stock interest is in respect of loan stock held by Marlborough Ltd as an investment. The amount of £14,500 is the amount received and accrued to 31 March 2018.

2   Rental income

The rental income is in respect of a warehouse which is held as an investment and is let out to an unconnected company. The rental received of £18,000 is also the amount accrued to 31 March 2018.

3   Professional fees

Professional fees are as follows:

	£
Accountancy and audit fees	4,600
Debt collection of trade debts	5,000
Legal fees in connection with renewing a 25 year lease	1,300
Legal fees in connection with director's motoring offences	2,000
	12,900

4   Repairs and renewals

Repairs and renewals include:

	£
Extension to factory	7,988
Repainting exterior of company's offices	6,000

5   Other expenses

Other expenses include:

	£
100 pens with an advertisement for company, given to customers	2,100
Qualifying charitable donation	5,000

6 Loan interest

The loan interest relates to the warehouse let out (see note (2)). The amount shown is the amount paid and accrued to 31 March 2018.

7 Plant and machinery

On 1 April 2017 the tax written down value of the main pool was £22,500. The following transactions took place during the year ended 31 March 2018:

		Cost/(Proceeds) £
10 June 2017	Purchased general plant	20,200
25 January 2018	Sold a van (original cost £17,000)	(11,500)
15 March 2018	Purchased a motor car CO_2 emissions 128g/km	10,600

The motor car purchased on 15 March 2018 is used by the company's sales manager: 30% of the mileage is for private journeys.

(a) What are Marlborough Ltd's trading profits for the year ended 31 March 2018? Start with the profit before taxation figure of £546,800 and list all of the items in the statement of profit or loss indicating by the use of a zero (0) any items that do not require adjustment.

(b) What are Marlborough Ltd's taxable total profits for the year ended 31 March 2018?

Answer

(a) **Marlborough Ltd – trading profits for y/e 31 March 2018**

	£	£
Profit before taxation		546,800
Add:		
Salaries (trade)	0	
Depreciation (capital)	37,900	
Loss on sale of non-current asset (capital loss)	1,400	
Impairment losses (trade)	0	
Accountancy and audit fees	0	
Debt collection (trade)	0	
Legal fees – renewal of short lease	0	
Legal fees – motoring offences (not trade)	2,000	
Repairs and renewals: extension (capital)	7,988	
Repairs and renewals: repainting (revenue)	0	
Other expenses: pens (<£50, advertisement)	0	
Other expenses: qualifying charitable donation	5,000	
Loan interest (non-trading loan relationship)	12,000	
		66,288
Deduct:		
Loan stock interest (non-trading loan relationship)	14,500	
Rental income (property business income)	18,000	
Capital allowances (W)	24,088	
		(56,588)
Profit adjusted for tax purposes		556,500

Working

Capital allowances on plant and machinery

	AIA £	Main pool £	Allowances £
TWDV b/f		22,500	
Additions qualifying for AIA			
10.6.17 General plant	20,200		
AIA	(20,200)		20,200
Additions not qualifying for AIA			
15.3.18 Car		10,600	
Disposal			
25.1.18 Van		(11,500)	
		21,600	
WDA @ 18%		(3,888)	3,888
TWDV c/f		17,712	
Allowances			24,088

Note. The private use of the car by the employee is not relevant for capital allowance purposes. No adjustment is ever made to a company's capital allowances to reflect the private use of an asset.

(b)   **Marlborough Ltd – taxable total profits for y/e 31 March 2018**

	£	£
Trading profit (part (a))		556,500
Non-trading loan relationship credit (loan stock)	14,500	
Less non-trading loan relationship debit (warehouse loan)	(12,000)	
		2,500
Property business income		18,000
Total profits		577,000
Less qualifying charitable donation		(5,000)
Taxable total profits		572,000

8 Long periods of account

FAST FORWARD

Long periods of account are split into two accounting periods: the first 12 months and the remainder.

As we saw earlier in this chapter, if a company has a long period of account exceeding 12 months, it is split into two accounting periods: the first 12 months and the remainder.

Where the period of account differs from the corporation tax accounting periods, profits are **allocated to the relevant periods** as follows:

- **Trading income** before capital allowances and **property income** are apportioned on a **time basis**.

- **Capital allowances** and balancing charges are **calculated for each accounting period**.

- **Other income is allocated to the period to which it relates** (eg interest accrued). Miscellaneous income, however, is apportioned on a time basis.

- **Chargeable gains and losses** are allocated to the **period in which they are realised**.

- **Qualifying charitable donations** are deducted in the accounting **period in which they are paid**.

Xenon Ltd makes up an 18 month set of accounts to 30 September 2018 with the following results.

	£
Trading income (no capital allowances claimed)	180,000
Interest income	
18 months @ £500 accruing per month	9,000
Capital gain (1 August 2018 disposal)	250,000
Less qualifying charitable donation (paid 31 March 2018)	(50,000)
	389,000

What are the taxable total profits for each of the accounting periods based on the above accounts?

Answer

The 18 month period of account is divided into:

Year ending 31 March 2018
6 months to 30 September 2018

Results are allocated:

	Y/e 31.3.18 £	6m to 30.9.18 £
Trading income 12:6	120,000	60,000
Interest income		
12 × £500	6,000	
6 × £500		3,000
Capital gain (1.8.18)		250,000
Total profits	126,000	313,000
Less qualifying charitable donation (31.3.18)	(50,000)	
Taxable total profits	76,000	313,000

9 Computing the corporation tax liability

 One of the competencies you require to fulfil Performance Objective 15 Tax computations and assessments of the PER is to prepare or contribute to the computation or assessment of tax computations for single companies, groups or other entities. You can apply the knowledge you obtain from this section of the Study Text to help to demonstrate this competence.

9.1 Rate of corporation tax

FAST FORWARD There is a single rate of corporation tax which is applied to a company's taxable total profits to compute the corporation tax liability.

For financial year 2017, there is a single rate of corporation tax (the main rate) which is 19%. This rate is applied to the company's taxable total profits to compute the corporation tax liability. The rate of corporation tax for financial years 2015 and 2016 was 20%.

Exam focus point The rates of corporation tax will be given in the Tax Rates and Allowances in the exam.

Question

Apricot Ltd had taxable total profits of £1,142,000 in the year to 31 March 2018. Compute Apricot Ltd's corporation tax liability.

Answer

£1,142,000 × 19%   £216,980

9.2 Accounting period in more than one financial year

An accounting period **may fall within more than one financial year. If the rates for corporation tax are the same in both financial years, tax can be computed for the accounting period as if it fell within one financial year.**

However, **if the rates for corporation tax are different in the financial years, taxable total profits are time apportioned between the financial years**. The rate of corporation tax in the financial year 2016 was 20% so if the accounting period spans 31 March 2017, apportionment will be needed.

Question

Wentworth Ltd makes up its accounts to 31 December each year. For the year to 31 December 2017, it has taxable total profits of £480,000. Compute Wentworth Ltd's corporation tax liability.

Answer

	£
FY 2016 (1.1.17 to 31.3.17 – 3 months)	
£480,000 × 3/12 = 120,000 × 20%	24,000
FY 2017 (1.4.17 to 31.12.17 – 9 months)	
£480,000 × 9/12 = 360,000 × 19%	68,400
Corporation tax liability for year to 31 December 2017	92,400

10 Choice of business medium

FAST FORWARD

An individual can choose between trading as a sole trader or trading through a company. Trading through a company may reduce the overall tax and national insurance liability.

10.1 Trading as a sole trader or through a company   9/16

An individual starting in business must decide whether to trade as a sole trader or as a company. If a company is used, the individual can be both a director and a shareholder of the company.

A sole trader pays **income tax on trading income** and also **Class 2 and Class 4 national insurance contributions.**

A company pays corporation tax on its taxable total profits. Any director's salary and its associated Class 1 employer's national insurance contributions are deducted in computing those profits. The employment allowance is not available if the director is the only employee. An amount equal to the **remaining profits after corporation tax** can then be **paid out to shareholders as a dividend.** The **individual as a director pays income tax on employment income** and **Class 1 employee's contributions**

on cash earnings. The **individual as a shareholder pays income tax on dividend income**. There are **no national insurance contributions on dividends**.

10.2 Example: Sole trader or company?

Sharif is starting a new business and expects to make profits of £42,000 before tax and national insurance.

Sharif wants to know how much net income he would receive from the business if he trades as a sole trader or, alternatively, through a company of which he would be the sole shareholder, director and employee, with the company paying him a salary of £8,200 (in order to maintain Class 1 national insurance contributions) and then an amount equal to the company's remaining profits (after corporation tax) as a dividend. Sharif has no other income.

As a sole trader

	£
Profits	42,000
Less personal allowance	(11,500)
Taxable income	30,500
Income tax on £30,500 × 20%	6,100
National Insurance Classes 2 (52 × £2.85) and 4 (£(42,000 – 8,164) × 9%)	3,193
	9,293
Net income £(42,000 – 9,293)	32,707

Through a company

	£
Profits	42,000
Less director's salary	(8,200)
Less employer's Class 1 contributions (8,200 – 8,164) × 13.8%	(5)
Taxable profits	33,795
Less corporation tax 19% × £33,795	(6,421)
Net profits	27,374

The employment allowance is not available as Sharif is the only employee of the company and a director of the company.

A dividend of £27,374 can be paid to Sharif.

	Non-savings income	Dividend income	Total
	£	£	£
Earnings	8,200		
Dividend		27,374	
Net income	8,200	27,374	30,430
Less personal allowance	(8,200)	(3,300)	
Taxable income	0	24,074	24,074
Dividend income			
£5,000 × 0%			0
£19,074 (24,074 – 5,000) × 7.5%			1,431
Income tax liability			1,431

		£
Net income		£
Salary		8,200
Dividend		27,374
	£	35,574
Less: income tax	1,431	
employee's Class 1 contributions		
£(8,200 – 8,164) × 12%	4	
		(1,435)
Net income		34,139

If Sharif trades through a company, he will receive £(34,139 – 32,707) = £1,432 more net income from the business than if he trades as a sole trader.

<table>
<tr><td>Exam focus point</td><td>

This topic was tested, in the context of extraction of profits from a company, in Question 31 Joe in the September 2016 exam. The examining team commented that although there were many good attempts at this question, various aspects consistently caused problems including:

- The majority of candidates did not appreciate that where all of a company's profits are paid out as director's remuneration (and the related employer's class 1 NIC) then there is not any corporation liability.

- Similarly, it was not appreciated that with director's remuneration of just £8,000 (which is below the NIC lower thresholds) then there are no NICs.

- Many candidates incorrectly calculated NICs on the dividends.

</td></tr>
</table>

Chapter Roundup

- Companies pay corporation tax on their taxable total profits.

- An accounting period cannot exceed 12 months in length so a long period of account must be split into two accounting periods. The first accounting period of a long period of account is always 12 months in length.

- Tax rates are set for financial years.

- A company is UK resident if it is incorporated in the UK or if it is incorporated overseas and its central management and control are exercised in the UK.

- Taxable total profits comprises the company's income and chargeable gains (total profits) less some losses and qualifying charitable donations. It does not include dividends received from other companies.

- Income includes trading income, property income, income from non-trading loan relationships (interest) and miscellaneous income.

- The adjustment of profits computation for companies broadly follows that for computing business profits subject to income tax. There are, however, some minor differences.

- Qualifying charitable donations are deducted from total profits when computing taxable total profits.

- Long periods of account are split into two accounting periods: the first 12 months and the remainder.

- There is a single rate of corporation tax which is applied to a company's taxable total profits to compute the corporation tax liability.

- An individual can choose between trading as a sole trader or trading through a company. Trading through a company may reduce the overall tax and national insurance liability.

Quick Quiz

1 When does an accounting period end?

2 What is the difference between a period of account and an accounting period?

3 Zed Ltd has been trading for many years, preparing accounts to 31 October. It decides to prepare accounts for the 15 month period ending 31 January 2018. What are Zed Ltd's accounting period(s) for the long period of account?

    A   1 November 2016 to 31 January 2018
    B   1 November 2016 to 31 October 2017 and 1 November 2017 to 31 January 2018
    C   1 November 2016 to 31 January 2017 and 1 February 2017 to 31 January 2018
    D   1 November 2016 to 31 March 2017 and 1 April 2017 to 31 January 2018

4 Should interest paid on a trading loan be adjusted in the trading income computation?

5 How is trading income (before capital allowances) of a long period of account divided between accounting periods?

    A   On a receipts basis
    B   On an accruals basis
    C   On a time basis
    D   On any basis the company chooses

6 What is the rate of corporation tax for financial year 2017?

1   An accounting period ends on the earliest of:

       (a)   12 months after its start

       (b)   The end of the company's period of account

       (c)   The commencement of the company's winding up

       (d)   The company ceasing to be resident in the UK

       (e)   The company ceasing to be liable to corporation tax

2   A period of account is the period for which a company prepares accounts. An accounting period is the period for which corporation tax is charged. If a company prepares annual accounts the two will coincide.

3   B. 1 November 2016 to 31 October 2017 and 1 November 2017 to 31 January 2018. The first accounting period of a long period of account is always 12 months in length.

4   Interest paid on a trading loan should not be adjusted in the trading income computation as it is an allowable expense, computed on the accruals basis.

5   C. Trading income (before capital allowances) is apportioned on a time basis.

6   The corporation tax rate for financial year 2017 is 19%.

Now try the questions below from the Practice Question Bank

Number	Type	Marks	Time
Q127	Section A	2	4 mins
Q128	Section A	2	4 mins
Q129	Section A	2	4 mins
Q130	Section B	2	4 mins
Q131	Section B	2	4 mins
Q132	Section B	2	4 mins
Q133	Section B	2	4 mins
Q134	Section B	2	4 mins
Q135	Section C	15	27 mins

Chargeable gains for companies

20

Topic list	Syllabus reference
1 Corporation tax on chargeable gains	E3(a)
2 Indexation allowance	E3(b)
3 Disposal of shares by companies	E3(d)–(f)
4 Relief for replacement of business assets (rollover relief)	E3(g)

Introduction

We studied chargeable gains for individuals earlier in this Study Text. In this chapter, we will consider the treatment of chargeable gains for companies.

Companies pay corporation tax on their chargeable gains, rather than capital gains tax. The computation of gains for companies is slightly more complicated than for individuals because companies are entitled to indexation allowance.

We also consider the matching rules for companies which dispose of shares in other companies. Again, these rules are slightly more complicated than for individuals.

Finally, we look at how the relief for replacement of business assets applies to companies.

In the next chapters we will deal with losses and groups.

Study guide

		Intellectual level
E3	**Chargeable gains for companies**	
(a)	Compute and explain the treatment of chargeable gains.	2
(b)	Explain and compute the indexation allowance available.	2
(d)	Understand the treatment of disposals of shares by companies and the identification rules including the same day and nine day matching rules.	2
(e)	Explain and apply the pooling provisions.	2
(f)	Explain and apply the treatment of bonus issues, rights issues, takeovers and reorganisations.	2
(g)	Explain and apply rollover relief.	2

Exam guide

There will be a 15 mark question on corporation tax in Section C. This may include the gains of a company so it is important that you can deal with the aspects covered in this chapter. Corporation tax may also be tested in 10 mark questions in Sections B or C. A Section A question may test a specific point such as computation of the indexation allowance.

Exam focus point

> ACCA's article **Chargeable gains,** written by a member of the Taxation (TX – UK) examining team, in Part 1 looks at **chargeable gains** in either a **personal or corporate context**. Part 2 focuses on **shares, reliefs,** and the way in which **gains made by limited companies are taxed**.

1 Corporation tax on chargeable gains

FAST FORWARD

> Chargeable gains for companies are computed in broadly the same way as for individuals, but indexation allowance applies and there is no annual exempt amount.

Companies do not pay capital gains tax. Instead their chargeable gains are included in the calculation of taxable total profits.

A company's capital gains or allowable losses are computed in a similar way to individuals but with a few major differences:

- There is relief for inflation called the indexation allowance
- **No annual exempt amount** is available
- Different matching rules for shares apply if the shareholder is a company

2 Indexation allowance   9/16, 12/16, 6/17

FAST FORWARD

> The indexation allowance gives relief for the inflation element of a gain.

The purpose of having an indexation allowance is to remove the inflation element of a gain from taxation.

Companies are entitled to indexation allowance from the date of acquisition until the date of disposal of an asset. It is based on the movement in the Retail Price Index (RPI) between those two dates.

For example, if J Ltd bought a painting on 2 January 2004 and sold it on 19 November 2017 the indexation allowance is available from January 2004 until November 2017.

The indexation factor is:

$$\frac{\text{RPI for month of disposal} - \text{RPI for month of acquisition}}{\text{RPI for month of acquisition}}$$

The calculation is expressed as a decimal and is rounded to three decimal places.

Indexation allowance is available on the allowable cost of the asset from the **date of acquisition** (including incidental costs of acquisition). It is also available on **enhancement expenditure from the month in which such expenditure becomes due and payable. Indexation allowance is not available on the costs of disposal**.

Question
The indexation allowance

An asset is acquired by a company on 15 February 2003 (RPI = 179.3) at a cost of £5,000. Enhancement expenditure of £2,000 is incurred on 10 April 2004 (RPI = 185.7). The asset is sold for £15,500 on 20 December 2017 (assumed RPI = 274.8). Incidental costs of sale are £500. Calculate the chargeable gain arising.

Answer

The indexation allowance is available until December 2017 and is computed as follows.

	£
$\frac{274.8 - 179.3}{179.3} = 0.533 \times £5,000$	2,665
$\frac{274.8 - 185.7}{185.7} = 0.480 \times £2,000$	960
	3,625

The computation of the chargeable gain is as follows.

	£
Proceeds	15,500
Less incidental costs of sale	(500)
Net proceeds	15,000
Less allowable costs £(5,000 + 2,000)	(7,000)
Unindexed gain	8,000
Less indexation allowance (see above)	(3,625)
Indexed gain	4,375

Indexation allowance cannot create or increase an allowable loss. If there is a gain before the indexation allowance, the allowance can reduce that gain to zero but no further. If there is a loss before the indexation allowance, there is no indexation allowance.

If the indexation allowance calculation gives a negative figure, treat the indexation as nil: do not add to the unindexed gain.

3 Disposal of shares by companies   6/17

FAST FORWARD

There are special rules for matching shares sold by a company with shares purchased. Disposals are matched with acquisitions on the same day, the previous nine days and the FA 1985 share pool.

3.1 The matching rules

We have discussed the share matching rules for individuals earlier in this Study Text. We also need special rules for companies.

For companies the matching of shares sold is in the following order.

(a)   Shares acquired on the **same day**

(b)   Shares acquired in the **previous nine days**, if more than one acquisition on a 'first in, first out' (FIFO) basis

(c)   Shares from the **FA 1985 pool**

The composition of the FA 1985 pool in relation to companies which are shareholders is explained below.

Exam focus point

Learn the 'matching rules' because a crucial first step to getting a shares question right is to correctly match the shares sold to the original shares purchased.

3.2 Example: Share matching rules for companies

Nor Ltd acquired the following shares in Last plc:

Date of acquisition	No of shares
9.11.02	15,000
15.12.04	15,000
11.7.17	5,000
15.7.17	5,000

Nor Ltd disposed of 20,000 of the shares on 15 July 2017.

We match the shares as follows:

(a)   Acquisition on same day: 5,000 shares acquired 15 July 2017
(b)   Acquisitions in previous 9 days: 5,000 shares acquired 11 July 2017
(c)   FA 1985 share pool: 10,000 shares out of 30,000 shares in FA 1985 share pool (9.11.02 and 15.12.04)

3.3 The FA 1985 share pool

Exam focus point

The examining team has stated that a detailed question will not be set on the pooling provisions. However, work through the examples below as you are expected to understand how the pool works.

The FA 1985 pool comprises the following shares of the same class in the same company.

•   **Shares held by a company on 1 April 1985 and acquired by that company on or after 1 April 1982**

•   **Shares acquired by that company on or after 1 April 1985**

We must keep track of:

(a)   The **number** of shares
(b)   The **cost** of the shares ignoring indexation
(c)   The **indexed cost** of the shares

The first step in constructing the FA 1985 share pool is to calculate the value of the pool at 1 April 1985 by indexing the cost of each acquisition before that date up to April 1985.

3.4 Example: The FA 1985 pool

Oliver Ltd bought 1,000 shares in Judith plc for £2,750 in August 1984 and another 1,000 for £3,250 in December 1984. RPIs are August 1984 = 89.9, December 1984 = 90.9 and April 1985 = 94.8. The FA 1985 pool at 1 April 1985 is as follows.

	No of shares	Cost £	Indexed cost £
August 1984 (a)	1,000	2,750	2,750
December 1984 (b)	1,000	3,250	3,250
	2,000	6,000	6,000

Indexation allowance

$\dfrac{94.8 - 89.9}{89.9} = 0.055 \times £2,750$ 151

$\dfrac{94.8 - 90.9}{90.9} = 0.043 \times £3,250$ 140

Indexed cost of the pool at 1 April 1985   6,291

Disposals and acquisitions of shares which affect the indexed value of the FA 1985 pool are termed **'operative events'. Prior to reflecting each such operative event within the FA 1985 share pool, a further indexation allowance (an 'indexed rise') must be computed up to the date of the operative event concerned from the date of the last such operative event** (or from the later of the first acquisition and April 1985 if the operative event in question is the first one).

Indexation calculations within the FA 1985 pool (after its April 1985 value has been calculated) **are not rounded to three decimal places**. This is because rounding errors would accumulate and have a serious effect after several operative events.

If there are several operative events between 1 April 1985 and the date of a disposal, the indexation procedure described above will have to be performed several times over.

Question	Value of FA 1985 pool

Following on from the above example, assume that Oliver Ltd acquired 2,000 more shares on 10 July 1986 at a cost of £4,000. Recalculate the value of the FA 1985 pool on 10 July 1986 following the acquisition. RPI July 1986 = 97.5.

Answer

	No of shares	Cost £	Indexed cost £
Value at 1.4.85 b/f	2,000	6,000	6,291
Indexed rise $\dfrac{97.5 - 94.8}{94.8} \times £6,291$			179
	2,000	6,000	6,470
Acquisition	2,000	4,000	4,000
Value at 10.7.86	4,000	10,000	10,470

In the case of a disposal, following the calculation of the indexed rise to the date of disposal, the cost and the indexed cost attributable to the shares disposed of are deducted from the amounts within the FA 1985 pool. The proportions of the cost and indexed cost to take out of the pool should be computed by using the proportion that the shares disposed of bear to the total number of shares held.

The indexation allowance is the indexed cost taken out of the pool minus the cost taken out. As usual, the indexation allowance cannot create or increase a loss.

Continuing the above exercise, suppose that Oliver Ltd sold 3,000 shares on 10 July 2017 for £24,000. Compute the gain, and the value of the FA 1985 pool following the disposal. Assume RPI July 2017 = 271.0.

Answer

	No of shares	Cost £	Indexed cost £
Value at 10.7.86	4,000	10,000	10,470
Indexed rise			
$\dfrac{271.0-97.5}{97.5} \times £10,470$	____	____	18,631
	4,000	10,000	29,101
Disposal	(3,000)		
Cost and indexed cost $\dfrac{3,000}{4,000} \times £10,000$ and £29,101	____	(7,500)	(21,826)
Value at 10.7.17	1,000	2,500	7,275

The gain is computed as follows:

	£
Proceeds	24,000
Less cost	(7,500)
Unindexed gain	16,500
Less indexation allowance £(21,826 – 7,500)	(14,326)
Indexed gain	2,174

3.5 Bonus and rights issues

When **bonus issue shares are issued**, all that happens is that **the size of the original holding is increased**. Since **bonus issue shares are issued at no cost** there is **no need to adjust the original cost** and there is **no operative event for the FA 1985 pool** (so no indexation allowance needs to be calculated).

When **rights issue shares are issued**, the **size of the original holding is increased** in the same way as for a bonus issue. So if the original shareholding was part of the FA 1985 pool, the rights issue shares are added to that pool. This might be important for the matching rules if a shareholding containing the rights issue shares is sold shortly after the rights issue.

However, in the case of a rights issue, the **new shares are paid for and this results in an adjustment to the original cost**. For the purpose of **calculating the indexation allowance, expenditure on a rights issue is taken as being incurred on the date of the issue** and not the date of the original holding.

3.6 Example: Bonus and rights issue

S Ltd bought 10,000 shares in T plc in May 2000 (RPI = 170.7) at a cost of £45,000.

There was a 2 for 1 bonus issue in October 2002.

There was a 1 for 3 rights issue in June 2006 (RPI = 198.5) at a cost of £4 per share. S Ltd took up all of its rights entitlement.

S Ltd sold 20,000 shares in T plc for £120,000 in January 2018 (assumed RPI = 275.5).

FA 1985 share pool

		No. of shares	Cost £	Indexed cost £
5.00	Acquisition	10,000	45,000	45,000
10.02	Bonus 2:1	20,000		
		30,000		
6.06	Indexed rise			
	$\dfrac{198.5-170.7}{170.7} \times £45,000$			7,329
	Rights 1:3	10,000	40,000	40,000
		40,000	85,000	92,329
1.18	Index rise			
	$\dfrac{275.5-198.5}{198.5} \times £92,329$			35,815
				128,144
	Disposal	(20,000)	(42,500)	(64,072)
c/f		20,000	42,500	64,072

The gain is:

	£
Proceeds	120,000
Less cost	(42,500)
Unindexed gain	77,500
Less indexation allowance £(64,072 − 42,500)	(21,572)
Indexed gain	55,928

3.7 Reorganisations and takeovers

The rules on reorganisation and takeovers apply in a similar way for company shareholders as they do for individuals.

In the case of a **reorganisation, the new shares or securities take the place of the original shares. The original cost and the indexed cost of the original shares is apportioned between the different types of capital issued on the reorganisation.**

Where there is a takeover of shares which qualifies for the 'paper for paper' treatment, the cost and indexed cost of the original holding is passed onto the new holding which take the place of the original holding.

Question   Takeover

J Ltd acquired 20,000 shares in G Ltd in August 1990 (RPI = 128.1) at a cost of £40,000. It acquired a further 5,000 shares in December 2006 (RPI = 202.7) at a cost of £30,000.

In September 2017, G Ltd was taken over by K plc and J Ltd received one ordinary share and two preference shares in K plc for each one share held in G Ltd. Immediately following the takeover, the ordinary shares in K plc were worth £4 per share and the preference shares in K plc were worth £1 per share.

(a) Show the cost and indexed cost of the ordinary shares and the preference shares in K plc.

(b) Calculate the gain arising if J Ltd sells 10,000 of its ordinary shares in K plc for £45,000 in February 2018 (assumed RPI = 275.8).

(a)   G Ltd FA 1985 share pool

		No. of shares	Cost £	Indexed cost £
8.90	Acquisition	20,000	40,000	40,000
12.06	Indexed rise			
	$\dfrac{202.7 - 128.1}{128.1} \times £40,000$			23,294
	Acquisition	5,000	30,000	30,000
		25,000	70,000	93,294

Note that the takeover is not an operative event because the pool of cost is not increased or decreased and so it is not necessary to calculate an indexed rise to the date of the takeover.

Apportionment of cost/indexed cost to K plc shares

	No. of shares	MV £	Cost £	Indexed cost £
Ords × 1	25,000	100,000	46,667	62,196
Prefs × 2	50,000	50,000	23,333	31,098
Totals		150,000	70,000	93,294

(b)   K plc ordinary shares FA 1985 share pool

		No. of shares	Cost £	Indexed cost £
12.06	Acquisition (deemed)	25,000	46,667	62,196
2.18	Indexed rise			
	$\dfrac{275.8 - 202.7}{202.7} \times £62,196$			22,430
				84,626
	Disposal	(10,000)	(18,667)	(33,850)
		15,000	28,000	50,776

Note that the indexation allowance on the ordinary shares is calculated from the December 2006, not from the date of the takeover.

The gain is:

	£
Proceeds	45,000
Less cost	(18,667)
Unindexed gain	26,333
Less indexation allowance £(33,850 – 18,667)	(15,183)
Indexed gain	11,150

4 Relief for replacement of business assets (rollover relief)

Rollover relief for replacement of business assets is available to companies to defer gains arising on the disposal of business assets.

4.1 Conditions for relief

As for individuals, **a gain may be deferred by a company where the proceeds on the disposal of a business asset are spent on a replacement business asset under rollover relief.**

The conditions for the relief to apply to company disposals are:

(a)   The old assets sold and the new asset bought are both used only in the trade of the company (apportionment into business and non-business parts available for buildings).

(b)   The old asset and the new asset both fall within one (but not necessarily the same one) of the following classes.

   (i)   **Land and buildings** (including parts of buildings) occupied as well as used only for the purposes of the trade

   (ii)   Fixed plant and machinery

(c)   Reinvestment of the proceeds received on the disposal of the old asset takes place in a period beginning one year before and ending three years after the date of the disposal.

(d)   The new asset is brought into use in the trade on its acquisition.

Note that goodwill is not a qualifying asset for the purposes of corporation tax.

A claim for the relief must be made by the later of four years of the end of the accounting period in which the disposal of the old asset takes place and four years of the end of the accounting period in which the new asset is acquired.

4.2 Operation of relief   9/16

Deferral is obtained by deducting the indexed gain from the cost of the new asset. For full relief, the whole of the proceeds must be reinvested. If only part is reinvested, a gain equal to the amount not invested, or the full gain, if lower, will be chargeable to tax immediately.

The new asset will have a base cost for chargeable gains purposes of its purchase price less the gain rolled over.

Question   Rollover relief

D Ltd acquired a factory in April 2000 (RPI = 170.1) at a cost of £120,000. It used the factory in its trade throughout the period of its ownership.

In August 2017 (assumed RPI = 271.7), D Ltd sold the factory for £250,000. In November 2017, it acquired another factory at a cost of £220,000.

Calculate the gain chargeable on the sale of the first factory and the base cost of the second factory.

Chargeable gain on sale of first factory

	£
Proceeds	250,000
Less cost	(120,000)
Unindexed gain	130,000
$\dfrac{271.7 - 170.1}{170.1} = 0.597 \times £120,000$	(71,640)
Indexed gain	58,360
Less rollover relief (balancing figure)	(28,360)
Chargeable gain: amount not reinvested £(250,000 − 220,000)	30,000

Base cost of second factory

	£
Cost of second factory	220,000
Less rolled over gain	(28,360)
Base cost	191,640

4.3 Depreciating assets

9/16

The relief for investment into depreciating assets works in the same way for companies as it does for individuals.

The indexed gain is calculated on the old asset and is deferred until the gain crystallises on the earliest of:

(a) The disposal of the replacement asset
(b) The date the replacement asset ceases to be used in the trade
(c) Ten years after the acquisition of the replacement asset

Chapter Roundup

- Chargeable gains for companies are computed in broadly the same way as for individuals, but indexation allowance applies and there is no annual exempt amount.

- The indexation allowance gives relief for the inflation element of a gain.

- There are special rules for matching shares sold by a company with shares purchased. Disposals are matched with acquisitions on the same day, the previous nine days and the FA 1985 share pool.

- Rollover relief for replacement of business assets is available to companies to defer gains arising on the disposal of business assets.

Quick Quiz

1   A company is entitled to an annual exempt amount against its chargeable gains. True/False?

2   Indexation allowance runs from the date of _____ to date of _____. Fill in the blanks.

3   What are the share matching rules for company shareholders?

4   J Ltd bought 10,000 ordinary shares for £20,000 in K Ltd in December 2015 (RPI 260.6). In October 2017 (RPI 272.9), there was a 2 for 1 rights issue in K Ltd at £2.50 per share and J Ltd took up all its rights issue shares. What is the indexed cost of the FA 1985 share pool immediately after the rights issue?

5   H Ltd sells a warehouse for £400,000. The warehouse cost £220,000 and the indexation allowance available is £40,000. The company acquires another warehouse ten months later for £375,000. What is the amount of rollover relief?

1   False. A company is not entitled to an annual exempt amount against its chargeable gains.

2   Indexation allowance runs from the date of **acquisition** to date of **disposal**.

3   The matching rules for shares disposed of by a company shareholder are:

    (a)   Shares acquired on the same day
    (b)   Shares acquired in the previous nine days
    (c)   Shares from the FA 1985 pool

4   *FA 1985 share pool*

		No. of shares	Indexed cost £
12.15	Acquisition	10,000	20,000
10.17	Indexed rise		
	$\dfrac{272.9-260.6}{260.6} \times £20,000$		944
	Rights 2:1 @ £2.50	20,000	50,000
		30,000	70,944

5   The gain on the sale of first warehouse is:

	£
Proceeds	400,000
Less cost	(220,000)
Unindexed gain	180,000
Less indexation allowance	(40,000)
Indexed gain	140,000
Less rollover relief (balancing figure)	(115,000)
Chargeable gain: amount not reinvested £(400,000 – 375,000)	25,000

Now try the questions below from the Practice Question Bank

Number	Type	Marks	Time
Q136	Section A	2	4 mins
Q137	Section A	2	4 mins
Q138	Section A	2	4 mins
Q139	Section B	2	4 mins
Q140	Section B	2	4 mins
Q141	Section B	2	4 mins
Q142	Section B	2	4 mins
Q143	Section B	2	4 mins
Q144	Section C	10	18 mins

Losses

Topic list	Syllabus reference
1 Trading losses – overview	E2
2 Carry forward trade loss relief	E2(e)
3 Trade loss relief against total profits	E2(f)
4 Choosing loss reliefs and other planning points	E2(g)
5 Other losses	E2(d), E3(c)

Introduction

In the previous three chapters we have seen how a company calculates its taxable total profits and the corporation tax payable.

We now look at how a company may obtain relief for losses.

In the next chapter we will look at groups, and in particular how losses can be relieved by group relief.

Study guide

		Intellectual level
E2	**Taxable total profits**	
(d)	Compute property business profits and understand how relief for a property business loss is given.	2
(e)	Understand how trading losses can be carried forward.	2
(f)	Understand how trading losses can be claimed against income of the current or previous accounting periods.	2
(g)	Recognise the factors that will influence the choice of loss relief claim.	2
E3	**Chargeable gains for companies**	
(c)	Explain and compute the treatment of capital losses.	1

Exam guide

Losses could form part of a 15 mark question or a 10 mark question in Section C. They may also be included in Section A or B questions, for example dealing with carry forward loss relief. Dealing with losses involves a methodical approach: first establish what loss is available for relief, second identify the different reliefs available, and third evaluate the options. Do check the question for specific instructions; you may be told that loss relief should be taken as early as possible.

1 Trading losses – overview

FAST FORWARD

Trading losses may be relieved by deduction from current total profits, from total profits of earlier periods or from future trading income.

In summary, the following reliefs are available for trading losses incurred by a company:

(a)　Claim to deduct the loss from current total profits

(b)　Claim to deduct the loss from earlier total profits

(c)　Make no claim and automatically carry forward the loss to be deducted from future trading profits of the same trade

These **reliefs may be used in combination**. The options open to the company are:

(a)　Do nothing, so that the loss is automatically carried forward against future trading profits

(b)　Claim to deduct the loss from current total profits, then automatically carry forward any remaining unrelieved loss to be deducted from future trading profits

(c)　Claim to deduct the loss from current total profits, then claim to carry any unused loss back and deduct from earlier total profits, and then automatically carry any remaining unrelieved loss forward to be deducted from future trading profits.

The reliefs are explained in further detail later in this chapter.

Exam focus point

Remember that total profits is income and gains before the deduction of qualifying charitable donations. This may lead to qualifying charitable donations becoming unrelieved.

2 Carry forward trade loss relief　　　　　　　　　　　　　　　　12/16

FAST FORWARD

Trading losses carried forward can only be deducted from future trading profits arising from the same trade.

A company must deduct a trading loss which is carried forward against trading profits from the same trade in future accounting periods (unless it has been otherwise relieved by making a claim to deduct it from total profits). **Relief is against the first available profits.**

Question   Carry forward trade loss relief

A Ltd has the following results for the three years to 31 March 2018.

	Year ended		
	31.3.16	*31.3.17*	*31.3.18*
	£	£	£
Trading profit/(loss)	(8,550)	3,000	6,000
Property income	0	1,000	1,000
Qualifying charitable donation	300	1,400	1,700

Calculate the taxable total profits for all three years showing any losses available to carry forward at 1 April 2018 and the amounts of any qualifying charitable donations which become unrelieved.

Answer

	Year ended		
	31.3.16	*31.3.17*	*31.3.18*
	£	£	£
Trading profits	0	3,000	6,000
Less carry forward loss relief		(3,000)	(5,550)
	0	0	450
Property income	0	1,000	1,000
Total profits	0	1,000	1,450
Less qualifying charitable donation	0	(1,000)	(1,450)
Taxable total profits	0	0	0
Unrelieved qualifying charitable donation	300	400	250

Note that the trading loss carried forward is deducted from the trading profit in future years. It cannot be deducted from the property income.

Loss memorandum

	£
Loss for y/e 31.3.16	8,550
Less used y/e 31.3.17	(3,000)
Loss carried forward at 1.4.17	5,550
Less used y/e 31.3.18	(5,550)
Loss carried forward at 1.4.18	0

3 Trade loss relief against total profits   9/16

FAST FORWARD

Loss relief by deduction from total profits is given before qualifying charitable donations and so qualifying charitable donations may become unrelieved.

3.1 Current year relief

A company may claim to deduct a trading loss incurred in an accounting period from total profits. This may make qualifying charitable donations unrelieved because such donations are deducted from total profits after this loss relief to compute taxable total profits.

3.2 Carry back relief

> Loss relief by deduction from total profits may be given by deduction from current period profits and from the previous 12 months.

Such a loss may then be carried back and deducted from total profits of an accounting period falling wholly or partly within the 12 months prior to the start of the period in which the loss was incurred. Again, this may cause qualifying charitable donations to be unrelieved.

> A claim for current period loss relief can be made without a claim for carry back relief. However, if a loss is to be carried back, a claim for current period relief must have been made first.

Any possible loss relief claim for the period of the loss must be made before any excess loss can be carried back to a previous period.

Any carry back is to more recent periods before earlier periods. Relief for earlier losses is given before relief for later losses.

Any loss remaining unrelieved after any loss relief claims against total profits is automatically carried forward to be deducted from future profits of the same trade.

Question — Loss relief against total profits

Helix Ltd has the following results.

	y/e 30.11.16 £	y/e 30.11.17 £
Trading profit/(loss)	22,500	(19,500)
Bank interest received	500	500
Chargeable gains	0	4,000
Qualifying charitable donation	250	250

Calculate the taxable total profits for both years affected assuming that loss relief by deduction from total profits is claimed. Show the amount of any qualifying charitable donations which become unrelieved.

Answer

	y/e 30.11.16 £	y/e 30.11.17 £
Trading profit	22,500	0
Investment income	500	500
Chargeable gains	0	4,000
Total profits	23,000	4,500
Less current period loss relief	0	(4,500)
	23,000	0
Less carry back loss relief	(15,000)	(0)
	8,000	0
Less qualifying charitable donation	(250)	0
Taxable total profits	7,750	0
Unrelieved qualifying charitable donation		250
Loss memorandum		
Loss incurred in y/e 30.11.17		19,500
Less used: y/e 30.11.17		(4,500)
y/e 30.11.16		(15,000)
Loss available to carry forward		0

If a period falls partly outside the prior 12 months, loss relief is limited to the proportion of the period's profits (before qualifying charitable donations) equal to the proportion of the period which falls within the 12 months.

Question | Short accounting period and loss relief

Tallis Ltd had the following results for the three accounting periods to 31 December 2017.

	y/e 30.9.16 £	3 months to 31.12.16 £	y/e 31.12.17 £
Trading profit (loss)	20,000	12,000	(39,000)
Building society interest received	1,000	400	1,800
Qualifying charitable donations	600	500	0

Calculate the taxable total profits for all years and show any qualifying charitable donations which become unrelieved. Assume loss relief is claimed by deduction from total profits where possible.

Answer

	y/e 30.9.16 £	3 months to 31.12.16 £	y/e 31.12.17 £
Trading profit	20,000	12,000	0
Interest income	1,000	400	1,800
Total profits	21,000	12,400	1,800
Less current period loss relief			(1,800)
	21,000	12,400	0
Less carry back loss relief	(15,750)	(12,400)	
	5,250	0	0
Less qualifying charitable donations	(600)		0
Taxable total profits	4,650	0	0
Unrelieved qualifying charitable donations	0	500	0

Loss memorandum	£
Loss incurred in y/e 31.12.17	39,000
Less used y/e 31.12.17	(1,800)
Less used p/e 31.12.16	(12,400)
Less used y/e 30.9.16 £21,000 × 9/12 (max)	(15,750)
C/f	9,050

Notes

1. The loss can be carried back to set against total profits of the previous 12 months. This means total profits in the y/e 30.9.16 must be time apportioned by multiplying by 9/12.
2. Losses remaining after the loss relief claims against total profits are carried forward to set against future trading profits.

3.3 Claims

A claim for relief by deduction from current or earlier period total profits must be made within two years of the end of the accounting period in which the loss arose. Any claim must be for the *whole* loss (to the extent that profits are available to relieve it). The loss can however be reduced by not claiming full capital allowances, so that higher capital allowances are given (on higher tax written down values) in future years (see later in this chapter).

3.4 Interaction with losses brought forward

A trading loss carried back is relieved after any trading losses brought forward have been offset.

Question	Losses carried forward and back

Chile Ltd has the following results.

	Year ended		
	30.11.16	30.11.17	30.11.18
	£	£	£
Trading profit/(loss)	21,000	(20,000)	40,000
Bank interest received	1,000	1,500	500
Chargeable gains	0	2,000	0
Qualifying charitable donations	500	500	500

Chile Ltd had a trading loss of £16,000 carried forward at 1 December 2015.

Compute the taxable trading profits for all the years affected assuming that loss relief by deduction from total profits is claimed. Show the amount of any qualifying charitable donations which become unrelieved.

Answer	

The loss of the year to 30 November 2017 is relieved by deduction from current year total profits and from total profits of the previous twelve months. The trading loss brought forward at 1 December 2015 is relieved in the year ended 30 November 2016 before the loss brought back.

	Year ended		
	30.11.16	30.11.17	30.11.18
	£	£	£
Trading profit	21,000	0	40,000
Less carry forward loss relief	(16,000)	0	(10,500)
	5,000	0	29,500
Interest income	1,000	1,500	500
Chargeable gains	0	2,000	0
Total profits	6,000	3,500	30,000
Less current period loss relief	0	(3,500)	0
	6,000	0	30,000
Less carry back loss relief	(6,000)	0	0
	0	0	30,000
Less qualifying charitable donation	0	0	(500)
Taxable total profits	0	0	29,500
Unrelieved qualifying charitable donations	500	500	

	£
Loss memorandum (1)	
Loss brought forward at 1 December 2015	16,000
Less used y/e 30.11.16	(16,000)
	0

	£
Loss memorandum (2)	
Loss incurred in y/e 30.11.17	20,000
Less used: y/e 30.11.17	(3,500)
y/e 30.11.16	(6,000)
	10,500
Less used: y/e 30.11.18	(10,500)
C/f	0

3.5 Terminal trade loss relief

Trading losses in the last 12 months of trading can be carried back and deducted from total profits of the previous three years.

For trading losses incurred in the 12 months up to the cessation of trade the carry back period is extended from 12 months to three years, later years first.

Question

Terminal losses

Brazil Ltd had the following results for the accounting periods up to the cessation of trade on 30 September 2017.

	y/e 30.9.14 £	y/e 30.9.15 £	y/e 30.9.16 £	y/e 30.9.17 £
Trading profits	60,000	40,000	15,000	(180,000)
Gains	0	10,000	0	6,000
Property income	12,000	12,000	12,000	12,000

You are required to show how the losses are relieved assuming the maximum use is made of loss relief by deduction from total profits.

Answer

	y/e 30.9.14 £	y/e 30.9.15 £	y/e 30.9.16 £	y/e 30.9.17 £
Trading profits	60,000	40,000	15,000	0
Property income	12,000	12,000	12,000	12,000
Gains	0	10,000	0	6,000
Total profits	72,000	62,000	27,000	18,000
Less current period loss relief				(18,000)
				0
Less carry back loss relief	(72,000)	(62,000)	(27,000)	
Taxable total profits	0	0	0	0

Loss memorandum

Loss in y/e 30.9.17	180,000
Less used y/e 30.9.17	(18,000)
Loss of y/e 30.9.17 available for 3 year carry back	162,000
Less used y/e 30.9.16	(27,000)
	135,000
Less used y/e 30.9.15	(62,000)
	73,000
Less used y/e 30.9.14	(72,000)
Loss remaining unrelieved	1,000

4 Choosing loss reliefs and other planning points

When selecting a loss relief, consider the timing of the relief and the extent to which relief for qualifying charitable donations might be lost.

One of the competencies you require to fulfil Performance Objective 17 Tax planning and advice of the PER is to mitigate and/or defer tax liabilities through the use of standard reliefs, exemptions and incentives. You can apply the knowledge you obtain from this section of the Study Text to help to demonstrate this competence.

4.1 Alternative loss reliefs

Several alternative loss reliefs may be available. In making a choice consider:

- **Timing of relief**: loss relief against total profits gives relief for the loss more quickly than carry forward loss relief and so it is generally preferable to carrying forward the loss. It also has the advantage of enabling a carry back of the loss to a prior accounting period, potentially saving tax at a higher rate.

- **The extent to which relief for qualifying charitable donations might be lost.**

Question — The choice between loss reliefs

M Ltd has had the following results.

| | Year ended 31 March | | | |
| | 2016 | 2017 | 2018 | 2019 |
	£	£	£	£
Trading profit/(loss)	2,000	(500,000)	200,000	138,000
Chargeable gains	35,000	250,000	0	0
Qualifying charitable donations	30,000	20,000	20,000	20,000

Recommend appropriate loss relief claims, and compute the corporation tax for all years based on your recommendations. Assume that future years' profits will be similar to those of the year ended 31 March 2019 and that the rate of corporation tax is 20% in financial years 2015 and 2016 and 19% in financial years 2017 and 2018.

Answer

A loss relief against total profits claim for the year ended 31 March 2017 will obtain relief quickly. However, it will waste the qualifying charitable donations.

Taxable total profits in the previous year are £7,000 (£35,000 + £2,000 – £30,000). Carry back would waste qualifying charitable donations of £30,000 and would use £37,000 of loss to save tax at 20% on £7,000.

If no current period loss relief claim is made, £200,000 of the loss will be carried forward and will obtain relief in the year ended 31 March 2018, with £20,000 of qualifying charitable donations being wasted. The remaining £300,000 of the loss, would be carried forward to the year ended 31 March 2019 and later years.

To conclude, a loss relief claim by deduction from total profits should be made for the year of the loss but not in the previous year. £20,000 of qualifying charitable donations would be wasted in the current year, but relief on £250,000 would be obtained quickly. Carrying the loss back would mean that £30,000 of qualifying charitable donations would become unrelieved. Therefore it would be more advantageous to carry the loss forward.

The final computations are as follows:

	Year ended 31 March			
	2016	2017	2018	2019
	£	£	£	£
Trading income	2,000	0	200,000	138,000
Less carry forward loss relief	0	0	(200,000)	(50,000)
	2,000	0	0	88,000
Chargeable gains	35,000	250,000	0	0
Total profits	37,000	250,000	0	88,000
Less current period loss relief	0	(250,000)	0	0
	37,000	0	0	88,000
Less qualifying charitable donations	(30,000)	0	0	(20,000)
Taxable total profits	7,000	0	0	68,000
CT at 20%/19%	1,400	0	0	12,920
Unrelieved qualifying charitable donations	0	20,000	20,000	0

4.2 Capital allowances and loss relief

A company with losses should consider claiming less than the maximum amount of capital allowances available. This will result in a higher tax written down value to carry forward and therefore higher capital allowances in future years.

Reducing capital allowances in the current period reduces the loss available for relief against total profits. As this relief, if claimed, must be claimed for all of a loss available, a reduced capital allowance claim could be advantageous where qualifying charitable donations may be wasted in the current (or previous) period if the maximum claim is made. Also a large loss cannot be used in the current (or previous) accounting period if there is no other income or gains, but would have to be carried forward. In that case, it may be advantageous to make a reduced capital allowance claim so that any loss in future accounting periods is greater. An increased loss in a future accounting period can be used against other income and gains in that period (compared with a brought forward loss that can only be used against trading income of the same trade) or can be group relieved (see later in this Study Text).

5 Other losses

5.1 Capital losses   12/16

> **FAST FORWARD**
>
> Capital losses can only be set against capital gains in the current or future accounting periods.

Capital losses can only be set against capital gains in the same or future accounting periods, never against income. Capital losses must be set against the first available gains and cannot be carried back.

5.2 Property business losses   12/16

> **FAST FORWARD**
>
> Property business losses are set off first against total profits in the current period and then carried forward against future total profits.

Property business losses are first deducted from the company's total profits of the current accounting period. Any excess is then:

(a)   **Carried forward to the next accounting period** and treated as a loss made by the company in that period; or

(b)   Available for surrender as **group relief** (see later in this Study Text).

Chapter Roundup

- Trading losses may be relieved by deduction from current total profits, from total profits of earlier periods or from future trading income.

- Trading losses carried forward can only be deducted from future trading profits arising from the same trade.

- Loss relief by deduction from total profits is given before qualifying charitable donations and so qualifying charitable donations may become unrelieved.

- Loss relief by deduction from total profits may be given by deduction from current period profits and from profits of the previous 12 months.

- A claim for current period loss relief can be made without a claim for carry back relief. However, if a loss is to be carried back, a claim for current period relief must have been made first.

- Trading losses in the last 12 months of trading can be carried back and deducted from total profits of the previous three years.

- When selecting a loss relief, consider the timing of the relief and the extent to which relief for qualifying charitable donations might be lost.

- Capital losses can only be set against capital gains in the current or future accounting periods.

- Property business losses are set off first against total profits in the current period and then carried forward against future total profits.

Quick Quiz

1 Against what profits may trading losses carried forward be set?

    A   Against all trading profits
    B   Against total profits
    C   Against profits from the same trade
    D   Against trading profits and gains

2 To what extent may losses be carried back?

3 Why might a company make a reduced capital allowances claim?

4 W plc made a chargeable gain of £40,000 in the year ended 31 March 2016 and a capital loss of £8,000 in the year ended 31 March 2017. Can W plc carry back the £8,000 loss against the gain of £40,000?

5 What loss reliefs are available to a company, which is not in a group, that has a property business loss?

Answers to Quick Quiz

1   C. Against profits from the same trade.

2   A loss may be carried back and set against total profits of the previous 12 months. The loss carried back is the trading loss left unrelieved after a claim to deduct the loss from total profits of the loss making accounting period has been made. A loss arising on the final 12 months of trading can be carried back and deducted from profits arising in the previous 36 months.

3   Reducing capital allowances in the current accounting period reduces the loss available for relief by deduction from total profits. Such a loss relief claim means that all of the available loss is utilised, possibly making qualifying charitable donations unrelieved. Reducing capital allowances reduces the size of the available loss and so may preserve relief for qualifying charitable donations. It may also generate a larger trading loss in future accounting periods which can be set against other income and gains (rather than a carried forward loss which can only be set against trading profits of the same trade) or group relieved.

4   No. Capital losses cannot be carried back.

5   Deduct from the company's total profits of the current accounting period. Excess carried forward the next accounting period and treated as a loss made by the company in that period.

Now try the questions below from the Practice Question Bank

Number	Type	Marks	Time
Q145	Section A	2	4 mins
Q146	Section A	2	4 mins
Q147	Section A	2	4 mins
Q148	Section C	10	18 mins

Groups

Topic list	Syllabus reference
1 Group relief	E5(a), E6
2 Chargeable gains group	E5(b), E6

Introduction

In the previous chapters in this section we have covered corporation tax on single companies, including the reliefs for losses.

In this chapter we consider the extent to which tax law recognises group relationships between companies. Companies in a group are still separate entities with their own tax liabilities, but tax law recognises the close relationship between group companies. They can, if they meet certain conditions, share their losses and also pass assets between each other without chargeable gains.

In the next chapter we consider administrative aspects of corporation tax.

Study guide

		Intellectual level
E5	**The effect of a group corporate structure for corporation tax purposes**	
(a)	Define a 75% group, and recognise the reliefs that are available to members of such a group.	2
(b)	Define a 75% chargeable gains group, and recognise the reliefs that are available to members of such a group.	2
E6	**The use of exemptions and reliefs in deferring and minimising corporation tax liabilities**	

Exam guide

Section A questions on groups could include the identification of members of a 75% group relief group or a 75% chargeable gains group. Groups may also feature in your examination as part of the 15 mark corporation tax question in Section C or in a 10 mark question in that Section or in Section B. Your first step in dealing with any group question must be to establish the relationship between the companies and identify what group or groups exist. You may find it helpful to draw a diagram. You must be aware that 75% group relief groups and 75% chargeable gains groups do not always coincide.

One of the competencies you require to fulfil Performance Objective 15 Tax computations and assessments of the PER is to prepare or contribute to the computation or assessment of tax computations for single companies, groups or other entities. You can apply the knowledge you obtain from this chapter of the Study Text to help to demonstrate this competence.

Exam focus point

ACCA's article Groups, written by a member of the Taxation (TX – UK) examining team, states that it is important that Taxation (TX – UK) candidates know the **group relationship** that must exist for **reliefs to be available**. Working through the examples in this article will prepare you for anything that could be set in the exam.

1 Group relief

FAST FORWARD

Within a 75% group, current period trading losses, excess property business losses and excess qualifying charitable donations can be surrendered between UK companies. Group relief is available where the existence of a group is established through companies resident anywhere in the world.

1.1 Group relief provisions

The group relief provisions enable companies within a 75% group to transfer trading losses to other companies within the group, in order to set these against taxable total profits and reduce the group's overall corporation tax liability.

1.2 Definition of a 75% group

Key term

For one company to be a **75% subsidiary** of another, the holding company must have:

- At least 75% of the ordinary share capital of the subsidiary
- A right to at least 75% of the distributable income of the subsidiary
- A right to at least 75% of the net assets of the subsidiary were it to be wound up

Two companies are members of a 75% group where one is a 75% subsidiary of the other, or both are 75% subsidiaries of a third company.

Two companies are in a 75% group only if there is a 75% effective interest. Thus an 80% subsidiary (T) of an 80% subsidiary (S) is not in a 75% group with the holding company (H), because the effective interest is only 80% × 80% = 64%. However, S and T are in a 75% group and can claim group relief from each other. S **cannot** claim group relief from T and pass it on to H; it can only claim group relief for its own use.

A 75% group may include non-UK resident companies. **However, losses may generally only be surrendered between UK resident companies**.

Exam focus point

Relief for trading losses incurred by an overseas subsidiary is not examinable in your paper.

Illustration of a 75% group:

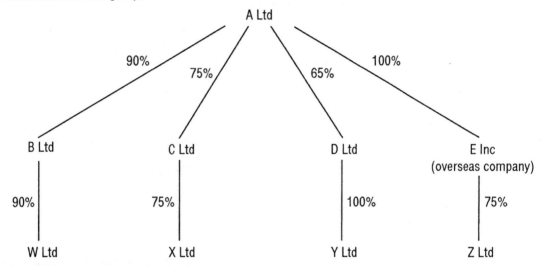

The companies in the 75% group are:

A Ltd
B Ltd
W Ltd (81% effective holding by A)
C Ltd
E Inc
Z Ltd (75% effective holding by A)

In addition C Ltd and X Ltd and also D Ltd and Y Ltd form their own separate mini-75% groups.

Note that a 75% group may also be called a 'group relief' group.

1.3 The relief

FAST FORWARD

A surrendering company can surrender any amount of its trading loss but a claimant company can only claim an amount up to its available taxable total profits.

1.3.1 Transfer of loss

A company which has made a loss (the surrendering company) may transfer its loss to another member of the 75% group (the claimant company).

1.3.2 The claimant company

A **claimant company** is **assumed to use its own current year losses** in working out the taxable total profits against which it may claim group relief, **even if it does not in fact claim relief for current losses against total profits**.

Furthermore, **group relief is set against taxable total profits after all other reliefs for the current period (for example qualifying charitable donations) or brought forward from earlier periods**.

Group relief is given before relief for any amounts carried back from later periods.

1.3.3 The surrendering company

The surrendering company may surrender **trading losses, excess property income losses and excess qualifying charitable donations to other group companies**. Qualifying charitable donations and property income losses can only be group relieved to the extent that they exceed total profits before taking account of any losses of the current period or brought forward or back from other accounting periods. Excess qualifying charitable donations must be surrendered before excess property income losses.

A surrendering company may group relieve a trading loss before setting it against its own total profits for the period of the loss. It may specify an amount less than the maximum amount to be surrendered.

Only current period losses are available for group relief.

Question	Group relief

K plc has one 75% subsidiary, L plc. The results for the group for the year ended 31 March 2018 are as follows:

	K plc	L plc
	£	£
Trading (loss)	(4,000)	(20,700)
Trading loss brought forward at 1 April 2017	0	(5,000)
Non-trading loan relationship income	10,000	2,900
Chargeable gain	15,000	0
Qualifying charitable donations	(2,000)	(3,200)

What is the maximum group relief that K plc can claim from L plc?

Answer

L plc can surrender losses under group relief as follows:

	£
Current year trading loss	20,700
Excess qualifying charitable donations £(3,200 – 2,900)	300
Total losses available for group relief	21,000

L plc cannot surrender its brought forward trading loss under group relief.

334   22: Groups | Part F Corporation tax

K plc has the following available taxable total profits:

	£
Non-trading loan relationship income	10,000
Chargeable gain	15,000
	25,000
Less current year trading loss	(4,000)
	21,000
Less qualifying charitable donations	(2,000)
Available taxable total profits	19,000
Maximum group relief that K plc can claim from L Ltd (lower of £21,000 and £19,000)	19,000

K plc must take account of its current year trading loss in working out available taxable total profits even if it does not actually make a claim for current year relief.

1.4 Corresponding accounting periods

FAST FORWARD

Profits and losses of corresponding accounting periods must be matched up.

Surrendered losses must be set against taxable total profits of a corresponding accounting period. If the accounting periods of a surrendering company and a claimant company are not the same this means that both the profits and losses must be apportioned so that only the results of the period of overlap may be set off. Apportionment is on a time basis. However, in the period when a company joins or leaves a group, an alternative method may be used if the result given by time-apportionment would be unjust or unreasonable.

Question
Corresponding accounting periods

	£
S Ltd incurs a trading loss for the year to 30 September 2017	(150,000)
H Ltd makes taxable total profits:	
for the year to 31 December 2016	200,000
for the year to 31 December 2017	100,000

What is the maximum group relief that H Ltd can claim from S Ltd?

Answer

H Ltd can claim group relief as follows.

	£
The lower of:	
For the year ended 31 December 2016 taxable total profits of the corresponding accounting period (1.10.16 – 31.12.16) are £200,000 × 3/12	50,000
Losses of the corresponding accounting period are £150,000 × 3/12	37,500

A claim for £37,500 of group relief may be made against H Ltd's taxable total profits for the year ended 31 December 2016.

	£
The lower of:	
For the year ended 31 December 2017 taxable total profits of the corresponding accounting period (1.1.17 – 30.9.17) are £100,000 × 9/12	75,000
Losses of the corresponding accounting period are £150,000 × 9/12	112,500

A claim for £75,000 of group relief may be made against H Ltd's taxable total profits for the year ended 31 December 2017.

If a claimant company claims relief for losses surrendered by more than one company, the total relief that may be claimed for a period that overlaps is limited to the proportion of the claimant's taxable total profits attributable to that period. Similarly, if a company surrenders losses to more than one claimant, the total losses that may be surrendered in a period that overlaps is limited to the proportion of the surrendering company's losses attributable to that period.

1.5 Claims

A claim for group relief is normally made on the claimant company's tax return. It is ineffective unless a notice of consent is also given by the surrendering company.

Group wide claims/surrenders can be made as one person can act for two or more companies at once.

Any payment by the claimant company for group relief, up to the amount of the loss surrendered, is ignored for all corporation tax purposes.

1.6 Alternative loss reliefs

Several alternative loss reliefs may be available, including group relief. In making a choice consider:

- **How quickly relief will be obtained**: obtaining loss relief by using group relief is quicker than carry forward loss relief and so generally preferable to carrying forward the loss.

- **The extent to which relief for qualifying charitable donations might be lost**: group relief is deducted after qualifying charitable donations in the claimant company, so relief for these donations is not lost. By contrast, if the loss-making company claims relief for the loss against its own current year total profits, relief for qualifying charitable donations in that company may be wasted.

1.7 Capital allowances and group relief

Companies with profits may benefit by reducing their claims for capital allowances in a particular year. This may leave sufficient profits to take advantage of group relief which may only be available for the current year. The amount on which writing-down allowances can be claimed in later years is increased accordingly.

2 Chargeable gains group

> **FAST FORWARD**
>
> A chargeable gains group consists of the top company plus companies in which the top company has a 50% effective interest, provided there is a 75% holding at each level.

2.1 Definition   12/16

Companies are in a chargeable gains group if:

(a)   At each level, there is a 75% holding
(b)   The top company has an effective interest of over 50% in the group companies

If A holds 75% of B, B holds 75% of C and C holds 75% of D, then A, B and C are in such a group, but D is outside the group because A's interest in D is only $75\% \times 75\% \times 75\% = 42.1875\%$. Furthermore, D is not in a group with C, because the group must include the top company (A).

The definition of a chargeable gains group is wider than that of a 75% group as only a effective 50% interest is needed compared to a 75% interest. However, a company can only be in one chargeable gains group although it may be a member of more than one 75% group.

Illustration of a chargeable gains group:

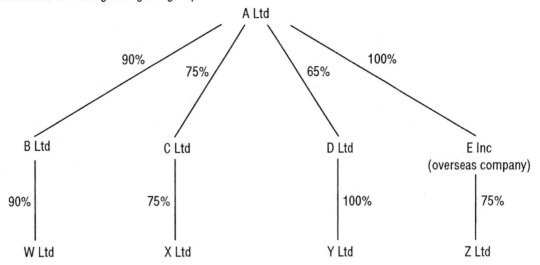

The companies in a group for chargeable gains purposes are:

A Ltd
B Ltd
W Ltd
C Ltd
X Ltd (75% subsidiary of 75% subsidiary, effective interest over 50%)
E Inc
Z Ltd

There is a separate chargeable gains group of D Ltd and Y Ltd.

2.2 Intra-group transfers

 Within a chargeable gains group, assets are transferred at no gain and no loss.

Companies in a chargeable gains group make intra-group transfers of chargeable assets without a chargeable gain or an allowable loss arising. No election is needed, as this relief is compulsory. The assets are deemed to be transferred at such a price as will give the transferor no gain and no loss (ie cost plus indexation allowance up to the date of transfer)

2.3 Matching group gains and losses

 Gains and losses can be matched within a group. This can be done by electing that all or part of any gain or loss is treated as transferred between group companies.

Two members of a chargeable gains group can elect to transfer a chargeable gain or allowable loss, or any part of a gain or loss, between them. This election must be made within two years of the end of the accounting period in which the gain or loss accrues in the company which is making the transfer.

Only current year losses can be transferred, not brought forward losses.

2.4 Rollover relief

Rollover relief is available in a chargeable gains group.

If a member of a chargeable gains group disposes of an asset eligible for chargeable gains rollover relief it may treat all of the group companies as a single unit for the purpose of claiming such relief. Acquisitions by other group members within the qualifying period of one year before the disposal to three years afterwards may therefore be matched with the disposal. If an asset is transferred at no gain and no loss between group members, that transfer does not count as the acquisition of an asset for rollover relief purpose.

Both the disposing company and the acquiring company must make the claim.

Exam focus point

Try to remember the following summary – it will be of great help in the exam.

Parent Co **owns** 75% or more of subsidiary (directly and effectively)

- Surrender trading losses, excess property business losses, excess qualifying charitable donations to companies with some taxable total profits for same time period

Parent Co **owns** 75% or more of subsidiary and subsidiary owns 75% or more of its subsidiaries

- Transfer assets between companies automatically at no gain/no loss
- Chargeable gains and losses can be matched between group member companies
- All companies treated as one for rollover relief purposes

Chapter Roundup

- Within a 75% group, current period trading losses, excess property business losses and excess qualifying charitable donations can be surrendered between UK companies. Group relief is available where the existence of a group is established through companies resident anywhere in the world.

- A surrendering company can surrender any amount of its trading loss but a claimant company can only claim an amount up to its available taxable total profits.

- Profits and losses of corresponding accounting periods must be matched up.

- A chargeable gains group consists of the top company plus companies in which the top company has a 50% effective interest, provided there is a 75% holding at each level.

- Within a chargeable gains group, assets are transferred at no gain and no loss.

- Gains and losses can be matched within a group. This can be done by electing that all or part of any gain or loss is treated as transferred between group companies.

- Rollover relief is available in a chargeable gains group.

Quick Quiz

1   List the types of losses which may be group relieved.

2   N Ltd and M Ltd are in a group relief group. N Ltd prepared accounts for the year to 31 March 2018 and had taxable total profits of £96,000. M Ltd prepared accounts for the nine month period ended 31 December 2017 and had a trading loss of £80,000. How much of M Ltd's loss for the period ended 31 December 2017 can be group relieved against N Ltd's taxable total profits for the year to 31 March 2018?

3   G Ltd owns 85% of the ordinary share capital of H Ltd and 70% of the ordinary share capital of J Ltd. H Ltd owns 80% of the ordinary share capital of K Ltd. Which of the companies are in a chargeable gains group with G Ltd?

4   When may assets be transferred intra-group at no gain and no loss?

5   How can chargeable gains and losses within a group be matched with each other?

Answers to Quick Quiz

1   Trading losses, excess property business losses and excess qualifying charitable donations.

2   £72,000. Corresponding period is 1 April 2017 to 31 December 2017. Lower of N Ltd's taxable total profits of the period of £96,000 × 9/12 = £72,000 and M Ltd's loss of the period of £80,000.

3   H Ltd and K Ltd. There is at least a 75% interest at each level and G Ltd has an effective interest of at least 50% in K Ltd. J Ltd is not a member of the chargeable gains group as G Ltd does not have at least a 75% interest in it.

4   No gain no loss asset transfers are mandatory between companies in a chargeable gains group.

5   Two members of a gains group can elect that all or part of a gain or loss is transferred between them within two years of the end of the accounting period in which the gain or loss accrued. This election allows the group to match its gains and losses in one company.

Now try the questions below from the Practice Question Bank

Number	Type	Marks	Time
Q149	Section A	2	4 mins
Q150	Section A	2	4 mins
Q151	Section A	2	4 mins
Q152	Section C	10	18 mins

Self assessment and payment of tax by companies

Topic list	Syllabus reference
1 Corporation tax self assessment	A3(b)
2 Returns, records and claims	A4(a), (d)
3 Compliance checks, appeals and disputes	A5(a), (b)
4 Payment of corporation tax and interest	A4(b), (c), A6(a)
5 Penalties	A6(a)

Introduction

We now complete our corporation tax studies by looking at the self assessment system for corporation tax, under which companies must file returns and pay the tax due.

In the following chapters we will turn our attention to VAT, which applies to both incorporated and unincorporated businesses.

Study guide

		Intellectual level
A3	**The systems for self-assessment and the making of returns**	
(b)	Explain and apply the features of the self-assessment system as it applies to companies, including the use of iXBRL.	2
A4	**The time limits for the submission of information, claims and payment of tax, including payments on account**	
(a)	Recognise the time limits that apply to the filing of returns and the making of claims.	2
(b)	Recognise the due dates for the payment of tax under the self-assessment system.	2
(c)	Explain how large companies are required to account for corporation tax on a quarterly basis and compute the quarterly instalment payments.	2
(d)	List the information and records that taxpayers need to retain for tax purposes.	1
A5	**The procedures relating to compliance checks, appeals and disputes**	
(a)	Explain the circumstances in which HM Revenue & Customs can make a compliance check into a self assessment tax return.	2
(b)	Explain the procedures for dealing with appeals and First and Upper Tier Tribunals.	2
A6	**Penalties for non-compliance**	
(a)	Calculate late payment interest and state the penalties that can be charged.	2

Exam guide

Section A questions on corporation tax administration could include the identification of filing dates and the calculation of interest on late paid tax or penalties. You may also be tested on these aspects in a Section B question. In Section C you might be asked to explain an aspect of the tax administration system such as the appeals process.

1 Corporation tax self assessment

FAST FORWARD

A company that does not receive a notice requiring a return to be filed must, if it is chargeable to tax, notify HMRC within 12 months of the end of the accounting period.

1.1 Introduction

One of the competencies you require to fulfil Performance Objective 16 Tax compliance and verification of the PER is to explain tax filing and payment requirements and the consequences of non-compliance to clients. You can apply the knowledge you obtain from this section of the Study Text to help to demonstrate this competence.

The self assessment system relies upon the company completing and filing a tax return and paying the tax due. The system is enforced by a system of penalties for failure to comply within the set time limits, and by interest for late payment of tax.

Dormant companies and companies which have not yet started to trade may not be required to complete tax returns. Such companies have a duty to notify HMRC when they should be brought within the self assessment system.

1.2 Notification of first accounting period

A company must notify HMRC of the beginning of its first accounting period (ie usually when it starts to trade) and the beginning of any subsequent period that does not immediately follow the end of a previous accounting period. The notice must be in the prescribed form and submitted within three months of the relevant date.

1.3 Notification of chargeability

A company that does not receive a notice requiring a return to be filed must, if it is chargeable to tax, **notify HMRC within twelve months of the end of the accounting period.**

2 Returns, records and claims

One of the competencies you require to fulfil Performance Objective 16 Tax compliance and verification of the PER is to verify and question client submissions and ensure timely submission of all relevant information to the tax authorities by the due date. You can apply the knowledge you obtain from this section of the Study Text to help to demonstrate this competence.

FAST FORWARD

A company must, in general, file a tax return within 12 months of the end of an accounting period.

2.1 Returns

A company's tax return must be filed electronically and must include a self assessment of any tax payable. Limited companies are also required to file electronically a copy of their accounts. The filing of accounts must be done in inLine eXtensible Business Reporting Language (iXBRL).

iXBRL is a standard for reporting business information in an electronic form which uses tags that can be read by computers. HMRC supplies software which can be used by small companies with simple accounts. This software automatically produces accounts and tax computations in the correct format. Other companies can use:

(a)   Other software that automatically produces iXBRL accounts and computations
(b)   A tagging service which will apply the appropriate tags to accounts and computations
(c)   Software that enables the appropriate tags to be added to accounts and computations

The tags used are contained in dictionaries known as taxonomies, with different taxonomies for different purposes. The tagging of tax computations is based on the corporation tax computational taxonomy, which includes over 1,200 relevant tags.

An obligation to file a return arises only when the company receives a notice requiring a return. A return is required for each accounting period ending during or at the end of the period specified in the notice requiring a return. A company also has to file a return for certain other periods which are not accounting periods (eg for a period when the company is dormant).

A notice to file a return may also require other information, accounts and reports. For a UK resident company the requirement to deliver accounts normally extends only to the accounts required under the Companies Act.

A return is due on or before the filing date. This is normally the later of:

(a)   **12 months after the end of the period to which the return relates**
(b)   **Three months from the date on which the notice requiring the return was made**

The relevant period of account is that in which the accounting period to which the return relates ends.

2.2 Amending a return

A company may amend a return within 12 months of the filing date.

HMRC may amend a return to correct obvious errors, or anything else that an officer has reason to believe is incorrect in the light of information available, within nine months of the day the return was filed, or if the correction is to an amended return, within nine months of the filing of an amendment. The company may amend its return so as to reject the correction. If the time limit for amendments has expired, the company may reject the correction by giving notice within three months.

2.3 Records

Companies must keep records until the latest of:

(a)   **Six years from the end of the accounting period**
(b)   **The date any compliance check enquiries are completed**
(c)   **The date after which a compliance check enquiry may not be commenced**

All business records and accounts, including contracts and receipts, must be kept or information showing that the company has prepared a complete and correct tax return.

If a return is demanded more than six years after the end of the accounting period, any records or information which the company still has must be kept until the later of the end of a compliance check enquiry and the expiry of the right to start one.

2.4 Claims

Wherever possible claims must be made on a tax return or on an amendment to it and must be quantified at the time the return is made.

If a company believes that it has paid excessive tax, for example as a result of an error in its tax return, a claim may be made within four years from the end of the accounting period. An appeal against a decision on such a claim must be made within 30 days. A claim may not be made if the return was made in accordance with a generally accepted practice which prevailed at the time.

Other claims must be made by four years after the end of the accounting period, unless a different time limit is specified.

If HMRC amend a self assessment or issue a discovery assessment then the company has a further period to make, vary or withdraw a claim (unless the claim is irrevocable) even if this is outside the normal time limit. The period is one year from the end of the accounting period in which the amendment or assessment was made, or one year from the end of the accounting period in which the compliance check enquiry was complete if the amendment is the result of a compliance check enquiry. The relief is limited where there has been fraudulent or negligent conduct by the company or its agent.

3 Compliance checks, appeals and disputes

One of the competencies you require to fulfil Performance Objective 16 Tax compliance and verification of the PER is to correspond appropriately and in a professional manner with the relevant parties in relation to both routine and specific matters/enquiries. You can apply the knowledge you obtain from this section of the Study Text to help to demonstrate this competence.

FAST FORWARD

HMRC can carry out compliance check enquiries on returns.

3.1 Compliance check enquiries

HM Revenue & Customs may decide to conduct a compliance check enquiry on a return, claim or election that has been submitted by a company, in the same way as for individuals.

The officer of HM Revenue & Customs must give written notice of his intention to conduct a compliance check enquiry. The notice must be given by:

(a) **The first anniversary of the due filing date** (most group companies) or **the actual filing date** (other companies), **if the return was delivered on or before the due filing date;** or

(b) **The quarter day following the first anniversary of the actual filing date, if the return is filed after the due filing date. The quarter days are 31 January, 30 April, 31 July and 31 October.**

If the company amends the return after the due filing date, the compliance check enquiry 'window' extends to the quarter day following the first anniversary of the date the amendment was filed. Where the compliance check enquiry was not started within the limit which would have applied had no amendment been filed, the enquiry is restricted to matters contained in the amendment.

3.2 Appeals and disputes

The procedure for HMRC internal reviews and appeals relating to individuals, discussed earlier in this Study Text, also applies to companies.

4 Payment of corporation tax and interest

One of the competencies you require to fulfil Performance Objective 16 Tax compliance and verification of the PER is to determine the incidence (timing) of tax liabilities and their impact on cash flow/financing requirements. You can apply the knowledge you obtain from this section of the Study Text to help to demonstrate this competence.

FAST FORWARD

In general, corporation tax is due nine months and one day after the end of an accounting period but large companies must pay their corporation tax in quarterly instalments.

4.1 Companies which are not large companies

Corporation tax is due for payment by **companies which are not large companies** (see below), **nine months and one day after the end of the accounting period.** For example, if a company, which is not a large company, has an accounting period ending on 31 December 2017, the corporation tax for the period is payable on 1 October 2018.

4.2 Large companies

4.2.1 Payment in instalments

Large companies must pay their corporation tax in instalments.

4.2.2 What is a large company?

A large company is one whose profits exceed the profit threshold.

For this purpose profits (which may be referred to as **augmented profits**) **are the taxable total profits of the company plus dividends received from other companies.**

The exception to this rule is that any dividends received from a 51% subsidiary company (sometimes called 'group dividends') **are ignored and so are not included.**

A company (company B) is a **51% subsidiary** of company A if more than 50% of company B's ordinary shares are owned directly or indirectly by company A.

Question
Profits

Q plc had the following results for the year ended 31 March 2018.

	£
Taxable total profits	1,142,000
Dividend received 1 May 2017 from 40% subsidiary	278,000
Dividend received 1 August 2017 from 90% subsidiary	378,000

What are Q plc's profits for determining whether it is a large company?

Answer

	£
Taxable total profits	1,142,000
Dividend from 40% subsidiary	278,000
Profits	1,420,000

The dividend from the 90% subsidiary is ignored because this is from a company which is a '51% subsidiary' of Q plc.

The profit threshold is £1,500,000 for a 12 month accounting period.

Exam focus point

The profit threshold will be given in the Tax Rates and Allowances in the exam.

The profit threshold is reduced in two circumstances:

(a) The company has a **short accounting period. In this case the threshold is scaled down.** For example, if a company has a three month accounting period, the threshold is (£1,500,000 × 3/12) = £375,000.

(b) The company has **related 51% group companies at the end of the immediately preceding accounting period**. The threshold is **divided by that number of related 51% group companies**, including the company itself.

Key term

A company (company B) is a related **51% group company** of another company (company A) if company A is a 51% subsidiary of company B or company B is a 51% subsidiary of company A or both company A and company B are 51% subsidiaries of another company. Non-UK resident company may be included as related 51% group companies. Companies which do not carry on a trade (dormant companies) are not related 51% group companies.

Question
Related 51% group companies

Y Ltd prepares accounts to 31 March each year. At 31 March 2017, Y Ltd had three wholly owned subsidiary companies – V Ltd, X Ltd and Z Ltd – and owned 45% of the ordinary shares of U Ltd. X Ltd did not carry on any trade or business during the year to 31 March 2017. Z Ltd is not resident in the UK.

Y Ltd acquired 75% of the ordinary shares of T Ltd on 1 July 2017.

What is the profit threshold for Y Ltd for determining corporation tax payment dates for the year ending 31 March 2018?

V Ltd and Z Ltd (residence not relevant) are related 51% group companies with Y Ltd so there are three related 51% group companies.

X Ltd is not a related 51% group company because it is dormant.

U Ltd is not a related 51% group company because it is not a 51% subsidiary of Y Ltd.

T Ltd was not a related 51% group company at the end of the previous accounting period and so does not reduce the profit threshold of Y Ltd in respect of the year ending 31 March 2018.

The profit threshold for Y Ltd for the year ending 31 March 2018 is therefore £(1,500,000/3) = £500,000.

4.2.3 Due dates for instalments

Instalments are due on the 14th day of the month, starting in the seventh month of the accounting period. Provided that the accounting period is 12 months long subsequent instalments are due in the tenth month during the accounting period and in the first and fourth months after the end of the accounting period. If an accounting period is less than 12 months long subsequent instalments are due at three monthly intervals but with the final payment being due in the fourth month of the next accounting period.

Question   Instalment due dates

D Ltd is a large company which has a 12 month accounting period which ends on 31 December 2017. What are the due dates for payment of D Ltd's instalments of corporation tax for this accounting period?

Answer

14 July 2017, 14 October 2017, 14 January 2018 and 14 April 2018.

4.2.4 Calculating the instalments

Instalments are based on the estimated corporation tax liability for the current period (not the previous period). **A company is therefore required to estimate its corporation tax liability before the end of the accounting period, and must revise its estimate each quarter.** It is extremely important for companies to forecast their tax liabilities accurately. Large companies whose directors are poor at estimating may find their companies incurring significant interest charges. **Companies can have instalments repaid if they later conclude the instalments ought not to have been paid.**

The amount of each instalment is computed by:

(a)   **Working out $3 \times CT/n$** where CT is the amount of the estimated corporation tax liability payable in instalments for the period and n is the number of months in the period

(b)   **Allocating the smaller of that amount and the total estimated corporation tax liability to the first instalment**

(c)   **Repeating the process for later instalments until the amount allocated is equal to the corporation tax liability**

If the company has an accounting period of 12 months, there will be four instalments and each instalment should be 25% of the estimated amount due.

Question

B Ltd is a large company which has a corporation tax liability of £440,000 for the year ended 31 March 2018. Show when the corporation tax liability is due for payment.

Answer

Due date	Amount
	£
14 October 2017	110,000
14 January 2018	110,000
14 April 2018	110,000
14 July 2018	110,000
	440,000

The position is slightly more complicated if the company has an accounting period of less than 12 months, as is shown in the following question.

Question

K plc is a large company which has a corporation tax liability of £880,000 for the eight month accounting period to 30 September 2017. Show when the corporation tax liability is due for payment.

Answer

£880,000 must be paid in instalments.

The amount of each instalment is $3 \times \dfrac{£880,000}{8} = £330,000$

The due dates and the amounts payable are:

	£
14 August 2017	330,000
14 November 2017	330,000
14 January 2018	220,000 (balance)

4.2.5 Exceptions

A company is not required to pay instalments in the first year that it is a large company, unless its profits exceed £10 million. The £10 million threshold is reduced proportionately by the number of related 51% group companies (including the company in question) at the end of the previous accounting period.

Any company whose corporation tax liability does not exceed £10,000 need not pay by instalments.

4.3 Interest on late or overpaid tax

Interest runs from the due date on over/underpaid instalments. The position is looked at cumulatively after the due date for each instalment. HMRC calculate the interest position after the company submits its corporation tax return.

Companies which do not pay by instalments are charged interest if they pay their corporation tax after the due date, and will receive interest if they overpay their tax or pay it early.

Interest paid/received on late payments or over payments of corporation tax is dealt with as investment income as interest paid/received on a non-trading loan relationship.

5 Penalties

One of the competencies you require to fulfil Performance Objective 16 Tax compliance and verification of the PER is to explain tax filing and payment requirements and the consequences of non-compliance to clients. You can apply the knowledge you obtain from this section of the Study Text to help to demonstrate this competence.

FAST FORWARD

Penalties may be levied for failure to notify the first accounting period, failure to notify chargeability, the late filing of returns, failure to keep records, and errors in returns.

5.1 Notification of first accounting period

Failure to notify, and provide information about, the first accounting period can mean a penalty of £300 plus £60 per day the information is outstanding, and a penalty of up to £3,000 for fraudulently or negligently giving incorrect information.

5.2 Notification of chargeability

The common penalty regime for late notification of chargeability discussed earlier in this Study Text in relation to individuals also applies to companies.

5.3 Late filing penalties

There is a £100 penalty for a failure to submit a return on time, rising to £200 if the delay exceeds three months. These penalties become £500 and £1,000 respectively when a return was late (or never submitted) for each of the preceding two accounting periods.

An additional tax geared penalty is applied if a return is more than six months late. The penalty is 10% of the tax unpaid six months after the return was due if the total delay is up to 12 months, and 20% of that tax if the return is over 12 months late.

There is a tax geared penalty for a fraudulent or negligent return and for failing to correct an innocent error without unreasonable delay. The maximum penalty is equal to the tax that would have been lost had the return been accepted as correct. HMRC can mitigate this penalty. If a company is liable to more than one tax geared penalty, the total penalty is limited to the maximum single penalty that could be charged.

5.4 Failure to keep records

Failure to keep records can lead to a **penalty of up to £3,000** for each accounting period affected.

5.5 Errors in returns

The common penalty regime for making errors in tax returns discussed earlier in this Study Text applies for corporation tax.

Chapter Roundup

- A company that does not receive a notice requiring a return to be filed must, if it is chargeable to tax, notify HMRC within 12 months of the end of the accounting period.

- A company must, in general, file a tax return within 12 months of the end of an accounting period.

- HMRC can carry out compliance check enquiries on returns.

- In general, corporation tax is due nine months and one day after the end of an accounting period, but large companies must pay their corporation tax in quarterly instalments.

- Penalties may be levied for failure to notify the first accounting period, failure to notify chargeability, the late filing of returns, failure to keep records, and errors in returns.

Quick Quiz

1   When must HMRC give notice to a non-group company that it is going to start a compliance check enquiry if the return was filed on or before the due filing date?

2   A plc has one wholly owned subsidiary, B plc which it has owned for many years. A plc prepared accounts for the nine-months to 31 December 2017. What is the profit threshold for this accounting period for A plc?

3   State the due dates for the payment of quarterly instalments of corporation tax for a 12 month accounting period.

4   Q plc submits its corporation tax return four months late. This is the first late return made by the company. What is the late filing penalty?

5   What is the maximum penalty if a company fails to keep records?

    A   £1,000
    B   £2,000
    C   £3,000
    D   £4,000

1   Notice must be given by the first anniversary of the actual filing date.

2   There are two related 51% group companies and a short accounting period. The profit threshold is therefore:

£1,500,000/2 × 9/12 = £562,500

3   14th day of:

   (a)   7th month in AP
   (b)   10th month in AP
   (c)   1st month after AP ends
   (d)   4th month after AP ends

4   £200 as the delay exceeds three months.

5   C. £3,000 for each accounting period affected.

Now try the questions below from the Practice Question Bank

Number	Type	Marks	Time
Q153	Section A	2	4 mins
Q154	Section A	2	4 mins
Q155	Section A	2	4 mins
Q156	Section B	2	4 mins
Q157	Section B	2	4 mins
Q158	Section B	2	4 mins
Q159	Section B	2	4 mins
Q160	Section B	2	4 mins
Q161	Section C	10	18 mins

Value added tax

24

An introduction to VAT

Topic list	Syllabus reference
1 The scope of VAT	F2
2 Zero-rated and exempt supplies	F2(f)
3 Registration	F1(a), (c)
4 Deregistration	F1(a)
5 Transfer of going concern	F2(a)
6 Pre-registration input tax	F1(b)
7 Accounting for and administering VAT	F2(a), (b)
8 The tax point	F2(c)
9 The valuation of supplies	F2(e)
10 The deduction of input tax	F2(g)
11 Relief for impairment losses	F2(h)

Introduction

The final topic in our studies is value added tax (VAT). We cover VAT in this and the next chapter.

VAT is a tax on turnover rather than on profits. As the name suggests, it is charged on the value added. The VAT is collected bit by bit along the chain of manufacturer, wholesaler, retailer, until it finally hits the consumer who does not add value, but uses up the goods.

In this chapter we look at the scope of VAT and then consider when a business must, or may, be registered for VAT. We also look at administration and accounting. VAT is a tax with simple computations but many detailed rules to ensure its enforcement. You may find it easier to absorb the detail if you ask yourself, in relation to each rule, exactly how it helps to enforce the tax.

Finally, we look at the rules regarding the deduction of input tax and relief for impairment losses on trade debts.

In the following chapter we will conclude our study of VAT and the Taxation (TX – UK) syllabus.

Study guide

		Intellectual level
F1	**The VAT registration requirements**	
(a)	Recognise the circumstances in which a person must register or deregister for VAT (compulsory) and when a person may register or deregister for VAT (voluntary).	2
(b)	Recognise the circumstances in which pre-registration input VAT can be recovered.	2
(c)	Explain the conditions that must be met for two or more companies to be treated as a group for VAT purposes, and the consequences of being so treated.	1
F2	**The computation of VAT liabilities**	
(a)	Calculate the amount of VAT payable/recoverable.	2
(b)	Understand how VAT is accounted for and administered.	2
(c)	Recognise the tax point when goods or services are supplied.	2
(e)	Explain and apply the principles regarding the valuation of supplies.	2
(f)	Recognise the principal zero rated and exempt supplies.	2
(g)	Recognise the circumstances in which input VAT is non-deductible.	2
(h)	Recognise the relief that is available for impairment losses on trade debts.	2

Exam guide

Section A questions on basic value added tax (VAT) topics could include identification of the date for registration and dealing with impairment losses. Section B questions could also include computing the amount of VAT payable or recoverable. In Section C, registration requirements may be examined in more detail; make sure that you know the difference between the historical test and the future test, and the dates by which HMRC must be notified and registration takes effect. Do not overlook pre-registration input VAT. You may also be required to calculate the VAT due for a return period; watch out for non deductible input tax and check the dates if there are impairment losses.

Exam focus point

> **ACCA's article Value added tax,** written by a member of the Taxation (TX – UK) examining team, in Part 1 considers **VAT registration and deregistration**, and **output and input** VAT.

1 The scope of VAT

FAST FORWARD

> VAT is charged on turnover at each stage in a production process, but in such a way that the burden is borne by the final consumer.

1.1 The nature of VAT

VAT is a tax on turnover, not on profits. The basic principle is that the VAT should be borne by the final consumer. Registered traders may deduct the tax which they suffer on supplies to them (input tax) from the tax which they charge to their customers (output tax) at the time this is paid to HMRC. Thus, at each stage of the manufacturing or service process, the net VAT paid is on the value added at that stage.

1.2 Example: The VAT charge

A forester sells wood to a furniture maker for £100 plus VAT. The furniture maker uses this wood to make a table and sells the table to a shop for £150 plus VAT. The shop then sells the table to the final consumer for £300 plus VAT of 20%. VAT will be accounted for to HMRC as follows.

	Cost £	Input tax 20% £	Net sale price £	Output tax 20% £	Payable to HMRC £
Forester	0	0	100	20.00	20.00
Furniture maker	100	20.00	150	30.00	10.00
Shop	150	30.00	300	60.00	30.00
					60.00

Because the traders involved account to HMRC for VAT charged less VAT suffered, their profits for income tax or corporation tax purposes are based on sales and purchases net of VAT.

1.3 Taxable supplies

FAST FORWARD

VAT is chargeable on taxable supplies made by a taxable person in the course or furtherance of any business carried on by him. Supplies may be of goods or services.

Key term

A **taxable supply** is a supply of goods or services made in the UK, other than an exempt supply.

PER alert

One of the competencies you require to fulfil Performance Objective 15 Tax computations and assessments of the PER is to prepare or contribute to computations or assessments of indirect tax liabilities. You can apply the knowledge you obtain from this section of the Study Text to help to demonstrate this competence.

A taxable supply is either standard-rated or zero-rated. The standard rate is 20%.

Certain supplies, which fall within the classification of standard rate supplies, are charged at a reduced rate of 5%. An example is the supply of domestic fuel.

Zero-rated supplies are taxable at 0%. A taxable supplier whose outputs are zero-rated but whose inputs are standard-rated will obtain repayments of the VAT paid on purchases.

An exempt supply is not chargeable to VAT. A person making exempt supplies is unable to recover VAT on inputs. The exempt supplier thus has to shoulder the burden of VAT. Of course, he may increase his prices to pass on the charge, but he cannot issue a VAT invoice which would enable a taxable customer to obtain a credit for VAT, since no VAT is chargeable on his supplies.

1.4 Example: Standard-rated, zero-rated and exempt supplies

Here are figures for three traders, the first with standard-rated outputs, the second with zero-rated outputs and the third with exempt outputs. All their inputs are standard-rated. The standard rate is 20%.

	Standard-rated £	Zero-rated £	Exempt £
Inputs	20,000	20,000	20,000
VAT	4,000	4,000	4,000
	24,000	24,000	24,000
Outputs	30,000	30,000	30,000
VAT	6,000	0	0
	36,000	30,000	30,000
Pay/(reclaim)	2,000	(4,000)	0
Net profit	10,000	10,000	6,000

VAT legislation lists zero-rated, reduced rate and exempt supplies. There is no list of standard-rated supplies. Therefore any supplies that do not appear on the zero-rated, reduced rate or exempt lists will be assumed to be standard-rated by default.

We look at the main categories of zero-rated and exempt supplies later in this chapter.

1.5 Supplies of goods

Goods are supplied if exclusive ownership of the goods passes to another person.

The following are treated as supplies of goods.

- The supply of any form of power, heat, refrigeration or ventilation, or of water

- The grant, assignment or surrender of a major interest (the freehold or a lease for over 21 years) in land

- Taking goods permanently out of the business for the non-business use of a taxable person or for other private purposes including the supply of goods by an employer to an employee for his private use

- Transfers under an agreement contemplating a transfer of ownership, such as a hire purchase agreement

Gifts of goods are normally treated as sales at cost (so VAT is due). **However, business gifts are not supplies of goods if:**

(a) **The total cost of gifts made to the same person does not exceed £50 in any 12 month period.** If the £50 limit is exceeded, output tax will be due in full on the total of gifts made. Once the limit has been exceeded a new £50 limit and new 12 month period begins.

(b) **The gift is a sample** (unlimited number of samples allowed).

1.6 Supplies of services

Apart from a few specific exceptions, **any supply which is not a supply of goods and which is done for a consideration is a supply of services**. A consideration is any form of payment in money or in kind, including anything which is itself a supply.

A supply of services also takes place if:

- Goods are lent to someone for use outside the business
- Goods are hired to someone
- Services bought for business purposes are used for private purposes

1.7 Taxable persons

The term 'person' includes individuals, partnerships (which are treated as single entities, ignoring the individual partners) **and companies. If a person is in business making taxable supplies, then the value of these supplies is called the taxable turnover. If a person's taxable turnover exceeds certain limits then he is a taxable person and should be registered for VAT** (see later in this Study Text).

2 Zero-rated and exempt supplies

FAST FORWARD

Some supplies are taxable (either standard-rated, reduced-rate or zero-rated). Others are exempt.

2.1 Types of supply

We have seen that a trader may make standard rated, reduced-rate, zero-rated or exempt supplies.

If a trader makes a supply we need to categorise that supply for VAT as follows:

Step 1   Consider the zero-rated list to see if it is zero-rated. If not:

Step 2   Consider the exempt list to see if it is exempt. If not:

Step 3   Consider the reduced rate list to see if the reduced rate of VAT applies. If not:

Step 4   The supply is standard rated.

Exam focus point

In the exam you will not be expected to categorise all the zero-rated and exempt supplies. The main supplies in each group are highlighted below.

2.2 Zero-rated supplies

The following are items on the **zero-rated list**.

(a)   Human and animal food

(b)   Sewerage services and water

(c)   Printed matter used for reading (eg books, newspapers)

(d)   Construction work on new homes or the sale of the freehold of new homes by builders

(e)   Transport of goods and passengers

(f)   Drugs and medicines on prescription or provided in private hospitals

(g)   Clothing and footwear for young children and certain protective clothing eg motor cyclists' crash helmets

2.3 Exempt supplies

The following are items on the **exempt** list.

(a)   Financial services

(b)   Insurance

(c)   Public postal services provided by the Royal Mail under its duty to provide a universal postal service (eg first and second class letters)

(d)   Betting and gaming

(e)   Certain education and vocational training

(f)   Health services

(g)   Burial and cremation services

(h)   Sale of freeholds of buildings (other than commercial buildings less than 3 years old) and leaseholds of land and buildings.

2.4 Exceptions to the general rule

The zero-rated, exempt and reduced rate lists outline general categories of goods or services which are either zero-rated or exempt or charged at a rate of 5%. However, the VAT legislation then goes into great detail to outline exceptions to the general rule.

For example the zero-rated list states human food is zero-rated. However, the legislation then states that food supplied in the course of catering (eg restaurant meals, hot takeaways) is not zero-rated. Luxury items of food (eg crisps, peanuts, chocolate covered biscuits) are also not zero-rated.

In the exempt list we are told that financial services are exempt. However the legislation then goes on to state that this does not include credit management, except if the credit management is by the person who also granted the credit. Investment advice is also not exempt.

Land and buildings is a complex topic. Broadly, sales of new homes are zero-rated, sales of new commercial buildings are standard rated and most other transactions are exempt.

Thus great care must be taken when categorising goods or services as zero-rated, exempt or standard-rated. It is not as straightforward as it may first appear.

3 Registration

FAST FORWARD

A trader becomes liable to register for VAT if the value of taxable supplies in any past period up to 12 months exceeds £85,000 or if there are reasonable grounds for believing that the value of the taxable supplies will exceed £85,000 in the next 30 days alone. A trader may also register voluntarily.

3.1 Compulsory registration   9/16, 12/16

3.1.1 Historical test

At the end of every month a trader must calculate his cumulative turnover of taxable supplies for the previous 12 months to date. Taxable supplies are the total of standard rated supplies and zero rated supplies, but not exempt supplies. **The trader becomes liable to register for VAT if the value of his cumulative taxable supplies** (excluding VAT) **exceeds £85,000**. The person is required to notify HMRC within 30 days of the end of the month in which the £85,000 limit is exceeded. HMRC will then register the person with effect from the end of the month following the month in which the £85,000 was exceeded, or from an earlier date if they and the trader agree.

Registration under this rule is not required if HMRC are satisfied that the value of the trader's taxable supplies (excluding VAT) in the year then starting will not exceed £83,000.

Question   VAT registration

Fred started to trade cutlery on 1 January 2017. Sales (excluding VAT) were £8,000 a month for the first nine months and £8,500 a month thereafter. From what date should Fred be registered for VAT?

Answer

	£
Sales to 31 October 2017	80,500
Sales to 30 November 2017	89,000 (exceeds £85,000)

Fred must notify his liability to register by 30 December 2017 (not 31 December) and will be registered and charge VAT from 1 January 2018.

3.1.2 Future test

A person is also liable to register **at any time** (not necessarily at the end of the month) if there are reasonable grounds for believing that his taxable supplies (excluding VAT) in the following 30 days will exceed £85,000. Only taxable turnover of that 30 day period is considered **not** cumulative turnover. HMRC must be notified by the end of the 30 day period and registration will be with effect from the beginning of that period.

Question	Future test

Constant Ltd started to trade on 1 February 2017 with sales of goods as follows

	VAT status	£ per month
Goods A	standard-rated	8,000
Goods B	zero-rated	3,000

On 1 June 2017 Constant Ltd signed a contract to provide £40,000 of Goods A and £35,000 of Goods B to Unicorn plc by 25 June 2017. This is in addition to normal sales.

From which date should Constant Ltd be registered for VAT?

Answer

Goods A and B are taxable supplies.

Cumulative turnover at end of May 2017 is £44,000.

Cumulative turnover at end of June 2017 is £130,000.

But on 1 June 2017 the company signed a contract and so 'knew' that within the next 30 days it would supply £86,000 of taxable supplies – this meets the future test conditions. Therefore the company needs to notify HMRC of its need to register within 30 days of 1 June 2017, ie by 30 June 2017.

HMRC will then register the company from 1 June 2017.

The historic test is met at the end of June 2017 (this would require notification by 30 July 2017 and registration from 1 August 2017).

However when a trader satisfies both tests HMRC will use the test that gives the earlier registration date.

In this case the future test gives the earliest date, 1 June 2017.

3.1.3 Other registration issues

When determining the value of a person's taxable supplies for the purposes of registration, supplies of goods and services that are *capital assets* of the business are to be disregarded, except for non zero-rated taxable supplies of interests in land.

When a person is liable to register in respect of a past period, it is his responsibility to pay VAT. If he is unable to collect it from those to whom he made taxable supplies, the VAT burden will fall on him. A person must start keeping VAT records and charging VAT to customers as soon as he is required to be registered. However, VAT should not be shown separately on any invoices until the registration number is known. The invoice should show the VAT inclusive price and customers should be informed that VAT invoices will be forwarded once the registration number is known. Formal VAT invoices should then be sent to such customers within 30 days of receiving the registration number.

Notification of liability to register must be made on form VAT 1. This can be downloaded from the HMRC website, can be requested by telephone, or an application to register can be made online through the website. Simply writing to, or telephoning, a local VAT office is not enough. On registration the VAT office will send the trader a certificate of registration. This shows the VAT registration number, the date of registration, the end of the first VAT period and the length of the VAT periods. We will look at VAT periods later in this chapter.

If a trader makes a supply before becoming liable to register, but gets paid after registration, VAT is not due on that supply.

3.2 Voluntary registration

A person may decide to become registered even though his taxable turnover falls below the registration limit. Unless a person is registered he cannot recover the input tax he pays on purchases.

Voluntary registration is advantageous where a person wishes to recover input tax on purchases. However, charging VAT may make the supply less competitive if customers are not VAT registered and the trader may have to absorb the VAT output tax thus reducing his profit.

Therefore, consideration needs to be given to the situation of the customer. For example, consider a trader who has one input during the period which cost £1,000 plus £200 VAT at 20%; he works on the input which becomes his sole output for the year and he decides to make a profit of £1,000.

(a)   If he is not registered he will charge £2,200 and his customer will obtain no relief for any VAT.

(b)   If he is registered he will charge £2,000 plus VAT of £400. His customer will have input tax of £400 which he will be able to recover if he, too, is registered.

If the customer is a non-taxable person he will prefer (a) as the cost to him is £2,200. If he is taxable he will prefer (b) as the net cost is £2,000. Thus, a decision whether or not to register voluntarily may depend upon the status of customers.

The decision to register may also depend on the image of the business the trader wishes to project (registration may give the impression of a substantial business). The **administrative burden of registration** should also be considered.

3.3 Group registration

FAST FORWARD

Two or more companies under common control can register as a group for VAT purposes. A single VAT return and payment are then made by a representative member for a VAT period but all members of the group are jointly and severally liable for VAT due. There is no need to account for VAT on supplies between group members.

Two or more companies under common control may apply for group registration.

The **effects and advantages of group registration** are as follows.

- Each VAT group must appoint a representative member which must **account for the group's output tax and input tax, completing one VAT return and paying VAT on behalf of the group. Thus this simplifies VAT accounting, saving administrative costs,** and allows payments and repayments of VAT to be netted off. However, **all members of the group are jointly and severally liable for any VAT due from the representative member.**

- **Any supply of goods or services by a member of the group to another member of the group is, in general, disregarded for VAT purposes,** reducing the VAT accounting required.

- Any other supply of goods or services by or to a group member is in general treated as a supply by or to the representative member.

- Any VAT payable on the import of goods by a group member is payable by the representative member.

Two or more companies are eligible to be treated as members of a group provided each of them is either established in the UK or has a fixed establishment in the UK, and:

- **One of them controls each of the others; or**
- **One person** (which could be an individual or a holding company) **controls all of them; or**
- **Two or more persons carrying on a business in partnership control all of them.**

An application to create, terminate, add to or remove a company from a VAT group may be made at any time.

It is not necessary for each company, which meets the requirements, to join a particular VAT group. It may be beneficial, for example, in the case of a company making largely zero-rated supplies (and so receiving VAT repayments) to remain outside the group and benefit from cash flow repayments from completing monthly VAT returns (see later in this Study Text).

4 Deregistration

A trader may deregister voluntarily if he expects the value of his taxable supplies in the following one year period will not exceed £83,000. Alternatively, a trader who no longer makes taxable supplies may be compulsorily deregistered.

4.1 Voluntary deregistration

A person is eligible for voluntary deregistration if HMRC are satisfied that the value of his taxable supplies (net of VAT and excluding supplies of capital assets) in the following one year period will not exceed £83,000. However, voluntary deregistration will not be allowed if the reason for the expected fall in value of taxable supplies is the cessation of taxable supplies or the suspension of taxable supplies for a period of 30 days or more in that following year.

HMRC will cancel a person's registration from the date the request is made or from an agreed later date.

4.2 Compulsory deregistration

A trader may be compulsorily deregistered if HMRC are satisfied that he is no longer making nor intending to make taxable supplies. Failure to notify a requirement to deregister within 30 days may lead to a penalty. Compulsory deregistration may also lead to HMRC reclaiming input tax which has been wrongly recovered by the trader since the date on which he should have deregistered.

4.3 The consequences of deregistration

VAT is chargeable on all goods and services on hand at the date of deregistration.

On deregistration, VAT is chargeable on all stocks and capital assets in a business on which input tax was claimed, since the registered trader is in effect making a taxable supply to himself as a newly unregistered trader. If the VAT chargeable does not exceed £1,000, it need not be paid.

5 Transfer of going concern

The transfer of a business as a going concern is outside the scope of VAT.

There is no VAT charge if a business (or a separately viable part of it) is sold as a going concern to another taxable person (or a person who immediately becomes a taxable person as a result of the transfer). Such a sale is outside the scope of VAT.

If a transfer of a going concern (TOGC) is from a VAT registered trader to a new owner who is not VAT registered, then it is possible to apply to transfer the registration number of the previous owner to the new owner. This would also transfer to the new owner the responsibility for the past VAT history of the old business. So, if the previous owner had committed any VAT misdemeanours the liability for those would transfer to the new owner of the business. As a result of this it may not be wise to apply to transfer the VAT registration number between old and new owners unless of course, it is a situation where there is a very close connection between the two.

If the VAT registration number is not transferred then the new owners do not have any responsibility for the VAT affairs of the previous owner of the business. This is probably a safer way to structure the transfer of a business.

6 Pre-registration input tax 9/16, 12/16

FAST FORWARD

VAT incurred on goods and services before registration can be treated as input tax and recovered from HMRC subject to certain conditions.

6.1 Introduction

VAT incurred before registration can be treated as input tax and recovered from HMRC subject to certain conditions.

Input tax cannot be recovered if it is attributable to onward supplies made before the date of registration by the trader who is becoming VAT registered. This rule applies whether the input tax is treated as being incurred before or after the date of registration.

6.2 Pre-registration goods

If the claim is for input tax suffered on goods purchased prior to registration then the following conditions must be satisfied.

(a)   The **goods were acquired for the purpose of the business** which either was carried on or was to be carried on by him at the time of supply.

(b)   The **goods have not been supplied onwards or consumed before the date of registration** (although they may have been used to make other goods which are still held).

(c)   The **VAT must have been incurred in the four years prior to the date of registration.**

6.3 Pre-registration services

If the claim is for input tax suffered on the supply of services prior to registration then the following conditions must be satisfied.

(a)   The **services were supplied for the purposes of the business** which either was carried on or was to be carried on by him at the time of supply.

(b)   **The services were supplied within the six months prior to the date of registration.**

7 Accounting for and administering VAT

7.1 Administration

FAST FORWARD

VAT is administered by HMRC. Appeals are heard by the Tax Tribunal.

7.1.1 Introduction

The administration of VAT is dealt with by HM Revenue & Customs (HMRC).

Local offices are responsible for the local administration of VAT and for providing advice to registered persons whose principal place of business is in their area. They are controlled by regional collectors.

From time to time a registered person will be visited by HMRC staff from a local office to ensure that the law is understood and is being applied properly. If a trader disagrees with any decision as to the application of VAT given by HMRC he can ask his local office to reconsider the decision. It is not necessary to appeal formally while a case is being reviewed in this way. Where an appeal can be settled by agreement, a written settlement has the same force as a decision by the Revenue and Customs Prosecution Office.

7.1.2 Assessments

HMRC may issue assessments of VAT due to the best of their judgement if they believe that a trader has failed to make returns or if they believe those returns to be incorrect or incomplete. The time limit for making assessments is normally four years after the end of a VAT period, but this is extended to 20 years in the case of fraud, dishonest conduct, certain registration irregularities and the unauthorised issue of VAT invoices.

HMRC sometimes write to traders, setting out their calculations, before issuing assessments. The traders can then query the calculations.

7.1.3 Appeals

A trader may appeal to the Tax Tribunal in the same way as an appeal may be made for income tax and corporation tax (see earlier in this Study Text). VAT returns and payments shown thereon must have been made before an appeal can be heard.

7.2 VAT periods

VAT is accounted for on regular returns – most are submitted electronically. Extensive records must be kept.

The VAT period (also known as the tax period) is the period covered by a VAT return. It is usually three calendar months. The return shows the total input and output tax for the tax period.

HMRC allocate VAT periods according to the class of trade carried on (ending in June, September, December and March; July, October, January and April; or August, November, February and May), to spread the flow of VAT returns evenly over the year. When applying for registration a trader can ask for VAT periods which fit in with his own accounting year. It is also possible to have VAT periods to cover accounting systems not based on calendar months.

A registered person whose input tax will regularly exceed his output tax can elect for a one month VAT period, but will have to balance the inconvenience of making 12 returns a year against the advantage of obtaining more rapid repayments of VAT.

Certain small businesses may submit an annual VAT return (see later in this Study Text).

7.3 Electronic filing   9/16, 12/16, 6/17

Nearly all VAT registered businesses must file their VAT returns online and make payments electronically.

The time limit for submission and payment is one month plus seven days after the end of the VAT period. For example, a business which has a VAT quarter ending 31 March 2018 must file its VAT return and pay the VAT due by 7 May 2018.

7.4 Substantial traders

Once a trader's total VAT liability for the 12 months or less to the end of a VAT period exceeds £2,300,000, the trader must start making payments on account of each quarter's VAT liability during each quarter.

Two payments on account of each quarter's VAT liability must usually be made. The first is due one month before the end of the quarter and the second is due at the end of the month which is the final month of the quarter. The amount of each payment on account made during the quarter is 1/24 of the trader's annual VAT liability in the period in which the threshold is exceeded. For the purposes of calculating the payments on account (but not for the purposes of the £2,300,000 threshold for entry into the scheme), a trader's VAT due on imports from outside the EU is ignored.

If the VAT liability for the quarter exceeds the total of the payments on account, a balancing payment is due one month after the end of the quarter to bring the total payments for that quarter to the amount of the VAT liability. If the VAT liability for the quarter is less than the total of the payments on account, HMRC will make a repayment to the trader.

Payments must be made and the quarterly VAT return submitted by the last day of the relevant month ie there is no additional seven days. **Payments must be made electronically.**

The default surcharge (see later in this Study Text) applies to late payments.

Question	Substantial traders

Large Ltd is liable to make payments on account of VAT calculated at £250,000 each for the quarter ended 31 December 2017.

What payments/repayment are due if Large Ltd's VAT liability for the quarter is calculated as:

(a) £680,000?
(b) £480,000?

Answer

(a)

Date	Payment
30 November 2017	Payment on account of £250,000
31 December 2017	Payment on account of £250,000
31 January 2018	Balancing payment of £(680,000 – 250,000 – 250,000) = £180,000 with submission of VAT return for quarter

(b)

Date	Payment/repayment
30 November 2017	Payment on account of £250,000
31 December 2017	Payment on account of £250,000
31 January 2018	Repayment by HMRC of £(480,000 – 250,000 – 250,000) = £(20,000) on submission of VAT return for quarter

Once a trader is in the scheme, the payments on account are reviewed annually at a set time. However, **the trader can apply to reduce payments on account at any time if the total VAT liability for the latest four returns is less than 80% of the total on which the payments on account are currently based,** ie the VAT liability decreases by 20% or more. **Conversely, HMRC may increase the payments on account in between annual reviews if the trader's total 12 month VAT liability increases by 20% or more,** ie the VAT for the last four periods is at least 120% of the amount on which the payments on account are currently based.

A trader can apply to leave the scheme if his 12 month VAT liability is below £1,800,000. A trader whose VAT liability at the annual review was below £2,300,000 will be automatically removed from the scheme six months later.

A trader may elect to pay his actual VAT liability monthly instead of making payments on account. For example, the actual liability for January would be due at the end of February. The trader can continue to submit quarterly returns as long as HMRC is satisfied the trader is paying sufficient monthly amounts.

7.5 Refunds of VAT

There is a four year time limit on the right to reclaim overpaid VAT. This time limit does not apply to input tax which a business could not have reclaimed earlier because the supplier only recently invoiced the VAT, even though it related to a purchase made some time ago. Nor does it apply to overpaid VAT penalties.

If a taxpayer has overpaid VAT and has recovered excessive input tax by reason of the same mistake, HMRC can set off any tax, penalty, interest or surcharge due to them against any repayment due to the taxpayer and repay only the net amount. In such cases the normal four year time limit for recovering VAT, penalties, interest, etc by assessment does not apply.

HMRC can refuse to make any repayment which would unjustly enrich the claimant. They can also refuse a repayment of VAT where all or part of the tax has, for practical purposes, been borne by a person other than the taxpayer (eg by a customer of the taxpayer) except to the extent that the taxpayer can show loss or damage to any of his businesses as a result of mistaken assumptions about VAT.

8 The tax point   6/17

FAST FORWARD ⟩⟩

> The tax point is the deemed date of supply. The basic tax point is the date on which goods are removed or made available to the customer, or the date on which services are completed. If a VAT invoice is issued or payment is received before the basic tax point, the earlier of these dates becomes the actual tax point. If the earlier date rule does not apply, and the VAT invoice is issued within 14 days of the basic tax point, the invoice date becomes the actual tax point.

8.1 The basic tax point

The tax point of each supply is the deemed date of supply. The basic tax point is the date on which the goods are removed or made available to the customer, or the date on which services are completed.

The tax point determines the VAT period in which output tax must be accounted for and credit for input tax will be allowed. The tax point also determines which rate applies if the rate of VAT or a VAT category changes (for example when a supply ceases to be zero-rated and becomes standard-rated).

8.2 The actual tax point

If a VAT invoice is issued or payment is received before the basic tax point, the earlier of these dates automatically becomes the tax point. If the earlier date rule does not apply and if the VAT invoice is issued within 14 days after the basic tax point, the invoice date becomes the tax point (although the trader can elect to use the basic tax point for all his supplies if he wishes). This 14 day period may be extended to accommodate, for example, monthly invoicing; the tax point is then the VAT invoice date or the end of the month, whichever is applied consistently.

Question   Tax point

Julia sells a sculpture to the value of £1,000 net of VAT. She receives a payment on account of £250 plus VAT on 25 April 2017. The sculpture is delivered on 28 May 2017. Julia's VAT return period is to 30 April 2017. She issues an invoice on 4 June 2017.

Outline the tax point(s) and amount(s) due.

Answer

A separate tax point arises in respect of the £250 deposit and the £750 balance payable.

Julia should account for VAT as follows.

(a) Deposit

     25 April 2017: tax at 20% × £250 = £50. This is accounted for in her VAT return to 30 April 2017. The charge arises on 25 April 2017 because payment is received before the basic tax point (which is 28 May 2017 – date of delivery).

(b)   Balance

4 June 2017: tax at 20% × £750 = £150. This is accounted for on the VAT return to 31 July 2017. The charge arises on 4 June because the invoice was issued within 14 days of the basic tax point of 28 May 2017 (delivery date).

8.3 Miscellaneous points

Goods supplied on sale or return are treated as supplied on the earlier of adoption by the customer or 12 months after despatch.

Continuous supplies of services paid for periodically normally have tax points on the earlier of the receipt of each payment and the issue of each VAT invoice, unless one invoice covering several payments is issued in advance for up to a year. The tax point is then the earlier of each due date or date of actual payment. However, for connected businesses the tax point will be created periodically, in most cases based on 12 month periods.

9 The valuation of supplies

FAST FORWARD

In order to ascertain the amount of VAT on a supply, the supply must be valued. If a discount is offered for prompt payment, VAT is chargeable on the amount received.

9.1 Value of supply

The value of a supply is the VAT-exclusive price on which VAT is charged. The consideration for a supply is the amount paid in money or money's worth.

Thus with a standard rate of 20%:

Value + VAT = consideration
£100 + £20.00 = £120.00

The VAT proportion of the consideration is known as the 'VAT fraction'. It is:

$$\frac{\text{rate of tax}}{100 + \text{rate of tax}} = \frac{20}{100 + 20} = \frac{1}{6}$$

Provided the consideration for a bargain made at arm's length is paid in money, the value for VAT purposes is the VAT exclusive price charged by the trader. If it is paid in something other than money, as in a barter of some goods or services for others, it must be valued and VAT will be due on the value.

If the price of goods is effectively reduced with money off coupons, the value of the supply is the amount actually received by the taxpayer.

9.2 Discounts

If the trader offers a discount for prompt payment, output VAT is charged on the actual amount received for the supply. The trader must either provide details of the discount on the sales invoice or issue an invoice for the full amount and then issue a credit note if the discount is taken up.

| Question | Discounts |

Melissa sells furniture. She makes a standard-rated supply to a customer, Chris, on 10 March 2018 for £5,000 plus VAT. However, the invoice states that Chris is entitled to a 10% discount if he pays within 14 days. What is the output tax payable on the supply if:

(a)   Chris pays on 20 March 2018; or
(b)   Chris pays on 30 March 2018?

(a) **Payment on 20 March 2018 (within 14 days)**

	£
Full amount	5,000
Less discount 10% × £5,000	(500)
Discounted amount	4,500
VAT @ 20% on £4,500	£900

(b) **Payment on 30 March 2018 (more than 14 days)**

	£
Full amount	5,000
VAT @ 20% on £5,000	1,000

9.3 Miscellaneous

For goods supplied under a hire purchase agreement VAT is chargeable on the cash selling price at the start of the contract.

When goods are permanently taken from a business for non-business purposes VAT must be accounted for on their market value. Where business services are put to a private or non-business use, the value of the resulting supply of services is the cost to the taxable person of providing the services. If services bought for business purposes are used for non-business purposes (without charge), then VAT must be accounted for on their cost, but the VAT to be accounted for is not allowed to exceed the input tax deductible on the purchase of the services.

10 The deduction of input tax

10.1 Input tax recovery

FAST FORWARD Not all input VAT is deductible, eg VAT on most motor cars.

For input tax to be deductible, the payer must be a taxable person, with the supply being to him in the course of his business. In addition a VAT invoice must be held (except for payments of up to £25 including VAT which are for telephone calls, or car park fees, or which are made through cash operated machines).

Input tax recovery can be denied to any business that does not hold a valid VAT invoice and cannot provide alternative evidence to prove the supply took place.

10.2 Capital items

The distinction between capital and revenue which is important in other areas of tax **does not apply to VAT.** Thus a manufacturer buying plant subject to VAT will be able to obtain a credit for all the VAT immediately. The plant must of course be used to make taxable supplies, and if it is only partly so used only part of the VAT can be reclaimed. Conversely, if plant is sold second-hand then VAT should be charged on the sale and is output tax in the normal way.

10.3 Non-deductible input tax   12/16

Exam focus point

In the Taxation (TX – UK) exam students are **not required** to know actual cases where VAT decisions were made. They are included below for your information only.

The following input tax is not deductible even for a taxable person with taxable outputs.

(a) **VAT on motor cars not used wholly for business purposes.** VAT on cars is never reclaimable unless the car is acquired new for resale or is acquired for use in or leasing to a taxi business, a self-drive car hire business or a driving school (see further below).

(b) **VAT on business entertaining** where the cost of the entertaining is not a tax deductible trading expense, unless the entertainment is of overseas customers in which case the input tax is deductible.

If the items bought are used partly for non-deductible entertaining and partly for other purposes, an apportionment of the expenses is required.

(c) **VAT on expenses incurred on domestic accommodation for directors.**

(d) **VAT on non-business items passed through the business accounts.** However, when goods are bought partly for business use, the purchaser may:

(i) Deduct all the input tax, and account for output tax in respect of the private use; or
(ii) Deduct only the business proportion of the input tax

Where services are bought partly for business use, only method (ii) may be used. If services are initially bought for business use but the use then changes, a fair proportion of the input tax (relating to the private use) is reclaimed by HMRC by making the trader account for output tax.

(e) **VAT which does not relate to the** making of supplies by the buyer in the course of a **business.**

10.4 Irrecoverable VAT

Exam focus point

ACCA's article Motor cars, written by a member of the Taxation (TX – UK) examining team explains the implications of acquiring, running, or having the use of a motor car for income tax, corporation tax, value added tax (VAT) and national insurance contribution (NIC).

Where all (as with many cars) or some (as for partial business use) of the input tax on a purchase is not deductible, the **non-deductible VAT is included in the cost for income tax, corporation tax, capital allowance or capital gains purposes. Deductible VAT is omitted from costs, so that only net amounts are included in accounts. Similarly, sales** (and proceeds in chargeable gains computations) **are shown net of VAT**, because the VAT is paid over to HMRC.

10.5 Motoring expenses   9/16

10.5.1 Cars

The VAT incurred on the purchase of a car not used wholly for business purposes is not recoverable (except as mentioned above). If accessories are fitted after the original purchase and a separate invoice is raised then the VAT on the accessories can be treated as input tax so long as the accessories are for business use. **If VAT is not recoverable on a car because it is not used wholly for business purposes, then VAT is not charged if the car is subsequently sold.**

If a car is used wholly for business purposes (including leasing, so long as the charges are at the open market rate), the input tax is recoverable but the buyer must account for VAT when he sells the car.

If a car is leased, the lessor recovered the input tax when the car was purchased and the lessee makes some private use of the car (for example private use by employees), **the lessee can only recover 50% of the input tax on the lease charges. A hiring of five days or less is assumed to be for wholly business use.**

If a car is used for business purposes then any VAT charged on repair and maintenance costs can be treated as input tax. No apportionment has to be made for private use.

10.5.2 Fuel

> If fuel is supplied for private purposes all input VAT incurred on the fuel is allowed and the business will normally account for output VAT using a set of scale charges.

If a business pays for fuel which is only used for business purposes, it can claim all the input tax paid on that fuel. However, many businesses will pay for fuel which is used for private motoring by employees.

If a business does provide fuel to an employee for private and business use but the employee reimburses the business the full cost of the private fuel, there is an actual taxable supply by the business valued at the amount received from that employee. The business can claim its input tax on all fuel, but then must account for output tax on the amount paid by the employee. HM Revenue & Customs will accept that the full cost of all private fuel has been reimbursed where a log is kept recording private miles and the employee pays a fuel-only mileage rate that covers the average fuel cost (on its website, HM Revenue & Customs publish a set of such rates for different sizes of engine).

If a business provides fuel to its employees for private use without charge or at a charge below the full cost, there is a deemed taxable supply. The business then has the following options for how to account for VAT on fuel:

(a) **Not to claim any input tax in respect of fuel** purchased by the business. **No output tax is charged.** In effect, the fuel is not brought into the VAT system at all.

(b) **Claim input VAT only on the fuel purchased for business journeys.** This requires the business to keep detailed mileage records of business and private use. **No output tax is charged in respect of private use.** In effect, the private fuel is not brought into the VAT system.

(c) **Claim input tax on all fuel purchased and charge output tax based either on the full cost of the private fuel supplied** (again, this requires detailed mileage records to be kept) **or the fuel scale charge which reflects the deemed output in respect of private use. The fuel scale charge is based on the CO_2 emissions of the car.**

Exam focus point

> In the Taxation (TX – UK) exam, questions on the treatment of private use fuel will normally involve the use of the fuel scale charge.

The above rules apply **even where employees pay for the fuel themselves and the business reimburses them**: as long as the business obtains VAT invoices for the fuel, it can treat the fuel as its own purchase/input.

Question   Fuel scale charge

Iain is an employee of ABC Ltd. He has the use of a car with CO_2 emissions of 176 g/km for one month and a car with CO_2 emissions of 208 g/km for two months during the quarter ended 31 August 2017.

ABC Ltd pays all the petrol costs in respect of both cars without requiring Iain to make any reimbursement in respect of private fuel. Total petrol costs for the quarter amount to £360 (including VAT). ABC Ltd wishes to use the fuel scale charge as detailed records of private mileage have not been kept.

What is the VAT effect of the above on ABC Ltd?

VAT scale rates (VAT inclusive) for three month periods

CO_2 emissions	£
175	351
205	436

Value added tax for the quarter:

	£
Car 1	
£351 × 1/3 =	117
Car 2	
£436 × 2/3 =	291
	408
Output tax:	
1/6 × £408	£68
Input tax	
1/6 × £360	£60

11 Relief for impairment losses

FAST FORWARD

Relief for VAT on impairment losses is available if the debt is over six months old (measured from when the payment is due) and has been written off in the trader's accounts.

Where a supplier of goods or services has accounted for VAT on the supply and the customer does not pay, the supplier may claim a refund of VAT on the amount unpaid. **Relief is available for VAT for impairment losses (bad debts) on trade debts if the debt is over six months old (measured from when payment is due) and has been written off in the creditor's accounts.** Where payments on account have been received, they are attributed to debts in chronological order. If the debtor later pays all or part of the amount owed, a corresponding part of the VAT repaid must be paid back to HMRC.

Impairment loss relief claims must be made within four years of the time the impairment loss became eligible for relief (in other words, within four years and six months from when the payment was due). The creditor must have a copy of the VAT invoice, and records to show that the VAT in question has been accounted for and that the debt has been written off. The VAT is reclaimed on the creditor's VAT return as an amount of input tax.

A business which has claimed input tax on a supply, but which has not paid the supplier of the goods or services within six months of date of supply (or the date on which the payment is due, if later), must repay the input tax, irrespective of whether the supplier has made a claim for bad debt relief. The input tax will be repaid by making an adjustment to the input tax on the VAT return for the accounting period in which the end of the six months falls.

Exam focus point

Watch out for the six month rule when claiming relief for impairment losses.

Question   Impairment loss relief

Elixir Ltd has VAT accounting periods ending on 31 March, 30 June, 30 September and 31 December. The company sold standard rated goods to Ben on 1 July 2017. The VAT inclusive amount on the invoice was £2,000 and payment was due by 15 July 2017. Ben paid Elixir Ltd £500 as part payment on 1 October 2017 but then became untraceable and Elixir Ltd has written off the remaining debt.

State how much impairment loss relief can be claimed by Elixir Ltd and the earliest VAT return on which the claim can be made.

The amount of the loss is £(2,000 – 500) = £1,500.

The VAT on the loss is £1,500 × 1/6 = £250, so this amount can be claimed as impairment loss relief.

Payment was due on 15 July 2017 and so the six month period ended on 15 January 2018. The earliest VAT return on which an impairment loss relief claim is that for the quarter ending 31 March 2018.

Chapter Roundup

- VAT is charged on turnover at each stage in a production process, but in such a way that the burden is borne by the final consumer.

- VAT is chargeable on taxable supplies made by a taxable person in the course or furtherance of any business carried on by him. Supplies may be of goods or services.

- Some supplies are taxable (either standard-rated, reduced-rate or zero-rated). Others are exempt.

- A trader becomes liable to register for VAT if the value of taxable supplies in any period up to 12 months exceeds £85,000 or if there are reasonable grounds for believing that the value of the taxable supplies will exceed £85,000 in the next 30 days alone. A trader may also register voluntarily.

- Two or more companies under common control can register as a group for VAT purposes. A single VAT return and payment are then made by a representative member for a VAT period but all members of the group are jointly and severally liable for VAT due. There is no need to account for VAT on supplies between group members.

- A trader may deregister voluntarily if he expects the value of his taxable supplies in the following one year period will not exceed £83,000. Alternatively, a trader who no longer makes taxable supplies may be compulsorily deregistered.

- VAT is chargeable on all goods and services on hand at the date of deregistration.

- The transfer of a business as a going concern is outside the scope of VAT.

- VAT incurred on goods and services before registration can be treated as input tax and recovered from HMRC subject to certain conditions.

- VAT is administered by HMRC. Appeals are heard by the Tax Tribunal.

- VAT is accounted for on regular returns – most are submitted electronically. Extensive records must be kept.

- The tax point is the deemed date of supply. The basic tax point is the date on which goods are removed or made available to the customer, or the date on which services are completed. If a VAT invoice is issued or payment is received before the basic tax point, the earlier of these dates becomes the actual tax point. If the earlier date rule does not apply, and the VAT invoice is issued within 14 days of the basic tax point, the invoice date becomes the actual tax point.

- In order to ascertain the amount of VAT on a supply, the supply must be valued. If a discount is offered for prompt payment, VAT is chargeable on the amount received.

- Not all input VAT is deductible, eg VAT on most motor cars.

- If fuel is supplied for private purposes all input VAT incurred on the fuel is allowed and the business will normally account for output VAT using a set of scale charges.

- Relief for VAT on impairment losses is available if the debt is over six months old (measured from when the payment is due) and has been written off in the trader's accounts.

Quick Quiz

1 On what transactions will VAT be charged?

2 What is a taxable person?

3 What are the two advantages of group registration?

4 When may a person choose to be deregistered?

5 What is the time limit in respect of claiming pre-registration input tax on goods?

6 On what amount is VAT charged if a discount is offered for prompt payment?

7 What input tax is never deductible?

8 What relief is available for impairment losses?

Answers to Quick Quiz

1   VAT is charged on taxable supplies of goods and services made in the UK by a taxable person in the course or furtherance of any business carried on by him.

2   Any 'person' whose taxable turnover exceeds the registration limit. The term 'person' includes individuals, partnerships and companies.

3   The two advantages of group registration are:

    •   Saving on administrative costs: only one VAT return needs to be completed for the group
    •   No VAT on supplies between group members

4   A person is eligible for voluntary deregistration if HMRC are satisfied that the value of his taxable supplies in the following year will not exceed £83,000.

5   The VAT must have been incurred in the four years prior to the effective date of registration.

6   VAT is chargeable on the actual amount received for the supply.

7   VAT on:

    •   Motor cars
    •   UK business entertaining
    •   Expenses incurred on domestic accommodation for directors
    •   Non-business items passed through the accounts
    •   Items which do not relate to making business supplies

8   Where a supplier has accounted for VAT on a supply and the customer fails to pay, then the supplier may claim a refund of the VAT accounted for to HMRC but never actually collected from the customer.

Number	Type	Marks	Time
Q162	Section A	2	4 mins
Q163	Section A	2	4 mins
Q164	Section A	2	4 mins
Q165	Section B	2	4 mins
Q166	Section B	2	4 mins
Q167	Section B	2	4 mins
Q168	Section B	2	4 mins
Q169	Section B	2	4 mins
Q170	Section C	10	18 mins
Q171	Section C	10	18 mins

Now try the questions below from the Practice Question Bank

24: An introduction to VAT | Part G Value added tax

25

Further aspects of VAT

Topic list	Syllabus reference
1 VAT invoices and records	F2(d)
2 Penalties	F2(i)
3 Imports, exports, acquisitions and despatches	F2(j)
4 Special schemes	F3(a)(i)–(iii)

Introduction

In the previous chapter we looked at the scope of VAT and when businesses must, or may, register for VAT.

In this chapter we consider the contents of a valid VAT invoice and the main penalties used to enforce the VAT system.

VAT needs to be applied to imports, so that people do not have a tax incentive to buy abroad, and VAT is taken off many exports in order to encourage sales abroad. We see how this is achieved for transactions both within and outside the European Union.

Finally we look at the three special schemes which are intended to reduce the administrative burden for small businesses.

This chapter concludes our study of UK taxation and the Taxation (TX – UK) syllabus.

Study guide

		Intellectual level
F2	**The computation of VAT liabilities**	
(d)	List the information that must be given on a VAT invoice.	1
(i)	Understand when the default surcharge, a penalty for an incorrect VAT return, and default interest will be applied.	1
(j)	Understand the treatment of imports, exports and trade within the European Union.	2
F3	**The effect of special schemes**	
(a)	Understand the operation of, and when it will be advantageous to use, the VAT special schemes:	
(a)(i)	Cash accounting scheme.	2
(a)(ii)	Annual accounting scheme.	2
(a)(iii)	Flat rate scheme.	2

Exam guide

The topics in this chapter could be examined in any of Sections A, B or C. Penalties are an important topic as they are used to enforce the VAT system, but the special schemes are designed to make life simpler for small businesses. You may be asked to advise on the VAT treatment of imports and exports outside the European Union (EU) and on trade within the EU. The flat rate scheme may also lead to a small extra profit for the business, depending on the flat rate percentage and the level of inputs.

Exam focus point

> ACCA's article **Value added tax,** written by a member of the Taxation (TX – UK) examining team, in Part 2 covers **VAT returns, VAT invoices, penalties, overseas aspects of VAT,** and **special VAT schemes**.

1 VAT invoices and records

1.1 VAT invoices 9/16

FAST FORWARD

> A taxable person making a taxable supply to another registered person must supply a VAT invoice within 30 days.

A taxable person making a taxable supply to another VAT registered trader must supply a VAT invoice within 30 days of the time of supply, and must keep a copy. There is no requirement to supply a VAT invoice if the supply is exempt or if the supply is to a non-VAT registered customer.

The invoice must show:

(a) The supplier's name, address and registration number

(b) The date of issue, the tax point and an invoice number

(c) The name and address of the customer

(d) A description of the goods or services supplied, giving for each description the quantity, the unit price, the rate of VAT and the VAT exclusive amount

(e) The rate of any cash discount

(f) The total invoice price excluding VAT (with separate totals for zero-rated and exempt supplies)

(g) Each VAT rate applicable and the total amount of VAT

If an invoice is issued, and a change in price then alters the VAT due, a credit note or debit note to adjust the VAT must be issued.

Credit notes must give the reason for the credit (such as 'returned goods'), and the number and date of the original VAT invoice. If a credit note makes no VAT adjustment, it should state this.

A less detailed VAT invoice may be issued by a taxable person where the invoice is for a total including VAT of up to £250. Such an invoice must show:

(a) The supplier's name, address and registration number
(b) The date of the supply
(c) A description of the goods or services supplied
(d) The rate of VAT chargeable
(e) The total amount chargeable including VAT

Zero-rated and exempt supplies must not be included in less detailed invoices.

VAT invoices are not required for payments of up to £25 including VAT which are for telephone calls, or car park fees, or made through cash operated machines. In such cases, input tax can be claimed without a VAT invoice.

1.2 Records

Every VAT registered trader must keep records for six years.

Every VAT registered trader must keep records for six years, although HMRC may sometimes grant permission for their earlier destruction. They may be kept on paper, on microfilm or microfiche or on computer. However, there must be adequate facilities for HMRC to inspect records.

All records must be kept up to date and in a way which allows:

- The calculation of VAT due
- Officers of HMRC to check the figures on VAT returns

The following records are needed.

- Copies of VAT invoices, credit notes and debit notes issued
- A summary of supplies made
- VAT invoices, credit notes and debit notes received
- A summary of supplies received
- A VAT account
- Order and delivery notes, correspondence, appointment books, job books, purchases and sales books, cash books, account books, records of takings (such as till rolls), bank paying-in slips, bank statements and annual accounts
- Records of zero-rated and exempt supplies, gifts or loans of goods, taxable self-supplies and any goods taken for non-business use

2 Penalties

2.1 The default surcharge   12/16

A default occurs when a trader either submits his VAT return late, or submits the return on time but pays the VAT late. A default surcharge is applied if there is a default on payment during a default surcharge period.

A default occurs when a trader either submits his VAT return late, or submits the return on time but pays the VAT late. If a trader defaults, HMRC will serve a surcharge liability notice on the trader. The notice specifies a surcharge period running from the date of the notice to the anniversary of the end of the period for which the trader is in default.

If a further default occurs in respect of a return period ending during the specified surcharge period, the original surcharge period will be extended to the anniversary of the end of the period to which the new default relates. In addition, if the default involves the late payment of VAT (as opposed to simply a late return) **a surcharge is levied.**

The surcharge depends on the number of defaults involving late payment of VAT which have occurred in respect of periods ending in the surcharge period, as follows.

Default involving late payment of VAT in the surcharge period	Surcharge as a percentage of the VAT outstanding at the due date
First	2%
Second	5%
Third	10%
Fourth or more	15%

Surcharges at the 2% and 5% rates are not normally demanded unless the amount due would be at least £400 but for surcharges calculated using the 10% or 15% rates there is a minimum amount of £30 payable.

A trader must submit one year's returns on time and pay the VAT shown on them on time in order to break out of the surcharge liability period and the escalation of surcharge percentages.

Question

Default surcharge

Peter Popper has an annual turnover of around £300,000. His VAT return for the quarter to 31 December 2015 is late. He then submits returns for the quarters to 30 September 2016 and 31 March 2017 late as well as making late payment of the tax due of £12,000 and £500 respectively.

Peter's VAT return to 31 March 2018 is also late and the VAT due of £1,100 is also paid late. All other VAT returns and VAT payments are made on time. Outline Peter Popper's exposure to default surcharge.

Answer

A surcharge liability notice will be issued after the late filing on the 31 December 2015 return outlining a surcharge period extending to 31 December 2016.

The late 30 September 2016 return is in the surcharge period so the period is extended to 30 September 2017. The late VAT payment triggers a 2% penalty. 2% × £12,000 = £240. Since £240 is less than the £400 de minimis limit it is not collected by HMRC.

The late 31 March 2017 return is in the surcharge period so the period is now extended to 31 March 2018. The late payment triggers a 5% penalty. 5% × £500 = £25. Since £25 is less than the £400 de minimis limit it is not collected by HMRC.

The late 31 March 2018 return is in the surcharge period. The period is extended to 31 March 2019. The late payment triggers a 10% penalty 10% × £1,100 = £110. This is collected by HMRC since the £400 de minimis does not apply to penalties calculated at the 10% (and 15%) rate.

Peter will have to submit all four quarterly VAT returns to 31 March 2019 on time and pay the VAT on time to 'escape' the default surcharge regime.

A default will be ignored for all default surcharge purposes if the trader can show that the return or payment was sent at such a time, and in such a manner, that it was reasonable to expect that HMRC would receive it by the due date. A default will also be ignored if the trader can demonstrate a reasonable excuse for the late submission or payment.

The application of the default surcharge regime to small businesses is modified. **A small business is one with a turnover below £150,000.** When a small business is late submitting a VAT return or paying VAT it

will receive a letter from HMRC offering help. No penalty will be charged. If a further default occurs within 12 months a surcharge liability notice will be issued.

2.2 Penalties for errors

FAST FORWARD

There is a common penalty regime for errors in tax returns, including VAT. Errors in a VAT return up to certain amounts may be corrected in the next return.

2.2.1 Common penalty regime

The common penalty regime for making errors in tax returns discussed earlier in this Study Text applies for value added tax.

2.2.2 Errors corrected in next return

Errors on a VAT return not exceeding the greater of:

- **£10,000** (net under-declaration minus over-declaration)
- **1% x net VAT turnover for return period** (maximum £50,000)

may be **corrected on the next return**.

Other errors should be notified to HMRC in writing eg by letter.

In both cases, a penalty for the error may be imposed. Correction of an error on a later return is not, of itself, an unprompted disclosure of the error and fuller disclosure is required for the penalty to be reduced.

Default interest (see below) on the unpaid VAT as a result of the error is only charged where the limit is exceeded for the error to be corrected on the next VAT return.

2.3 Interest on unpaid VAT (default interest)

FAST FORWARD

Default interest is charged on unpaid VAT if HMRC raise an assessment of VAT or the trader makes a voluntary payment before the assessment is raised. It runs from the date the VAT should have been paid to the actual date of payment but cannot run for more than three years before the assessment or voluntary payment.

Interest (not deductible in computing taxable profits) **is charged on VAT which is the subject of an assessment** (where returns were not made or were incorrect), **or which could have been the subject of an assessment but was paid before the assessment was raised. It runs from the reckonable date until the date of payment.** This interest is sometimes called 'default interest'.

The reckonable date is when the VAT should have been paid (usually one month and seven days from the end of the return period), or in the case of VAT repayments, seven days from the issue of the repayment order. However, where VAT is charged by an assessment, interest does not run from more than three years before the date of the assessment; where the VAT was paid before an assessment was raised, interest does not run for more than three years before the date of payment.

In practice, interest is only charged when there would otherwise be a loss to the Exchequer. It is not, for example, charged when a company failed to charge VAT but if it had done so another company would have been able to recover the VAT.

3 Imports, exports, acquisitions and despatches

3.1 Introduction

The terms **import and export** refer to purchases and sales of goods with countries **outside the European Union (EU)**.

The terms **acquisition and despatch** refer to purchases and sales of goods with countries **in the EU**.

3.2 Trade in goods outside the European Union

FAST FORWARD ⟫ Imports of goods from outside the EU are subject to VAT and exports of goods to outside the EU are zero-rated.

3.2.1 Imports

Goods imported into the UK from outside the EU are effectively treated in the same way as goods that are purchased within the UK. This is because imports are chargeable to VAT if the same goods supplied in the home market by a registered trader would be chargeable to VAT. The rate of VAT is the same as that which would have applied if the supply had been made in the home market.

An importer of goods from outside the EU must calculate VAT on the value of the goods imported and account for it at the point of entry into the UK. He can then deduct the VAT payable as input tax on his next VAT return. HMRC issue monthly certificates to importers showing the VAT paid on imports. VAT is chargeable on the onward sale of the goods in the UK in the normal way.

If security (such as a bank guarantee) can be provided, the deferred payment system can be used whereby VAT is automatically charged to the importer's bank account each month rather than payment being made for each import when the goods arrive in the UK. Approved importers are able to provide reduced (and in some cases zero) security in respect of the deferred payment scheme. Such importers need to seek the approval of HMRC.

3.2.2 Exports

There is a general zero-rating where a UK VAT registered trader exports goods outside of the EU.

It is not sufficient merely to export goods. The zero-rating only applies if HMRC 'are satisfied' that the supplier has exported the goods. Evidence of the export must therefore be retained by the trader and must take the form specified by HMRC.

3.3 Trade in goods within the European Union

FAST FORWARD ⟫ Sales of goods to registered traders in other EU states are zero-rated. Taxable acquisitions of goods to the UK from other EU states are subject to VAT in the UK as both output tax and input tax.

3.3.1 Sales (despatches)

Where goods are sold by a UK registered trader to a customer in another EU member state, the supply is usually zero-rated if the supply is made to a VAT registered trader.

3.3.2 Purchases (acquisitions)

Goods acquired in the UK by a VAT registered trader from another EU member state are liable to UK VAT. Consequently, output tax has to be accounted for by that UK trader on the relevant VAT return. **The 'tax point' for such acquisitions is the earlier of:**

- **The fifteenth day of the month following the month of acquisition**
- **The date of issue of an invoice**

The transaction is entered on the UK trader's VAT return as an output and an input so the effect is usually neutral. Thus the UK trader is effectively in the same overall position as he would have been if he had acquired the goods from another UK VAT registered trader.

Although the end result is the same as with an import from outside the EU, the difference with an EU acquisition is that there is no need to actually pay the VAT subsequent to its recovery as input VAT.

3.4 Supplies of services

FAST FORWARD ⟫

Services supplied to a business customer are generally treated as being supplied in the country where that customer is situated. Therefore, if the customer is a UK VAT registered trader, output VAT is payable by that trader on the supply. Supplies of services by a UK VAT registered trader to business customers outside the UK are generally outside the scope of UK VAT.

3.4.1 Place of supply of services

Services supplied to a business customer are generally treated as **being supplied in the country where that customer is situated.** A 'business customer' is anyone carrying on a business anywhere in the world, not just VAT registered traders and not just customers in the EU.

3.4.2 Supplies of services to a UK business customer

Where a UK business customer receives services from outside the UK, the place of supply will be the UK. Therefore, if the business customer is a VAT registered trader, **output tax has to be accounted for by that UK trader on the relevant VAT return.**

The tax point for a supply of such services is the earlier of:

* **The time the service is completed**
* **The time the service is paid for**

The transaction is entered on the UK trader's VAT return as an output and an input so the effect is usually neutral. Thus the UK trader effectively in the same overall position as if the services have been supplied by another UK VAT registered trader.

3.4.3 Supplies of services by a UK trader

Supplies of services by a UK VAT registered trader to business customers outside the UK are generally outside the scope of UK VAT. This is because the place of supply is not in the UK.

Exam focus point

The rules on international services are complex. For Taxation (TX – UK) purposes, you only need to know the rules in outline as explained in this section.

4 Special schemes

FAST FORWARD ⟫

Special schemes include the cash accounting scheme, the annual accounting scheme and the optional flat rate scheme. These schemes can make VAT accounting easier and ease cash flow for certain types of trader.

One of the competencies you require to fulfil Performance Objective 15 Tax computations and assessments of the PER is to explain the basis of tax calculations, and interpret the effect of current legislation and case law. You can apply the knowledge you obtain from this section of the Study Text to help to demonstrate this competence.

4.1 The cash accounting scheme

The cash accounting scheme enables businesses to account for VAT on the basis of cash paid and received. That is, the date of payment or receipt determines the return in which the transaction is dealt with. This means that the cash accounting scheme gives automatic impairment loss relief (bad debt relief) because VAT is not due on a supply until payment has been received.

The scheme can only be used by a trader whose taxable turnover (exclusive of VAT) for the 12 months starting on their application to join the scheme is not expected to exceed £1,350,000. A trader can join the scheme only if all returns and VAT payments are up to date (or arrangements have been made to pay outstanding VAT by instalments).

If the value of taxable supplies exceeds £1,600,000 in the 12 months to the end of a VAT period a trader must leave the cash accounting scheme immediately.

Businesses which leave the scheme (either voluntarily or because they have breached the £1,600,000 limit) can account for any outstanding VAT due under the scheme on a cash basis for a further six months.

4.2 The annual accounting scheme

The annual accounting scheme is only available to traders who regularly pay VAT to HMRC, not to traders who normally receive repayments. It is available for traders **whose taxable turnover (exclusive of VAT) for the 12 months starting on their application to join the scheme is not expected to exceed £1,350,000.**

Under the annual accounting scheme traders file annual VAT returns but throughout the year they must make payments on account of their VAT liability by direct debit. The year for which each return is made may end at the end of any calendar month. Unless HMRC agree otherwise, the trader must pay 90% of the previous year's net VAT liability during the year by means of nine monthly payments commencing at the end of the fourth month of the year. The balance of the year's VAT is then paid with the annual return. There is an option for businesses to pay three larger interim instalments.

Late payment of instalments is not a default for the purposes of the default surcharge.

An annual VAT return must be submitted to HMRC along with any balancing payment due within two months of the end of the year.

It is not possible to use the annual accounting scheme if input tax exceeded output tax in the year prior to application. In addition, all VAT payments must be up to date.

If the expected value of a trader's taxable supplies exceeds £1,600,000, notice must be given to HMRC within 30 days and he may then be required to leave the scheme. If the £1,600,000 limit is in fact exceeded, the trader must leave the scheme.

If a trader fails to make the regular payments required by the scheme or the final payment for a year, or has not paid all VAT shown on returns made before joining the scheme, he may be expelled from the scheme. HMRC can also prevent a trader using the scheme 'if they consider it necessary to do so for the protection of the revenue'.

Advantages of annual accounting:

- Only **one VAT return each year** so fewer occasions to trigger a default surcharge
- Ability to **manage cash flow** more accurately
- **Avoids need for quarterly calculations for input tax recovery**

Disadvantages of annual accounting:

- Need to **monitor future taxable supplies** to ensure turnover limit not exceeded
- **Timing of payments have less correlation to turnover** (and hence cash received) by business
- **Payments based on previous year's turnover may not reflect current year turnover** which may be a problem if the scale of activities has reduced.

4.3 Flat rate scheme

The optional flat rate scheme enables businesses to calculate VAT due simply by applying a flat rate percentage to their turnover.

Under the scheme, businesses calculate VAT by applying a fixed percentage to their **tax inclusive turnover**, ie the total turnover, **including all reduced rate, zero-rated and exempt income.** However, the businesses **cannot reclaim any input tax suffered.**

The percentage usually depends upon the trade sector into which a business falls. It ranges from 4% for retailing food, confectionery or newspapers to 14.5% for accountancy and bookkeeping services.

A 1% reduction off the flat rate % can be made by businesses **in their first year of VAT registration.**

Exam focus point

> The flat rate percentage will be given to you in your examination.

Businesses using the scheme must issue VAT invoices to their VAT registered customers but they do not have to record all the details of the invoices issued or purchase invoices received to calculate the VAT due. Invoices issued will show VAT at the normal rate rather than the flat rate.

To join the flat rate scheme businesses must have a VAT exclusive annual taxable turnover of up to £150,000. A business must leave the flat rate scheme if the total value of its VAT inclusive supplies in the year (excluding sales of capital assets) is more than £230,000.

Question
Flat rate scheme (1)

Brian is an accountant who has been registered for VAT for many years and undertakes work for individuals and for business clients. In a VAT year, the business client work amounts to £70,000 and Brian issues VAT invoices totalling £84,000 (£70,000 plus VAT at 20%). Turnover from work for individuals totals £18,000, inclusive of VAT. Brian provides some exempt financial services which amount to £2,000 in a VAT year. The flat rate percentage for an accountancy business is 14.5%. Brian also incurs annual standard rated expenses of £4,800 inclusive of VAT.

Advise Brian whether he should register for the flat rate scheme.

Answer

Under the flat rate scheme VAT due to HMRC will be £(84,000 + 18,000 + 2,000) = £104,000 (VAT inclusive amount) × 14.5%= £15,080.

Under the normal VAT rules the net VAT due to HMRC would be:

	£
£70,000 × 20%	14,000
£18,000 × 1/6	3,000
Output VAT	17,000
Less input VAT £4,800 × 1/6	(800)
VAT due to HMRC	16,200

Brian should therefore register for the flat rate scheme as he will save VAT of £(16,200 – 15,080) = £1,120. The reduced VAT administration cost of using the flat rate scheme should also be taken into account.

From April 2017, there is a special flat rate of 16.5% which applies if the trader either does not purchase any goods or purchases only a limited amount of goods.

In Taxation (TX – UK) you will not be expected to establish whether the flat rate of 16.5% is applicable but a question could be set where you are told that this rate applies.

If the 16.5% rate is applicable, it will usually not be advantageous for a trader to use the flat rate scheme unless the amount of input VAT is very low.

Question
Flat rate scheme (2)

Clare has been registered for VAT for many years and has been using the flat rate scheme. In a VAT year, she makes only standard rated sales which amount to £100,000 exclusive of VAT. From April 2017, the applicable flat rate percentage for Clare is 16.5%. Clare also incurs annual standard rated expenses of £18,000 inclusive of VAT. Advise Clare whether she should continue to use the flat rate scheme.

Answer

Under the flat rate scheme VAT due to HMRC will be £(100,000 × 120/100) = £120,000 (VAT inclusive amount) × 16.5% = £19,800.

Under the normal VAT rules the net VAT due to HMRC would be:

	£
Output VAT £100,000 × 20%	20,000
Less input VAT £18,000 × 1/6	(3,000)
VAT due to HMRC	17,000

Clare should therefore deregister from the flat rate scheme as she will save VAT of £(19,800 – 17,000) = £2,800 although she should also take into account the extra costs of administration under the normal VAT rules.

Chapter Roundup

- A taxable person making a taxable supply to another registered person must supply a VAT invoice within 30 days.

- Every VAT registered trader must keep records for six years.

- A default occurs when a trader either submits his VAT return late, or submits the return on time but pays the VAT late. A default surcharge is applied if there is a default on payment during a default surcharge period.

- There is a common penalty regime for errors in tax returns, including VAT. Errors in a VAT return up to certain amounts may be corrected in the next return.

- Default interest is charged on unpaid VAT if HMRC raise an assessment of VAT or the trader makes a voluntary payment before the assessment is raised. It runs from the date the VAT should have been paid to the actual date of payment but cannot run for more than three years before the assessment or voluntary payment.

- Imports of goods from outside the EU are subject to VAT and exports of goods to outside the EU are zero-rated.

- Sales of goods to registered traders in other EU states are zero-rated. Taxable acquisitions of goods to the UK from other EU states are subject to VAT in the UK as both output tax and input tax.

- Services supplied to a business customer are generally treated as being supplied in the country where that customer is situated. Therefore, if the customer is a UK VAT registered trader, output VAT is payable by that trader on the supply. Supplies of services by a UK VAT registered trader to business customers outside the UK are generally outside the scope of UK VAT.

- Special schemes include the cash accounting scheme, the annual accounting scheme and the optional flat rate scheme. These schemes can make VAT accounting easier and ease cash flow for certain types of trader.

Quick Quiz

1. How long must a VAT trader keep records?

2. What is a default?

3. Dylan makes an error in his VAT for the quarter ending 31 March 2018 which results in a net under-declaration of £5,000. His net VAT turnover for the period is £150,000. How can Dylan correct the error?

4. Are goods despatched to the EU standard-rated or zero-rated?

5. Higgins is registered for VAT in the UK. Higgins is supplied with services by a French business on 1 September 2017. The value of the supply is £50,000. What are the VAT consequences of the supply?

6. How does the cash accounting scheme operate?

7. The turnover limits for the annual accounting scheme are not exceeding £_____m to join the scheme and once turnover exceeds £_____m the trader must leave the scheme. Fill in the blanks.

8. What is the optional flat rate scheme?

1   A VAT trader must keep records for six years.

2   A default occurs when a trader either submits his VAT return late or submits the return on time but pays the VAT late.

3   Dylan can correct the error in his VAT return for the quarter ending 30 June 2018. This is because the error of £5,000 is less than the greater of £10,000 and 1% of his net VAT turnover for the return period (£1,500).

4   In general, despatches to the EU are zero-rated.

5   Higgins will have to account for output tax of £50,000 × 20% = £10,000 on the supply and also £10,000 of input tax. The supply is therefore tax neutral for him.

6   The cash accounting scheme operates by a trader accounting for VAT on the basis of cash paid and received (rather than invoices). The date of payment or receipt determines the return in which the transaction is dealt with. The scheme gives automatic impairment loss relief because VAT on a supply is not due until payment is received.

7   The turnover limits for the annual accounting scheme are not exceeding **£1.35m** to join the scheme and once turnover exceeds **£1.6m** the trader must leave the scheme.

8   The optional flat rate scheme enables businesses to calculate VAT simply by applying a percentage to their tax-inclusive turnover. Under the scheme, businesses calculate VAT due by applying a flat rate percentage to their tax inclusive turnover, ie the total turnover generated, including all reduced-rate, zero-rated and exempt income. The percentage depends upon the trade sector in which a business falls or may be 16.5% if the trader makes no, or limited, purchases of goods.

Now try the questions below from the Practice Question Bank

Number	Type	Marks	Time
Q172	Section A	2	4 mins
Q173	Section A	2	4 mins
Q174	Section A	2	4 mins
Q175	Section B	2	4 mins
Q176	Section B	2	4 mins
Q177	Section B	2	4 mins
Q178	Section B	2	4 mins
Q179	Section B	2	4 mins
Q180	Section C	10	18 mins

Practice question and answer bank

Introduction to the UK tax system MCQs   4 mins each

1   Which of the following are functions of HM Revenue & Customs (HMRC) in the UK tax system?

   (1)   Formally imposes taxation
   (2)   Produces a wide range of explanatory notes
   (3)   Provides advice on minimising tax liability
   (4)   Has the administrative function for collection of tax.

   A   1 and 2
   B   2 and 3
   C   1 and 4
   D   2 and 4   (2 marks)

2   Which of the following are NOT revenue taxes?

   (1)   Income tax
   (2)   Capital gains tax
   (3)   National insurance
   (4)   Inheritance tax

   A   1 and 2
   B   2 and 4
   C   3 and 4
   D   2 and 3   (2 marks)

3   You work for a firm of accountants. A few weeks ago, you prepared a tax return for Serena. Serena
     has now told you that she forgot to include some bank interest in the return but that she does not
     intend to tell HMRC of the omission.

     Which of the following actions should you take?

     (1)   Inform Serena in writing that it is not possible for your firm to act for her.

     (2)   Inform HMRC that your firm is no longer acting for Serena.

     (3)   Inform HMRC about the details of Serena's omission.

     (4)   Report to your firm's Money Laundering Reporting Officer Serena's refusal to disclose the
            omission to HMRC and the facts surrounding it.

     A   1, 2 and 3
     B   2, 3 and 4
     C   1, 2 and 4
     D   1, 3 and 4   (2 marks)

Computing taxable income and the income tax liability MCQs

4 mins each

4   Which of the following types of income are exempt from income tax?

   (1)   Dividends from a company
   (2)   Interest received from an Individual Savings Account
   (3)   £50 Premium Bond prize
   (4)   Interest on NS&I Savings Certificates
   (5)   Interest on government securities (gilts)

   A   1, 2 and 4
   B   2, 3 and 5
   C   2, 3 and 4
   D   1, 4 and 5   **(2 marks)**

5   In 2017/18, Robert had property business income of £108,000. This was his only income in 2017/18. Robert also paid a gross personal pension contribution of £3,000 in December 2017.

   What is the personal allowance available to Robert for the tax year 2017/18?

   A   £6,500
   B   £7,500
   C   £9,000
   D   £11,500   **(2 marks)**

6   Peter has taxable income for the tax year 2017/18 as follows:

   Non-savings income   £2,000
   Savings income   £6,410

   What is Peter's income tax liability for the tax year 2017/18?

   A   £882
   B   £482
   C   £1,082
   D   £1,682   **(2 marks)**

7   Rhoda has taxable income of £175,000 in 2017/18 which is all employment income. PAYE of £40,000 was deducted.

   What is Rhoda's income tax payable for the tax year 2017/18?

   A   £64,550
   B   £19,375
   C   £24,550
   D   £23,300   **(2 marks)**

8   John is a widower and has two children aged 14 and 12. He receives child benefit of £1,788 in 2017/18. John has net income of £53,400 in 2017/18 and he made a gift aid donation of £300 (gross) in January 2018.

   What is John's child benefit income tax charge for the tax year 2017/18?

   A   £536
   B   £554
   C   £608
   D   £1,788   **(2 marks)**

9 Sandeep, Harriet and Romelu

18 mins

(a) Sandeep had not previously been UK-resident prior to the tax year 2017/18. He arrived in the UK on 6 April 2017 and remained in the UK for 190 days. Sandeep does not work during 2017/18.

Required

Explain why Sandeep is UK resident in the tax year 2017/18.   **(2 marks)**

(b) Harriet had always been UK-resident prior to the tax year 2017/18, but she has not spent more than 90 days in the UK in the two previous tax years. Harriet is self-employed and does substantive (but not full-time) work in the UK during 2017/18. She has no close family. Harriet owns a house in the UK. On 6 April 2017, she started to rent an overseas apartment in which she lived for 255 days. She then returned to the UK where she lived in her house for the remainder of the tax year 2017/18.

Required

Explain why Harriet is UK resident in the tax year 2017/18.   **(4 marks)**

(c) Romelu had not previously been UK-resident prior to the tax year 2017/18 and has never spent more than 60 days in the UK in previous tax years. His wife is UK resident. Romelu arrived in the UK on 6 April 2017 and remained in the UK for 92 days during which time he lived in a rented flat. He also has a home outside the UK where he spent the rest of 2017/18. Romelu does not work during 2017/18.

Required

Explain why Romelu is non-UK resident in the tax year 2017/18.   **(4 marks)**

(Total = 10 marks)

10 John and Helen

27 mins

John and Helen are a married couple. They have a 12 year old son, Marcus. John and Helen received the following income in 2017/18.

	John £	Helen £
Salary (before tax deducted)	68,090	23,500
PAYE tax deducted	15,936	2,400
Dividends	6,211	7,820
Bank deposit interest	1,000	1,095
Building society interest	990	525

Required

(a) Compute the tax payable by John and by Helen for 2017/18.   **(13 marks)**

(b) Explain the tax implications if Helen had received child benefit of £1,076 during 2017/18.

(2 marks)

(Total = 15 marks)

11 Michael and Josie

27 mins

Michael and Josie are a married couple. They received the following income in 2017/18.

	Michael £	Josie £
Salary (before tax deducted)	163,540	100,000
PAYE tax deducted	59,390	28,700
Dividends	17,111	7,820
Bank deposit interest	7,500	150
Building society interest	7,400	550

Josie made a gift aid donation of £1,600 in December 2017.

Required

Compute the tax payable by Michael and Josie for 2017/18.

(15 marks)

Employment income MCQs

4 mins each

12   Jacob works part time for Z Ltd at a salary of £8,000 a year. He is not a director of Z Ltd. On 30 November 2017, Jacob received a bonus of £1,800 in respect of Z Ltd's trading results for the year ended 31 October 2017. He expects to receive a bonus of £2,400 in November 2018 in respect of Z Ltd's results for the year ended 31 October 2018.

What is Jacob's employment income for the tax year 2017/18?

A   £8,000
B   £9,800
C   £10,050
D   £10,400

(2 marks)

13   You are a tax advisor for the following clients.

(1)   Ben, who is a computer systems advisor. He works in the Bristol office one day a week and spends the rest of his time visiting clients in London and Manchester.

(2)   Colin, who is a computer technician. He works two days a week at the Bristol workshop depot and three days a week at the Swindon workshop.

(3)   Diane, who works for an accountancy firm. She is based in the Birmingham office but has been seconded to the Bristol office for 12 months.

(4)   Erica, who works permanently in the same Birmingham office as Diane. She occasionally travels from home to visit a client in Bristol.

Which of your clients can claim tax relief for travelling expenses between home and Bristol?

A   1 and 2
B   2 and 3
C   3 and 4
D   1 and 4

(2 marks)

14   Sarah is employed by Y plc. She uses her own car for business purposes and is reimbursed 35p per mile by Y plc. In 2017/18, Sarah travelled 15,000 miles on business.

What is the employment income consequence of the reimbursement for business mileage?

A   £5,250 taxable benefit
B   £(500) allowable expense
C   £(1,500) allowable expense
D   £(5,750) allowable expense

(2 marks)

Danni

4 mins each

The following scenario relates to questions 15 to 19.

Danni joined a UK company, Clifton plc, as purchasing director on 1 July 2017, based at their Nottingham office.

Salary and bonus

Until 31 December 2017, Danni's monthly salary as a director was £6,000. From 1 January 2018, her salary increased by 2.5%.

Clifton plc awarded Danni a bonus of £10,000 in relation to a special purchasing project during Clifton plc's period of account ended 31 March 2018. This bonus was determined by the board of directors on 15 March 2018, credited in the company's accounts on 10 April 2018, which was also the date when Danni became entitled to payment of the bonus. The bonus was paid to Danni on 31 May 2018.

Travel to Clifton plc's offices

From 1 July 2017, Danni travelled to Clifton plc's office in Nottingham from home using the Nottingham Tram Network. Danni bought a monthly tram season ticket for each of the months from July 2017 to December 2017.

From 1 January 2018, Danni was seconded to Clifton plc's office in Manchester for a period of six months. Danni bought a monthly rail season ticket for each month of her secondment.

Travel to clients

Danni also used her own car for journeys to meet clients in Leicester, which is 24 miles from Nottingham. She made five return journeys between 1 July 2017 and 5 April 2018. Clifton plc paid Danni 30p per mile for these journeys.

Subscriptions

Danni is a member of the Chartered Institute of Purchasing and Supply (MCIP) and paid her annual membership fee on 31 December 2017. Danni is also a member of her local tennis club at which she sometimes meets potential suppliers for Clifton plc and paid her annual membership fee on 1 September 2017.

Payroll giving

Clifton plc has a payroll giving scheme. Danni made monthly contributions through the scheme from 31 December 2017.

15   What is the amount of Danni's employment income from her salary and bonus taxable in the tax year 2017/18?

     A   £64,000
     B   £54,450
     C   £64,450
     D   £54,000   **(2 marks)**

16   Which of the following of Danni's travel to Clifton plc's offices will be qualifying travel expenses?

     (1)   Travel from home to Clifton plc's office in Nottingham.
     (2)   Travel from home to Clifton plc's office in Manchester

     A   1 only
     B   2 only
     C   Both 1 and 2
     D   Neither 1 nor 2   **(2 marks)**

17   What are the employment income consequences of using her own car for journeys to meet clients in Leicester?

     A   £72 taxable benefit
     B   £108 allowable deduction
     C   £12 taxable benefit
     D   £36 allowable deduction   **(2 marks)**

18   Which of the following of Danni's subscriptions will be deductible in computing her employment income?

     (1)   Chartered Institute of Purchasing and Supply (MCIP)
     (2)   Tennis club

     A   1 only
     B   2 only
     C   Both 1 and 2
     D   Neither 1 nor 2   **(2 marks)**

19   How is tax relief given for Danni's contributions through the payroll giving scheme?

	By whom	How tax relief given
A	Clifton plc	Deducting the donation from Danni's gross pay before calculating PAYE
B	Clifton plc	Increasing the basic rate tax limit when computing PAYE on Danni's gross pay
C	Danni	Making contributions net of basic rate tax
D	Danni	Making a claim in her self assessment tax return **(2 marks)**

Taxable and exempt benefits. The PAYE system MCQs

4 mins each

20   Lenny is employed by B plc at a salary of £42,000 each tax year. He is provided with a car available for private use throughout 2017/18. The car has CO_2 emissions of 103 g/km and a list price of £20,000. B plc paid £18,000 for the car as a result of a dealer discount. The car has a diesel engine. No private fuel is provided.

What is Lenny's taxable car benefit for the tax year 2017/18?

A   £3,800
B   £4,400
C   £3,960
D   £3,420   **(2 marks)**

21   Bernie is employed by N Ltd. N Ltd provided Bernie with the use of free accommodation (not job related) from 6 April 2017 to 5 August 2017. The accommodation cost Bernie's employer £99,000 in February 2015 and was previously occupied by another employee. The accommodation had a market value of £123,000 in April 2017 and an annual value of £3,780.

What is Bernie's total taxable benefit in respect of the accommodation for the tax year 2017/18?

A   £1,260
B   £200
C   £1,460
D   £1,660   **(2 marks)**

22   Julia is employed by C plc at a salary of £20,000 each tax year. For the tax year 2017/18 C plc paid Julia's corporate gym membership at a cost of £1,200. Julia receives no other benefits from C plc. C plc does not payroll any of the benefits provided to employees.

Which form, if any, does C plc use to report this benefit to HM Revenue & Customs (HMRC) and by what date must it be submitted to HMRC?

	Form	Date by when must be submitted to HMRC
A	P11D	31 May 2018
B	P11D	6 July 2018
C	P60	31 May 2018
D	P60	6 July 2018 **(2 marks)**

Clara

4 mins each

The following scenario relates to questions 23 to 27.

You should assume that the current date is 6 April 2017.

Clara is setting up in business as a sole trader and will employ 12 individuals, including Burton, Jessica and Lewis. In addition to paying these three employees a salary, Clara will provide them with the following additional payments and benefits for the tax year 2017/18.

Burton will be required to travel on business in the UK and will be paid £8 per night to cover private incidental expenses if he stays away from home overnight. Burton will spend 50 such nights away from home. Burton will travel by train on business journeys and will spend £1,200 on train fares. This amount will be reimbursed in full by Clara.

Jessica will be required to attend Clara's office every working day and will be provided with workplace parking for which Clara will pay the car park provider £500 per year. Jessica will be provided with childcare vouchers for her one-year old son at a cost of £67 per week for 45 weeks. Jessica is a basic rate employee.

Lewis will be provided with a company van from 6 August 2017 which he will park overnight at home and use to travel to Clara's office every working day. He will also be allowed to use the van on non-working days. All fuel will be provided for the van. The van will have a diesel engine and CO_2 emissions of 161 g/km. It will have a list price of £15,000.

Clara understands that she will need to operate the Pay As You Earn (PAYE) system for income tax and national insurance contributions (NICs). She will not be payrolling benefits.

23   What is the total amount that Clara will report to HM Revenue & Customs (HMRC) on form P11D for Burton for the tax year 2017/18?

    A   £150
    B   £400
    C   £1,350
    D   £1,600   **(2 marks)**

24   What is the total amount that Clara will report to HMRC on form P11D for Jessica for the tax year 2017/18?

    A   £540
    B   £1,040
    C   £3,015
    D   £3,515   **(2 marks)**

25   What is the total amount that Clara will report to HMRC on form P11D for Lewis for the tax year 2017/18?

    A   £8,522
    B   £3,840
    C   £2,560
    D   £0   **(2 marks)**

26   By when must Clara make her Full Payment Submission (FPS) for PAYE and by when must she pay the corresponding tax and national insurance contributions if she does so electronically?

	Report	*Payment*
A	End of tax month	14 days after end of tax month
B	End of tax month	17 days after end of tax month
C	On or before any day when she pays someone	14 days after end of tax month
D	On or before any day when she pays someone	17 days after end of tax month

    (2 marks)

27   Clara makes both her first and second FPSs each six weeks late.

What are the monthly penalties that HMRC will impose?

	First FPS	*Second FPS*
A	£0	£200
B	£200	£200
C	£0	£100
D	£100	£100

    (2 marks)

28 Azure plc

18 mins

The following items have been provided by a UK company, Azure plc, to various employees.

(a)   A loan of £16,000 at 0.25% a year to Andrew on 6 October 2017. The loan was not for a qualifying interest purpose.

(b)   A flower arrangement costing £45 given to Penelope on 6 April 2017 on the occasion of her wedding.

(c)   The loan of a TV to Charles from 6 June 2017, the asset having cost the company £800 in 2013 and having had a market value of £500 in June 2017.

(d)   A long service award in December 2017 to Demelza, the company secretary, comprising a gold wrist watch costing £1,000. Demelza has been employed by the company since December 1990.

(e)   Removal expenses of £9,500 to Janet in September 2017 who moved 200 miles from Plymouth to Liverpool to take up a new position in the Liverpool office in July 2017.

(f)   The provision of two mobile phones to Lawrence on 6 April 2017 both of which were available solely for private use. Azure plc paid £120 for the hire of each of the mobile phones for the tax year. The market value of each of the phones was £500. The cost of the calls made during the year was £300 for one of the phones and £400 for the other phone.

Required

State in detail how each of the above items would be treated for 2017/18, computing the amount of any taxable benefit.

(10 marks)

Pensions MCQs

4 mins each

29   In the tax year 2017/18, Treena earned £3,500 from part time work, trading income of £2,000 and gross bank interest of £500.

What is the maximum gross pension contribution that Treena could have made during the tax year 2017/18 on which there would have been tax relief?

A   £3,500
B   £5,500
C   £3,600
D   £6,000

(2 marks)

30   In the tax year 2017/18, Jemima earned a salary of £90,500 and she paid a contribution of £15,000 to her employer's occupational pension scheme. Jemima has no other sources of income.

What is Jemima's taxable income for the tax year 2017/18?

A   £90,500
B   £75,500
C   £64,000
D   £60,250

(2 marks)

31   Rio started in business as a sole trader on 6 April 2015 and had the following results:

2015/16   £20,000
2016/17   £30,000
2017/18   £85,000

Rio had not made any pension provision prior to 2016/17 but on 6 April 2016 he joined a personal pension scheme and made a contribution of £17,000 (gross) on that date. He now wishes to make a pension contribution in March 2018.

What is the maximum gross pension contribution that Rio can make in March 2018 on which there will be tax relief without incurring an annual allowance charge?

A   £63,000
B   £103,000
C   £85,000
D   £40,000   **(2 marks)**

Gary, George and Geraldine   4 mins each

The following scenario relates to questions 32 to 36.

Gary

Gary has taxable income of £45,900 for 2017/18, all from employment income and after deduction of his personal allowance. He paid £4,000 (net) into his personal pension scheme in 2017/18.

George

George has trading income of £15,000 for 2017/18. In this tax year he also has property business income from a furnished holiday letting of £8,000 and gross bank interest of £1,200. George wants to know the tax consequences of accessing his pension fund of £500,000 when he reaches the age of 55 under flexi-access drawdown.

Geraldine

Geraldine had trading income of £60,000 in 2016/17. She paid £25,000 (net) into her personal pension scheme in 2016/17. This was the first year in which she had been a member of a registered pension scheme. She has trading income of £130,000 in 2017/18. She now wishes to make a personal pension contribution in March 2018. Geraldine hopes to build up a pension fund of £1,500,000 by the time she is aged 55 when she will start taking pension benefits. She will take the excess of the fund over the lifetime allowance as a lump sum.

32   What is Gary's income tax payable for the tax year 2017/18?

A   £11,660
B   £10,860
C   £10,660
D   £9,180   **(2 marks)**

33   What are George's relevant earnings for 2017/18?

A   £3,600
B   £15,000
C   £23,000
D   £24,200   **(2 marks)**

34   What are the tax consequences of George accessing his pension fund under flexi-access drawdown?

A   Lump sum taxable at 55%, pension income taxable at 25%
B   Tax-free lump sum of up to 25% of pension fund, remainder taxable as pension income
C   Tax-free lump sum of up to 50% of pension fund, remainder taxable as pension income
D   All withdrawals taxable as pension income   **(2 marks)**

35   What is the maximum net personal pension contribution that Geraldine will be able to make in March 2018, obtaining tax relief and without resulting in a tax charge?

A   £40,000
B   £48,750
C   £32,000
D   £39,000   **(2 marks)**

36   What will Geraldine's tax position be if she takes the excess of the fund over the lifetime allowance as a lump sum?

    A   She will be subject to income tax at her marginal rate of tax on the lump sum

    B   She will be subject to income tax at the rate of 55% on the lump sum

    C   She will be subject to income tax at the rate of 25% on the lump sum

    D   She will not be subject to income tax on the lump sum   **(2 marks)**

Property income MCQs   4 mins each

37   Paul rents out a house which is fully furnished. The house does not qualify as a furnished holiday letting. Paul paid the following expenses in relation to the letting:

	£
New chairs for garden (not previously provided) bought July 2017	600
Replacement cooker (upgrade, similar cooker to original would have cost £650, no scrap value for old cooker) bought September 2017	900
Central heating breakdown cover premium paid 1 January 2018 for year to 31 December 2018 (not previously covered)	580

What is the amount of Paul's allowable expenses for calculating his property business income in the tax year 2017/18?

    A   £1,395

    B   £1,045

    C   £795

    D   £1,230   **(2 marks)**

38   Laura granted an 11-year lease on a property to a tenant for a premium of £30,000.

What is the amount of the premium on which will Laura be chargeable to income tax?

    A   £23,400

    B   £6,000

    C   £30,000

    D   £24,000   **(2 marks)**

39   Andrea rents out a house. In the tax year 2017/18, she had the following income and expenses:

	£
Rent receiveable	20,000
Mortage: capital repayments	2,000
Mortage: interest paid	5,000

What is Andrea's property business income for the tax year 2017/18?

    A   £13,000

    B   £16,000

    C   £14,000

    D   £15,000   **(2 marks)**

40 Rafe   18 mins

On 1 May 2017, Rafe started to invest in rented properties using capital inherited from his grandfather. He bought two houses in the first three months, as follows.

House 1

Rafe bought house 1 for £62,000 on 1 May 2017. It needed a new roof before it was fit to be let out. Rafe paid £5,000 for the work to be done in May. He then let it unfurnished for £600 a month from 1 June to 30 November 2017. The first tenant then left, and the house was empty throughout December 2017. On 1 January 2018, a new tenant moved in. The house was again let unfurnished. The rent was £6,000 a year, payable annually in advance.

Rafe paid a buildings insurance premium of £480 for the period from 1 June 2017 to 31 May 2018.

House 2

Rafe bought house 2 for £45,000 on 1 July 2017. He spent £1,200 on routine redecoration and £5,300 on new furniture in July, and let the house fully furnished from 1 August 2017 for £7,800 a year, payable annually in advance. Rafe paid a buildings insurance premium of £920 for the period from 1 July 2017 to 30 June 2018 and a boiler insurance premium of £180 for the period from 1 August 2017 to 31 July 2018. In March 2018, the tenant damaged a sofa which was part of the furniture bought in July 2017 and Rafe bought an identical replacement sofa for £800. The damaged sofa was scrapped with no value.

During 2017/18 Rafe also rented out one furnished room of his main residence. He received £7,850 and incurred allowable expenses of £875.

Required

Compute Rafe's property business income for 2017/18. **(10 marks)**

Computing trading income MCQs 4 mins each

41 Which TWO of the following items of expenditure will Walter NOT be allowed to deduct in calculating his tax-adjusted trading profit before capital allowances?

(1) Installing air conditioning in his workshop

(2) Repairing the central heating in his offices

(3) Redecorating his showroom

(4) Making initial repairs to a recently acquired second-hand office building which was not usable until the repairs were carried out

A 1 and 2
B 2 and 3
C 1 and 4
D 2 and 4 **(2 marks)**

42 Allie is a sole trader and has a profit of £160,000 on her statement of profit or loss for the year ended 31 December 2017. Included within this figure are these expenses:

(1) £3,000 legal fees in connection with renewing a 15-year lease of Allie's business premises
(2) £180 car parking fines incurred by Allie whilst visiting clients
(3) £40 hamper of food for customer

What is Allie's tax adjusted profit for the year ended 31 December 2017?

A £160,040
B £163,180
C £163,220
D £160,220 **(2 marks)**

43 Terry has been in business for many years preparing accounts to 5 April each year. On 6 July 2017 leased a car with CO_2 emissions of 155g. The leasing costs were £400 per month. In the period from 6 July 2017 to 5 April 2017, Terry drove 13,500 miles, of which 10,800 were on business.

What is the deductible expense for Terry in repect of the car for the year ended 5 April 2018?

A £2,880
B £2,448
C £3,060
D £3,600 **(2 marks)**

Margaret

4 mins each

The following scenario relates to questions 44 to 48.

On 6 April 2017, Margaret acquired a country house called The Cedars and immediately started a sole trader guest house business in it. Two-thirds of The Cedars was used by guests and one-third by Margaret. The following information is relevant for the year to 5 April 2018.

(1)   Revenue was £36,000 of which £500 was owed as receivables at 5 April 2018.

(2)   Furniture for guest use was acquired for £2,500.

(3)   A plot of land was acquired to provide parking solely for the use of guests for £7,500.

(4)   Gas and electricity bills relating to the whole of The Cedars amounted to £7,400. Cleaning and gardening costs, again relating to the whole of The Cedars, amounted to £1,800. Margaret also spent £2,000 on providing food eaten by her and the guests. There were no amounts outstanding at 5 April 2018. The fixed rate adjustment for private use of business premises for one occupant is £350 per month.

(5)   Margaret purchased a motor car on 6 April 2017. She drove 15,000 miles in the car during the year of which 12,000 miles were for journeys relating to the guest house business.

(6)   Other allowable expenses were £2,000 of which £900 was owed as payables at 5 April 2018.

Margaret will elect to use the cash basis for accounting for the tax year 2017/18 and will use fixed rate expenses where available. She expects to make a loss in period of account ending 5 April 2019.

44   What is the amount of revenue that will be taxable in the tax year 2017/18 and the amount of other allowable expenses that will be allowable in that tax year?

	Revenue	Other allowable expenses
A	£36,000	£2,000
B	£36,000	£1,100
C	£35,500	£2,000
D	£35,500	£1,100

(2 marks)

45   What are the amounts which are allowable in relation to the furniture and the plot of land for guest parking?

	Furniture	Land for guest parking
A	£2,500	£7,500
B	£2,500	£Nil
C	£450	£7,500
D	£450	£Nil

(2 marks)

46   What is the amount of a household expenses in item (4) that are allowable under the cash basis?

A	£11,200
B	£7,467
C	£7,000
D	£5,000

(2 marks)

47   What is the amount of the allowable motoring expenses?

A	£5,000
B	£3,000
C	£5,750
D	£5,400

(2 marks)

BPP
LEARNING MEDIA

48   How will Margaret be able to relieve the loss that she expects to make in the tax year 2018/19?

(1)   Against general income of 2018/19
(2)   Against general income of 2017/18
(3)   Carry forward against future trading profits of the guest house business

A   1, 2 and 3
B   3 only
C   1 and 2 only
D   1 and 3 only   (2 marks)

49 Archie   27 mins

Archie's statement of profit or loss for the year to 31 March 2018 was as follows.

	£	£
Gross profit		246,250
Other income		
Impairment trade losses recovered (previously written off)	373	
Profit on sale of office	5,265	
Building society interest	1,900	
		7,538
Expenses		
General expenses	73,611	
Repairs and renewals	15,000	
Legal and accountancy charges	1,200	
Subscriptions and donations	7,000	
Impairment losses (trade)	500	
Salaries and wages	30,000	
Travel	8,000	
Depreciation	15,000	
Rent and rates	1,500	
		(151,811)
Net profit		101,977

Notes

(1)   *General expenses include the following.*

	£
Entertaining staff	1,000
Entertaining suppliers	600

(2)   *Repairs and renewals include the following.*

	£
Redecorating existing premises	300
Renovations to new premises to remedy wear and tear of previous owner (the premises were usable before these renovations)	500

(3)   *Legal and accountancy charges are made up as follows.*

	£
Debt collection service	200
Staff service agreements	50
Tax consultant's fees for advice on tax efficient personal investments	30
45 year lease on new premises	100
Audit and accountancy	820
	1,200

(4)   *Subscriptions and donations include the following.*

	£
Donations under the gift aid scheme	5,200
Donation to a political party	500
Sports facilities for staff	600
Subscription to trade association	100

(5)   Travel expenses included Archie's motoring expenses of £2,000. 25% of his use of his car was for private purposes.

(6)   Capital allowances amounted to £2,200.

Required

Compute Archie's taxable trading profit for the accounting period to 31 March 2018. You should start with net profit figure of £101,977 and you should indicate by the use of zero (0) any items which do not require adjustment.   **(15 marks)**

Capital allowances MCQs   4 mins each

50   Which TWO of the following items COULD be plant which is eligible for capital allowances?

    (1)   Refrigerator for coffee shop
    (2)   Extension to office building
    (3)   Sound insulation in a recording studio
    (4)   A bridge

    A   1 and 4
    B   2 and 3
    C   2 and 4
    D   1 and 3   **(2 marks)**

51   Julian is a sole trader who prepares accounts to 5 April each year. He acquired a car for both business and private purposes on 1 October 2017. The car has a CO_2 emission rate of 165 grams per kilometre and cost £21,000. The private mileage for Julian's period of account to 5 April 2018 was 25% of the total mileage for that year.

What is the maximum amount of capital allowances that Julian can claim in respect of the car for the year ended 5 April 2018?

    A   £1,260
    B   £3,780
    C   £2,835
    D   £1,680   **(2 marks)**

52   Olive started trading on 1 October 2017 and prepared her first set of accounts to 31 December 2017. On 10 October 2017 she acquired machinery at a cost of £60,000.

What is the maximum amount of capital allowances that Olive can claim for the period ended 31 December 2017?

    A   £60,000
    B   £51,800
    C   £50,450
    D   £50,000   **(2 marks)**

Sylvester

The following scenario relates to questions 53 to 57.

Sylvester is the sole proprietor of a small engineering business. He has previously prepared accounts annually to 5 April but has decided to prepare accounts for the nine-month period to 31 December 2017. The following tax written down values are brought forward on 6 April 2017:

Main pool	£56,800
Special rate pool	£500
Motor car for Sylvester's use (30% private use)	£6,000

The following disposals and additions were made during the period ended 31 December 2017.

Disposals:	20 April 2017	–	Plant £12,000 (original cost £10,000)
	21 May 2017	–	Motor car for Sylvester's own use £7,200 (original cost £8,923)
	20 June 2017	–	Plant £800 (original cost £3,000)
Additions:	21 May 2017	–	New motor car for Sylvester's own use £19,000 CO_2 emissions 150 g/km. Private use of this car is 20%.

Sylvester is considering buying a new motor car for use by sales representative in January 2018. He is considering two cars. Motor car [1] has CO_2 emissions of 70g/km. Motor car [2] has CO_2 emissions of 140g/km. The motor car will be the only acquisition in the year to 31 December 2018.

53   What is the balancing charge that arises on the disposal of Sylvester's car?

  A   £1,200
  B   £840
  C   £360
  D   £2,046   (2 marks)

54   What is the maximum writing down allowance on Sylvester's new car for the period to 31 December 2017?

  A   £912
  B   £1,520
  C   £1,140
  D   £1,216   (2 marks)

55   What is the maximum writing down allowance on the main pool for the period to 31 December 2017?

  A   £6,210
  B   £5,940
  C   £8,280
  D   £7,920   (2 marks)

56   What is the maximum writing down allowance on the special rate pool for the period to 31 December 2017?

  A   £68
  B   £40
  C   £500
  D   £30   (2 marks)

57   How will the purchase of the motor car for use by the sales representative be treated if Sylvester wishes to claim maximum capital allowances in the year to 31 December 2018?

      (1)   It will be given a 100% first year allowance

      (2)   It will be added to the main pool and given writing down allowances of 18% as part of the pool

      (3)   It will be added to the special rate pool and given writing down allowances of 8% as part of the pool

	Motor car [1]	Motor car [2]
A	1	2
B	2	3
C	2	1
D	1	3

                                                              (2 marks)

58 Tom   27 mins

Tom prepares accounts to 30 June. Despite substantial investment in new equipment, business has been indifferent and he will cease trading on 31 December 2021. His last accounts will be prepared for the six months to 31 December 2021.

The tax written down values at 1 July 2017 were as follows.

	£
Main pool	33,500
Short life asset (acquired 1 May 2016)	4,400

Additions and disposals have been as follows.

		£
20.9.17	Plant cost	27,000
15.7.18	Car for own use cost	13,400
14.7.20	Plant sold for	340
10.5.21	Short life asset sold for	2,900

Private use of the car was 20% for all years. The car emits CO_2 of 105g/km.

At the end of 2021, the plant will be worth £24,000 and the car £10,600.

Required

Calculate the capital allowances for the periods from 1 July 2017 to 31 December 2021, assuming the capital allowances rates for 2017/18 apply throughout.   **(15 marks)**

Assessable trading income MCQs   4 mins each

59   Frank started trading on 1 January 2017. He prepared his first set of accounts for the 13-month period to 31 January 2018. His tax adjusted trading profit for this period was £19,500.

      What are Frank's overlap profits?

      A   £1,500

      B   £3,250

      C   £4,500

      D   £3,000   **(2 marks)**

60   Fredericka stopped trading on 31 March 2018. Her tax adjusted profits for the last two periods of account were:

y/e 31.1.18	£10,000
p/e 31.3.18	£2,500

      Fredericka had £1,000 of overlap profit when she started trading.

What is Fredericka's taxable trading income for the tax year 2017/18?

A   £12,500
B   £11,500
C   £9,833
D   £1,500   (2 marks)

61   Renee commenced trading on 1 January 2017. She prepared her first set of accounts for the
      18 month period to 30 June 2018.

      What is Renee's basis period for the tax year 2017/18?

      A   1 July 2017 to 30 June 2018
      B   6 April 2017 to 5 April 2018
      C   1 January 2017 to 31 December 2017
      D   1 January 2017 to 5 April 2017   (2 marks)

62 Clive   27 mins

Clive starts a business as a sole trader on 1 January 2018.

His business plan shows that his monthly profits are likely to be as follows.

January 2018 to June 2018 (inclusive)	£800	a month
July 2018 to December 2018 (inclusive)	£1,200	a month
Thereafter	£2,000	a month

Clive is considering two alternative accounting dates, 31 March and 30 April, in each case commencing
with a period ending in 2018.

Required

Show the taxable trading profits which will arise for each of the first four tax years under each of the two
alternative accounting dates, and recommend an accounting date.   (15 marks)

63 Fiona   27 mins

Fiona started to trade as a baker on 1 January 2018 and prepared her first accounts to 30 April 2019.
Adjusted profits before capital allowances are as follows.

	£
Period to 30 April 2019	47,030
Year to 30 April 2020	24,787

Fiona incurred the following expenditure on plant and machinery.

Date	Item	£
1.1.18	Desk and other office furniture	2,625
4.1.18	General plant	8,070
1.3.18	Second-hand oven	5,300
25.3.18	Delivery van	5,450
15.4.18	General plant	8,555
15.5.18	Car for Fiona	6,600
30.1.20	General plant	10,000
30.4.20	Mixer	1,200

The private use of the car is 35%. The car has CO_2 emissions of 103g/km.

Required

Calculate the taxable profits for the first four tax years and the overlap profits carried forward. Assume that
the capital allowances rates applicable in 2017/18 apply throughout.   (15 marks)

Trading losses MCQs

4 mins each

64   Which TWO of the following statements about trading loss relief for an individual are correct?

(1)   A claim to set a trading loss against general income can be restricted so that the individual has enough net income to use the personal allowance.

(2)   A trading loss carried forward must be set against the first available profits of the same trade.

(3)   A trading loss carried forward can only be used in the following six tax years.

(4)   A trading loss claim for relief against general income must be made by 31 January 22 months after the end of the tax year of the loss.

A   1 and 2
B   1 and 3
C   3 and 4
D   2 and 4   (2 marks)

65   Shelley has been a sole trader for many years, preparing accounts to 31 January each year. In the year to 31 January 2017 she made a profit of £9,000 and in the year to 31 January 2018 she made a loss of £24,000. In 2016/17 she had property business income of £4,000. She has no other income in 2017/18.

How much of the loss of the tax year 2017/18 remains to carry forward to the tax year 2018/19 if Shelley makes a loss relief claim against general income for the tax year 2016/17?

A   £22,000
B   £11,000
C   £20,000
D   £15,000   (2 marks)

66   William has been a sole trader for many years, preparing accounts to 31 March each year. In the year to 31 March 2017, William made a profit of £15,000 and in the year to 31 March 2018 he made a loss of £180,000. William has property business income of £260,000 in the tax year 2016/17. He has no other income in 2017/18.

What is the amount of the loss that William can set against his general income for the tax year 2016/17?

A   £65,000
B   £50,000
C   £83,750
D   £68,750   (2 marks)

67 Morgan

18 mins

Morgan has been in business as a sole trader for many years. He has the following expected results.

Year ending 5 April		£
2018	Profit	15,000
2019	Loss	(40,000)
2020	Profit	45,000

In addition to his trading income, Morgan has savings income of £12,000 a year.

Required

(a)   Outline the ways in which Morgan could obtain relief for his loss.   (5 marks)

(b) Prepare a statement showing how the loss would be relieved assuming that relief were to be claimed as soon as possible. Assume that the rates and allowances applicable in 2017/18 apply in later years. Comment on whether this is likely to be the best relief.

(5 marks)

(Total = 10 marks)

Partnerships and limited liability partnerships MCQs

4 mins each

68 Jess and Kate have been in partnership for many years preparing accounts to 31 December each year. Laura joined the partnership on 1 January 2018. From this date, the profits were shared equally between the three partners. The partnership had a trading profit of £60,000 for the year ended 31 December 2018.

What is Laura's taxable trading income from the partnership for the tax year 2017/18?

A £15,000
B £5,000
C £20,000
D £10,000

(2 marks)

69 Quayle and Partridge have been in partnership for many years sharing profits equally and preparing accounts to 31 March each year. From 1 May 2017 the profits were divided 1 part to Quayle and 2 parts to Partridge. The partnership had a trading profit of £96,000 for the year ended 31 March 2018.

What is Quayle's taxable trading income from the partnership for the tax year 2017/18?

A £29,333
B £4,000
C £33,333
D £32,000

(2 marks)

70 Victor is a 50% partner in a partnership which prepares accounts to 5 April each year. In the year to 5 April 2018, the partnership makes a loss of £(180,000) and Victor has other income of £60,000 in 2017/18.

What is the amount of loss relief that Victor can claim against general income in 2017/18?

A £15,000
B £50,000
C £60,000
D £90,000

(2 marks)

Anne, Betty and Chloe

4 mins each

The following scenario relates to questions 71 to 75.

Anne and Betty had been in partnership since 1 January 2011. Anne was entitled to a salary of £6,000 per year and the remainder of the profits were shared 30% to Anne and 70% to Betty. On 30 September 2017 Betty resigned as a partner and was replaced on 1 October 2017 by Chloe. From that date, profits were shared 60% to Anne and 40% to Chloe with no salaries being payable.

The partnership's taxable trading profits/(losses) are as follows:

	£
Year ended 31 December 2017	60,000
Year ended 31 December 2018	42,000
Year ended 31 December 2019 (estimated)	(18,000)

As at 6 April 2017 Anne and Betty each had unrelieved overlap profits of £3,000.

71   What is Anne's taxable trading profit for the period between 1 January 2017 and
      30 September 2017?

      A   £12,150
      B   £21,150
      C   £16,650
      D   £17,700   (2 marks)

72   What is Betty's taxable trading profit for the tax year 2017/18?

      A   £25,350
      B   £28,500
      C   £28,350
      D   £39,000   (2 marks)

73   What is Chloe's taxable trading profit for the tax year 2017/18?

      A   £4,200
      B   £6,000
      C   £16,800
      D   £10,200   (2 marks)

74   How can Anne relieve her trading loss for the tax year 2019/20?

      (1)   Against general income of 2019/20 and/or 2018/19
      (2)   Carry forward against future trading income of the partnership
      (3)   Carry back against trading income of 2018/19, 2017/18 and 2016/17 later years first
      (4)   Carry back against general income of 2016/17, 2017/18 and 2018/19 earlier years first

      A   1 and 2
      B   2 and 3
      C   1, 2 and 3
      D   1, 2 and 4   (2 marks)

75   How can Chloe relieve her trading loss for the tax year 2019/20?

      (1)   Against general income of 2019/20 and/or 2018/19
      (2)   Carry forward against future trading income of the partnership
      (3)   Carry back against trading income of 2018/19, 2017/18 and 2016/17 later years first
      (4)   Carry back against general income of 2016/17, 2017/18 and 2018/19 earlier years first

      A   1, 2 and 4
      B   1, 2 and 3
      C   1 and 2
      D   2 and 4   (2 marks)

National insurance contributions MCQs   4 mins each

76   Natalie is a sole trader and has taxable trading profits of £42,000 for her period of account ended
      31 August 2017.

      What is the TOTAL amount of national insurance contributions (NIC) that Natalie has to pay for the
      tax year 2017/18?

      A   £3,045
      B   £3,928
      C   £3,193
      D   £4,208   (2 marks)

77   Nigel is an employee earning £36,000 a year, payable in equal monthly amounts. In February 2018 he received a bonus of £8,000.

What are Nigel's class 1 (employee's) national insurance contributions (NIC) in respect of February 2018?

A   £1,238
B   £513
C   £358
D   £368   (2 marks)

78   Gina was paid an annual salary of £45,000 during 2017/18. In addition, her employer provided her with a computer for private use for which the taxable benefit is £300.

What are the national insurance contributions (NIC) liabilities?

A   Class 1 employee's and employer's contributions on £45,000

B   Class 1 employee's contributions on £45,000, Class 1 employer's contributions on £45,300

C   Class 1 employee's contributions on £45,300, Class 1 employer's contributions on £45,000, Class 1A contributions on £300

D   Class 1 employee's contributions on £45,000, Class 1 employer's contributions on £45,000, Class 1A contributions on £300   (2 marks)

Derek and Denise   4 mins each

The following scenario relates to questions 79 to 83.

Derek

Derek is the sole employee of Rose, a sole trader. In the tax year 2017/18, Derek was paid a salary of £55,000. He was also provided with a car from 6 November 2017. The car was available for private use and had a list price of £12,000 and had CO_2 emissions of 46 g/km. Derek was not provided with any fuel.

Denise

Denise started business on 6 January 2018 as a designer dressmaker. She prepared her first set of accounts for the four month period to 5 May 2018 and had taxable profits of £15,000. There are 14 contribution weeks in the period from 6 January 2018 to 5 April 2018 and five contribution weeks in the period from 6 April 2018 to 5 May 2018.

79   What are the employee's Class 1 national insurance contributions payable by Derek for 2017/18?

A   £3,515
B   £4,420
C   £5,620
D   £4,620   (2 marks)

80   What are the employee's Class 1 national insurance contributions payable by Rose for 2017/18?

A   £3,463
B   £2,620
C   £6,463
D   £2,283   (2 marks)

81   What are the Class 1A national insurance contributions payable by Rose for 2017/18?

A   £124
B   £62
C   £54
D   £149   (2 marks)

82   What are the Class 2 contributions payable by Denise in 2017/18 and by when are they payable?

   A   £40 by 31 January 2019
   B   £54 by 31 July 2018
   C   £40 by 31 July 2018
   D   £54 by 31 January 2019   (2 marks)

83   What are the Class 4 contributions payable by Denise in 2017/18?

   A   £615
   B   £370
   C   £278
   D   £1,012   (2 marks)

84 Sasha   27 mins

Sasha is a computer programmer. Until 5 April 2017 she was employed by Net Computers plc, but since then has worked independently from home. Sasha's income for the year ended 5 April 2018 is £60,000. All of this relates to work done for Net Computers plc. Her expenditure for the year ended 5 April 2018 is as follows:

(1)   The business proportion of light, heat and telephone for Sasha's home is £880.

(2)   Computer equipment was purchased on 6 April 2017 for £4,000.

(3)   A motor car was purchased by Sasha on 6 April 2017 for £10,000 with CO_2 of 115g/km. Motor expenses for the year ended 5 April 2018 amount to £3,500, of which 40% relate to journeys between home and the premises of Net Computers plc. The other 60% relate to private mileage.

Required

(a)   List eight factors that will indicate that a worker should be treated as an employee rather than as self-employed.   (4 marks)

(b)   (i)   Calculate the amount of taxable trading profits if Sasha is treated as self-employed during 2017/18.

       (ii)   Calculate the amount of Sasha's taxable earnings if she is treated as an employee during 2017/18.   (7 marks)

(c)   (i)   Calculate Sasha's liability to Class 2 and Class 4 NIC if she is treated as self-employed during 2017/18.

       (ii)   Calculate Sasha's liability to Class 1 NIC if she is treated as an employee during 2017/18.
                                                                                     (4 marks)

                                                                          (Total = 15 marks)

Computing chargeable gains MCQs   4 mins each

85   Which TWO of the following assets will ALWAYS be exempt from capital gains tax?

   (1)   A qualifying corporate bond (QCB)
   (2)   Investments held in individual savings accounts (ISAs)
   (3)   A plot of land
   (4)   A decoration for bravery

   A   1 and 2
   B   2 and 3
   C   2 and 4
   D   1 and 4   (2 marks)

86   Joe has chargeable gains of £16,700 and allowable capital losses of £3,000 in the tax year 2017/18. He also has allowable capital losses of £4,000 brought forward from the tax year 2016/17.

What is the correct use of these amounts for the tax year 2017/18?

A   £16,700 – £3,000 (current year loss) – £4,000 (brought forward loss) = £9,700
B   £16,700 – £3,000 (current year loss) – £2,400 (brought forward loss) = £11,300
C   £16,700 – £4,000 (brought forward loss) – £1,400 (current year loss) = £11,300
D   £16,700 – £3,000 (current year loss) = £13,700

(2 marks)

87   Melanie purchased a ten-acre plot of land for £80,000. In January 2018, she sold three of the acres for £36,000 with expenses of sale amounting to £1,000. The market value of the remaining seven acres of land in January 2018 was £90,000.

What is Melanie's chargeable gain on the disposal of the three acres of land in the tax year 2017/18?

A   £12,600
B   £13,600
C   £13,143
D   £12,143

(2 marks)

88 Peter   18 mins

Peter made the following disposals of assets during the tax year 2017/18.

30 June 2017

Residential investment property for £150,000 less costs of disposal £1,280. Acquired for £79,000.

27 July 2017

Part of a plot of land used for agricultural purposes. The proceeds of sale were £35,000. The costs of disposal were £700. The original cost of the land was £54,000. The remainder of the land is worth £70,000.

1 September 2017

A vase which was destroyed. It cost £12,000. Compensation of £20,000 was received on 30 September 2017. Peter bought a new vase as a replacement for £17,000 on 21 December 2017.

Peter had taxable income of £29,100 in 2017/18.

Required

Calculate Peter's capital gains tax payable for the year 2017/18.   (10 marks)

Chattels and the principal private residence exemption MCQs   4 mins each

89   Edward purchased a painting for £1,500, incurring purchase costs of £75. In October 2017 he sold the painting for £7,000, incurring disposal costs of £350.

What is Edward's chargeable gain in the tax year 2017/18?

A   £1,667
B   £5,500
C   £5,075
D   £1,083

(2 marks)

90 Belinda purchased a necklace for £7,500, incurring purchase costs of £400. In January 2018 she sold the necklace for £4,000, incurring disposal costs of £200.

What is Belinda's allowable loss in the tax year 2017/18?

A £1,500
B £1,900
C £2,100
D £4,100

(2 marks)

91 Roger purchased a house on 1 January 1994 and lived in it until 31 December 2005. On 1 January 2006 Roger went to live with his parents and the house was unoccupied for six years. Roger then lived in the house from 1 January 2012 until it was sold on 31 December 2017.

How many years of Roger's period of ownership of the house will be chargeable to capital gains tax?

A Three years
B Six years
C 21 years
D 10 and a half years

(2 marks)

John and Elsie

4 mins each

The following scenario relates to questions 92 to 96.

John

John purchased a property in England on 1 August 2005 and lived in it until 31 July 2006 when he moved overseas to take up an offer of employment. He returned to the UK on 1 August 2011 and moved back into the house until 31 January 2012 when he moved out permanently and went to live with his mother. The house was let out between 1 February 2015 and 31 January 2017. The house was then put up for sale and was finally sold on 31 July 2017 realising a gain of £72,000.

Elsie

Elsie made the following disposals of assets during the tax year 2017/18.

(1) An oil painting for £5,000 (net of £400 commission). She had purchased the painting for £11,500.

(2) A vase for gross proceeds of £7,500. Elsie spend £75 advertising the vase for sale. She had purchased the vase for £4,000.

92 How many exempt months are there for the purposes of computing principal private residence relief on John's disposal?

A 84 months
B 132 months
C 144 months
D 96 months

(2 marks)

93 How many extra exempt months would there have been if John had moved back into the house between 1 February 2017 and the date of sale?

A 6 months
B 48 months
C 36 months
D No extra months

(2 marks)

94 How many months would be covered by letting relief assuming John did NOT move back into the house on 1 February 2017?

  A   No months
  B   12 months
  C   18 months
  D   24 months   (2 marks)

95 What is Elsie's allowable loss on the disposal of the oil painting?

  A   £6,500
  B   £10,833
  C   £5,900
  D   £5,500   (2 marks)

96 What is Elsie's chargeable gain on the disposal of the vase?

  A   £2,500
  B   £2,375
  C   £3,425
  D   £3,500   (2 marks)

Business reliefs MCQs   **4 mins each**

97 Jane has two chargeable gains in the tax year 2017/18:

  £10,000 – claim made for entrepreneurs' relief
  £13,200 – no claim made for entrepreneurs' relief and not residential property

  She has taxable income of £25,000 in the tax year 2017/18.

  What is Jane's capital gains tax liability for the tax year 2017/18?

  A   £3,640
  B   £2,380
  C   £1,380
  D   £2,320   (2 marks)

98 Norman is a sole trader. He sold Shop A in July 2017 for £80,000, realising a chargeable gain of £25,000. Norman used the proceeds to buy a Shop B for £70,000 and used the remainder as working capital.

  What is the cost of Shop B for capital gains tax purposes if Norman makes a claim for replacement of business assets (rollover) relief?

  A   £60,000
  B   £65,000
  C   £45,000
  D   £55,000   (2 marks)

99 On which TWO of the following gifts can a claim be made for gift relief?

  (1)   10% shareholding in an unlisted investment company

  (2)   Factory owned by an individual and used in the trade of that individual's personal company

  (3)   Premises owned by a sole trader of which two thirds are used for trade purposes and one third is used for private purposes

  (4)   2% shareholding in a trading company listed on the London Stock Exchange

  A   1 and 2
  B   2 and 3
  C   2 and 4
  D   1 and 4   (2 marks)

Roy and Graham

4 mins each

The following scenario relates to questions 100 to 104.

Roy was a sole trader for many years. He had bought a factory for use in his trade on 10 July 2010 for £150,000. On 1 December 2017, Roy sold his sole trader business as a going concern to his son, Graham. The market value of the factory at that time was £260,000 and the consideration paid by Graham for the factory was £180,000.

Due to restructuring of the business, Graham let out the factory to an unconnected company from 1 December 2017. However, on 1 March 2018 he ceased trading and sold the factory to a developer for £320,000.

The factory is the only chargeable asset owned by either Roy or Graham. Both Roy and Graham are higher rate taxpayers.

100 What is the capital gains tax payable by Roy for the tax year 2017/18 if a claim is not made for gift relief?

    A   £19,740
    B   £11,000
    C   £27,636
    D   £9,870   **(2 marks)**

101 What is the capital gains tax payable by Graham for the tax year 2017/18 if a claim is not made for gift relief?

    A   £4,870
    B   £12,000
    C   £9,740
    D   £13,636   **(2 marks)**

102 What is the capital gains tax payable by Roy for the tax year 2017/18 if a claim is made for gift relief?

    A   £3,000
    B   £1,870
    C   £6,870
    D   £0   **(2 marks)**

103 What is the capital gains tax payable by Graham for the tax year 2017/18 if a claim is made for gift relief?

    A   £25,740
    B   £31,740
    C   £12,870
    D   £28,000   **(2 marks)**

104 Why is it beneficial for Roy and Graham not to make a claim for gift relief on the factory?

    A   The CGT liability would be payable earlier
    B   It enables Roy to use his annual exempt amount
    C   Graham would have to pay Roy more for the factory
    D   More of the gain is covered by a lower rate of CGT   **(2 marks)**

105 Kai

18 mins

Kai started in business as a sole trader in August 2011. He acquired a freehold shop for £105,000 and a warehouse for £150,000.

Kai sold his business as a going concern to Jibran in December 2017 and received £75,000 for goodwill, £90,000 for the shop and £180,000 for the warehouse. Kai also sold a plot of land to Jibran which he had not used in his business and is not residential property. The land cost £10,000 and Jibran paid £26,100 for it.

Other than those listed above, Kai had never undertaken any transactions which were relevant for capital gains tax purposes.

Kai's taxable income in 2017/18 was £20,000.

Required

Compute the capital gains tax payable by Kai for 2017/18, assuming that he makes any beneficial claims. State the date by which any claim must be made. **(10 marks)**

Shares and securities MCQs

4 mins each

106   On 14 March 2018, Caroline gave her daughter 10,000 shares in A plc. On that date the shares were quoted at £2.20 – £2.22.

What is the value of gift for capital gains tax purposes?

A   £22,100
B   £22,000
C   £22,200
D   £22,050   **(2 marks)**

107   Bill bought 1,000 shares in B plc on 10 March 2010. He purchased a further 500 B plc shares on 31 July 2017 and 250 B plc shares on 10 August 2017. Bill sold 800 B plc shares on 31 July 2017.

How are the 800 B plc shares sold on 31 July 2017 matched?

A   Against 250 of the shares acquired on 10 August 2017 and then against 550 of the shares acquired on 10 March 2010

B   Against 500 of the shares acquired on 31 July 2017 and then against 300 of the shares acquired on 10 March 2010

C   Against 500 of the shares acquired on 31 July 2017, then against 250 of the shares acquired on 10 August 2017 and then against 50 of the shares acquired on 10 March 2010

D   Against 800 of the shares acquired on 10 March 2010   **(2 marks)**

108   Which TWO of the following statements about shares and securities owned by an individual are correct?

(1)   A disposal of government securities ('gilts') by an individual is chargeable to capital gains tax.

(2)   If a company makes a 2 for 1 bonus issue, each shareholder will receive 1 extra share for each 2 shares held without payment.

(3)   In a rights issue the rights issue shares are paid for by the shareholder resulting in an adjustment to the cost of the shareholding.

(4)   A chargeable gain does not usually arise on a takeover where new shares are exchanged for old shares.

A   1 and 3
B   3 and 4
C   2 and 4
D   1 and 2   **(2 marks)**

109 Melissa

18 mins

Melissa bought shares in Fisher plc as follows:

12 July 2002	3,000 shares for £21,000
17 January 2005	Bonus issue 1 share for each 1 share held
14 December 2007	Rights issue 1 share for each 3 shares held at £3.25 per share
11 July 2017	4,000 shares for £16,000

She sold 10,000 shares for £42,000 on 2 July 2017.

Required

Compute Melissa's gain on sale.

(10 marks)

Self assessment and payment of tax for individuals MCQs

4 mins each

110 Steven and Rita wish to file their personal tax returns for 2017/18 electronically. The notice to file by HM Revenue & Customs (HMRC) to Steven was issued on 31 May 2018. The notice to file by HMRC to Rita was issued on 30 November 2018.

What is the latest filing date for each of Steven and Rita?

	Steven	*Rita*
A	31 October 2018	28 February 2019
B	31 October 2018	31 January 2019
C	31 January 2019	28 February 2019
D	31 January 2019	31 January 2019

(2 marks)

111 Tony is self-employed and his trading income is his only source of income. His income tax liabilities and Class 4 national insurance contributions (NIC) for 2016/17 and 2017/18 are as follows:

	2016/17	*2017/18*
	£	£
Income tax	10,000	12,500
Class 4 NIC	2,000	2,500
	12,000	15,000

How will Tony pay his income tax and Class 4 NIC for the tax year 2017/18?

A £15,000 on 31 January 2019
B £7,500 on 31 January and 31 July 2018
C £5,000 on 31 January 2018, 31 July 2018 and 31 January 2019
D £6,000 on 31 January and 31 July 2018, £3,000 on 31 January 2019   **(2 marks)**

112 Pepe has a trading loss of £30,000 for the tax year 2017/18. Due to carelessness he enters £38,000 on his tax return and makes a loss relief claim for £38,000 against his property business income for the tax year 2017/18. The property business income would otherwise have been taxed at 40%.

What is the maximum penalty that could be charged by HM Revenue & Customs (HMRC) in respect of the error?

A £3,200
B £960
C £2,400
D £640

(2 marks)

Ash

The following scenario relates to questions 113 to 117.

Ash is employed and also has a bank deposit account and owns some shares.

Ash's income tax liability for the tax year 2016/17 was £16,800. Of this £7,200 was paid under the PAYE system. Ash had made payments on account for the tax year totalling £3,600. On 31 March 2018, Ash filed his tax return for 2016/17. The late filing was due to Ash's carelessness and was not deliberate.

On 5 May 2018, HM Revenue & Customs issued a notice to Ash to file his tax return for the tax year 2017/18. Ash's income tax liability for the tax year 2017/18 was £22,000. £7,100 of this was paid under PAYE system. Ash did not make any claim in respect of his payments on account for 2017/18. On 30 April 2019, Ash paid the balancing payment for 2017/18.

113   What is the penalty for late filing of Ash's tax return for the tax year 2016/17?

    A   Greater of 100% of tax liability which would have been shown on return and £300
    B   Greater of 70% of tax liability which would have been shown on return and £300
    C   Greater of 5% of tax liability which would have been shown on return and £300
    D   £100   **(2 marks)**

114   What is the amount of the balancing payment for the tax year 2016/17?

    A   £16,800
    B   £6,000
    C   £13,200
    D   £9,600   **(2 marks)**

115   What is the amount of each of the payments on account (POAs) for the tax year 2017/18?

    A   £4,800
    B   £16,800
    C   £9,600
    D   £8,400   **(2 marks)**

116   What are the due dates for the payments on account for the tax year 2017/18?

	First POA	Second POA
A	31 July 2018	31 January 2019
B	14 July 2018	14 January 2019
C	31 January 2018	31 July 2018
D	5 April 2018	5 October 2018

                                                                 (2 marks)

117   What is the penalty for late payment of the balancing payment of Ash's tax liability for the tax year 2017/18?

    A   £100
    B   5% of the unpaid tax
    C   10% of the unpaid tax
    D   15% of the unpaid tax   **(2 marks)**

Inheritance tax: scope and transfers of value MCQs

4 mins each

118   Bernard made a gross chargeable lifetime transfer of £260,000 in August 2013. In November 2017, he gave £420,000 to a trust for the benefit of his son and daughter. Bernard agreed to pay any lifetime IHT due.

How much inheritance tax will be payable by Bernard on transfer of value in November 2017?

     A   £87,250
     B   £69,800
     C   £88,750
     D   £22,500   **(2 marks)**

119   Andy and Hilda had been married for many years when Andy died in June 2007. 60% of Andy's nil rate band was unused on his death. The nil rate band at Andy's death was £300,000. Hilda died in December 2017. Her only lifetime transfers of value were cash gifts of £6,000 to her nephew in January 2017 and £10,000 to her niece in March 2017.

What is the maximum nil rate band available for use against Hilda's death estate?

     A   £504,000
     B   £520,000
     C   £510,000
     D   £495,000   **(2 marks)**

120   On 15 July 2017 Yvette gave £500,000 to a trust for the benefit of her grandchildren. Yvette died on 27 December 2017.

What are the due dates for inheritance tax to be paid on this transfer of value?

	Lifetime tax	*Death tax*
A	31 January 2018	30 June 2018
B	30 April 2018	30 June 2018
C	31 January 2018	30 April 2018
D	30 April 2018	30 April 2018 **(2 marks)**

Colin and Diane

4 mins each

The following scenario relates to questions 121 to 125.

Colin

Colin always used his annual exemption in April each year. On 21 January 2009 he gave cash of £352,000 to a trust. Colin paid the inheritance tax due. The nil rate band in 2008/09 was £312,000.

On 10 November 2015, Colin gave a further amount of cash to the trust. The trustees paid the inheritance due. Colin died on 15 June 2017. Additional inheritance tax was payable by the trustees as a result of his death.

Diane

Diane died on 20 December 2017. During her lifetime, she used her annual exemption in April each year and also made the following gifts.

Date	Gift	Donee
20.8.12	Shares worth £15,000	Daughter
19.6.13	Shares worth £360,000	Trustees (Trustees paid the IHT)

The nil rate band in both 2012/13 and 2013/14 was £325,000.

121 What was the amount of lifetime inheritance tax paid by Colin on the gift made by him on 21 January 2009?

    A   £8,500

    B   £10,000

    C   £6,750

    D   £8,000   (2 marks)

122 What were the due dates for payment of inheritance tax on the gift made by Colin on 10 November 2015?

	Lifetime tax	Death tax
A	30 April 2016	30 April 2018
B	31 May 2016	31 December 2017
C	30 April 2016	31 December 2017
D	31 May 2016	30 April 2018

    (2 marks)

123 What was the amount of lifetime inheritance tax paid by the trustees on the gift made by Diane on 19 June 2013?

    A   £5,800

    B   £8,750

    C   £10,000

    D   £7,000   (2 marks)

124 What was the amount of taper relief which could be set against the inheritance tax payable on Diane's death on the gift made by her on 19 June 2013?

    A   £12,000

    B   £5,600

    C   £8,000

    D   £5,000   (2 marks)

125 Which one of the following is NOT an advantage of making a lifetime transfer of value?

    A   There is no capital gains tax on a lifetime transfer of value if the donor dies after seven years of making it.

    B   If the donor makes a chargeable lifetime transfer and survives seven years, he has reduced his estate for IHT and the only inheritance tax payable is that on the lifetime transfer at lifetime rates.

    C   The values of lifetime transfers cannot exceed the transfer of value when made.

    D   If the donor makes a potentially exempt transfer and survives seven years, he has reduced his estate for IHT but the transfer is exempt.   (2 marks)

126 Simona   18 mins

Simona died on 19 January 2018, leaving the following assets:

	£
Shares in MS plc	320,000
Life assurance policy	see note
Main residence	205,000
Household furniture	20,000
Cash in bank	97,750
Car	5,000

Simona also had the following debts at her death:

	£
Repayment mortgage secured on main residence	110,000
Credit card bills	7,000
Income tax	3,000
Gas bill	250

Note. The value of the insurance policy immediately before Simona's death was £60,000. The proceeds payable as a result of Simona's death were £250,000.

The personal representative of Simona's estate paid funeral expenses of £2,500.

Simona had made a chargeable lifetime transfer (after exemptions) of £90,000 in May 2015.

In her will, Simona left her shares in MS plc to her husband and the remainder of her estate to her children.

Required

(a)   Compute Simona's chargeable death estate.   **(6 marks)**

(b)   Explain and compute the amount of the nil rate bands available to be set against Simona's death estate.   **(2 marks)**

(c)   Using your answer to part (b), compute the inheritance tax payable on Simona's death estate.   **(2 marks)**

(Total = 10 marks)

Computing taxable total profits and the corporation tax liability MCQs   4 mins each

127   H Ltd started trading on 1 December 2016 and prepared its first set of accounts to 31 March 2018.

What are H Ltd's accounting period(s) for the period of account to 31 March 2018?

A   1 December 2016 to 31 March 2017 and 1 April 2017 to 31 March 2018
B   1 December 2016 to 5 April 2017 and 6 April 2017 to 31 March 2018
C   1 December 2016 to 30 November 2017 and 1 December 2017 to 31 March 2018
D   1 December 2016 to 31 March 2018   **(2 marks)**

128   L Ltd is a trading company which prepares accounts to 31 March each year. In its statement of profit or loss for the year to 31 March 2018, it has included a deduction of £3,200 in respect of the annual leasing cost for a car. The car has a recommended list price of £16,000 and CO_2 emissions of 140g/km.

What is the allowable expense in respect of the leasing cost for the accounting period ended 31 March 2018?

A   £2,720
B   £480
C   £3,360
D   £3,200   **(2 marks)**

129   Z Ltd is a trading company which prepared accounts to 30 June 2017. In addition to its trading activities, Z Ltd lets out an unfurnished house for an annual rent of £14,400 payable in monthly instalments. The tenant is due to pay each instalment in arrears on the last day of each month but did not pay the June 2017 instalment until 14 July 2017. There was interest of £7,500 accrued during the year to 30 June 2017 on a mortgage taken out by Z Ltd to acquire the house and Z Ltd also made capital repayments on the mortgage of £300 during that year.

How much must Z Ltd include in its taxable total profits as its property business income for the accounting period ended 30 June 2017?

A   £13,200
B   £6,900
C   £5,400
D   £14,400   (2 marks)

Red plc and Green plc   4 mins each

The following scenario relates to questions 130 to 134.

Red plc

Red plc previously prepared accounts to 31 December. A decision has been made to change its year end to 31 March. The following information relates to the 15 month period of account from 1 January 2017 to 31 March 2018.

Red plc had a tax written down value of £24,000 on its main pool at 1 January 2017. It bought a car with CO_2 emissions of 120g/km for use by an employee in November 2017 at a cost of £12,000. It also bought some machinery in February 2018 at a cost of £290,000, and a new car with CO_2 emissions of 60g/km for £10,000 in March 2018.

Green plc

Green plc previously made its accounts up to 31 December. A decision has been made to change its year end to 31 May. The following information relates to the 17 month period of account from 1 January 2016 to 31 May 2017.

	£
Trading profits	391,000
Bank interest accrued and received	
31.5.16	15,000
31.12.16	6,000
31.5.17	2,500
Chargeable gain on property sold on	
1.9.16	5,000
Qualifying charitable donations paid	
28.2.16	15,000
31.8.16	15,000
28.2.17	40,000

130   What are the maximum capital allowances for Red plc for the first accounting period in the period of account to 31 March 2018?

A   £16,320
B   £4,320
C   £2,700
D   £6,480   (2 marks)

131 What is the maximum amount of the annual investment allowance which can be claimed on the expenditure on machinery in February 2018?

    A   £290,000
    B   £50,000
    C   £250,000
    D   £200,000   **(2 marks)**

132 What are the maximum capital allowances for Red plc in respect of the car purchased in March 2018 in the accounting period of purchase?

    A   £2,500
    B   £10,000
    C   £1,800
    D   £450   **(2 marks)**

133 What are the taxable total profits for Green plc for the first accounting period in the period of account to 31 May 2017?

    A   £272,000
    B   £130,000
    C   £302,000
    D   £115,000   **(2 marks)**

134 What are the taxable total profits for Green plc for the second accounting period in the period of account to 31 May 2017?

    A   £117,500
    B   £234,500
    C   £77,500
    D   £289,500   **(2 marks)**

135 Elderflower Ltd   27 mins

Elderflower Ltd is a company which trades as a manufacturer of specialist soft drinks. The company's statement of profit or loss for the year ended 31 March 2018 is as follows:

	£	£
Gross profit		510,000
Other income		
Profit on disposal of office building (note 1)		54,000
Bank interest (note 2)		7,000
Expenses		
Depreciation	54,690	
Professional fees (note 3)	22,000	
Repairs and renewals (note 4)	29,700	
Other expenses (note 5)	24,400	
		(130,790)
Finance costs		
Interest payable (note 6)		(23,000)
Profit before taxation		417,210

Notes

(1)   *Disposal of office building*

The profit of £54,000 is in respect of a freehold office building that was sold on 30 June 2017 for £380,000. The chargeable gain on sale has been computed to be £45,580.

(2)   *Bank interest received*

The bank interest was received on 31 March 2018 and is the amount accrued to that date. The bank deposit is held for non-trading purposes.

(3)   *Professional fees*

Professional fees are as follows:

	£
Accountancy and audit fee	5,900
Legal fees in connection with the issue of share capital	8,800
Legal fees in connection with the issue of loan notes (see note 6)	6,400
Legal fees in connection with fine for breach of health and safety legislation	900
	22,000

(4)   *Repairs and renewals*

The figure of £29,700 for repairs includes £9,700 for constructing an extension to the company's manufacturing premises and £5,400 for repainting the interior of the company's offices.

(5)   *Other expenses*

Other expenses include £2,310 for entertaining customers and a qualifying charitable donation of £500.

(6)   *Interest payable*

Elderflower Ltd issued loan notes on 1 October 2017. The capital raised was used for trading purposes. Interest of £23,000 in respect of the first six months of the loan was paid on 31 March 2018.

(7)   *Plant and machinery*

On 1 April 2017 the tax written down values of plant and machinery were as follows:

	£
Main pool	27,500
Special rate pool (consisting of car with CO_2 emissions of 176g/km)	14,700

The following transactions took place during the year ended 31 March 2018:

		Cost/(Proceeds) £
10 May 2017	Purchased plant	20,200
5 January 2018	Sold the special rate pool motor car	(9,700)
20 March 2018	Sold a delivery van	(11,600)
31 March 2018	Purchased a motor car CO_2 emissions 107g/km	9,600

The van sold on 20 March 2018 for £11,600 originally cost £18,500. The motor car purchased on 31 March 2018 is used by the sales manager: 25% of the mileage is for private journeys.

Required

(a)   Calculate Elderflower Ltd's trading profit for the year ended 31 March 2018. Your answer should commence with the profit before taxation figure of £417,210 and should list all of the items in the statement of profit or loss indicating by the use of a zero (0) any items that do not require adjustment. You should assume that the company claims the maximum available capital allowances.

(12 marks)

(b)   Calculate Elderflower Ltd's taxable total profits for the year ended 31 March 2018.   **(2 marks)**

(c)   Calculate Elderflower Ltd's corporation tax liability for the year ended 31 March 2018.   **(1 mark)**

(Total = 15 marks)

Chargeable gains for companies MCQs   **4 mins each**

136   U Ltd acquires an asset in April 2002 (RPI = 175.7) for £12,000, incurring costs of acquisition of £800. U Ltd sells the asset in August 2017 (RPI = 271.7) for £17,500, incurring costs of disposal of £1,000.

What is the chargeable gain or allowable loss (if any) on the sale?

A   £3,700 gain
B   £(3,289) loss
C   £(2,852) loss
D   Neither a gain nor a loss   **(2 marks)**

137   D Ltd sold a factory for £640,000 on 15 March 2018. It had paid £120,000 for the factory on 12 January 2013. D Ltd incurred expenses of £8,000 in buying the factory and £6,000 in selling the factory. The assumed indexation factor for the period January 2013 to March 2018 is 0.124.

What is D Ltd's chargeable gain on the disposal?

A   £489,384
B   £490,128
C   £491,120
D   £506,000   **(2 marks)**

138   F Ltd sells a factory for £200,000. The factory cost £110,000 and the indexation allowance available is £20,000. The company acquires another factory 15 months later for £187,500.

What is the amount of rollover relief which F Ltd can claim?

A   £12,500
B   £70,000
C   £77,500
D   £57,500   **(2 marks)**

Long Ltd, Tall Ltd and Short Ltd   **4 mins each**

The following scenario relates to questions 139 to 143.

Long Ltd

On 16 October 2017, Long Ltd sold 6,000 £1 ordinary shares in Shallow Ltd for £45,000. Long Ltd had purchased 10,000 shares in Shallow Ltd on 21 May 2008 for £40,000.

Tall Ltd

Tall Ltd purchased 5,000 shares in Middle plc on 10 June 2002 for £14,000. On 28 October 2017, Middle plc made a 1 for 1 rights issue at £4 per share. Tall Ltd took up its full entitlement to rights issue shares.

Short Ltd

Short Ltd purchased 10,000 shares in Far plc on 20 June 2002 for £34,000. On 7 March 2018 Far plc was taken over by Deep plc. Short Ltd received two £1 ordinary shares and one £1 preference share in Deep plc for each £1 ordinary share held in Far plc. Immediately after the takeover each £1 ordinary share in Deep plc was quoted at £5 and each £1 preference share was quoted at £2.50.

RPIs (actual and assumed)

June 2002 = 176.2   May 2008 = 215.1   October 2017 = 272.9

139   Which TWO of the following statements about chargeable gains for companies are true?

(1)   There is an annual exempt amount available to set against chargeable gains
(2)   There is relief for inflation called the indexation allowance
(3)   A company pays corporation tax on its gains at a rate of 10%
(4)   A company is liable to corporation tax on its net chargeable gains as part of its total profits

A   1 and 3
B   1 and 4
C   2 and 4
D   2 and 3   **(2 marks)**

140   What is the correct order of matching share disposals for companies?

(1)   Shares acquired on the same day
(2)   Shares from the FA 1985 pool
(3)   Shares acquired in the previous nine days

A   1, then 2, then 3
B   1, then 3, then 2
C   2, then 1, then 3
D   2, then 3, then 1   (2 marks)

141   What is the chargeable gain on the disposal by Long Ltd on 16 October 2017?

A   £14,551
B   £3,251
C   £21,000
D   £14,544   (2 marks)

142   What is the indexed cost of the Middle plc shares following the rights issue on 28 October 2017?

A   £52,659
B   £21,683
C   £34,000
D   £41,683   (2 marks)

143   What are the costs of the ordinary shares and the preference shares in Deep plc held by Short Ltd following the takeover on 7 March 2018?

	Ordinary shares	Preference shares
A	£22,667	£11,333
B	£27,200	£6,800
C	£20,000	£10,000
D	£100,000	£25,000

(2 marks)

144 Xeon Ltd   18 mins

Xeon Ltd made the following disposals in the year ended 31 March 2018.

(a)   On 31 May 2017, Xeon Ltd sold a warehouse used in its trade for £125,000. The company had bought the warehouse for £65,000 on 1 July 2003. Xeon Ltd had bought another warehouse for use in its trade for £105,000 on 1 July 2016.

(b)   On 18 June 2017, Xeon Ltd sold two acres of land for £30,000. These two acres were part of a five acre plot of land which was purchased for £21,000 on 1 April 2000. The remaining three acres were valued at £40,000 in June 2017. Xeon Ltd spent £1,000 in December 2012 on improving the two acres of land sold in June 2017.

Xeon Ltd made any beneficial claims in respect of these gains.

Required

Compute Xeon Ltd's chargeable gains for the year ended 31 March 2018 and show the cost for chargeable gains purposes of the warehouse bought on 1 July 2016.   (10 marks)

RPIs (actual and assumed)

April 2000 = 170.1   May 2017 = 270.2
July 2003 = 181.3   June 2017 = 270.6
December 2012 = 246.8

Losses

145 Which TWO of the following statements about loss reliefs for a company are correct?

(1) Property business losses of a company cannot be set against total profits of the same accounting period

(2) Trade losses of a company carried forward can only be used against profits of the same trade

(3) Trade loss relief may be given by deduction from current period total profits and those in the previous 12 months

(4) Capital losses made by a company can be used against chargeable gains of the previous accounting period

A 1 and 2
B 2 and 3
C 1 and 4
D 2 and 4

(2 marks)

146 E plc prepares accounts to 31 December each year. In the year ended 31 December 2016 E plc had total profits of £36,000 and it made a qualifying charitable donation of £1,000. In the year ended 31 December 2017 E plc made an adjusted trading loss of £40,000, had other taxable income of £10,000 and made a qualifying charitable donation of £3,000.

What is the loss that E plc can claim to carry back to the year ended 31 December 2016?

A £30,000
B £33,000
C £36,000
D £35,000

(2 marks)

147 The following information relates to T plc for the year ended 31 March 2018:

	£
Trading income	165,000
Income from non-trading loan relationships	27,000
Chargeable gain	14,000
Trading loss b/f at 1 April 2017	(170,000)
Capital loss b/f at 1 April 2017	(3,000)

What are T plc's taxable total profits for the year ended 31 March 2018?

A £33,000
B £27,000
C £41,000
D £38,000

(2 marks)

148 Ferraro Ltd

Ferraro Ltd has the following results.

	y/e 31.3.16 £	9m to 31.12.16 £	y/e 31.12.17 £
Trading profit (loss)	6,200	4,320	(100,000)
Bank deposit interest accrued	80	240	260
Rents receivable	1,420	1,440	1,600
Chargeable gain	0	7,680	0
Qualifying charitable donations	0	1,000	1,500

BPP
LEARNING MEDIA

Required

Compute all taxable total profits, claiming loss reliefs as early as possible. State the amounts of any losses carried forward as at 31 December 2017. **(10 marks)**

Groups
4 mins each

149 C Ltd had the following results for the year ended 31 March 2018:

	£
Trading income	(16,000)
Income from non-trading loan relationships	1,000
Capital loss	(5,000)

C Ltd paid a qualifying charitable donation of £4,000 on 2 February 2018.

What is the maximum amount that C Ltd can surrender for group relief?

A   £16,000
B   £20,000
C   £19,000
D   £21,000   **(2 marks)**

150 O Ltd owns 100% of P Ltd. In the year to 31 December 2017 O Ltd made a trading loss of £60,000. P Ltd had taxable total profits of £54,000 for the year to 31 March 2018.

What group relief can P Ltd claim from O Ltd which can be set against its taxable total profits for the year to 31 March 2018?

A   £40,500
B   £54,000
C   £45,000
D   £60,000   **(2 marks)**

151 A Ltd group has the following structure:

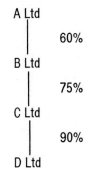

Which ONE of the following is a chargeable gains group?

A   A Ltd, B Ltd and C Ltd
B   B Ltd and C Ltd
C   B Ltd, C Ltd and D Ltd
D   C Ltd and D Ltd   **(2 marks)**

152 P Ltd

18 mins

P Ltd owns the following holdings in ordinary shares in other companies.

Q Ltd	83%
R Ltd	77%
S Ltd	67%
M Ltd	80%
T Ltd	70%

The following are the results of the above companies for the year ended 31 March 2018.

	P Ltd £	Q Ltd £	R Ltd £	S Ltd £	M Ltd £	T Ltd £
Trading profit	0	14,000	210,000	0	20,000	70,000
Trading loss	226,000	0	0	8,000	0	0
Property business income	6,000	4,000	0	0	0	0
Qualifying charitable donation paid	4,500	2,000	5,000	0	14,000	0

P Ltd and S Ltd are not expected to become profitable for several years and have no capacity to carry back losses.

Required

Compute the overall corporation tax payable for the above accounting period for the above companies. Assume that loss relief is claimed in the most beneficial manner.

(10 marks)

Self assessment and payment of tax by companies

4 mins each

153 N Ltd is not a large company and prepares accounts to 31 December every year.

What are the dates by which N Ltd must file its tax return and pay its corporation tax for the accounting period ended 31 December 2017 to avoid penalties and interest?

	Return date	*Tax payable date*
A	31 January 2019	31 January 2019
B	31 December 2018	1 October 2018
C	31 January 2019	1 October 2018
D	31 December 2018	31 January 2019

(2 marks)

154 Q plc has a 15-month period of account ending 31 March 2018.

What is the date by which Q plc must file its corporation tax return for the first accounting period in this period of account to avoid penalties and interest?

A   31 March 2019
B   30 June 2018
C   31 December 2018
D   1 October 2018

(2 marks)

155 M Ltd prepared accounts for the year ended 31 March 2018.

What is the earliest date until which M Ltd must retain its business records related to this year, assuming that no compliance check is made, and what is the maximum penalty for non-compliance?

(1)   Retention date: 31 March 2020
(2)   Retention date: 31 March 2024
(3)   Maximum penalty: £2,000
(4)   Maximum penalty: £3,000

A   1 and 3
B   2 and 3
C   1 and 4
D   2 and 4   (2 marks)

Skyblue Ltd and Turquoise plc   4 mins each

The following scenario relates to questions 156 to 160.

Skyblue Ltd

Skyblue Ltd prepares accounts to 30 September each year. HM Revenue & Customs sent Skyblue Ltd a notice on 15 December 2017 requiring it to file a corporation tax return for the accounting period ended 30 September 2017. Skyblue Ltd is not a member of a group of companies.

Turquoise plc

Turquoise plc prepares accounts to 31 March each year. In its return for the year ending 31 March 2018, loss relief for £100,000 was claimed, resulting in a reduction of £20,000 in the company's corporation tax. In fact, the loss relief available was only £10,000. The error was deliberate but not concealed.

156   How must Skyblue Ltd file its corporation tax return for the year ended 30 September 2017 and what is the latest filing date?

	Return	Filing date
A	Paper return	31 January 2019
B	Electronic return	31 January 2019
C	Paper return	30 September 2018
D	Electronic return	30 September 2018	(2 marks)

157   What is the penalty charged on Skyblue Ltd if it files its return four months late, if either it has always submitted its returns on time or has submitted late returns for each of the preceding two accounting periods?

	On time	Last two returns late
A	£100	£200
B	£200	£500
C	£200	£1,000
D	£100	£500	(2 marks)

158   What is the latest date by which HM Revenue & Customs can give written notice to Skyblue Ltd of a compliance check on the return if it is filed either on the due date or four months late?

	Due date	Four months late
A	Quarter day following the first anniversary of the filing date	Quarter day following the first anniversary of the filing date
B	First anniversary of the filing date	Quarter day following the first anniversary of the filing date
C	Quarter day following the first anniversary of the filing date	First anniversary of the filing date
D	First anniversary of the filing date	First anniversary of the filing date	(2 marks)

159 What is the maximum penalty that may be imposed on Turquoise plc for its error?

- A £5,400
- B £18,000
- C £12,600
- D £7,000

(2 marks)

160 What is the minimum percentage of potential lost revenue that may be imposed as a penalty on Turquoise plc if it either makes an unprompted disclosure or a prompted disclosure of the error?

	Unprompted	Prompted
A	20%	35%
B	0%	15%
C	70%	100%
D	30%	50%

(2 marks)

161 Cyan plc and Crimson plc   18 mins

Cyan plc

Cyan plc prepared its accounts to 31 March for many years. In May 2017, Cyan plc decided to change its accounting date to 31 December and so prepared accounts to 31 December 2017. Its taxable total profits for this nine-month period were £1,350,000. Cyan plc did not receive any dividends during the period and it has no related 51% group companies. In the year to 31 March 2017, Cyan plc had taxable total profits of £1,632,000.

Crimson plc

Crimson plc prepares accounts to 31 March each year. In the year ended 31 March 2018 it had taxable total profits of £450,000.

Crimson plc has owned 55% of the ordinary shares of Tangerine plc and 45% of the ordinary share capital of Russet plc for many years. Tangerine plc has owned 96% of the ordinary share capital of Rouge plc for many years.

Crimson plc bought 80% of the ordinary shares of Chestnut plc on 1 July 2017.

Crimson plc received a dividend of £30,000 from Russet plc on 1 February 2018 and a dividend of £50,000 from Tangerine plc on 1 March 2018.

Required

(a) Calculate the corporation tax payable by Cyan plc for the accounting period ended 31 December 2017. **(2 marks)**

(b) Show how the corporation tax liability in part (a) will be paid. **(3 marks)**

(c) Explain which companies are related 51% group companies with Crimson plc for the calculation of the profits threshold to determine whether Crimson plc is a large company in the year ended 31 March 2018. **(2 marks)**

(d) Using your answer to part (c), determine whether Crimson plc is a large company in the year ended 31 March 2018. **(3 marks)**

(Total = 10 marks)

An introduction to VAT MCQs

162 Alec has been in business since 1 June 2017 making water bottles. He will prepare his first set of accounts for the 12 months ending 31 May 2018. Alec's total taxable turnover for the seven months ended 31 December 2017 amounted to £45,000. On 1 January 2018 he received an order for water bottles amounting to £85,500 to be delivered later that month. Alec registered for VAT only when he was required to do so.

From what date will HM Revenue & Customs (HMRC) register Alec for value added tax (VAT) purposes?

A   1 January 2018
B   1 February 2018
C   1 June 2018
D   1 March 2018   **(2 marks)**

163 B plc is registered for value added tax (VAT). In the quarter ended 31 October 2017 it made taxable supplies (before taking account of any discounts) of £60,000, exclusive of VAT. All supplies are standard rated. On each sales invoice, B plc offers a discount of 4% to all of its customers who settle their invoices within 30 days. Only 25% of all customers (representing a quarter of the £60,000 above) pay within this time.

How much output VAT should B plc show on its VAT return for the quarter ended 31 October 2017 in respect of the above supplies?

A   £11,880
B   £11,640
C   £11,520
D   £12,000   **(2 marks)**

164 K Ltd received an order for machine parts on 14 December 2017. K Ltd dispatched these to the customer on 18 December 2017. An invoice was issued on 31 December 2017 and full payment was received on 15 January 2018.

What is the tax point for the sale of the machine parts?

A   18 December 2017
B   31 December 2017
C   15 January 2018
D   14 December 2017   **(2 marks)**

Justin

The following scenario relates to questions 165 to 169.

Justin has the following transactions in the quarter ended 31 December 2017. All amounts exclude any VAT unless otherwise stated.

	£
Purchases	
Furniture for resale	275,000
Restaurant bills: two-thirds for entertaining UK customers, one-third for entertaining non-UK customers	1,800
Petrol for car owned by Justin and used by an employee for business and private use (VAT inclusive)	600
Sales	
Furniture	490,000
Books on interior design	2,400

The employee uses the car provided by Justin 30% for private use. Justin has opted to use the fuel scale for the employee's car. The appropriate fuel scale charge for the quarter is £365 inclusive of VAT.

Justin is considering buying a car for his own use which will be used for both business and private purposes.

165   What is the output VAT payable on the sales of furniture and books?

    A   £81,667

    B   £98,480

    C   £98,000

    D   £82,067   **(2 marks)**

166   What is the net VAT payable or recoverable by Justin for petrol for the employee's car?

    A   £39 recoverable

    B   £61 recoverable

    C   £9 recoverable

    D   £61 payable   **(2 marks)**

167   What is the amount of the input VAT recoverable on the restaurant bills?

    A   £240

    B   £120

    C   £360

    D   £Nil   **(2 marks)**

168   When must Justin submit his VAT return for the quarter to 31 December 2017 and by when must he pay the associated VAT?

	Submission	Payment
A	31 January 2018	7 February 2018
B	14 February 2018	14 February 2018
C	7 February 2018	7 February 2018
D	31 January 2018	14 February 2018

        (2 marks)

169   What will be the VAT treatment of the car purchased for use by Justin?

	Input tax	Sale
A	Full recovery of input VAT	Full charge to output tax on sale
B	No recovery of input VAT	Full charge to output tax on sale
C	Business use recovery of input VAT	Business use charge to output tax on sale
D	No recovery of input VAT	No charge to VAT on sale

        (2 marks)

170 Newcomer Ltd and Au Revoir Ltd   18 mins

(a)   Newcomer Ltd commenced trading on 1 October 2017. Its forecast sales are as follows.

		£
2017	October	18,500
	November	21,900
	December	23,400
2018	January	22,300
	February	22,700
	March	19,200

The company's sales are all standard-rated, and the above figures are exclusive of VAT.

Required

Explain when Newcomer Ltd will be required to compulsorily register for VAT.   **(6 marks)**

(b)   Au Revoir Ltd has been registered for VAT for many years and its sales are all standard-rated. The company has recently seen a downturn in its business activities, and sales for the years ended 31 October 2017 and 2018 are forecast to be £77,000 and £75,500 respectively. Both of these figures are exclusive of VAT.

Required

Explain why Au Revoir Ltd will be permitted to voluntarily deregister for VAT, and from what date deregistration will be effective.   **(4 marks)**

(Total = 10 marks)

171 Ongoing Ltd   18 mins

Ongoing Ltd is registered for VAT, and its sales and purchases are all standard-rated. The following information relates to the company's VAT return for the quarter ended 30 April 2017:

(1)   Standard-rated sales amounted to £120,000. Ongoing Ltd offers its customers a 5% discount for prompt payment, and this discount is taken by half of the customers. The discount is detailed on the sales invoice.

(2)   Standard-rated purchases and expenses amounted to £35,640. This figure includes £480 for entertaining UK customers.

(3)   On 15 April 2017 the company wrote off impairment losses (bad debts) of £2,100 and £840 in respect of invoices due for payment on 10 August 2016 and 5 December 2016 respectively.

(4)   On 30 April 2017 the company purchased a motor car at a cost of £16,450 for the use of a salesperson, and machinery at a cost of £21,150. Both these figures are inclusive of VAT. The motor car is used for both business and private mileage.

(5)   On 30 April 2017 the company sold a motor car for £12,000 which had been used for both business and private mileage.

Unless stated otherwise, all of the above figures are exclusive of VAT. Ongoing Ltd does not operate the cash accounting scheme.

Required

Calculate the amount of VAT payable by Ongoing Ltd for the quarter ended 30 April 2017.

(10 marks)

Further aspects of VAT MCQs   4 mins each

172   Which TWO of the following statements about the value added tax (VAT) cash accounting scheme are correct?

(1)   All VAT returns must be up to date before a trader can join the scheme.

(2)   Trader must pay 90% of the previous year's net VAT liability during the year by means of nine monthly payments.

(3)   Trader's taxable turnover (exclusive of VAT) in 12 months before application must not exceed £1,350,000.

(4)   Scheme gives automatic impairment loss relief (bad debt relief).

A   1 and 2
B   2 and 3
C   1 and 4
D   2 and 4   **(2 marks)**

173 Iris is a UK value added tax (VAT) registered trader. She sold goods with a VAT exclusive price of £30,000 to Heinrich in February 2018. Heinrich runs a business in Germany and is VAT registered in that country. Iris quoted the Heinrich's VAT number on the invoice and has proof of delivery to him in Germany. The rate of VAT in Germany on the goods would be 19%.

What is the VAT that Iris must charge on this supply?

A   £5,000
B   £6,000
C   £5,700
D   £Nil   (2 marks)

174 X plc is registered for value added tax (VAT) and uses the flat rate scheme. In its VAT quarter ended 30 June 2017 it had a tax inclusive turnover of £110,000. This comprises of standard rated sales of £80,000, zero-rated sales of £20,000 and exempt sales of £10,000. The flat rate scheme percentage for the company's trading sector is 9%.

What is the VAT payable to HMRC by X plc for the quarter ended 30 June 2017?

A   £9,900
B   £7,200
C   £9,000
D   £8,100   (2 marks)

Jason   4 mins each

The following scenario relates to questions 175 to 179.

Jason is a sole trader who has recently registered for value added tax (VAT). He buys and sells goods from and to other businesses situated elsewhere in the European Union (EU) and also, occasionally, businesses outside the EU. He also supplies services to business customers outside the EU.

Jason bought some goods from a trader in Germany on 20 July 2017. An invoice was issued by the German trader on 18 August 2017 and was paid by Jason on 28 August 2017.

175 How will the supplies of goods made by Jason be treated for UK VAT if made to a VAT registered trader in another EU state or to a customer outside the EU?

	EU registered trader	Outside EU
A	Standard rated	Zero rated
B	Zero rated	Zero rated
C	Standard rated	Outside the scope of VAT
D	Zero rated	Outside the scope of VAT

(2 marks)

176 How Jason will deal with the VAT implications of buying goods from Germany?

	Output tax	Input tax
A	Output tax at UK rate at point of entry	Input tax at UK rate in next VAT return
B	Output tax at UK rate on next VAT return	Input tax at German rate in next VAT return
C	Output tax at UK rate at point of entry	Input tax at German rate in next VAT return
D	Output tax at UK rate on next VAT return	Input tax at UK rate in next VAT return

(2 marks)

177 What is the tax point for the purchase by Jason of goods from Germany?

A   28 August 2017
B   18 August 2017
C   15 August 2017
D   20 July 2017   (2 marks)

178 How will Jason deal with the VAT implications of his occasional import of goods from outside the EU?

	Output tax	Input tax
A	Output tax at UK rate at point of entry	No input tax
B	Output tax at UK rate on next VAT return	No input tax
C	Output tax at UK rate at point of entry	Input tax at UK rate in next VAT return
D	Output tax at UK rate on next VAT return	Input tax at UK rate in next VAT return

(2 marks)

179 What is the VAT treatment of supplies of services by Jason to business customers outside the EU?

A   Outside the scope of VAT
B   Standard rated
C   Zero rated
D   Exempt   (2 marks)

180 K Ltd and L Ltd   18 mins

(a) K Ltd is registered for value added tax (VAT). The directors of K Ltd have recently heard about the annual accounting scheme and asked you for advice on this matter.

Required

Prepare draft notes, for a meeting with the directors of K Ltd, outlining:

(i)   The rules and qualifying conditions that the company must satisfy in order to join and continue to use the VAT annual accounting scheme.   (4 marks)

(ii) The advantages and disadvantages of using the scheme.   (3 marks)

(b) L Ltd carries on a business as a wholesale adult clothing outlet and is registered for VAT. In recent months, L Ltd has had difficulty in obtaining payment of its invoices from its customers which has led to cash flow problems.

The directors of L Ltd have heard that there is a VAT scheme which may be advantageous for L Ltd to use. It wishes to continue to submit quarterly VAT returns.

Required

State the VAT scheme which would be advantageous for L Ltd to use and advise the directors of the conditions to join the scheme.   (3 marks)

(Total = 10 marks)

Introduction to the UK tax system MCQs

1   D   2 and 4

HM Revenue & Customs (HMRC) produces a wide range of explanatory notes and has the administrative function for collection of tax.

HM Treasury formally imposes taxation. Advice on minimising tax liability is provided by professional advisors such as accountants.

2   B   2 and 4

Inheritance tax and capital gains tax are capital taxes.

Income tax and national insurance are revenue taxes. Corporation tax is both a revenue tax (in respect of its income) and a capital tax (in respect of its chargeable gains).

3   C   1, 2 and 4

Inform Serena in writing that it is not possible for your firm to act for her, inform HMRC that your firm is no longer acting for Serena, and report Serena's refusal to disclose the omission and the facts surrounding it to your firm's Money Laundering Reporting Officer.

You are not required to inform HMRC about the details of Serena's omission.

Computing taxable income and the income tax liability MCQs

4   C   2, 3 and 4

Interest received from an individual savings account, Premium Bond prizes, and interest on NS&I Savings Certificates are exempt from income tax.

Dividends from a company and interest on government securities (gilts) are chargeable to income tax.

5   C   £9,000

	£
Net income	108,000
Less personal pension contribution	(3,000)
Adjusted net income	105,000
Less income limit	(100,000)
Excess	5,000
Personal allowance	11,500
Less half excess £5,000 × ½	(2,500)
Available personal allowance	9,000

6   A   £882

	£
£2,000 × 20%	400
£(5,000 − 2,000) = 3,000 × 0% (savings starting rate band)	0
£1,000 × 0% (savings income nil rate band)	0
£(6,410 − 3,000 − 1,000) = 2,410 × 20%	482
Tax liability	882

Non-savings income is taxed at 20%. Savings income is taxed at 0% where such income falls within the first £5,000 of taxable income and then at 0% on the amount of the savings income nil rate band of £1,000. The remainder of the savings income is then taxed at 20%.

7   C   £24,550

	£
£33,500 × 20%	6,700
£(150,000 – 33,500) = 116,500 × 40%	46,600
£(175,000 – 150,000) = 25,000 × 45%	11,250
Tax liability	64,550
Less PAYE deducted	(40,000)
Tax payable	24,550

8   B   £554

	£
Net income	53,400
Less gift aid donation (gross)	(300)
Adjusted net income	53,100
Less threshold	(50,000)
Excess	3,100
÷ £100	31
Child benefit income tax charge: 1% × £1,788 × 31	554

9 Sandeep, Harriet and Romelu

> **Tutorial note.** When answering a question on residence status, start by considering whether the individual is automatically non-UK resident. If this test is not satisfied, then consider whether the individual is automatically UK resident. Again, if this test is not satisfied, then consider whether the combination of days in the UK and sufficient UK ties makes the individual UK resident.

(a)   Sandeep is not automatically non-UK resident for the tax year 2017/18 because he spends 46 days or more in the UK during that tax year and does not work full-time overseas (and, in any case, has spent more than 90 days in the UK for the tax year).

He is automatically UK resident for the tax year 2017/18 because he spends 183 days or more in the UK during that tax year.

(b)   Harriet was previously resident in the UK. She does not satisfy any of the automatic overseas tests since she spends 16 days or more in the UK and does not work full-time overseas.

Harriet does not satisfy any of the automatic UK tests since she spends less than 183 days in the UK, during the tax year 2017/18, has an overseas home and does not work full-time in the UK.

The 'sufficient ties' test is therefore relevant. Harriet has two UK ties:

(i)   Substantive work in the UK
(ii)   Available accommodation in the UK in which she spends at least one night in the tax year

Harriet spends between 91 and 120 days in the UK in 2017/18. These two ties are therefore sufficient to make her UK resident for the tax year 2017/18.

(c)   Romelu was not previously resident in the UK. He does not satisfy any of the automatic overseas tests since he spends 46 days or more in the UK during the tax year 2017/18 and does not work full-time overseas.

Romelu does not satisfy any of the automatic UK tests as he spent less than 183 days in the UK, has an overseas home and does not work in the UK.

The 'sufficient ties' test is therefore relevant. Romelu has two UK ties:

(i)   UK resident close family (spouse)

(ii)   Available accommodation in the UK in which he spends at least one night in the tax year

Romelu spends between 91 and 120 days in the UK in 2017/18 and so he would need three UK ties to be UK resident for that tax year. Since Romelu has only two ties with the UK, he is therefore non-UK resident for the tax year 2017/18.

10 John and Helen

Tutorial note. In part (a), John's dividend income is between the basic rate limit and the higher rate limit, so the excess over the dividend nil rate band is taxed at 32.5%. Helen's dividends in excess of the dividend nil rate band, however, fall below the basic rate limit and are consequently taxed at 7.5%. In part (b), John's adjusted net income is the same as his net income, since he has not made any personal pension contributions or gift aid donations in 2017/18.

(a)   *John and Helen 2017/18*

	Non-savings income	*Savings income*	*Dividend income*	*Total*
John	£	£	£	£
Employment income	68,090			
Dividends			6,211	
Bank deposit interest		1,000		
Building society interest		990		
Net income	68,090	1,990	6,211	76,291
Less personal allowance	(11,500)			
Taxable income	56,590	1,990	6,211	63,291

	£
Non savings income	
£33,500 × 20%	6,700
£23,090 (56,590 − 33,500) × 40%	9,236
Savings income	
£500 × 0% (higher rate taxpayer)	0
£1,490 (1,990 − 500) × 40%	596
Dividend income	
£5,000 × 0%	0
£1,211 (6,211 − 5,000) × 32.5%	394
Tax liability	16,926
Less: PAYE	(15,936)
Tax payable	990

	Non-savings income £	Savings income £	Dividend income £	Total £
Helen				
Employment income	23,500			
Dividends			7,820	
Bank deposit interest		1,095		
Building society interest		525		
Net income	23,500	1,620	7,820	32,940
Less personal allowance	(11,500)			
Taxable income	12,000	1,620	7,820	21,440

	£
Non-savings income	
£12,000 × 20%	2,400
Savings income	
£1,000 × 0% (basic rate taxpayer)	0
£620 (1,620 – 1,000) × 20%	124
Dividend income	
£5,000 × 0%	0
£2,820 (7,820 – 5,000) × 7.5%	211
Tax liability	2,735
Less PAYE	(2,400)
Tax payable	335

(b) John will be liable to the child benefit income tax charge for the tax year 2017/18 because his spouse has received child benefit during this tax year and he has adjusted net income in excess of £50,000 that is higher than that of Helen. Since John's adjusted net income exceeds £60,000, the child benefit income tax charge is the full amount of child benefit (£1,076) received by Helen in 2017/18. This charge will be collected under the self assessment system.

11 Michael and Josie

> **Tutorial note.** Michael is not entitled to a personal allowance because his net income is more than £123,000. Josie is entitled to a reduced personal allowance because her adjusted net income is between £100,000 and £123,000.

	Non-savings income £	Savings income £	Dividend income £	Total £
Michael				
Employment income	163,540			
Dividends			17,111	
Bank deposit interest		7,500		
Building society interest		7,400		
Net income/Taxable income	163,540	14,900	17,111	195,551

	£
Non savings income	
£33,500 × 20%	6,700
£116,500 (150,000 – 33,500) × 40%	46,600
£13,540 (163,540 – 150,000) × 45%	6,093
Savings income	
£14,900 × 45%	6,705
Dividend income	
£5,000 × 0%	0
£12,111 (17,111 – 5,000) × 38.1%	4,614
	70,712
Less PAYE	(59,390)
Tax payable	11,322

No savings income nil rate band available because Michael is an additional rate taxpayer.

	Non-savings income £	Savings income £	Dividend income £	Total £
Josie				
Employment income	100,000			
Dividends			7,820	
Bank deposit interest		150		
Building society interest		550		
Net income	100,000	700	7,820	108,520
Less personal allowance (W1)	(8,240)			
Taxable income	91,760	700	7,820	100,280

	£	£
Non-savings income		
£35,500 (W2) × 20%		7,100
£56,260 (91,760 – 35,500) × 40%		22,504
Savings income		
£500 × 0% (higher rate taxpayer)		0
£200 (700 – 500) × 40%		80
Dividend income		
£5,000 × 0%		0
£2,820 (7,820 – 5,000) × 32.5%		916
Tax liability		30,600
Less: PAYE		(28,700)
Tax payable		1,900

Workings

1   Personal allowance

	£
Net income	108,520
Less gross gift aid donation £1,600 × 100/80	(2,000)
Adjusted net income	106,520
Less income limit	(100,000)
Excess	6,520

		£
Personal allowance		11,500
Less half excess £6,520 × ½		(3,260)
Revised personal allowance		8,240

2   Basic rate limit and higher rate limit

£33,500 + (£1,600 × 100/80)	£35,500
£150,000 + (£1,600 × 100/80)	£152,000

Employment income MCQs

12   B   £9,800

	£
Salary	8,000
Bonus received 30 November 2017 (receipts basis)	1,800
Employment income 2017/18	9,800

13   C   3 and 4

Diane is employed in a temporary workplace for less than 24 months, so travel from home to her temporary workplace is allowable. Erica's journey from home to Bristol is travel in the performance of duties so travel from home to the client is allowable.

Ben has a permanent workplace in Bristol and is not entitled to deduct travelling expenses from home to his workplace. Colin has two permanent workplaces so he is not entitled to deduct travelling expenses to either of them.

14   B   £(500) allowable expense

	£
Amount reimbursed 15,000 × 35p	5,250
Less: statutory allowance	
10,000 miles × 45p	(4,500)
5,000 miles × 25p	(1,250)
Allowable expense	(500)

Danni

> **Tutorial note.** Tax relief is not available for an employee's normal commuting costs but relief is available where the employee has a temporary workplace where the secondment is expected to last up to 24 months.

15   C   £64,450

	£
Salary	
1.7.17 – 31.12.17	
£6,000 × 6	36,000
1.1.18 – 31.3.18	
£(6,000 × 102.5%) × 3	18,450
Bonus	
31 March 2018 (receipts basis)	10,000
Taxable in tax year 2017/18	64,450

As Danni is a director of Clifton plc, bonus is received on the earliest of:

- The time when payment is made (31 May 2018)

- The time when she becomes entitled to payment of the bonus (10 April 2018)

- The time when the amount is credited in the company's accounting records (10 April 2018)

- The end of the company's period of account (as the amount was determined on 15 March 2018 which is within the period of account) (31 March 2018)

The earliest of these dates is provided by the last test and so the date of receipt is 31 March 2018.

16	B	2 only

Home to permanent workplace: not qualifying travel expenses
Home to temporary workplace expected to last less than 24 months: qualifying travel expenses

17	D	£36 allowable deduction

24 miles × 2 (return journey) × 5 = 240 miles

Excess over statutory mileage allowance 240 × (0.45 − 0.30) = £(36) allowable deduction

18	A	1 only

Chartered Institute of Purchasing and Supply (MCIP): Subscription to professional body relevant to the duties of the employment

Tennis club: not incurred wholly, exclusively and necessarily in the performance of the duties of the employment

19	A	By Clifton plc deducting the donation from Danni's gross pay before calculating PAYE

Taxable and exempt benefits. The PAYE system MCQs

20	B	£4,400

CO_2 emissions are 103 g/km, round down to 100 g/km

Appropriate percentage: (100 − 95) = 5 g/km in excess of threshold

5/5 = 1%

18% + 1% + 3% = 22%

List price £20,000 × 22% = £4,400

21	C	£1,460

	£
Annual value	3,780
Additional amount £(99,000 − 75,000) × 2.5%	600
	4,380
× 4/12	1,460

Accommodation provided for private use by an employer is taxed on the annual value plus an additional amount if the accommodation cost the company more than £75,000. The market value is only used if the accommodation was acquired more than six years prior to being provided. Both benefits are pro-rated for occupation for part of the tax year.

22	A	Form P11D by 6 July 2018

Clara

23 B £400

£8 × 50 = £400

Private incidental expenses are only exempt if they are no more than £5 for each night spent in the UK. As this limit is exceeded, all of the expenses are taxable, not just the excess.

Reimbursed expenses such as on travel are automatically treated as exempt, provided that the amount of the deduction is at least equal to the amount of the expense, and so do not have to be reported on form P11D.

The answer £150 taxes the excess private incidental expenses over the £5 limit. The answer £1,350 taxes the excess private incidental expenses over the £5 limit and the train fares. The answer £1,600 taxes the whole of the private incidental expenses and the train fares.

24 A £540

£(67 − 55) = 12 × 45 = £540

The excess over the limit of £55 per week for a basic rate employee is taxable.

Workplace parking is an exempt benefit.

The answer £500 taxes the workplace parking only. The answer £1,040 taxes both the childcare vouchers and the workplace parking. The answer £3,015 taxes only the childcare vouchers but the whole amount. The answer £3,515 taxes the workplace parking and the childcare vouchers in full.

25 C £2,560

£(3,230 + 610) = 3,840 × 8/12 = £2,560

No taxable benefit applies where an employee takes a van home (ie uses the van for home to work travel) but only if they are not allowed any other private use which is not the case here as Lewis uses the van on non-working days.

The answer £8,522 uses the car benefit rules. The answer £3,840 is the full tax year benefit. The answer £0 assumes there is no private use of the van.

26 D Report on or before any day when she pays someone, payment 17 days after end of tax month if paid electronically

27 A First FPS £0, second FPS £200

The first late submission of the tax year is ignored. Further late submissions will attract penalties based on the number of employees. Since Clara has between 10 and 49 employees, the penalty on the second FPS is £200.

28 Azure plc

> **Tutorial note.** The calculation of benefits is particularly important for exam purposes. Ensure that you pro-rate the benefits if they are not available for the entire year.

(a)   A taxable benefit must be computed for Andrew. The benefit will equal the difference between the interest which would have arisen at the official rate and the actual interest paid. The benefit for 2017/18 is therefore £16,000 × (2.5 − 0.25)% × 6/12 months = £180.

(b)   The flower arrangement costing £45 given to Penelope is a trivial benefit, so the taxable benefit is nil.

(c)   Charles will have a taxable benefit of the annual value of the TV, which will be computed as 20% of the value of the asset when first provided as a benefit to any employee. If the TV had been lent to an employee when it was bought, the benefit for 2017/18 would be £800 × 20% = £160 × 10/12 = £133. If the TV was first provided as a benefit in June 2017, the benefit would be £500 × 20% = £100 × 10/12 = £83.

(d)   Long service awards of tangible property to employees with at least 20 years service are not taxed provided the cost to the employer does not exceed £50 for each year of service and no similar award has been made to the same person within the previous ten years. In Demelza's case the limit on value would be £50 × 25 = £1,250, so there will be no taxable benefit.

(e)   The first £8,000 of removal expenses payable to Janet will be an exempt benefit because:

   (i)   She does not already live within a reasonable daily travelling distance of her new place of employment, but will do so after moving, and

   (ii)   The expenses are incurred or the benefits provided by the end of the tax year following the tax year of the start of employment at the new location.

   Janet will be taxable on the excess removal expenses £(9,500 − 8,000) = £1,500.

(f)   The private use of one mobile phone is an exempt benefit. The private use of the second phone is a taxable benefit. Lawrence can choose which phone is exempt and should therefore choose the one which has the higher phone charges.

   The taxable benefit on the second phone is calculated as follows.

	£
Greater of:	
20% of market value (20% × £500 = £100)	
Hire charge £120	
ie	120
Cost of calls	300
Taxable benefit	420

Pensions MCQs

29   B   £5,500

   The maximum amount of contributions attracting tax relief which could be made by Treena in 2017/18 is the higher of:

   (a)   Relevant earnings which is the total of her employment income of £3,500 and her trading income of £2,000; and

   (b)   Basic amount of £3,600.

   Bank interest is not relevant earnings.

30 **C** £64,000

	£
Earnings	90,500
Less occupational pension contribution	(15,000)
Net income	75,500
Less personal allowance	(11,500)
Taxable income	64,000

Under net pay arrangements (most occupational pension schemes) the gross contribution is deducted from earnings so that tax relief is given at all rates of tax. Under tax relief at source (most personal pension schemes), the payment is made net of basic rate tax and higher rate relief and additional rate relief are given by increasing the basic rate and higher rate limits in the tax computation.

31 **A** £63,000

	£
Annual allowance 2017/18	40,000
Annual allowance unused in 2016/17 £(40,000 – 17,000)	23,000
Maximum gross pension contribution in 2017/18	63,000

The annual allowance for 2015/16 is not available as Rio was not a member of a pension scheme in that year.

Gary, George and Geraldine

Tutorial note. In question 35, Geraldine's relevant earnings of £130,000 exceed the gross pension contributions of £48,750, so she can obtain tax relief on this contribution.

32 **C** £10,660

	£
£38,500 (W) × 20%	7,700
£7,400 × 40%	2,960
45,900	10,660

Working

Basic rate limit £33,500 + (£4,000 × 100/80) = 38,500

33 **C** £23,000

	£
Trading income	15,000
FHL property income	8,000
Relevant earnings	23,000

34 **B** Tax-free lump sum of up to 25% of pension fund, remainder taxable as pension income

35 **D** £39,000

In 2016/17, Geraldine had made a gross contribution of £(25,000 × 100/80) = £31,250. She therefore has an unused annual allowance of (40,000 – 31,250) = £8,750. This will be brought forward and added to her annual allowance of £40,000 for 2017/18, giving a total of £(8,750 + 40,000) = £48,750. The net equivalent (ie the amount she would actually pay) is £48,750 × 80% = £39,000.

36 **B** She will be subject to income tax at the rate of 55% on the lump sum.

The lump sum is in excess of the lifetime allowance of £1,000,000 and so it taxable at the rate of 55%.

Property income MCQs

37 C £795

	£
Chairs – no relief for new furniture	0
Cooker – cost of replacing original only	650
Central heating breakdown cover (accruals basis)	
£580 × 3/12	145
Allowable expenses	795

38 D .£24,000

	£
Premium received	30,000
Less £30,000 × 2% × (11 – 1)	(6,000)
Amount chargeable to income tax	24,000

39 B £16,000

	£
Rent receivable	20,000
Less mortgage interest £5,000 × 80%	(4,000)
Property business income	16,000

The mortgage capital repayments are not allowable in computing property business income. The remaining mortgage interest will be relieved in the income tax computation as a basic rate tax reducer.

40 Rafe

> **Tutorial note.** Remember to accrue the rents receivable and expenses payable for the tax year. Where you disallow an expense, such as the new roof, note this in your computation to show that you have considered it.

	£	£
Rent		
House 1: first letting £600 × 6		3,600
House 1: second letting £6,000 × 3/12		1,500
House 2: £7,800 × 8/12		5,200
		10,300
Expenses		
House 1: new roof, disallowable because capital	0	
House 1: buildings insurance £480 × 10/12	400	
House 2: redecoration	1,200	
House 2: new furniture	0	
House 2: buildings insurance £920 × 9/12	690	
House 2: boiler insurance £180 × 8/12	120	
House 2: replacement domestic items relief on replacement sofa	800	
		(3,210)
Income from houses 1 and 2		7,090
Rent a room (W)		350
Total property business income		7,440

Working

Rafe should claim rent a room relief in respect of the letting of the furnished room in his main residence, since this is more beneficial than the normal basis of assessment (£7,850 – £875 = £6,975). This means that Rafe will be taxed on an additional £350 (£7,850 – £7,500) of property business income.

Computing trading income MCQs

41   C   1 and 4

Installing air conditioning in his workshop and making initial repairs to a recently acquired second-hand office building which was not usable until the repairs were carried out (see *Law Shipping Co Ltd v CIR 1923*) are capital expenditure. They are not allowable as expense in calculating trading profits.

Repairing the central heating in his offices and redecorating the showroom are allowable expenses in calculating trading profits.

42   D   £160,220

	£
Profit per accounts	160,000
Add: parking fines	180
hamper	40
Tax-adjusted profit	160,220

The legal fees in relation to the short lease are allowable as this involves a renewal of a short lease rather than the grant of a new lease. Parking fines for the owner of a business are never allowable. Gifts of food are not allowable.

43   B   £2,448

	£
Lease payments £400 × 9	3,600
Less 15% disallowed for high emission car	(540)
	3,060
Business use proportion 10,800/13,500 × 3,060	2,448

Margaret

> **Tutorial note**. The fixed rate adjustment for the private use of a trader's business premises is not the amount which is allowable, but instead reduces the allowable amount.

44   D   Revenue £35,500, other allowable expenses £1,100

Under the cash basis, revenue and expenses are recognised on the amounts actually received and paid in the period of account.

45   B   Furniture £2,500, plot of land for guest parking £Nil

Business expenses for the cash basis of accounting include capital expenditure on plant and machinery such as furniture but not other capital expenses such as the acquisition of the land for guest parking.

46   C   £7,000

	£
Gas and electricity	7,400
Cleaning and gardening	1,800
Food	2,000
	11,200
Less fixed rate private use proportion £350 × 12	(4,200)
Allowable household expenses	7,000

		£
First 10,000 miles @ 45p		4,500
Next 2,000 miles @ 25p		500
Allowable motoring expenses		5,000

48   B   3 only

A net cash deficit (ie a loss) under the cash basis can only be relieved against future cash surpluses (ie future trading profits). Cash basis traders cannot offset a loss against general income.

49 Archie

Tutorial note. You are extremely likely to be required to adjust accounts profit in your exam to arrive at taxable trading profits. The best way to familiarise yourself with the adjustments required is to practise plenty of questions like this.

	£	£
Net profit		101,977
Add: general expenses: entertaining staff	0	
general expenses: entertaining suppliers	600	
repairs and renewals: redecoration	0	
repairs and renewals: renovation	0	
legal and accountancy: debt collection	0	
legal and accountancy: staff service agreements	0	
legal and accountancy: tax consultancy (not for purposes of trade)	30	
legal and accountancy: grant of short lease on new premises	100	
legal and accountancy: audit and accountancy	0	
subscription and donations: gift aid donation	5,200	
subscription and donations: political donation	500	
subscription and donations: sports facilities for staff	0	
subscription and donations: trade association	0	
impairment losses (trade)	0	
salaries and wages	0	
travel: private travel expenses 25% × £2,000	500	
depreciation	15,000	
rent and rates	0	
		21,930
Less: profit on sale of office	5,265	
impairment losses recovered	0	
capital allowances	2,200	
building society interest	1,900	
		(9,365)
Taxable trading profit		114,542

Capital allowances MCQs

50 D 1 and 3

Refrigeration equipment and sound insulation (provided mainly to meet the particular requirements of the trade) are items which could be plant for the purposes of capital allowances.

Expenditure on a building such as an office extension could not qualify as plant. A bridge is a structure and is therefore also not plant.

51 A £1,260

	Car £	Allowances 75% £
y/e 5 April 2018		
Addition	21,000	
WDA @ 8%	(1,680)	1,260
TWDV c/f	19,320	
Maximum capital allowances		1,260

52 C £50,450

	AIA £	Main pool £	Allowances £
p/e 31 December 2017			
Addition qualifying for AIA			
Machinery	60,000		
AIA £200,000 × 3/12	(50,000)		50,000
	10,000		
Transfer balance to main pool	(10,000)	10,000	
WDA @ 18% × 3/12		(450)	450
TWDV c/f		9,550	
Maximum capital allowances			50,450

Sylvester

> **Tutorial note.** Balancing adjustments where there has been private use of the asset are restricted to the business use element.

53 B £840

	Sylvester's car (70%) £	Allowances/ (charges) £
TWDV b/f	6,000	
Disposal	(7,200)	
Balancing charge	(1,200) × 70%	(840)

54 A £912

	Sylvester's car (80%)	Allowances/ (charges)
Private use car	19,000	
WDA 8% × 9/12	(1,140) × 80%	912
TWDV c/f	17,860	

55   A   £6,210

	Main pool £	Allowances/(charges) £
TWDV b/f	56,800	
Disposals		
(10,000 + 800)	(10,800)	
	46,000	
WDA 18% × 9/12	(6,210)	6,210
TWDV c/f	39,790	

The disposal proceeds on the plant sold on 20 April 2017 are restricted to cost.

56   C   £500

A writing down allowance equal to unrelieved expenditure in the special rate pool for a 9 month period of account can be claimed where this is £750 (£1,000 × 9/12) or less.

57   D   Motor car [1] will be given a first year allowance, Motor car [2] will be added to the special rate pool and given writing down allowances of 8% as part of the pool.

A 100% first year allowance (FYA) is available for expenditure incurred on new low emission motor cars. A low emission car is one which has CO_2 emissions of 75g/km or less.

Expenditure on motor cars which emit over 130g/km is added to the special rate pool.

58 Tom

> **Tutorial note.** The key to being able to deal with a capital allowances computation correctly is to get the layout right. Once you have done this, the figures should fall into place.

	AIA £	Main pool £	Private use car (80%) £	Short life asset £	Allowances £
1.7.17 – 30.6.18					
Brought forward		33,500		4,400	
Addition qualifying for AIA					
Plant	27,000				
AIA	(27,000)				27,000
	0				
WDA @ 18%		(6,030)		(792)	6,822
Carried forward		27,470		3,608	
Allowances					33,822
1.7.18 – 30.6.19					
Addition (not AIA)			13,400		
WDA @ 18%		(4,945)	(2,412) × 80%	(649)	7,524
Carried forward		22,525	10,988	2,959	
Allowances					7,524
1.7.19 – 30.6.20					
WDA @ 18%		(4,055)	(1,978) × 80%	(533)	6,170
Carried forward		18,470	9,010	2,426	
Allowances					6,170

	AIA £	Main pool £	Private use car (80%) £	Short life asset £	Allowances £
1.7.20 – 30.6.21					
Brought forward		18,470	9,010	2,426	
Disposals		(340)		(2,900)	
		18,130		(474)	
Balancing charge				474	(474)
WDA @ 18%		(3,263)	(1,622) × 80%		4,561
Carried forward		14,867	7,388		
Allowances					4,087
1.7.21 – 31.12.21					
Disposals		(24,000)	(10,600)		
		(9,133)	(3,212)		
Balancing charges		9,133	3,212 × 80%		(11,703)

> **Tutorial note.** The capital allowances are restricted as a result of the private use of an asset by the owner of the business.

Assessable trading income MCQs

59 D £3,000

First tax year (2016/17)
Actual basis
Basis period 1.1.17 to 5.4.17

Second tax year (2017/18)
Period of account in 2nd year at least 12 months so basis period is 12 months to that accounting date
Basis period 1.2.17 to 31.1.18

Overlap profits
Period of overlap 1.2.17 to 5.4.17 (two months)

2/13 × £19,500   £3,000

60 B £11,500

Last tax year (2017/18)
Basis period 1.2.17 to 31.3.18

	£
y/e 31.1.18	10,000
p/e 31.3.18	2,500
	12,500
Less overlap profits	(1,000)
	11,500

61 B 6 April 2017 to 5 April 2018

2017/18 is the second year of trading. There is no period of account ending in 2017/18, so the basis period is the tax year.

62 Clive

> **Tutorial note.** Significant cash flow advantages can be gained with a careful choice of accounting date.

Taxable profits for the four years 2017/18 to 2020/21

The accounts profits will be as follows.

Period ending in	Working	Accounting date 31 March £	30 April £
2018	3 × £800	2,400	
	4 × £800		3,200
2019	3 × £800 + 6 × £1,200 + 3 × £2,000	15,600	
	2 × £800 + 6 × £1,200 + 4 × £2,000		16,800
2020	12 × £2,000	24,000	24,000
2021	12 × £2,000	24,000	24,000

The taxable profits will be as follows.

		Accounting date 31 March £	30 April £
2017/18	Actual basis (1 January 2018 to 5 April 2018)	2,400	
	£3,200 × 3/4 (work to nearest month)		2,400
2018/19	Year to 31.3.19	15,600	
	First 12 months (1 January 2018 to 31 December 2018)		
	£3,200 + £16,800 × 8/12		14,400
2019/20	Year to 31.3.20	24,000	
	Year to 30.4.19		16,800
2020/21	Year to 31.3.21	24,000	
	Year to 30.4.20		24,000
		66,000	57,600

30 April is the better choice of accounting date as it will give a considerable cash flow advantage.

63 Fiona

> **Tutorial note.** In a question like this, work out the capital allowances for each period of account before you think about allocating profits to tax years.
>
> Writing down allowances and the annual investment allowance are time apportioned in a long period of account.

We must first work out the capital allowances.

	AIA £	Main pool £	Private use car (65%) £	Allowances £
1.1.18 – 30.4.19				
Additions qualifying for AIA				
Desk and office furniture (1.1.18)	2,625			
General plant (4.1.18)	8,070			
Second-hand oven (1.3.18)	5,300			
Delivery van (25.3.18)	5,450			
General plant (15.4.18)	8,555			
	30,000			
AIA £200,000 × 16/12 = £266,667	(30,000)			30,000

	AIA	Main pool	Private use car (65%)	Allowances
	£	£	£	£
Addition not qualifying for AIA				
Car (15.5.18)			6,600	
WDA @ 18% × 16/12		—	(1,584) × 65%	1,030
Carried forward		0	5,016	
Allowances				31,030
1.5.19 – 30.4.20				
Additions qualifying for AIA				
General plant (30.1.20)	10,000			
Mixer (30.4.20)	1,200			
	11,200			
AIA	(11,200)			11,200
WDA @ 18%			(903) × 65%	587
Carried forward			4,113	
Allowances				11,787

Profits are as follows.

Period	Profit	Capital allowances	Adjusted profit
	£	£	£
1.1.18 – 30.4.19	47,030	31,030	16,000
1.5.19 – 30.4.20	24,787	11,787	13,000

The taxable profits are as follows.

Year	Basis period	Working	Taxable profit
			£
2017/18	1.1.18 – 5.4.18	£16,000 × 3/16	3,000
2018/19	6.4.18 – 5.4.19	£16,000 × 12/16	12,000
2019/20	1.5.18 – 30.4.19	£16,000 × 12/16	12,000
2020/21	1.5.19 – 30.4.20		13,000

The overlap profits are the profits from 1 May 2018 to 5 April 2019: £16,000 × 11/16 = £11,000.

Trading losses MCQs

64   D   2 and 4

A trading loss carried forward must be set against the first available profits of the same trade. A trading loss claim for relief against general income must be made by 31 January 22 months after the end of the tax year of the loss.

A claim to set a trading loss against general income cannot be restricted so that the individual has enough net income to use the personal allowance. A trading loss can be carried forward indefinitely.

65	B	£11,000	

	2016/17 £
Trading income	9,000
Property business income	4,000
	13,000
Less loss relief against general income c/b from 2017/18	(13,000)
Net income	0

The trading loss available to carry forward to 2018/19 is £(24,000 – 13,000) = <u>£11,000</u>.

66	C	£83,750	

	2016/17 £
Trading income	15,000
Property business income	260,000
Total income	275,000
Less loss relief against general income	(83,750)
Net income	191,250

In 2016/17, the loss relief cap does not apply to loss relief against the trading income of £15,000. However, the cap does apply to the loss relief against non-trading income. The cap is £275,000 × 25% = £68,750. The total loss relief claim for 2016/17 is therefore £(15,000 + 68,750) = £83,750.

67 Morgan

> **Tutorial note**. Take care to consider all available reliefs. When deciding on the best relief you must consider both the rate of tax saved and the timing of the relief.

(a) Loss relief could be claimed:

  (i) Against general income of the year of loss (2018/19), the savings income of £12,000

  (ii) Against general income of the preceding year (2017/18). This would be trading profits of £15,000 plus savings income of £12,000

  (iii) Against the first available future profits of the same trade. This would be trading profits of £45,000 in 2019/20

(b) **The quickest claim**

The quickest way to obtain relief would be for Morgan to use loss relief against general income in both years. The tax computations would then be as follows.

	2017/18 £	2018/19 £
Trading profits	15,000	0
Savings income	12,000	12,000
Total income	27,000	12,000
Less loss relief against general income	(27,000)	(12,000)
Net income	0	0

The balance of the loss, £1,000, would be carried forward and relieved against future trading income in 2019/20.

Although this proposal produces loss relief quickly, it has the disadvantage of wasting Morgan's personal allowance and savings income nil rate band in both years. Morgan could, if he chose, delay his relief by carrying the loss forward. The loss would then be set off only against trading income, with the savings income using his personal allowance and the savings income nil rate band in 2019/20.

Partnerships and limited liability partnerships MCQs

68 B £5,000

y/e 31 December 2018

Profit share £60,000 × 1/3	£20,000

2017/18 basis period is 1 January 2018 to 5 April 2018 so 3/12 of this amount is taxable in 2017/18 ie £5,000.

69 C £33,333

y/e 31 March 2018

	£
1.4.17 – 30.4.17	
Profit share £96,000 × 1/12 × 1/2	4,000
1.5.17 – 31.3.18	
Profit share £96,000 × 11/12 × 1/3	29,333
	33,333

Current year basis applies as there is no commencement or cessation, simply a change in profit sharing ratios.

70 B £50,000

Victor's share of the loss is 50% ie £90,000. However, the amount of loss relief that Victor can claim against general income of £60,000 is restricted to the greater of £50,000 and 25% of Victor's adjusted total income (ie 25% × £60,000 = £15,000) ie £50,000.

Anne, Betty and Chloe

> **Tutorial note**. Each partner can make a separate loss relief claim for her share of the partnership loss.

71 C £16,650

	£
1.1.17 – 30.9.17	
Salary £6,000 × 9/12	4,500
PSR £([60,000 × 9/12] - 4,500) × 30%	12,150
	16,650

72 A £25,350

	£
2017/18	
Basis period 1.1.17 – 30.9.17	
PSR £([60,000 × 9/12] - 4,500) × 70%	28,350
Less overlap profits relieved on cessation	(3,000)
	25,350

73 D £10,200

	£
2017/18	
Basis period 1.10.17 – 5.4.18	
1.10.17 – 31.12.17	
PSR £(60,000 × 3/12) × 40%	6,000
1.1.18 – 5.4.18	
PSR £(42,000 × 3/12) × 40%	4,200
	10,200

74 A 1 and 2

Against general income of 2019/20 and/or 2018/19 and against future trading profits.

75 A 1, 2 and 4

Against general income of 2019/20 and/or 2018/19, against future trading profits and against general income of 2016/17, 2017/18 and 2018/19 earlier years first (early years loss relief).

National insurance contributions MCQs

76 C £3,193

	£
Class 2	148
£2.85 × 52	
Class 4	
£(42,000 – 8,164) = 33,836 × 9%	3,045
Total NIC 2017/18	3,193

77 B £513

Total earnings received in February 2018 are £11,000 (£3,000 + £8,000)

The NIC employee's limits for each month are £8,164/12 = £680 and £45,000/12 = £3,750.

NIC payable is therefore:

	£
£(3,750 – 680) = 3,070 × 12%	368
£(11,000 – 3,750) = 7,250 × 2%	145
NIC February 2018	513

78 D Class 1 employee's contributions on £45,000, Class 1 employer's contributions on £45,000, Class 1A contributions on £300

Class 1 employee's and employer's contributions are generally payable on cash earnings. Class 1A contributions are payable on non-cash benefits by the employer only.

Derek and Denise

> **Tutorial note.** It is important that you can calculate and distinguish NICs for the self-employed and employed individuals.

79 D £4,620

	£
£(45,000 – 8,164) = 36,836 × 12%	4,420
£(55,000 – 45,000) = 10,000 × 2%	200
	4,620

80   A   £3,463

		£
£(55,000 − 8,164) = 46,836 × 13.8%		6,463
Less Employment Allowance (only employee of sole trader)		(3,000)
		3,463

81   B   £62

£(12,000 × 9% × 5/12) × 13.8%	62

82   A   £40 by 31 January 2019

14 × £2.85 = £40 payable under self assessment by 31 January following the end of the tax year.

83   C   £278

Basis period for 2017/18 is 6.1.18 to 5.4.18 (3 months)

£([15,000 × 3/4] − 8,164) = 3,086 × 9% = £278

84 Sasha

> **Tutorial notes**
>
> 1   Strictly, expenses are only deductible in calculating net taxable earnings if they are incurred wholly, necessarily and exclusively in the performance of the duties. In practice, however, HM Revenue & Customs allow an apportionment between private and business use as here.
>
> 2   Capital allowances are available to an employee who provides plant and machinery necessarily for use in the performance of his duties, in the same way as a sole trader.
>
> 3   The use of the car for travel between home and work is ordinary commuting and not business use.
>
> 4   'Earnings' for Class 4 NIC purposes are trading profits. However, earnings for Class 1 NIC purposes are gross earnings before the deductions of any expenses.

(a)   Factors that will indicate that a worker should be treated as an employee rather than as self-employed are:

(i)   Control by employer over employee's work

(ii)   Employee must accept further work if offered (and employer must offer work)

(iii)   Employee does not provide own equipment

(iv)   Employee does not hire own helpers

(v)   Employee does not take substantial financial risk

(vi)   Employee does not have responsibility for investment and management of business and cannot benefit from sound management

(vii)   Employee cannot work when he chooses but when an employer tells him to work

(viii)   Described as an employee in any agreement between parties

(b)   (i)   *Income assessable as trading profits*

	£	£
Gross income		60,000
Less: business expenses on heating etc	880	
computer – AIA	4,000	
business expenses re car (£3,500 × 40%)	1,400	
WDA @ 18% on business car (CO_2 up to 130g/km)		
£10,000 × 18% × 40% (business proportion)	720	(7,000)
Assessable as trading profits		53,000

(ii) *Net taxable earnings*

	£	£
Gross income		60,000
Less: business expenses on heating etc	880	
computer – AIA	4,000	(4,880)
Net taxable earnings		55,120

If Sasha is an employee, car journeys between home and her place of work are treated as private motoring so there is no allowable deduction at all for the use of the car.

(c) (i) *Class 2 and Class 4 NIC*

		£
Class 2	£2.85 × 52	148
Class 4	£(45,000 – 8,164) = 36,836 × 9%	3,315
	£(53,000 – 45,000) = 8,000 × 2%	160
Total		3,623

(ii) *Class 1 NIC (Employee's)*

	£
£(45,000 – 8,164) = 36,836 × 12%	4,420
£(60,000 – 45,000) = 15,000 × 2%	300
Total	4,720

Computing chargeable gains MCQs

85 A 1 and 2

Qualifying corporate bonds (QCBs) are exempt assets. Investments held in individual savings accounts (ISAs) are exempt assets.

A plot of land is a chargeable asset. Decorations for bravery are exempt assets only if awarded, not purchased.

86 B £16,700 – £3,000 (current year loss) – £2,400 (brought forward loss) = £11,300

Current year losses must always be used in full against the current year gains.

If losses are brought forward then they must be used against the first available gains after the current year losses and then only enough to reduce the current year's net gains to the annual exempt amount limit of £11,300.

Therefore in this case the £3,000 must be used first and only £2,400 of the brought forward figure needs to be used.

87 D £12,143

The amount of the cost attributable to the part sold is:

$$\frac{£36,000}{£36,000 + £90,000} \times £80,000 = £22,857$$

	£
Proceeds £(36,000 – 1,000)	35,000
Less cost (see above)	(22,857)
Gain	12,143

88 Peter

> **Tutorial note**. The first disposal is a basic computation. The second disposal tests the A/(A+B) formula and the third part tests compensation for the destruction of an asset.

Peter CGT payable 2017/18

Summary

	Residential property £	Other gains £
Residential investment property (W1)	69,720	
Non-residential land (W2)		16,300
Destroyed asset (W3)		3,000
	69,720	19,300
Less annual exempt amount (best use)	(11,300)	(0)
Taxable gains	58,420	19,300
CGT		
£(33,500 − 29,100) = £4,400 @ 18%	792	
£(58,420 − 4,400) = £54,020 @ 28%	15,126	
	15,918	
£19,300 @ 20%		3,860
CGT 2017/18 £(15,918 + 3,860)		19,778

Note. The same amount of tax would be payable if the other gains were taxed first:

	Residential property £	Other gains £
Taxable gains	58,420	19,300
CGT		
£(33,500 − 29,100) = £4,400 @ 10%		440
£(19,300 − 4,400) = £14,900 @ 20%		2,980
		3,420
£58,420 @ 28%	16,358	
CGT 2017/18 £(3,420 + 16,358)		19,778

Workings

1 *Investment property*

	£
Proceeds	150,000
Less cost of disposal	(1,280)
Net proceeds	148,720
Less cost	(79,000)
Gain	69,720

2   Land

	£
Proceeds	35,000
Less cost of disposal	(700)
Net proceeds	34,300
Less cost	
£54,000 × $\dfrac{35,000}{35,000 + 70,000}$	(18,000)
Gain	16,300

3   Vase

	£
Proceeds	20,000
Less cost	(12,000)
Gain	8,000
Gain immediately chargeable	
£(20,000 – 17,000)	3,000

Remainder £(8,000 – 3,000) = £5,000 rolled into base cost of new vase.

Chattels and the principal private residence exemption MCQs

89   A   £1,667

	£
Proceeds less disposal costs £(7,000 – 350)	6,650
Less cost and purchase costs £(1,500 + 75)	(1,575)
Gain	5,075

The maximum gain is 5/3 × £(7,000 – 6,000) = £1,667

The chargeable gain is the lower of £5,075 and £1,667 ie £1,667

90   C   £2,100

	£
Proceeds (assumed)	6,000
Less disposal costs	(200)
	5,800
Less cost and purchase costs £(7,500 + 400)	(7,900)
Allowable loss	(2,100)

91   A   Three years

		Exempt	Chargeable
1.1.94 – 31.12.05	Actual occupation	12	
1.1.06 – 31.12.08	Up to 3 years any reason	3	
1.1.09 – 31.12.11	Unoccupied		3
1.1.12 – 31.12.17	Actual occupation	6	—
Total		21	3

Any periods up to three years are exempt if the house is then reoccupied, so only the remaining three years of the period when Roger was staying with his parents are chargeable as Roger then went back to occupy his house.

John and Elsie

> **Tutorial note**. The last 18 months of ownership are always treated as a period of occupation, if at some time the residence has been the taxpayer's main residence.

92 D   96 months

	Exempt months
1.8.05 – 31.7.06 – actual residence	12
1.8.06 – 31.7.11 – employed abroad any period	60
1.8.11 – 31.1.12 – actual residence	6
1.2.16 – 31.7.17 – last 18 months ownership	18
	96

93 C   36 months

Because John had a period of actual occupation after a period of absence, he can claim 36 months deemed occupation for any reason during the period of absence from 1.2.12 to 31.1.16.

94 B   12 months

The property is let between 1.2.15 and 31.1.17. However, the period 1.2.16 to 31.1.17 is already covered by the last 18 months exemption. The remainder of the let period to be covered by letting relief is therefore 1.2.15 to 31.1.16 = 12 months.

95 C   £5,900

	£
Proceeds (deemed)	6,000
Less costs of disposal	(400)
Net proceeds	5,600
Less cost	(11,500)
Loss	(5,900)

96 A   £2,500

	£
Proceeds	7,500
Less costs of disposal	(75)
Net proceeds	7,425
Less cost	(4,000)
Gain	3,425
Cannot exceed £(7,500 – 6,000) × 5/3	2,500

Business reliefs MCQs

97   C   £1,380

	£
Entrepreneurs' relief claimed	1,000
£10,000 × 10%	
No entrepreneurs' relief claimed	
£(13,200 − 11,300) = £1,900 × 20%	380
Total CGT	1,380

Gain on which entrepreneurs' relief is claimed is taxed at 10%. The other gain will be reduced by the annual exempt amount and then taxed at 20% because the entrepreneurs' relief gain is treated as using up the remainder of the basic rate band.

98   D   £55,000

	£
Chargeable gain on Shop A	25,000
Less amount not reinvested £(80,000 − 70,000)	(10,000)
Amount eligible for rollover relief	15,000
Original cost of Shop B	70,000
Less rollover relief	(15,000)
Cost of Shop B for CGT	55,000

99   B   2 and 3

Gift relief can be claimed for the factory owned by an individual and used in the trade of that individual's personal company. It can also be claimed for premises owned by a sole trader of which two thirds are used for trade purposes and one third is used for private purposes (although the relief will be restricted to the business part of the premises).

Gift relief is not available on investment company shares. It is only available on listed trading company shares if the company is the individual's personal company: a 2% shareholding is too small to meet this test.

Roy and Graham

> **Tutorial note.** When dealing with a sole trader, you should bear in mind that entrepreneurs' relief may apply to reduce the rate of tax on the gain. In questions 101 and 103, entrepreneurs' relief is not available for Graham's disposal because he has not used the factory in his own business.

100   D   £9,870

	£
Market value	260,000
Less cost	(150,000)
Gain	110,000
Less annual exempt amount	(11,300)
Taxable gain	98,700
CGT payable @ 10% (entrepreneurs' relief claimed)	9,870

101 C £9,940

	£
Proceeds	320,000
Less cost	(260,000)
Gain	60,000
Less annual exempt amount	(11,300)
Taxable gain	48,700
CGT payable @ 20%	9,740

102 B £1,870

Partial gift relief is available as payment is made by Graham.

	£
Gain before gift relief	110,000
Less gift relief (balancing figure)	(80,000)
Gain after gift relief £(180,000 – 150,000) (cash gain)	30,000
Less annual exempt amount	(11,300)
Taxable gain	18,700
CGT payable @ 10%	1,870

103 A £25,740

	£
Proceeds	320,000
Less cost £(260,000 – 80,000)	(180,000)
Gain	140,000
Less annual exempt amount	(11,300)
Taxable gain	128,700
CGT payable @ 20%	25,740

104 D More of the gain is covered by a lower rate of CGT

If Roy and Graham make a claim for gift relief, the total tax payable is £(1,870 + 25,740) = £27,610. If they do not make a claim for gift relief, the total tax payable is £(9,870 + 9,740) = £19,610, which is £8,000 less than if a gift relief claim is made. This is due to the availability of entrepreneurs' relief for Roy and so more of the gain is covered by a lower rate of CGT.

105 Kai

> **Tutorial note.** Gains qualifying for entrepreneurs' relief use up the basic rate band in priority to gains not qualifying for the relief.

	£	Gains £	CGT £
Gains qualifying for entrepreneurs' relief			
Goodwill		75,000	
Shop	90,000		
Less cost	(105,000)		
Gain		(15,000)	
Warehouse	180,000		
Less cost	(150,000)		
Warehouse		30,000	
Taxable gains		90,000	
CGT @ 10% on £90,000			9,000
Gains not qualifying for entrepreneurs' relief			
Land	26,100		
Less cost	(10,000)		
Gain		16,100	
Less annual exempt amount (best use)		(11,300)	
Taxable gain		4,800	
CGT @ 20% on £4,800 (N)			960
Total CGT due			9,960

The claim for entrepreneurs' relief must be made by 31 January 2020.

Notes

1   Where there is a material disposal of business assets which results in both gains and losses, losses are netted off against gains to give a single chargeable gain on the disposal of the business assets.

2   The basic rate band is used first by income (£20,000), then by gains qualifying for entrepreneurs' relief (£90,000). The remaining gain is therefore above the basic rate limit and so taxable at 20%.

Shares and securities MCQs

106   A   £22,100

$$\frac{2.22 - 2.20}{2} + 2.20 = 2.21 \times 10,000 \qquad \underline{£22,100}$$

107   C   Against 500 of the shares acquired on 31 July 2017, then against 250 of the shares acquired on 10 August 2017 and then against 50 of the shares acquired on 10 March 2010.

The matching rules are first against same day acquisitions, then shares in the following 30 days and then the share pool.

108   B   3 and 4

In a rights issue the rights issue shares are paid for by the shareholder resulting in an adjustment to the cost of the shareholding. A chargeable gain does not usually arise on a takeover where new shares are exchanged for old shares ('paper for paper' takeover).

A disposal of gilts by an individual is exempt from capital gains tax. If a company makes a 2 for 1 bonus issue, each shareholder will receive 2 extra shares for each 1 share held without payment.

109 Melissa

> **Tutorial note.** The matching rules are very important and must be learnt.

First match the disposal with the acquisition in the next 30 days:

	£	£
Proceeds $\dfrac{4,000}{10,000} \times £42,000$	16,800	
Less cost	(16,000)	800

Next match the remaining shares with the share pool:

	£	£
Proceeds $\dfrac{6,000}{10,000} \times £42,000$	25,200	
Less cost (W)	(20,625)	4,575
Total gains		5,375

Working

	No. of shares	Cost £
12 July 2002 acquisition	3,000	21,000
17 January 2005 bonus issue 1 for 1	3,000	0
	6,000	21,000
14 December 2007 rights issue 1 for 3 @ £3.25 per share	2,000	6,500
	8,000	27,500
2 July 2017 disposal	(6,000)	(20,625)
c/f	2,000	6,875

Self assessment and payment of tax for individuals MCQs

110   C   Steven 31 January 2019, Rita 28 February 2019

The latest filing date for a personal tax return is usually 31 January following the end of the tax year. However, if the notice to file the tax return is issued to the taxpayer after 31 October following the end of the tax year, the latest filing date is the end of 3 months following the notice.

111   D   £6,000 on 31 January and 31 July 2018, £3,000 on 31 January 2019

Payments on account will be made on 31 January and 31 July 2018, with the balance being paid on 31 January 2019.

Payments on account for 2017/18 are payable based on 50% of the relevant amount (income tax plus Class 4 NIC) for 2016/17.

112   B   £960

The maximum penalty for a careless error is 30% of the potential lost revenue (PLR). The PLR in this instance is 40% × £8,000 = £3,200. The penalty is therefore 30% × £3,200 = £960.

Ash

> **Tutorial note**. In relation to a late payment penalty, the penalty date is 30 days after the due date for the payment of tax. For the late filing penalty, the penalty date is the date on which the return is overdue.

113 D £100

The penalty date for late filing of the tax return is the date on which the return will be overdue (ie 1 February 2018 which is the day after the filing date). The date of filing is not more than three months after the penalty date. The late payment penalty is therefore £100.

114 B £6,000

The balancing payment in respect of Ash's 2016/17 tax liability was calculated as follows:

	£
2016/17 income tax liability	16,800
Less: PAYE	(7,200)
	9,600
Less payments on account	(3,600)
Balancing payment	6,000

115 A £4,800

Ash's payments on account for 2017/18 are based on the excess of the 2016/17 tax liability over amounts deducted under the PAYE system:

	£
2016/17 tax liability	16,800
Less: PAYE	(7,200)
'Relevant amount'	9,600

The two payments on account for 2017/18 were therefore £4,800 (£9,600/2) each.

116 C First POA 31 January 2018, Second POA 31 July 2018

117 B 5% of the unpaid tax

The penalty date for late payment of tax is 30 days after the due date. The date of payment is therefore not more than five months after the penalty date. The late payment penalty is therefore 5% of the unpaid tax at the penalty date.

Inheritance tax: scope and transfers of value MCQs

118 A £87,250

	£
Gift	420,000
Less AEs 2017/18, 2016/17 b/f	(6,000)
Net chargeable transfer	414,000
Less nil band remaining £(325,000 – 260,000)	(65,000)
	349,000
IHT @ 20/80	87,250

The gross chargeable transfer in August 2013 is after any exemptions but the gift in November 2017 must have the annual exemptions deducted to find the net chargeable transfer.

119 C £510,000

	£
Andy's unused nil band	
60% × £325,000	195,000
Hilda's unused nil band	
£(325,000 – 10,000)	315,000
	510,000

The transfer by Hilda to her nephew is covered by her annual exemptions for 2016/17 and 2015/16 b/f.

120 B Lifetime tax 30 April 2018, death tax 30 June 2018

For chargeable lifetime transfers the due date is the later of 30 April just after the end of the tax year of the transfer and six months after the end of the month of the transfer. The due date for the tax arising on death is six months from the end of the month of death.

Colin and Diane

> **Tutorial note.** In question 123, the PET is treated as exempt during Diane's lifetime so does not enter into cumulation whilst Diane is alive.

121 B £10,000

No chargeable transfers were made in the seven years prior to 21.1.09 so all of the nil band of £312,000 remained available for use.

	£
Net transfer of value	352,000

IHT			£
	£312,000	× 0% =	Nil
	£ 40,000	× 20/80 =	10,000
	£352,000		10,000

122 B Lifetime tax 31 May 2016, Death tax 31 December 2017

123 D £7,000

The trustees pay the IHT due so no grossing up is required.

	£
Gross transfer of value	360,000

IHT			£
	£325,000	× 0% =	Nil
	£ 35,000	× 20% =	7,000
	£360,000		7,000

124 C £8,000

The PET has come into charge so the available nil rate band is £(325,000 – 15,000) = £310,000.

	£
Gross transfer of value	360,000

IHT			£
	£310,000	× 0% =	Nil
	£ 50,000	× 40% =	20,000
	£360,000		20,000

	£
Taper relief (4 to 5 years) 40% × £20,000	8,000

125 A There is no capital gains tax on a lifetime transfer of value if the donor dies after seven years of making it.

This statement is not true. There may be capital gains tax on the gift if this is of a chargeable asset, and the market value of the asset is such that a gain arises. The seven year period is only relevant for inheritance tax purposes.

126 Simona

> **Tutorial note.** The available residence nil rate band is the lower of £100,000 and the net value of the main residence. The amount of £100,000 is in the Tax Rates and Allowances in the exam.

(a) **Simona's death estate**

	£	£
Shares in MS plc		320,000
Life assurance policy (amount of proceeds payable as result of death)		250,000
Main residence	205,000	
Less repayment mortgage secured on main residence	(110,000)	
		95,000
Household furniture		20,000
Cash in bank		97,750
Car		5,000
Less: credit card bills	7,000	
income tax	3,000	
gas bill	250	
funeral expenses	2,500	(12,750)
Net death estate		775,000
Less spouse exemption (value of shares in MS plc)		(320,000)
Chargeable death estate		455,000

(b) Simona's residence nil rate band available to be set against her death estate is the lower of the maximum residence nil rate band of £100,000 and the net value of the main residence which is £95,000 and so is £95,000.

Simona's nil rate band available to be set against her death estate is the maximum nil rate band at the date of her death of £325,000 reduced by the chargeable lifetime in May 2015 and so is £(325,000 – 90,000) = £235,000.

(c) The IHT on Simona's death estate is:

	£
£95,000 × 0% (residence nil rate band)	0
£235,000 × 0% (nil rate band)	0
£125,000 × 40%	50,000
£455,000	50,000

Computing taxable total profits and the corporation tax liability MCQs

127 C   1 December 2016 to 30 November 2017 and 1 December 2017 to 31 March 2018

If a company has a long period of account it is divided into one accounting period of 12 months and one accounting period of the remainder.

128 A   £2,720

	£
Leasing cost	3,200
Less £3,200 × 15% disallowable	(480)
Allowable deduction	2,720

129 D   £14,400

Rent (accruals)	£14,400

The mortgage is a non-trading loan relationship and so the interest is a debit which must be set against credits from other non-trading loan relationships. Capital repayments are not relevant to the computation of property business income.

Red plc and Green plc

> **Tutorial note.** Where a company has a long period of account, it has two accounting periods: first 12 months and then the remainder.

130 D   £6,480

	Main pool £	Allowances £
12 months ended 31.12.17		
TWDV b/f	24,000	
Addition not qualifying for AIA		
11.17 Car	12,000	
	36,000	
WDA @ 18%	(6,480)	6,480

131 B   £50,000

The purchase of the machinery takes place in the second accounting period from 1 January 2018 to 31 March 2018 which is three months long. The annual investment allowance is therefore £200,000 × 3/12 = £50,000.

132 B   £10,000

This a new low emission car and so 100% FYA is available regardless of the length of the accounting period.

133   A   £272,000

	1.1.16 - 31.12.16 (12m) £
Trading profits (12/17)	276,000
Investment income (15,000 + 6,000)	21,000
Chargeable gain	5,000
Total profits	302,000
Less qualifying charitable donations (15,000 + 15,000)	(30,000)
Taxable total profits	272,000

134   C   £77,500

	1.1.17 - 31.5.17 (5m) £
Trading profits (5/17)	115,000
Investment income	2,500
Total profits	117,500
Less qualifying charitable donation	(40,000)
Taxable total profits	77,500

135 Elderflower Ltd

Tutorial notes. You must use the layout shown when adjusting profits for taxation. The notes have been added for tutorial purposes.

(a)   **Trading profit for y/e 31 March 2018**

	£	£
Profit before taxation		417,210
Add:		
Depreciation	54,690	
Accountancy and audit	0	
Legal fees – share capital (N1)	8,800	
Legal fees – loan notes (N1)	0	
Legal fees – health and safety (N1)	900	
Repairs and renewals: extension (N2)	9,700	
Repairs and renewals: repainting (N2)	0	
Other expenses: entertaining customers	2,310	
Other expenses: qualifying charitable donation	500	
Interest payable (N3)	0	
		76,900
Deduct:		
Office building profit	54,000	
Bank interest	7,000	
Capital allowances (W)	25,190	
		(86,190)
Profit adjusted for tax purposes		407,920

Notes

1. Costs relating to share capital need to be added back as they relate to a capital expense. However, the fees relating to the loan notes are a loan relationship expense and thus deductible as a trading expense because the debenture is for trade purposes. Legal fees in relation to the fine are not deductible as the fine is a payment contrary to public policy.

2. The cost of the extension has been added back as a capital expense but the cost of repainting is allowable as it is a repair and therefore a revenue expense.

3. No adjustment is needed for the interest because it relates to a trade purpose loan.

Working: Capital allowances on plant and machinery

	AIA £	Main pool £	Special rate pool £	Allowances £
TWDV b/f		27,500	14,700	
Additions qualifying for AIA				
10.5.17 Equipment	20,200			
AIA	(20,200)			20,200
Additions not qualifying for AIA				
31.3.18 Car (N1)		9,600		
Disposals				
5.1.18 Car			(9,700)	
			5,000	
20.3.18 Van		(11,600)		
		25,500		
WDA @ 18%		(4,590)		4,590
WDA @ 8% (N2)			(400)	400
TWDVs c/f		20,910	4,600	
Allowances				25,190

Notes.

1. The private use of the car by the employee is not relevant for capital allowance purposes. No adjustment is ever made to a company's capital allowances to reflect the private use of an asset.

2. Although the only asset in the special rate pool has been sold, the pool of expenditure continues to be written down. A balancing allowance on the special rate pool can only arise when the trade ceases.

(b) **Total taxable profits y/e 31 March 2018**

	£
Trading profit (part (a))	407,920
Chargeable gain	45,580
Investment income	7,000
Total profits	460,500
Less qualifying charitable donation	(500)
Taxable total profits	460,000

(c) **Corporation tax liability y/e 31 March 2018**

£460,000 × 19%	87,400

Chargeable gains for companies MCQs

136 D Neither a gain nor a loss

	£
Net proceeds £(17,500 – 1,000)	16,500
Less cost £(12,000 + 800)	(12,800)
Unindexed gain	3,700
Less indexation allowance $\frac{271.7 - 175.7}{175.7} = 0.546 \times £12,800$	(6,989)
Chargeable gain/allowable loss (indexation cannot create a loss)	0

137 B £490,128

	£
Net proceeds £(640,000 – 6,000)	634,000
Less cost £(120,000 + 8,000)	(128,000)
	506,000
Less indexation allowance 0.124 × £128,000	(15,872)
Chargeable gain	490,128

138 D £57,500

	£
Proceeds	200,000
Less cost	(110,000)
Unindexed gain	90,000
Less indexation allowance	(20,000)
Indexed gain	70,000
Less rollover relief (balancing figure)	(57,500)
Chargeable gain: amount not reinvested £(200,000 – 187,500)	12,500

Long Ltd, Tall Ltd and Short Ltd

139 C 2 and 4

There is relief for inflation called the indexation allowance and a company is liable to corporation tax on its net chargeable gains as part of its total profits.

140 B 1, then 3, then 2

Shares acquired on the same day, then shares acquired in the previous nine days and finally shares from the FA 1985 pool.

141 A £14,551

	£
Proceeds	45,000
Less cost £40,000 × 6,000/10,000	(24,000)
	21,000
Less indexation allowance $\frac{272.9 - 215.1}{215.1} \times £24,000$	(6,449)
Gain	14,551

142 D £41,683

	No. of shares	Indexed cost
		£
June 2002 Acquisition	5,000	14,000
October 2017 Indexed rise		
$\dfrac{272.9-176.2}{176.2} \times £14,000$		7,683
Rights 1:1 @ £4 per share	5,000	20,000
	10,000	41,683

143 B Ordinary shares £27,200, Preference shares £6,800

	No. of shares	MV	Cost
		£	£
Ordinary shares	20,000	100,000	27,200
Preference shares	10,000	25,000	6,800
	30,000	125,000	34,000

144 Xeon Ltd

> **Tutorial note.** When using the part disposal formula, remember that it only applies to cost which relates to the whole of the original asset, not to expenditure incurred just on the part being sold (which is deductible in full).

Warehouse sold in May 2017

	£
Proceeds	125,000
Less cost	(65,000)
	60,000
Less indexation allowance $\dfrac{270.2-181.3}{181.3}$ (0.490) × £65,000	(31,850)
Gain	28,150
Less rollover relief (balancing figure)	(8,150)
Gain left in charge £(125,000 − 105,000)	20,000

Cost of warehouse bought in July 2016

	£
Cost	105,000
Less rollover relief	(8,150)
Revised cost	96,850

Plot of land sold in June 2017

	£
Proceeds	30,000
Less cost	(9,000)
$\dfrac{30,000}{30,000+40,000} \times £21,000$	
expenditure in December 2012	(1,000)
	20,000
Less indexation allowance	
$\dfrac{270.6-170.1}{170.1}$ (0.591) × £9,000	(5,319)
$\dfrac{270.6-246.8}{246.8}$ (0.096) × £1,000	(96)
	14,585

Losses MCQs

145 B 2 and 3

Trade losses of a company carried forward can only be used against profits of the same trade. Trade loss relief may be given by deduction from current period total profits and those in the previous 12 months.

Property business losses of a company are set against total profits of the same accounting period. Capital losses can only be set against chargeable gains in the same or future accounting periods.

146 A £30,000

E plc must make a current year loss claim against total profits if it wishes to make a claim to carry a loss back so the loss available for carry back is £(40,000 – 10,000) = £30,000.
E plc cannot keep sufficient income to cover the qualifying charitable donation. The carry back is against total profits (ie before qualifying charitable donations).

147 D £38,000

	£
Trading income	165,000
Less trading loss b/f	(165,000)
	0
Non-trading loan relationship income	27,000
Chargeable gain £(14,000 – 3,000)	11,000
Taxable total profits	38,000

148 Ferraro Ltd

> **Tutorial note.** The pro forma for loss relief is important. If you learn the pro forma you should find that the figures slot into place. Note that the result of a losses claim may be that, as here, qualifying charitable donations become unrelieved.

	Accounting periods		
	12m to 31.3.16	9m to 31.12.16	12m to 31.12.17
	£	£	£
Trading profits	6,200	4,320	0
Investment income	80	240	260
Property business income	1,420	1,440	1,600
Chargeable gain	0	7,680	0
Total profits	7,700	13,680	1,860
Less current period loss relief	0	0	(1,860)
	7,700	13,680	0
Less carry back loss relief	(1,925)	(13,680)	(0)
Less qualifying charitable donations	(0)	(0)	(0)
Taxable total profits	5,775	0	0
Unrelieved qualifying charitable donations		1,000	1,500

	£
Loss memo	
Loss of y/e 31.12.17	100,000
Less used y/e 31.12.17	(1,860)
	98,140
Less used 9m/e 31.12.16	(13,680)
	84,460
Less used y/e 31.3.16 3/12 × £7,700	(1,925)
c/f against first available profits of the same trade	82,535

> **Tutorial note.** The loss is carried back to set against profits arising in the previous 12 months. This means that the set off in the y/e 31.3.16 is restricted to 3/12 × £7,700 = £1,925.

Groups MCQs

149   C   £19,000

	£
Trading loss	16,000
Excess qualifying charitable donation £(4,000 − 1,000)	3,000
Amount available for group relief	19,000

150   A   £40,500

The lower of:

P Ltd profits 1.4.17 – 31.12.17 £54,000 × 9/12	£40,500
O Ltd loss 1.4.17 – 31.12.17 £(60,000) × 9/12	£45,000

151   C   B Ltd, C Ltd and D Ltd

B Ltd owns 75% of C Ltd and so is in a chargeable gains group with it. B Ltd also has an effective interest in D Ltd of 75% × 90% = 67.5%. As this is 50% or more, D Ltd is also in this gains group.

A Ltd does not own 75% or more of B Ltd and so cannot be in a chargeable gains group with B Ltd or its subsidiaries.

152 P Ltd

> **Tutorial note.** It is helpful to use a pro forma as shown in the answer to work out.

S Ltd and T Ltd are outside the P Ltd group for group relief purposes so the loss of S Ltd cannot be group relieved.

A claim by P Ltd against its own total profits would waste its qualifying charitable donation and carrying the loss forward against future profits of P Ltd would not obtain relief for several years.

A claim for group relief should therefore be made. P Ltd's trading loss of £226,000 could be surrendered under group relief to Q Ltd, R Ltd and M Ltd. The amount to be surrendered is after taking account of qualifying charitable donations.

The following is one possible use of group relief (the overall corporation tax liability will be the same regardless of which group company ends up with taxable total profits of £1,000):

	P Ltd	Q Ltd	R Ltd	S Ltd	M Ltd	T Ltd	Overall CT
	£	£	£	£	£	£	
Trading profits	0	14,000	210,000	0	20,000	70,000	
Property business income	6,000	4,000	0	0	0	0	
Total profits	6,000	18,000	210,000	0	20,000	70,000	
Less qualifying charitable donation	(4,500)	(2,000)	(5,000)	0	(14,000)	0	
	1,500	16,000	205,000	0	6,000	70,000	
Less group relief	0	(16,000)	(205,000)	0	(5,000)	0	
Taxable total profits	1,500	0	0	0	1,000	70,000	
Corporation tax (FY17) @ 19%							
Corporation tax payable	285	0	0	0	190	13,300	13,775

Self assessment and payment of tax by companies MCQs

153 B Return date 31 December 2018, tax payable date 1 October 2018

The return must be submitted within 12 months of the end of the accounting period and the tax paid nine months and one day after the end of the accounting period.

154 A 31 March 2019

The tax return must be filed within 12 months of the end of the period of account because it is not more than 18 months long. Therefore the return for the first accounting period which ends on 31 December 2017 must be submitted by 31 March 2019.

155 D Retention date: 31 March 2024, maximum penalty: £3,000

A company must keep its records for six years from the end of the accounting period, if no compliance check is made.

Failure to keep records can lead to a maximum penalty of £3,000 for each accounting period affected.

Skyblue Ltd and Turquoise plc

Tutorial note. In question 159 first calculate the potential lost revenue (PLR) as a result of the error as the penalty will be a percentage of this amount.

156 D Electronic return filed by 30 September 2018

157 C On time £200, last two returns late £1,000

158 B Due date: first anniversary of the filing date, four months late: quarter day following the first anniversary of the filing date

159 C £12,600

	£
£(100,000 – 10,000) = £90,000 × 20%	18,000
The maximum penalty for a deliberate, but not concealed, error is:	
£18,000 × 70%	12,600

160 A Unprompted 20%, prompted 35%

161 Cyan plc and Crimson plc

> **Tutorial note.** Large companies must pay their CT liabilities in quarterly instalments. The profit threshold for determining whether a company is a large company must be adjusted for related 51% group companies and for short accounting periods.

(a) **Cyan plc – corporation tax payable p/e 31.12.17**

	£
Corporation tax £1,350,000 × 20% × 3/12 (FY 2016)	67,500
Corporation tax £1,350,000 × 19% × 9/12 (FY 2017)	192,375
	259,875

(b) **Cyan plc – payments of corporation tax for p/e 31.12.17**

Profit limit £1,500,000 × 9/12	1,125,000

Cyan plc is therefore a large company for the period.

Cyan plc is required to pay its corporation tax liability in instalments because it is a large company and this is not the first year that it is large.

The amount of each instalment and the due dates are as follows:

$$3 \times \frac{£259,875}{9} = £86,625 \text{ payable on 14 October 2017, 14 January 2018, 14 April 2018.}$$

(c) **Crimson plc - related 51% group companies**

Tangerine plc – related 51% group company as more than 50% of Tangerine plc's ordinary shares are owned directly by Crimson plc.

Russet plc - not related 51% group company as more than 50% of Russet plc's ordinary shares are not owned directly by Crimson plc.

Rouge plc - related 51% group company as more than 50% of Rouge plc's ordinary shares are owned indirectly by Crimson plc (55% × 96% = 52.8%).

Chestnut plc - related 51% group company as more than 50% of Chestnut plc's ordinary shares are owned directly by Crimson plc. However, since this relationship did not exist on 31 March 2017, it is not relevant for determining whether Crimson plc is a large company for the year ended 31 March 2018.

(d) **Crimson plc – whether large company in the year ended 31 March 2018**

	£
Taxable total profits	450,000
Dividend from 45% subsidiary (Russet plc)	30,000
Profits	480,000

The dividend from Tangerine plc is not included in the calculation of profits as it is received from a related 51% group company.

The profit threshold of £1,500,000 must be divided by three which is the total number of related 51% group companies including the company itself (Tangerine plc, Rouge plc and Crimson plc), and so is £500,000.

Therefore Crimson plc is not a large company in the year ended 31 March 2018.

An introduction to VAT MCQs

162 A   1 January 2018

Alec is liable to register for value added tax (VAT) when he is aware that his taxable turnover during the next 30 days will exceed the VAT registration limit of £85,000 (the future test). Alec must then charge VAT from the first day of that 30-day period, in this case 1 January 2018.

163 A   £11,880

VAT is charged on the amounts actually received. Therefore the VAT due is $£[(60,000 \times 25\% \times 96\%) + 60,000 \times 75\%) \times 20\% = \underline{£11,880}$.

164 B   31 December 2017

The tax point is generally the earliest of: the date of delivery, the invoice date and the cash receipt date. However, if as in this case, the invoice is issued within 14 days of delivery, then the invoice date becomes the tax point.

Justin

> **Tutorial note.** Note how the input and output VAT is accounted for in respect of petrol and that the VAT incurred on the entertaining for UK customers is blocked from recovery.

165 C   £98,000

	£
Output VAT	
Furniture: £490,000 × 20% (standard rated)	98,000
Books: £2,400 × 0% (zero rated)	0
	98,000

166 A   £39 recoverable

	£
Output VAT	
£365 × 1/6	61
Input VAT	
£600 × 1/6	(100)
Net VAT recoverable	(39)

167 B   £120

Non-UK customers only: £1,800 × 1/3 × 20% = £120

168 C   Submission 7 February 2018, payment 7 February 2018

169 D   No recovery of input VAT, no charge to VAT on sale

170 Newcomer Ltd and Au Revoir Ltd

> **Tutorial note.** This question is a typical question on registration and deregistration. Note the importance of the dates.

(a) The registration threshold is £85,000 during any consecutive 12-month period.

This is exceeded in January 2018:

		£
2017	October	18,500
	November	21,900
	December	23,400
2018	January	22,300
		86,100

Therefore, Newcomer Ltd must notify HM Revenue & Customs (HMRC) within 30 days of the end of the month the threshold was exceeded, ie by 1 March 2018.

Newcomer Ltd will be registered from the end of the month following the month in which the registration threshold was exceeded ie from 1 March 2018, or an earlier date agreed between the company and HMRC.

(b) A person is eligible for voluntary deregistration if HMRC are satisfied that the amount of his taxable supplies (net of VAT) in the following one year period will not exceed £83,000. However, voluntary deregistration will not be allowed if the reasons for the expected fall in value of taxable supplies is the cessation of taxable supplies or the suspension of taxable supplies for a period of 30 days or more in that following year. HMRC will cancel a person's registration from the date the request is made or an agreed later date.

171 Ongoing Ltd

> **Tutorial notes**
>
> 1 Where a discount is offered for prompt payment, VAT is chargeable on amount received.
>
> 2 VAT on business entertaining is generally not recoverable. However the cost of entertaining overseas customers is recoverable.
>
> 3 Impairment loss (bad debt) relief is only available for debts over six months old (measured from when the payment is due).
>
> 4 VAT incurred on the purchase of a car not used wholly for business purposes is not recoverable. However, the subsequent sale of the car is exempt from VAT.

	£	£
Output tax		
£[(120,000 × 50% × 95%) + (120,000 × 50%)] = 117,000 × 20% (note 1, note 4)		23,400
Input tax		
£(35,640 − 480) = 35,160 × 20% (note 2)	7,032	
£2,100 × 20% (note 3)	420	
£21,150 × 1/6 (note 4)	3,525	(10,977)
VAT payable for quarter ending 30 April 2017		12,423

Notes

1   VAT is calculated after the deduction of the prompt payment discount taken up.
2   UK entertaining is not an expense on which input tax can be recovered.
3   The debt must be six months old to claim bad debt relief. The discount was obviously not taken up.
4   Input tax on motor cars not used wholly for business purposes is irrecoverable. However, the sale of the car, on which input tax is irrecoverable, is exempt from VAT.

Further aspects of VAT MCQs

172   C   1 and 4

All VAT returns must be up to date before a trader can join the scheme and it gives automatic impairment loss relief (bad debt relief) because VAT is not due on a supply until payment has been received.

The turnover condition is that a trader can join the scheme if their taxable turnover (exclusive of VAT) for the 12 months starting on their application to join the scheme is not expected to exceed £1,350,000. The payment of VAT by monthly payments applies to the annual accounting scheme.

173   D   £Nil

Where goods are sold to another EU member state, the supply is zero-rated if the supply is made to a registered trader.

174   A   £9,900

The flat rate percentage is applied to the full tax inclusive turnover including all standard, zero and exempt supplies so the VAT liability is £110,000 × 9% = $\underline{£9,900}$.

Jason

> **Tutorial note.** Make sure that you are clear about the different procedures for dealing with VAT on goods acquired from outside and inside the EU. The overall effect will usually be the same, but there is an actual payment of VAT required for imports from outside the EU at the time of importation.

175   B   EU registered trader zero rated, outside EU zero rated
176   D   Output tax at UK rate in next VAT return, input tax at UK rate in next return
177   C   15 August 2017

The 'tax point' is the earlier of:

(a)   The fifteenth day of the month following the month of acquisition
(b)   The date of issue of an invoice

178   C   Output tax at UK rate at point of entry, input tax at UK rate in next VAT return
179   A   Outside the scope of VAT

Supplies of services by a UK VAT registered trader to business customers outside the EU are outside the scope of UK VAT as the place of supply is not in the UK.

180 K Ltd and L Ltd

> **Tutorial note.** In part (a), it is a good idea to present your answer as bullet points where you are asked to prepare notes for a meeting. The main advantage of the cash accounting scheme is automatic impairment loss relief so you should have spotted that this was the relevant scheme in part (b).

(a) **K Ltd – notes for meeting on annual accounting scheme**

    (i) *Rules and qualifying conditions*

- Must regularly pay VAT (rather than receive repayments) to HM Revenue & Customs (HMRC) .

- Taxable turnover (excluding VAT) must not be expected to exceed £1,350,000 in next 12 months

- All VAT returns must be up-to-date

- Nine payments on account required, commencing at the end of the fourth month of the year

- Payments are made by direct debt

- Each payment is 10% of the net VAT payable for the previous year

- Option to pay three larger interim instalments

- Annual return must be submitted within two months of the VAT year-end and any balance paid

- If the expected value of taxable supplies by the end of a year exceeds £1,600,000, notice must be given to HMRC within 30 days and may then be required to leave the scheme

- If by the end of that year the £1,600,000 limit is in fact exceeded, must leave the scheme

    (ii) *Advantages*

- Only one VAT return each year so fewer occasions to trigger a default surcharge
- Ability to manage cash flow more accurately
- Avoids need for quarterly calculations for input tax recovery

    Disadvantages

- Need to monitor future taxable supplies to ensure turnover limit not exceeded

- Timing of payments are less related to turnover (and therefore cash flow received) by business

- Payments based on previous year's turnover may not reflect current year turnover which may be a problem if the scale of activities has reduced

(b) **L Ltd – cash accounting scheme**

The cash accounting scheme will provide automatic impairment loss relief. This is because L Ltd will account for VAT on the basis of cash paid and received and so the date of payment or receipt determines the return in which the transaction is dealt with. Therefore, VAT will not be due on a supply until payment has been received.

L Ltd can use the cash accounting scheme if its expected taxable turnover for the next 12 months does not exceed £1,350,000. L Ltd must also be up-to-date with its VAT returns and VAT payments.

Tax tables

SUPPLEMENTARY INFORMATION

1. Calculations and workings need only be made to the nearest £.
2. All apportionments may be made to the nearest month.
3. All workings should be shown in Section C.

TAX RATES AND ALLOWANCES

The following tax rates and allowances are to be used in answering the questions.

Income tax

		Normal rates	Dividend rates
Basic rate	£1 – £33,500	20%	7.5%
Higher rate	£33,501 to £150,000	40%	32.5%
Additional rate	£150,001 and over	45%	38.1%

Savings income nil rate band – Basic rate taxpayers		£1,000
– Higher rate taxpayers		£500
Dividend nil rate band		£5,000

A starting rate of 0% applies to savings income where it falls within the first £5,000 of taxable income.

Personal allowance

	£
Personal allowance	11,500
Transferable amount	1,150
Income limit	100,000

Residence status

Days in UK	Previously resident	Not previously resident
Less than 16	Automatically not resident	Automatically not resident
16 to 45	Resident if 4 UK ties (or more)	Automatically not resident
46 to 90	Resident if 3 UK ties (or more)	Resident if 4 UK ties
91 to 120	Resident if 2 UK ties (or more)	Resident if 3 UK ties (or more)
121 to 182	Resident if 1 UK tie (or more)	Resident if 2 UK ties (or more)
183 or more	Automatically resident	Automatically resident

Child benefit income tax charge

Where income is between £50,000 and £60,000, the charge is 1% of the amount of child benefit received for every £100 of income over £50,000.

Car benefit percentage

The base level of CO_2 emissions is 95 grams per kilometre.

The percentage rates applying to petrol cars with CO_2 emissions up to this level are:

50 grams per kilometre or less	9%
51 grams to 75 grams per kilometre	13%
76 grams to 94 grams per kilometre	17%
95 grams per kilometre	18%

Car fuel benefit

The base figure for calculating the car fuel benefit is £22,600.

Individual savings accounts (ISAs)

The overall investment limit is £20,000.

Property income

Basic rate restriction applies to 25% of finance costs.

Pension scheme limits

Annual allowance	£40,000
Minimum allowance	£10,000
Income limit	£150,000

The maximum contribution that can qualify for tax relief without any earnings is £3,600.

Authorised mileage allowances: cars

Up to 10,000 miles	45p
Over 10,000 miles	25p

Capital allowances: rates of allowance

Plant and machinery

Main pool	18%
Special rate pool	8%

Motor cars

New cars with CO_2 emissions up to 75 grams per kilometre	100%
CO_2 emissions between 76 and 130 grams per kilometre	18%
CO_2 emissions over 130 grams per kilometre	8%

Annual investment allowance

Rate of allowance	100%
Expenditure limit	£200,000

Cash basis

Revenue limit	£150,000

Cap on income tax reliefs

Unless otherwise restricted, reliefs are capped at the higher of £50,000 or 25% of income.

Corporation tax

Rate of tax	– Financial year 2017	19%
	– Financial year 2016	20%
	– Financial year 2015	20%
Profit threshold		£1,500,000

Value Added Tax (VAT)

Standard rate	20%
Registration limit	£85,000
Deregistration limit	£83,000

Inheritance tax: tax rates

Nil rate band		£325,000
Residence nil rate band		£100,000
Rates of tax on excess	– Lifetime rate	20%
	– Death rate	40%

Inheritance tax: taper relief

Years before death	Percentage reduction
Over 3 but less than 4 years	20%
Over 4 but less than 5 years	40%
Over 5 but less than 6 years	60%
Over 6 but less than 7 years	80%

Capital gains tax

		Normal rates	Residential property
Rates of tax	– Lower rate	10%	18%
	– Higher rate	20%	28%
Annual exempt amount			£11,300
Entrepreneurs' relief	– Lifetime limit		£10,000,000
	– Rate of tax		10%

National insurance contributions

Class 1 Employee	£1 – £8,164 per year	Nil
	£8,165 – £45,000 per year	12%
	£45,001 and above per year	2%
Class 1 Employer	£1 – £8,164 per year	Nil
	£8,165 and above per year	13.8%
	Employment allowance	£3,000
Class 1A		13.8%
Class 2	£2.85 per week	
	Small profits threshold	£6,025
Class 4	£1 – £8,164 per year	Nil
	£8,165 – £45,000 per year	9%
	£45,001 and above per year	2%

Rates of Interest (assumed)

Official rate of interest	2.50%
Rate of interest on underpaid tax	2.75%
Rate of interest on overpaid tax	0.50%

Case bibliography

Bamford v ATA Advertising Ltd 1972 .... [1972] 48 TC 359
Blackwell v Mills 1945 .... [1945] 2 All ER 655
Brown v Bullock 1961 .... [1961] 3 All ER 129
Brown v Burnley Football and Athletic Co Ltd 1980 .... [1980] 53 TC 357

Caillebotte v Quinn 1975 .... [1975] 50 TC 22
Cape Brandy Syndicate v CIR 1921 .... [1921] 1 KB 64
Carmichael and Anor v National Power plc 1999 .... [1999] UKHL 47
CIR v Fraser 1942 .... [1942] 24 TC498
CIR v Scottish and Newcastle Breweries Ltd 1982 .... [1982] 55 TC 252
Cole Brothers Ltd v Phillips 1982 .... [1982] 55 TC 188

Donald Fisher (Ealing) Ltd v Spencer 1989 .... [1989] STC 256

Edwards v Clinch 1981 .... [1981] STC 617
Elwood v Utitz 1965 .... [1965] 42 TC 482

Fitzpatrick v IRC 1994 .... [1994] STC 237

Hampton v Fortes Autogrill Ltd 1979 .... [1979] 53 TC 691
Hall v Lorimer 1994 .... [1994] IRLR 171
Harvey v Caulcott 1952 .... [1952] 33TC159

Jarrold v John Good and Sons Ltd 1963 .... [1963] 40 TC 681

Law Shipping v CIR 1921 .... [1921] 12 TC 621
Lucas v Cattell 1972 .... [1972] 48 TC 353
Lupton v Potts 1969 .... [1969] 45 TC 643

Mallalieu v Drummond 1983 .... [1983] 57 TC 330
Martin v Lowry 1927 .... [1927] 1 KB 550
McKnight (HMIT) v Sheppard (1999) .... [1999] STC 669
McLaren v Mumford 1996 .... [1996] 69 TC 173
Munby v Furlong 1977 .... [1977] 50 TC 491

Odeon Associated Theatres Ltd v Jones 1971 .... [1971] 48 TC 257

Rutledge v CIR 1929 .... [1929] 14 TC 490

Samuel Jones & Co (Devondale) Ltd v CIR 1951 .... [1951] 32 TC 513
Sanderson v Durbridge 1955 .... [1955] 36 TC 239
Smith v Abbott 1994 .... [1994] STC 237
Strong & Co of Romsey Ltd v Woodifield 1906 .... [1906] AC 448

Vodafone Cellular Ltd and others v Shaw 1995 .... [1995] 69 TC 376

Wimpy International Ltd v Warland 1988 .... [1988] 61 TC 51
Wisdom v Chamberlain 1969 .... [1969] 45 TC 92

Yarmouth v France 1887 .... [1887] 19 QB D

Index

Please help us to ensure that the ACCA learning materials we produce remain as accurate and user-friendly as possible. We cannot promise to answer every submission we receive, but we do promise that it will be read and taken into account when we update this Study Text.

Name: _____   **Address:** _____

_____

_____

How have you used this Study Text?
(Tick one box only)

☐ On its own (book only)

☐ On a BPP in-centre course _____

☐ On a BPP online course

☐ On a course with another college

☐ Other _____

Why did you decide to purchase this Study Text? *(Tick one box only)*

☐ Have used BPP Study Texts in the past

☐ Recommendation by friend/colleague

☐ Recommendation by a lecturer at college

☐ Saw information on BPP website

☐ Saw advertising

☐ Other _____

During the past six months do you recall seeing/receiving any of the following?
(Tick as many boxes as are relevant)

☐ Our advertisement in *ACCA Student Accountant*

☐ Our advertisement in *Pass*

☐ Our advertisement in *PQ*

☐ Our brochure with a letter through the post

☐ Our website www.bpp.com

Which (if any) aspects of our advertising do you find useful?
(Tick as many boxes as are relevant)

☐ Prices and publication dates of new editions

☐ Information on Study Text content

☐ Facility to order books

☐ None of the above

Which BPP products have you used?

Study Text ☑   *Passcards* ☐   *Other* ☐

Kit ☐   *i-Pass* ☐

Your ratings, comments and suggestions would be appreciated on the following areas.

	Very useful	Useful	Not useful
Introductory section	☐	☐	☐
Chapter introductions	☐	☐	☐
Key terms	☐	☐	☐
Quality of explanations	☐	☐	☐
Examples	☐	☐	☐
Exam focus points	☐	☐	☐
Questions and answers in each chapter	☐	☐	☐
Fast forwards and chapter roundups	☐	☐	☐
Quick quizzes	☐	☐	☐
Question Bank	☐	☐	☐
Answer Bank	☐	☐	☐
Index	☐	☐	☐

Overall opinion of this Study Text.	Excellent ☐	Good ☐	Adequate ☐	Poor ☐

Do you intend to continue using BPP products?   Yes ☐   No ☐

On the reverse of this page is space for you to write your comments about our Study Text. We welcome your feedback.

The BPP Learning Media author of this edition can be emailed at: accaqueries@bpp.com

TELL US WHAT YOU THINK

Please note any further comments and suggestions/errors below. For example, was the text accurate, readable, concise, user-friendly and comprehensive?